Geographies of Dance

Geographies of Dance

Body, Movement, and Corporeal Negotiations

Edited by
Adam Pine and Olaf Kuhlke

LEXINGTON BOOKS
Lanham • Boulder • New York • Toronto • Plymouth, UK

Published by Lexington Books
A wholly owned subsidiary of Rowman & Littlefield
4501 Forbes Boulevard, Suite 200, Lanham, Maryland 20706
www.rowman.com

10 Thornbury Road, Plymouth PL6 7PP, United Kingdom

British Library Cataloguing in Publication Information Available

Library of Congress Cataloging-in-Publication Data Available

ISBN: 978-1-4985-2073-7 (pbk : alk, paper)
ISBN: 978-0-7391-7184-4 (cloth : alk. paper)—ISBN: 978-0-7391-7185-1 (electronic)

∞™ The paper used in this publication meets the minimum requirements of American National Standard for Information Sciences—Permanence of Paper for Printed Library Materials, ANSI/NISO Z39.48-1992.

Printed in the United States of America

Contents

Introduction

O body swayed to music,
O brightening glance,
How can we know the dancer from the dance?

—Yeats 1927

W. B. Yeats' question, posed at the end of his famous poem *Among School Children*, is perhaps the best possible opening for this book. What Yeats was questioning here, in poetic form, was the element of agency in the act of dancing. If we examine dance as a choreographed practice driven by social traditions, what is the relationship of individual dancer to the dance? How does the individual dancer interact with, conform to, interpret or challenge often prescribed movements? How does a dancer think about his or her relationship with dance as a form of art, often propelled by music? What is the dancer's role in dance as a form of practice or (re)presentation? All these questions, and more, have been addressed by dance scholars in a variety of fields ranging from the performing arts to dance studies, art history, anthropology, and sociology (Wolff 1995, Savigliano 1995, Skinner 2010, Reynolds and McCormick 2003, Osumare 2002, Nally 2009, Kloetzel and Pavlik 2010, Hagendoorn 2004, Foster 1996, Farrer 2004, Desmond 1997, Dempster 1995, Daly 1992).

Take, for example, Jane Desmond, who argues that dance is "both a product (particular dances as realized in production) and a process (dancing, the historical conditions of possibility for the production and reception of such texts and processes, as well as the articulation of systems of value)." She encourages us to think of this relationship between product and process, to interrogate "when, where and how we dance, with whom, under what conditions—and what gets danced, whether on the stage in the street or at party" (Desmond 1997, 2). Such work illustrates the deep commitment of dance scholars to examine the complex and multifaceted relationship between dancer, dance, audience, and stage.

More recently, *geographers* and other scholars engaged in *spatial theory* have joined in these discussions, and geographic research on dance has proliferated over the past decade. This body of literature is global in its scope of inquiry and multithreaded in its theoretical perspective, ranging from analyses of the racialized nature of the connections between bodies on the multicultural trance dance floors of Goa (Saldanha 2005, 2007), to the role of consumption in the globalized production of Spanish Flamenco dance (Aoyama 2007), to the tensions between tradition and authenticity in Balinese dance (Dunbar-Hall 2003). Linking together this diverse emerging area of geographic inquiry is its (1) active embrace of a diversity of research sites and social theories as a way of deciphering the connections between "place" and the globalization of culture; (2) commitment to creating new theory built on the unique corporeality and fluidity of dance as a research subject; and (3) its active engagement in interdisciplinary questions of performativity, choreography, and the meaning of the body at dance. In its global focus, commitment to the advancement of social theory, and innovative linking of the dancing body to national and global scale processes, dance scholarship in geography is an innovative and growing literature uniquely suited to add to existing debates within geography and engage in interdisciplinary dialogues with other scholars of dance, choreography, movement and performance studies.

The tension between "place" and globalized cultural production (Escobar 2001) figures prominently in geographic research on dance. Central to these debates are questions relating to the ability of authentic "local" dances to exist and even thrive amid capitalist cultural globalization, and the ability of innovative counter-hegemonic dance styles to emerge and survive. Cresswell (2006a), for example, examines how British attempts to avoid cultural hybridity involved regulating the introduction of "American" movements into British Ballroom dance, resulting in the creation of a carefully regimented and "encoded" British style of ballroom dance. In contrast, economic geographer Yuko Aoyama (2007) analyzes how the tensions between the place-based community of marginalized Andalusian gypsies which created flamenco dance and the "Flamenco art complex" in the United States and Japan which actively consumes this place-based "exotic" product (also see Aparicio 1998 and Waxer 2002 for similar analyses of the salsa music industry and Jazeel 2005 for the British-Asian music scene). This question of how the authenticity of "local" dance forms should be understood is explicitly treated by Dunbar-Hall (2003) who analyzes Balinese dance performances for tourists and concludes that "authenticity" is little more than a trope of tourism operators, and cultural transformation is an ongoing process in which transnational tourism is but one of many factors. Analyses of the cultural import of dance tackle both its mainstream and its subaltern variants and contribute to emerging literatures on alternative economies (Gibson-Graham 2006) and the importance of "geographies of play" (Katz 2004). Fraser and Ettlinger (2008), for example, analyze the prospects of a subaltern Drum and Bass economy of marginalized techno musicians in Britain, concluding that drum and bass can best be termed a "fragile" form of empowerment in that while the musicians have constructed an alternative economy, it is quintessentially interconnected with capitalism and subject to the problems inherent in a rapidly changing community propelled by technological innovation. Similarly Hubbard et al. (2008) analyze the unique geography "adult dance venues" through the lens of exclusion, gentrification, and sexuality studies.

The sweaty, loud, erotized and ritualized movements that are part and parcel of the dance floor are also being used by geographers to create understandings of how social theory interacts with the body, knowing, and consciousness. Dance scholarship has a unique ability to rethink social theory through its engagement in corporeality, a task that a variety of different non-geographers are involved in (for example see Grosz 1994, and Schneider 1997). Within geography, McCormack (2003) uses the rhythm of dancing bodies to rethink the process of academic production and Saldanha (2005) introduces the concept of "viscosity" to theorize the unique ways in which dancers and their bodies interact with one another on the dance floor to rethink the lived corporeality of race. A similar critical rethinking of the corporeality of "knowing" can be seen in the work of Somdahl-Sands (2006) who connects the body at dance with Edward Soja's conception of "Thirdspace," situating dance as a way of inscribing the body in space. This commitment to situating the body within geographic theory also adds to ongoing conversations around governmentality, as it struggles to understand how the body and the state are connected (Foucault 1991, Rose 1996).

The above examples show that that geographic work on dance, like that of non-geographers, is deeply committed to the representational aspects of dance and to decode the ideological underpinnings of bodily practice. While critical and post-structural theorists of dance have focused on decoding and deconstructing the various meanings of dance, the representations and contestations of identity represented by it, and the increasing hybridity of styles, geographic scholarship has been particularly innovative in its approach to dance by engaging in a different approach to corporeality—it has championed the development of "non-representational theory."

Following this interest in deciphering what is understood by the movement of bodies, it is particularly the work of Nigel Thrift, embracing the theories of Benjamin, de Certeau, Foucault, Deleuze and Guattari, that has embraced "non-representational theory" or the "theory of practices" (Thrift 1996, 1997). Thrift argues that the mundane, repeated actions of dance are unspeakable, but illustrative of how societies change and evolve over time. He provides a non-intentionalist account of the world, and argues that too often, the body is placed into discourse, analyzed and understood discursively, "without considering the other, expressive side of its existence" (Thrift 1997, 137). The expressive character of the body is underestimated, and denigrated as a surface upon which society is inscribed, without considering that the body can participate in expressions of identity that go beyond the textual. As Ford and Brown (2006, 162) highlight, for Thrift the non-representational view "asserts that rather than being about signs and meanings, the body is about the relation between body and things." Identification with and attachment to a certain place or a specific group of people is achieved by producing spaces through the things of nature, by the felt energy that connects people to places and each other. When we eat, see, move, and consequently when we dance, we are not only concerned about the representational meaning of our movement, but what equally—or perhaps pre-dominantly—matters is the sense of *communitas*, to borrow Victor Turner's words. Through the consumption of nature's goods or by movements in a certain place, the feeling, the energy of that material or place is absorbed by us, and absorbs us in it. Rather than absorbed by and controlled through discourse, rather than controlled by power and ideology, the body at dance is a body at play, meaning that the power of movement lies in "being able to articulate complexes of thought—with—feeling that words cannot name, let alone set forth. It is a way of accessing the world, not just a means of achieving ends that cannot be named (Radley 1995, 13). This ambiguity of meaning as it is present in dance is also captured by Isadora Duncan's famous theorem that "if I could tell you what it meant, there would be no point in dancing it" (as quoted by Thrift 1997, 139).

Thrift's ideas are also carefully reflected in the work of German philosopher Peter Sloterdijk. What Sloterdijk so brilliantly does in his work is to elaborate on the relationship between modern individuals and groups, and the desire and need of individuals to belong to a group. For Sloterdijk, modern individuals negotiate constantly between the multiple identities and groups that they belong to. Our sense of allegiance has never been and will never be monolithic and tied to just one religion, nation or region. With the demise of the authority of church and state, and the decline of "high culture" as a medium of identification, it is increasingly the popular forms of entertainment that have become part of our ways of belonging and our negotiations of identity. Yet, as Sloterdijk argues, it is particularly the non-representational forms of practice that have taken on a role in shaping who we are. Instead of overt, political and textual messages, modern societies more and more rely on sonispheric practices and movement to form communities. We dance, eat, listen to music, and so on to become part of a larger community, and these communities are multifaceted in their messages and ideas, not homogenous. It is only the practice, the food, the movement and the desire to return to some kind of archaic state of pre-linguistic infancy that unites people, not their political ideology.

As archaic as it might be, consumptive participation in the maternal milieu through one's *infans* voice is not the earliest form of absorption magic. Before the subject could experience the necessity of calling in order to eat, it was granted an even deeper form of participation that, as fetal, sanguine, endo-acoustic communion, offered the absolute maximum of absorbed life. That is where those who want neither to work nor to call strive to return in order to find the archaic homeostasis once more. Before the *infans*, the non-speaker, comes the *inclamans*, the non-caller. It is characteristic of modern mass culture that it has learned how to bypass the tables and altars of high culture and offer new, direct ways of fulfilling the desire for homeostatic communion. This is the psychodynamic purpose of pop music and all its derivatives: for its consumers, it stages the possibility of diving into a body of rhythmic noise in which critical ego functions become temporarily dispensable. Anyone who witnesses the behavioral gestures at discotheques and sound parades as an impartial observer must conclude that the current mass music audience strives for an enthusiastic self-sacrifice by plunging—voluntarily and at its own risk—into the sound crater. It creatively longs to be drawn inwards by the acoustic juggernaut and transformed inside its innards into a rhythmicized, oxygen-deprived, pre-subjective something. Pop music has overtaken religious communities—Christian ones—on the archaic wing by outdoing the chances of absorption found at altars with the offer to join psychoacoustic abdominal cavities and follow passing audio gods. (Sloterdijk 2011, 527)

Our interest in dance research is in direct communication with other interdisciplinary scholarship analyzing cultural forms such as music (Leyshon et al. 1998), youth cultures (Skelton and Valentine 1998); and "the body" (Nast and Pile 1998). In these collections, we package cutting edge research on dance that examines "geographies of dance" as they relate to issues such as transnationalism, citizenship, governmentality, feminist theory, queer theory, scale, mobility, ethnicity, and marginalization. While the existing literature has selectively addressed these important aspects of geographies of dance, there exists to date no comprehensive geographical compendium of this phenomenon. In these edited collections, our authors situate dance within contemporary debates in geography; they analyze the theoretical contributions that dance research has made to geographic theory, and position dance research within contemporary debate in social theory. We build our collection around two themes: (1) corporeal negotiations; and (2) globalization, hybridity and cultural identity, and present it in two separate volumes.

This first volume analyzes the dancing body as a corporeal actor that is choreographed and performed through the process of dance, but also as an entity that is expressive, spontaneous and either consciously or unconsciously evading discursive positioning. In using the dancing body as our object of inquiry we examine the essential corporeality of questions of identity, race and nationality. This book comments on contemporary debates involving performativity, governmentality, and liminality, suggesting that through the movement of the body at dance we see individuals *negotiating* the complex boundaries and questions of modern life.

The specific contribution of this book lies in its ability to draw together scholarly work that examines the above questions at a variety of different scales and geographies. It is not only important to question how and where dance does take place, but also why we dance, where we dance, and how dance is used in conjunction with landscapes (and through the medium of choreography) to create a meaningful form of representation that interprets space. Most importantly, how does the meaning of dance change as we contemplate the different interconnections between the diverse locations where dance occur?

Central to our discussion of the multiple meanings of the dancing body is our understanding of the various scales that influence the understanding, representation, and creation of dance. Importantly, scales are not preexisting containers of space, but are socially produced as a result of political, social, and economic processes. As Delaney and Leitner argue, "once our conception of scale is freed from the fixed categories inherited from the past and our conception of politics is similarly expanded and enlivened, the questions multiply and the analytic or interpretive problems involved in relating scale to politics become more obvious" (1997, 95).

Importantly, Kaiser and Nikiforova (2008) in their article "The Performativity of Scale" assert that scalar imaginaries become ingrained through the "reiterative and citational practices through which scale effects are socially produced"; thus in performing scale we more solidly create and solidify current scalar imaginaries. Although the scalar debates emerged from Marxist analyses of the expansion of capitalism (for examples, see Harvey 1990, Arrighi 1994, Brenner 2001), a central aspect of the scalar debate concerns the primacy of political and economic forces in the creation of scales, versus the ability and importance of cultural processes such as gender and social reproduction to also produce scales (Marston, 2000). Multiple scholars have entered this debate discussing the ways in which gender and race can be understood as constructing scales (Silvey 2006, Merrill and Carter 2002, Merrill 2004), and other such as Marston et al. (2005) have attempted to think through the confusing interconnections between sites by proposing the importance of "flat ontologies" and a stronger sense of the theoretical foundations of the site. To them, rather than reading social events through the lens of hierarchal scalar arrangements (pre-existing scalar theories), we should instead approach analyses of scale as qualitative researchers approach "the field" and look to construct theory from what we see. This embrace of a postmodern regime of "particularisms" should be tempered by the idea that "sites" are not all unique, instead they exhibit signs of interactions with other sites, patterns formed through shared "co-spatiality" and existence.

We view dance as a crucial venue through which to explore the interconnections across scales, and between sites because the body is a crucial space within which ideologies, actions, and emotions are made manifest. Inspired by the work of Paromita Kar that is leading off the case studies presented in this volume, we use the term *corporeal negotiations* as a way of naming the complex position of a dancing body. In her 2000 analysis of performativity in the geography literature, geographer Catherine Nash engages with ongoing debates in cultural studies and dance studies in questioning whether dance movements are essentially performative in nature (and thus reflect the true "natural" inner core of the participant), or choreographed in nature (and thus reflect merely repetitions of preordained movements chosen and designed by others). Within this paradigm dance is constructed as either a "true" and authentic" form of representation or simply a set of actions that serve as a container for transnational cultural production. This debate highlights the fluidity of dance and demands we contemplate the interaction between choreography and spontaneity as dancers use their bodies to negotiate the relationship be how they want to move and how the outside world will understand their movements.

Dance speaks to multiple audiences that are situated at various spatial scales. What we find in the intersecting conversations that these multiple audiences create is that the corporeality of the body becomes abstracted as its negotiations are broadcast in impersonal ways through technology, presentation, and curatorial decisions. For social dancers, the mirrors inside the dance studio permit students to examine their own bodies in ways seldom encountered in other venues. In this instance the dancer is both the performer and the audience, and dancers are in the unique situation of being forced to gaze upon themselves and view both their own corporeality and the maneuvers they are being asked to learn. Dance also speaks to a physical audience within the auditorium or performance space. While through dance notation it is possible to transform dance from a physical art form to written art form, most dance is experienced first hand in a space where there is a clear divide between dancer and audience. But the dancer is representing not only their movements, but also, as Bourdieu and Lefebvre remind us, a whole ensemble of social relationships which dictate what movements are most respected and how the audience is to respond to these movements. Other dance venues like films, movies, music videos, YouTube, and the TV show *Dancing With the Stars* create a spatial distinction between dancer and audience which allows for the images of the dance to be mediated through special effects, camera angles, and editing. In these instance also the social systems in which the dance is embedded is decontextualized.

The scale of the audience / dancer relationship is constantly evolving, and subject to negotiation. Therefore there is no set dance stage or dance venue. Instead *we create spaces of dance* based on what the dance means and the fluid relationship between dancer, audience and space. For example, dance venues like outdoor raves change with the weather, and dance clubs transform as the music switches. In this instance the nooks and crannies of the dance hall are alternately part of the dance floor and places of relaxation and conversation depending on the time. Similarly liturgical dance is often staged near the altar or in the aisles of the church, at weddings the crowd makes a space for the couples first dance to occur, and staged outdoor dances use rivers and landscapes as part of the choreography.

To this end, dance is important as a subject of scholarly attention because its performance, development, and philosophy all represent the interactions between specific cultural tradition *and by studying dance we come to know more about how culture, identity, and specific places have formed.* The aspects of culture that scholars focus on in this book are diverse, ranging from transnational identities to explorations of how new identities can be formed through the process of dance instruction. How does dance emerge from specific places, and what is globalization doing to the connection between place and dance? How are identities shaped dance and choreography, and what role does the audience play in this process?

Paromitra Kar in "Modernity, Post-modernity, and the Paradigmatic *Mudra*: Corporeal Negotiations in the Works of Toronto's Contemporary Bharatanatyam Choreographers" explores how the work of Toronto-based South Indian choreographers understand their place in the South Indian diaspora. She employs the beautiful metaphor of the *pas de deux* (a term from classical ballet) to investigate how the conflict between the Self and the (cultural, ethnic, or movement discipline) Other operates in their choreographic work. She argues that rather than engage with the other in superficial or shallow ways, the choreographers have engaged in contemporary movement disciplines in direct and physical ways: literally immersing themselves in the movement vocabulary of the other, transforming their choreography into a conversation between different ways of understanding movement. Of particular importance to Kar is the place of the body, which she reads as a "site of cultural expression" where specific gestures (such as *mudras)* signify the complex relationship between body, dance, and choreography: a relationship that the choreographers are constantly challenging.

Moriah McSharry McGrath in "Neighboring in Strip City: Local Conflict and Spaces of Exotic Dance in Portland, Oregon" understands the unique distribution and culture of strip clubs to be representations of 'frontier' culture in the West. She notes that in Portland there are more strip clubs per capita than other city, and exotic dance establishments are not regarded as locally unwanted land uses (LULUs) and zoned into specific isolated areas, but are instead present in many residential neighborhoods. To this end the "sexscape" of Portland is continually reformed through people becoming more aware and accepting of the sex industry because of liberal zoning codes. She explores the unique culture of exotic dance in Portland where these spatially diverse dance establishments where non-traditional body types, unique musical styles, and distinctive choreography make Portland strip clubs a reflection of the cultural ethos of the town. Dancers, for example, while still stigmatized in the larger dance community, do find a sense of empowerment working in Portland. McGrath, analyzing exotic dance at the city, neighborhood, and individual club scale sees the acceptance of contested—yet lucrative and popular—dance the emergence of new and more flexible understandings sexuality that are not more liberating and open than existing norms.

Teresa Heiland in "One Foot Inside the Circle: Contemporary Dance of Los Angeles Steps Outside Postmodernism and into Neo-Modernism-with-a-Twist" draws connections between the city of Los Angeles and the unique dance form of *HyperDance* which has emerged from this metropolis. For Heiland, the puzzle of a major American city with an enormous entertainment industry yet little reputation or institutional support for modern dance, serves as an entré into the connection between place and dance. She argues that the economic power of the Hollywood entertainment industry and its focus on spectacle, computer-aided special effects, intermixing of dance and movement styles, and a constant focus on innovation has served to create the unique place-based form of dance *HyperDance* which is focused on pushing the human body to its physical limits and creating ways of moving that have never been seen before. Heiland connects this hybrid dance form to Los Angeles's postmodern urban form and the culture of the city which revolves around newness and growth, asserting a dynamic connection between urban space and movement. Heiland draws on Bourdieu to argue that LA is a giant field out of which a postmodern pastiche of *Hyperdance* has emerged.

Tamara M. Johnson in "Some Dance to Remember: The Emotional Politics of Marginality, Reinvention, Embodied Memory, and All the (Cape) Jazz" explores the connections between memory, emotion, and history in the creation of the syncretic dance style that has come to be known as Cape Jazz. Johnson conducts "critical performance ethnography," dancing and listening to the narratives of Cape Jazz dancers. She explores how the embodied nature of dance make it a lived experience which can better be understood thorough an embrace of personal affect and emotion as opposed to concrete assurances that dance can be directly connected to a specific signifier or root. She connects the ephemeral nature of Cape Jazz to the process of forgetting that has been a strong part of South Africa's economic and political emergence from apartheid. To Johnson, the narratives that emerge out of the dancers of Cape Jazz assemble the dance as a commemorative and embodied reflection of the marginality and displacement experienced by the coloured community of Cape Town. To this end the dance is not global or local, rather she asserts that these terms are not static but formed through the complicated personal histories of oppression and collective identity that are part and parcel of Cape jazz.

Jonathan Skinner, in "Social Dance and Social Space," takes us to the vibrant salsa scene in Belfast, Northern Ireland. Skinner uses the concept of "social dance" to illustrate how dance serves as a way to cross real and perceived divides between immigrant cultures and locals and between catholic and protestant communities. To Skinner dance is one venue which can be used to open channels of communication for cross-cultural understanding. Social dance provides immigrants with a way to explore their birth identity while firmly immersed in Northern Irish Culture, and for locals to experiment with and navigate through an increasingly complex mix of immigrant dance cultures that offer exotic escapism. For him, transnational dancers in a transnational city temporarily play with identities not of their own, or recuperate an identity that they had perceived as lost or suppressed.

Georgia Connover in "Mediating the Other through Dance: Geopolitics, Social Ordering, and Meaning-Making in American and Improvisational Tribal Style Dance" reads the new dance form of American Tribal Style (ATS) as a *mediated text*, within which power relationships are inscribed and co-producers of the meanings of the dance. She argues that this new dance that is "not authentic to anywhere" was created by mostly white American women as a juxtaposition of different movement styles to be an intervention against the disempowering over-sexualized belly-dance type dances. This conscious co-opting of dance styles consciously destabilizes whiteness and "otherness" as dances are reformed in communities far from their origins. To Conover, these create something new and significant to themselves, but continue to construct the Orient as static and unchanging: especially in comparison to the newness of ATS. Similarly, in creating a new representation of belly dance, ATS writes Arab women out of the dance and the white female body becomes the rational norm against which others are to be judged.

The second question that our volume addresses is in regards to the expressive, non-representational power of the body. At what scale does the non-representational,

expressive power of corporeality begin to disrupt or counteract discourse that might
be inscribed in choreography or perceived by audiences? Is the non-representational
power of the body, and its ability to form communities of excitement, to use Peter Sloterdijk's words, limited in scale? How effective and permanent is expressive
embodiment through dance in creating communities of various scales? How does
it create community if not through representational practices that can be read and
interpreted by participants and audience alike? Can, as Sloterdijk has argued, an entire nation be drawn together by non-representational practice, and simply form, by
dance, a community of collective excitement that transcends traditional coherence
of representational regimes?

Four of the ten contributions in this volume address the possibilities and powers
of expressive embodiment, and the scaled interactions of a variety of dance productions that at least to some degree, either voluntarily or intentionally, escape or
challenge the realm of discursive construction. Our author's reflections begin with
Matthew Kurtz's analysis of the Inupiaq Alaska natives of Kotzebue, titled "Mimetic
Moves: Dance and Learning to Learn in Northwest Alaska." His work encourages us
to learn about dance, to understand its power from below, to drop our methodological gaze as outsiders looking in, and to shed our preconceived ideological notions.
He argues that dance scholars and geographers, as outsiders, have "read" and placed
Inupiak dance as a cultural practice into a certain discourse—one that is produced
for metropolitan visitors to tell a certain story of the Alaska natives and their relation
to the land. Instead, Kurtz asserts that what we must do is to see it as a playful mimesis. For example, it is practice among Inuit tribes such as the Inupiaq to socialize
and educate their children through forms of role-play, including moral dilemmas and
dramatizations. These activities encourage them to embrace uncertainty and foster
adaptability to changing circumstances rather than providing fixed answers and
normative behavior. These presentations, while instructive and providing a form of
learning, encourage learning through re-enactment and play, not words and recitation, and thus representation. Similarly, Inupiaq dance can of course be understood
as a cultural practice embedded in a certain socio-economic and historical discourse,
but such a perspective is that of an outsider. From within the native Alaskan community that Kurtz examined, dance must be understood as a form of mimesis, a form of
learning by doing that rather than a representation of values and norms. It must be
understood as performative, imitative, and instructive, yet leaves room for dilemma,
uncertainty, and multiple answers and expressions. Dance, according the Inupiaq
tradition, is thus a presentational form of play and mimesis that creates community,
sets boundaries, expectations, and behaviors, yet remains open to multiple interpretations. Kurtz's work is thus instructive of how dance can used as an epistemology,
a way of getting know the world, a playful non-representational exploration of the
relationship between individuals, their groups, and the landscapes they inhabit.

Frances Bronet, in "Dance, Architecture and Space in the Making," analyzes two
dance performances that actively and critically engage with architecture and the
built environment. Contrary to the common perception that dance is placed in a

given, fixed landscape that was intended by the choreographer and must be read or interpreted by the audience in a specific way, she shows us that the embodied practice in dance often allows for the creative reconstruction of physical and designed spaced space and thus challenges the perceived static relationship between dancer and audience. In both projects she addresses in her chapter, "Beating a Path," and "Spill Out," dancers work within and actively reconfigure architectural landscapes in highly mobile choreographies that blur the boundary between stage and landscape on the one side and dancer and audience on the other. Her work actively questions who is looking, gazing at, or viewing a performance and who is dancing, and with this raises the all-important question of non-representational theory: For whom, by whom and for what is meaning produced in performative acts, and how can we, if at all, distinguish these? Is it even important to do so?

Katrinka Somdahl-Sands, in "At Home in Motion: Networks, Nodes, and Navigation the Varied Flight Paths of Bird Brain Dance," shows us that the uncertainty of boundaries between landscape/stage and dancer/audience is not only visible in the immediate production site of event, as evident in the work of Bronet, but that such creative acts of can be extended to much larger scales. She chronicles the path of *Bird Brain Dance*, a production that is migratory and uses a variety of different sites for its production. Each site is characterized by a different landscape, different set-up and different audiences, thus complicating the meaning and interpretation of the event, and its ability to be read. Somdahl-Sands argues however, that it is precisely the moving and constantly changing character of the event, and its multi-year migratory path from performance site to performance site that makes it valuable and meaningful. She shows us that in *Bird Brain Dance*, the movement of dance in site and the movement of the site of dance, simultaneously, can show us something that best be conveyed when on the move, not in a static environment. Some things cannot be captured in a single choreography at a single site—especially when it comes to using dance as a teaching tool about a natural phenomenon such as bird migration.

Tovi Fenster, in "Belly Dancing in Israel: Body, Embodiment, Religion and Nationality," translates the ability of dance to explore, to play with different identities at different sites, to an analysis of the exploration of borders. She investigates how Israeli women step out of the performance of their everyday identities in political landscapes of clearly defined cultural and political borders, and enter the dance studio to explore the opposite. Yet belly dancing does not provide a fixed platform to immerse oneself in another fixed identity, to become someone else, to represent other values, to become "the other," albeit only for a short while. The studio is place where belly dancing, itself a performance art with a cultural identity that is geographically diverse, becomes a vehicle for women to explore, to play with, and to engage safely with identities that do not have to be named and demarcated. The studio and the dance become a vehicle to escape the often dangerous associations of the fixed geographies and identities of the world outside, where their acts of everyday life are necessarily bound to a much more fixed framework of meaning, and escape or opposition to that can be dangerous.

What emerges out of the contrasting theoretical approaches (both representational and non-representational), and the multitude of examples portrayed in this volume, is a complex picture of the corporeality of the dancing body, its limited power of representation, and its ability to resist such fixed meanings by engaging in spontaneous collective enjoyment that is defined not by text, but a pre-linguistic understanding of sound and motion. On the one hand, dance continuously navigates between the intentionality of choreography, the scripted and inscribed portrayal of meaning that intends to deliver a message to the viewer and the dancers themselves, to be perceived and read within a social context and given geographical landscape. On the other, non-representational theory and its exemplary work has pointed out that such understanding of dance is problematic in that it discounts spontaneous embodiment and the power of dance to create meaning by "experiencing the moment." Dance and dancer can either intentionally or spontaneously work against choreography, against or outside of a social context, and most importantly, utilize geographical environments, landscapes, and sites not only to represent a meaningful message, but instead create community and communion by immersion in a non-discursive, tactile, and audible environment. To return to our opening quote by W. B. Yeats, this volume intends to show that sometimes, it is possible to tell the dancer from the dance, and we can interpret the intentionality, motivation and meaning of a performance, yet sometimes we are best advised to delight in the messiness of being unable to separate the dancer from the dance, and to embrace this experience of human movement as the non-intentional, unselfconscious, expressive yet deeply meaningful experience it can be.

1

Modernity, Post-modernity, and the Paradigmatic *Mudra*

Corporeal Negotiations in the Works of Toronto's Contemporary Bharatanatyam Choreographers

Paromitra Kar, York University

Over two last decades, social anthropologists and theorists have increasingly engaged with questions of diasporic identities. They emphasize that identities of national belonging are rendered complex, multilayered, and continually mobile. This paper is a study of how identity is manifest in cultural production, focusing on the choreographic medium. I trace some of the dynamics of identity expressed in select choreographies by the Toronto-based choreographers Natasha Bakht, Nova Bhattacharya, Hari Krishnan, and Lata Pada. Each of these choreographers have been trained in the classical Indian dance form of Bharatanatyam, and they all venture outside the Bharatanatyam movement lexicon and repertoire in their choreographic work, to engage with contemporary dance movement vocabulary, form, and thematic matter to create works reflective of their quotidian experience and inquiries.

I employ the metaphor of the *pas de deux* to theorize the choreographic approach of these artists in their contemporary work in Toronto. The term pas de deux is an import from classical ballet vocabulary, usually used to refer to a partnering dance between the principal male dancer and principal female dancer in a full-length ballet. While duets are occasionally performed within Bharatanatyam performances, Bharatanatyam was essentially developed as a solo dance genre during its twentieth century revival. The full-length classical Bharatanatyam repertoire, known as the *margam*, was developed exclusively as solo dance repertoire. I use the term pas de deux to denote a dance between a "Self" and an "Other," or, essentially, two "Others."

In classical ballet, the two Others dancing a pas de deux are differentiated almost always by gender in its design as the dance between the principal male and female dancer. Often, they are also separated by a human/non-human divide, such as in the case of Prince Sigfried and Odette the Swan Queen in Petipa and Lev Ivanov's *Swan Lake*, or the Rose and the female protagonist in Michel Fokine's *Spectre de la Rose*.

Throughout the twentieth century, the balletic pas de deux saw a number of changes, such as in the gendering as in Matthew Bourne's *Swan Lake*, where the lead Swan is a male Swan, or in the incorporation of the *corps de ballet*, or the female ensemble dancers within the pas de deux, as in the ribbon dance in Frederick Ashton's *La Fille mal Gardee*. However, in most works, the pas de deux continues to remain a dance of two Others, characterized by a mutual desire between the two Others to engage with each other. I use the term Other not necessarily in binary opposition to a constructed Self, but rather see these notions as porous entities, with space for each to seep into the other. The term Other is used to denote dance movements, vocabulary and embodied philosophies, and aesthetics which lie outside of the Bharatanatyam canon.

Resonating the central question in the danced pas de deux, the engagement between others is often the central question for scholars in their explorations of the phenomenon of cosmopolitanism. Social anthropologist Ulf Hannerz posits a theory of cosmopolitanism in which he presents cosmopolitanism as a conscious willingness of an individual to engage with a culture outside his or her own (1990). Gita Rajan and Shailja Sharma point to the new cosmopolitan subject as an increasingly significant subject of study (2006). Ulrich Beck and Watan Sznaider point out that while cosmopolitanism is a contested term in that there is no uniform interpretation of the term in scholarship (2006), it remains identifiable as an intellectual movement. At the heart of this academic cosmopolitanism, they see two crux ideas; that the world today is more cosmopolitan than earlier, and that this must be addressed by a methodological cosmopolitanism in scholarship. Kendall, Woodland and Skrbis also point out that there are tensions between different conceptualizations of cosmopolitanism—that there are different types of cosmopolitanisms, and people are cosmopolitan in different ways (2009).

This paper is a study of how a cosmopolitan approach is manifest in cultural production, focusing on the choreographic work by Toronto-based choreographers of Bharatanatyam movement background. Nikos Papastergiadis examines cosmopolitanism in the field of cultural production, maintaining that there is an emerging trend of "globally oriented artistic practices," which require a new conceptual paradigm adequate for representing the mobilities and mixtures that constitute the social context of art (2012, 12). He contends that "artists are knowledge partners in the theories of cosmopolitanism and innovators in the modes of global belonging" (2012, 10). I argue that the metaphor of the pas de deux may be an apt lens of analysis; and further, the focus of this lens on the body as it negotiates through identities bridges the subject of cosmopolitanism with the subject of the body.

A study of a Self and an Other when analyzing contemporary dance works by Bharatanatyam-based choreographers is complicated by the complex and precarious identity of an Indian classical dance-trained choreographer of South Asian origin working in North America. Ananya Chatterjee describes how the simultaneous existence of various modes of Indian dance performance, often taken to signify "Indian dance" for a non-Indian audience in North America serve to complicate the construction of "South Asian contemporary dance," as these modes often produce multiple and often conflicting notions of "Indian dance" and "Indian culture." In particular, she points to "film dances," (2004, xii) and pop-culture's use and often appropriation of Indian dance, such as the Indian classical Odissi dance section in Michael Jackson's video, and how the widespread dissemination of the images of Indian dance creates certain expectations and images of "Indian dance." She attributes the confusion regarding the identity of South Asian contemporary dance partly to the "absence of a fully theorized contemporary genre" (2004, xii).

To this, I add that the multiplicity of contexts in which the term "contemporary South Asian dance" has come to be used further complicates an easy description of the field, as does the lack of a singular monolithic emblematic image accompanying the term "contemporary South Asian dance." Romila Thapar, in "The Tyranny of Labels," asserts that "labels, where they may include a variety of activity and experience, tend to force interpretations into a single category so that the infinite shades of difference between them disappear" (1996, 3). Perhaps then, it is the absence of a single monolithic category that leads to the confusion regarding the connotations of the term "South Asian contemporary dance." The word "contemporary" is not used in a singular sense by the different choreographers, and many modes of "contemporary Indian dance" coexist simultaneously. In India, a growing "contemporary dance" scene is taking shape, in which dancers and choreographers train and perform in "contemporary dance" as it is understood in the Euro-North American context, in relation to particular schools of technique and grammar.

Janet O'Shea views choreography as "strategy," and applies this to different eras in Bharatanatyam history. Four years ago, I witnessed noted Bharatanatyam exponent Navtej Johar perform a self-choreographed solo titled *Meenakshi* in Toronto. The piece was dedicated to the fish-eyed goddess, and throughout the piece, he used movements from classical Bharatanatyam idiom. In a certain memorable section, he dipped his hand in green powdery paint, and continued the piece with green hands, thereby changing the look of the piece, and also the context of the performance. Choreographers of classical Indian dance backgrounds working in a contemporary context thus contend with not only the existence of multiple forms of "contemporary South Asian" performance, but also continually changing modes of performance of classical Indian dance, in the use of the word "contemporary" as a descriptor for this work.

I am interested in tracing what negotiations of the body underlie the choreographic works in the genre of contemporary Indian dance, especially in the choreographic works of those trained in Indian classical dances. How do issues of representation and subjectivity intersect the work of choreographers, and how might these be traced in terms of the moving body? Drawing upon Janet O'Shea's system of reading choreography as "strategy," and therefore as a series of conscious choices, I argue that for the Bharatanatyam-based contemporary choreographers in Toronto, the body becomes the space and medium through which negotiations of identity occur, manifest as a pas de deux with an Other. Here, the Self is located in the realm of the corporeal, relating to both the body itself, as well as the body's training in a particular movement discipline.

The phenomenon of Bharatanatyam-trained choreographers creating in a contemporary context is a global one, and not exclusive to Toronto alone. The choreographers whose works I analyze participate in an international practice, prominent in North America, Europe, and India. In Canada itself, there are a number of noted choreographers working with this genre, such as the Montreal-based Roger Sinha, and Toronto-based Menaka Thakkar and Janak Khendry. An analysis of the works of all of these choreographers would be beyond the scope of this article, and hence I focus on close readings of the negotiations of the body in the works of my four selected choreographers. In particular, I engage in a reading of some of their works created between 2000 to 2010.

Among my research source materials are live performances, videos of performances, attendance at public talks and lectures by these artists, radio interviews, and textual transcripts of interviews. This is, therefore, also a study of how these choreographers engage with their own choreography at a self-reflexive, discursive level. My research on the subject coincided with the International Conference and Festival on Contemporary Choreography in Indian Dance, jointly hosted in Toronto by Kalanidhi Fine Arts of Canada and the Menaka Thakkar Dance Company in January 2009. Some of the performances described in this article were staged and viewed at the aforementioned conference, which featured live performance evenings at the Fleck Dance Theatre in downtown Toronto.

THE *MUDRA* AND THE BODY: SITES OF NEGOTIATION AND MANIFESTATION

My title is a nod in the direction of Ketu Katrak's "The Gestures of Bharata Natyam: Migrating into Diasporic Contemporary Indian Dance," in which Katrak examines the ways in which features from the Bharatanatyam tradition, such as the stylized hand gestures, the footwork, and mimetic interpretation of lyrics are employed and recontextualized by choreographers in the South Asian diaspora in California, especially by choreographer Shyamala Moorty, to represent the diasporic reality (Katrak 2008). The word mudra refers to the codified hand-gesture system, which is attributed to the *Natyashastra*, a treatise on the classical Indian performing arts, believed to have been written between 200 BC and 200 AD. The use of this unified, codified hand-gesture system is a characteristic of the majority of the Indian classical dance styles, even as a number of them also feature hand-gestures distinct to the respective style. The status of the mudra system as being codified allows the mudras in the dance to be recognizable as belonging to the Indian classical dance system. Kendall, Woodland, and Skrbis emphasize that objects have performative, symbolic qualities in that they are "interpretable markers of cultural origin and difference" (2009, 128). While the authors speak of "objects," largely in the case of material possessions, such as a foreign car, fashion object, or fruit, I find that this performative quality is equally applicable in the case of movement quotations. The mudra is possibly one of the most identifiable markers of classical Indian dance, and thus stands as paradigmatic reference to the Indian classical dance within these corporeal negotiations.

At present, the Indian government recognizes eight different classical dance forms, namely Bharatanatyam, Kathak, Odissi, Manipuri, Kuchipudi, Kathakali, Mohiniattam, and Sattriya. Each of these dance forms, originating in different regions in India, have distinct aesthetic traditions, embodied philosophies, and histories of revival. The four choreographers whose works I analyze each have their movement background in the discipline of Bharatanatyam. The Bharatanatyam dance form had its origins in the state of Tamil Nadu in India. It was among the first of the Indian classical dance forms to undergo a "revival" whereby it was adapted for the purpose of performance in the public arena, especially for the proscenium stage. Bharatanatyam's "revival" began in the 1930s, with the efforts of a number of individuals to resuscitate the *sadir* dance form, originally practiced by the temple-attendants in the southern state of Tamil Nadu in India, and present it on the urban, proscenium stage as the classical Bharatanatyam dance form. Two figures closely associated with the revival of Bharatanatyam are Rukmini Devi Arundale, and Balasaraswati, who spearheaded the Pandanallur/Kalakshetra and Thanjavur traditions of Bharatanatyam respectively. Bharatanatyam was thus the first recognized classical Indian dance form.

The traditional discourse surrounding Bharatanatyam links it to temple dance traditions rooted in antiquity. The rhetoric of scholars and practitioners was instrumental in the construction of this form as the authentic "ancient" classical dance form of India, and this rhetoric, in support of the revivalist project, dominated the discourse on Indian classical dance until the 1980s.

With *Angika* in 1985, the choreographer Chandralekha is considered to have ushered in the postmodern in the context of Indian dance and movement arts. Bharatanatyam features the use of a specific stylized movement vocabulary and a number of its repertoire pieces are dedicated to the depiction of characters and narratives. As Chatterjea notes, *Angika* interrupts the notion of the unadulterated "classical purity" of form by proposing the "contamination" of the movement of highly trained Bharatanatyam dancers through their "exposure" to other forms (2004, 195). Chandralekha's project brought together the lines of Bharatanatyam with the postures of *yogasanas*; it was a project that was invested in the body reclaiming agency and questioning its own function as the medium of entertainment and spectacle. Chandralekha's work was a departure from the "spectacle" features of Bharatanatyam; her dancers' costumes consisted of "rehearsal clothes," as opposed to the elaborate garments, jewelry, and makeup of Bharatanatyam.

Perhaps paralleling the shift in choreographic approach, since the 1980s, a number of scholars have questioned the revivalist rhetoric, especially in regards to twentieth century Bharatanatyam practice as having directly evolved from the temple dance practice and retaining unchanged elements over the centuries. Janet O'Shea looks at the politics of the Bharatanatyam revival, and examines the strategies undertaken by its key players. She views choreography as "strategy," and applies this to different eras in Bharatanatyam history, including the Bharatanatyam revival during the 1930s, and choreography during the late 1990s and early 2000s. Her approach involves looking at case studies of specific choreographies and analyzing the specific personal and socio-political contexts in which they were created. O'Shea suggests that an approach toward Bharatanatyam history which overlooks the individual choreographers, and the contexts in which they create, runs the risk of being similar to "an Orientalist notion of individuals replicating tradition, with practitioners being constrained by, rather than actively negotiating, their heritage" (2007, 12). In O'Shea's theory then, Bharatanatyam itself is seen as "contemporary," as opposed to being the Other to contemporary.

Addressing the problematic assumptions that underlie the usages of the terms "classical" and "contemporary" in the context of Indian dance, Alyssandra y Royo states that any performance that addresses itself to a contemporary audience may be called "contemporary" (2003). She argues that in the western context, the term "contemporary," when used with reference to Indian dance, is conflated with the idea of an "engagement with modernity, with a suggestion of temporariness," and that the idea of "contemporary," with reference to Indian dance, is further complicated by the existence of Indian practitioners of western contemporary techniques of dance (2003, 154). She labels the work of dance artists, whose works grow out of the traditional Indian movement repertoire, and yet who consciously identify their works as being located in a contemporary context as "post-classicist" or "Contemporary dance with a capital 'c'" (2003, 153). She gives the example of Mavin Khoo, a British practitioner trained in both Bharatanatyam and ballet, whom, Royo asserts, sees the two forms as extensions of each other (2004). She states that Khoo's relationship with classicism can be described as the "neo-classical" approach, whereby he works with two different dance forms which share the idea of being based on "classical principles." She also refers to the work of the influential choreographer Shobhana Jeyasinghe, originally a Bharatanatyam-trained artiste, who moved from a "traditionally authentic" position in her early work to neo-classical work in the late 1980s, to a distinctly post-modern approach in which she rejected labeling. Royo thus advocates for the multiplicity in the understandings of the term "contemporary" in the context of Indian dance in the diaspora.

While recent scholarship acknowledges the contemporary work by choreographers of Indian classical dance backgrounds, I contend that in scholarship on Indian classical and contemporary dance, the negotiations of the body remains largely underdeveloped. Helen Thomas observes that the body has become a major area of interest for scholars of dance studies and culture since the late 1980s (2003). She marks this historical shift of scholarly attention to the body, claiming that the body had been a marginal topic before the 1980s, before turning into a "veritable industry" in scholarship during the 1990s in a shift she terms the "body project." Ann Cooper Albright points out that while the body has become an important discursive site in cultural theory, it remains largely underdeveloped as a discursive site in dance scholarship and criticism (1997). Susan Foster asserts that the body is a site of meaning making, and that bodies develop their own system of signs, through physicality, with which to narrate their condition (1996). She points out that the presence of the body in writing about dance would "corpo-realize writing" (1996, xv).

Configurations and reconfigurations of the body remained central to scholarship on Chandralekha, as much as much as to the nature of her choreographic work itself. Ananya Chatterjea undertakes a reading of selected works from the repertoire of Zollar and Chandralekha, in which she maps the socio-political implications, and issues of choreographic agency in their works. The body makes a strong presence in her work; Chatterjea writes early on that her title "Butting Out" indicates a disruption of "linear neatness and spinal containment" (2004, 19). She argues for how the work of these choreographers is post-modern, "resistive," and draws upon the metaphor of the deeply flexed hip, often characteristic of several movement and life practices of Indian and African diasporic people (2004, 19). However, in scholarship on contemporary Indian dance outside of Chandralekha's work, especially on the work of South Asian dance artists engaging in contemporary choreographic work in the diaspora, the study of the body remains largely underdeveloped. There have been few instances of the corporeal presence in such scholarship. Priya Srinivasan uses the body, and its experiences to trace the production process involved behind the production, and visual consumption of Bharatanatyam. She details textures such as the patch of sweat on the dancer's armpit. Shyamala Moorty and Sandra Chatterjee highlight the often alienating experience of being a "hired body" engaged to represent a certain cultural identity, regardless of the actual lived experience or cultural complexity, drawing upon Susan Foster's notion of the "hired body" (2011).

In this paper, it is my intention to centralize the body, and to read the body as the site of cultural expression; accordingly, I propose to "corpo-realize" my readings of the choreographic works of the aforementioned Toronto-based choreographers. I seek to theorize their work as bodies moving in constant negotiation. I argue that while Bharatanatyam remains the common movement base of these choreographers, they display a desire to engage with the Other in their works, with my reading of the Other extending to the ethnic Other, cultural Other, as well as the Other in movement discipline. In their choreographic work, the body becomes a site where cosmopolitanism is embodied.

DANCING CONTEMPORARY INDIAN DANCE IN TORONTO

Toronto saw its first Bharatanatyam school in 1975, with the opening of Menaka Thakkar's Nrtyakala. Natasha Bakht and Nova Bhattacharya both trained extensively in Bharatanatyam at this institution. Hari Krishnan and Lata Pada trained extensively in India, and much of their current work is based in Toronto. Each of these four choreographers has a movement background deeply steeped in Bharatanatyam. While I use the term "Toronto-based," the relationship of some of these artists to Toronto is more complex, with some of them frequently traveling between Toronto and other locations.

Nova Bhattacharya trained in Bharatanatyam under Menaka Thakkar, Kitapa Pillai, and Kalanidhi Narayan. Prior to becoming an independent artist, she toured extensively with Menaka Thakkar and Company. She began her forays into creating contemporary works in the late 1990s, and founded Ipsita Nova Dance Projects in 2007 (Bhattacharya, 2011). Natasha Bakht had trained in Bharatanatyam for two decades under Menaka Thakkar, and, like Bhattacharya, toured extensively with Thakkar's company. During the 1990s, she began working and collaborating with a number of choreographers of Indian contemporary dance, such as Roger Sinha and Shobhana Jeyasinghe in England. She danced and toured with Shobhana Jeyasinghe's company for three seasons (Bakht, 2011). Hari Krishnan, in addition to presenting his contemporary works, also regularly performs and presents Bharatanatyam repertoire pieces. Krishnan is the founder and artistic director of the Toronto-based company inDance. Traveling between Middletown, Connecticut, where he teaches at Wesleyan University, Toronto, the home of inDance, and India, where he performs regularly, Krishnan engages with the Bharatanatyam form in a myriad of roles, ranging from scholar to teacher to performer to choreographer.

Lata Pada trained extensively in the Thanjavur style of Bharatanatyam. She is the founder and director of Sampradaya, which is based in Mississauga in 1990. She has been creating works of contemporary and often intercultural nature since the 1990s, while also choreographing and performing works in the Bharatanatyam repertoire. She trains a large number of students in traditional Bharatanatyam technique and repertoire at the Sampradaya Dance Academy. She and her company members and students perform frequently in Toronto. While they create works in the genre of contemporary Indian dance, both Lata Pada and Hari Krishnan are also deeply invested in performing, transmitting, and choreographing repertoire pieces in the traditional Bharatanatyam genre. They regularly present works in the traditional Bharatanatyam repertoire, in addition to their contemporary works.

Since its establishment in Canada in 1992, Kalanidhi Fine Arts of Canada, under the artistic directorship of Sudha Khandwani, has produced a number of international events which have showcased the contemporary South Asian choreographic works. Two of its landmark events in promoting this genre was the New Directions in Indian Dance festival and conference in 1993, and the Contemporary Choreography in Indian Dance 2009, jointly presented with the Menaka Thakkar Dance Company. Both events were held in Toronto, and were one of the major events at which contemporary Indian dance choreographers and scholars gathered.

Through the 1990s and continuing into the first decade of the 2000s, there has been an increasing number of contemporary Indian dance choreographers whose works address the Indian classical traditional movement arts and dance. Notable choreographers among these include, but are not limited to, the U.K.-based Akram Khan, Shobhana Jeyasinghe and Mavin Khoo, Canadian Roger Sinha, India-based Aditi Mangaldas, Daksha Seth, Astad Deboo, Santosh Nair, the late Manjusri Chaki-Sircar and Ranjabati Sircar, and the U.S.-based Post Natyam Collective. Each of these artists has distinct creative approaches in their inquiry into the "contemporary," and also in many cases, distinct styles of Indian classical dances as their choreographic points of reference.

In this context then, it is evident that the work of the selected four Toronto-based choreographers does not exist in isolation, but rather, participates in an international movement of Indian classical dancers exploring contemporary areas of inquiry in their work.

Nova Bakht, Natasha Bhattacharya, Hari Krishnan, and Lata Pada have been creating choreographies which engage with the notion of the "contemporary" since the 1990s. In the following section, I analyze some of their choreographic works, and trace the corporeal negotiations in these works, and also how the choreographers themselves relate to their works at a discursive level.

PAS DE DEUX: THE SELF AND THE OTHER

The film *Moments in Motion* documents the creative processes and philosophies of six celebrated Canadian choreographers. Featured among these four is Natasha Bakht, who discusses her choreographic process and strategies for creating her solo *Obiter Dictum*, which she had created at the end of her law school experience. As she dances, she discusses the different aspects and ideas which informed the creation and creative process of the piece. Her movements transition fluidly between the techniques of one movement tradition to another; she dances a number of phrases stamping her feet audibly on the ground, as characteristic in Bharatanatyam, and retaining the more earthy, grounded stances home to the Bharatanatyam form, before suddenly proceeding to execute swiveling attitude turns to the back. This sudden transition catches the spectator by surprise. In a more fluid transition, she then returns to the grounded and percussive footwork phrases, and then proceeds to include pedestrian movements such as walking.

Stuart Hall argues that cultural identity can be viewed in two distinct ways, one in which cultural identities in the diaspora are perceived as fixed, and the other which recognizes cultural identities as being continuously moving, changing, and in flux (1990). Bakht's at times seamless and at other times sudden transitions between movement disciplines perhaps embodies this constant and often uneasy negotiation through the various cultural identities that the South Asian diasporic dancer experiences. Also resonating with Hall's theory of the diasporic identity as being in continual flux, Bakht, speaking about *Obider Dictum* in the film, states that she wants the body to "never stop moving."

In her solo *White Space,* performed at the Contemporary Choreography in Indian Dance festival (2009), Bakht draws upon Bharatanatyam's vocabulary of hand gestures, body postures, and occasional frozen iconic poses. She also occasionally draws upon the footwork of Bharatanatyam. In *White Space*, her movement is characterized by a lightness more home to contemporary dance technique, though she occasionally draws upon the grounded, earth-bound centeredness of Bharatanatyam. Bakht negotiates her movements within the spaces and silences of the music, resisting the traditional system of dancing within the frame of the rhythm. Throughout her piece, one notices a sculpture-like quality to her body profiles, evoking the sculpturesque philosophy of Bharatanatyam itself. As in *Obider Dictum*, in *White Space* too, Bakht continues to slip in and out of evocations to the Bharatanatyam form. This shift, perhaps, embodies the fluid nature of the identity of the contemporary yet Bharatanatyam-based South Asian dance artist.

Throughout much of *Obider Dictum*, Bakht holds her palm in the *pataka* hand gesture, and occasionally sinks into deep *aramandi* plies of Bharatanatyam. Retaining gestural "quotations" from the Indian classical dance vocabulary, she continues to traverse through movement vocabularies and sartorial juxtapositions of two different movement tropes. Bakht's body becomes both site and medium for these negotiations. This is thus a dance which negotiates a pas de deux at a number of levels; a pas de deux with the different movement disciplines inhabiting the body, and an interdisciplinary pas de deux which negotiates with a predominantly contemporary, and Euro-North American costuming. Bakht's costume in *White Space*, designed by U.K.-based Ursula Bombshell, consists of a fitted white top, and a short, frilly white skirt made of Styrofoam pieces and string. Her body thus becomes a space for both a contemporary costuming and movement experiment as well as evocations to traditional lineage.

Nova Bhattacharya, in her solo *Unspoken*, performed at the Contemporary Choreography in Indian Dance Festival (2009), featured heavy use of facial expression, reminiscent of the *abhinaya* or mimetic dances from the Bharatanatyam repertoire. While she incorporated her corporeal mime or *abhinaya* in her choreography, her movement vocabulary largely investigated weight, momentum and resistance, movement characteristics more associated with contemporary dance. Further, the minimalism of her *abhinaya*, and contemporary costuming distances her dance from the character-narrative driven performance of traditional Bharatanatyam. Her movements represent, instead, an abstraction of the fundamental body position from the Bharatanatyam form. Bhattacharya's *Akshongay* (2009), a collaborative duet co-created and performed with Louis Laberge-Cote, features frequent contact between the two dancers. The type of contact displayed in the choreography, such as the clasping of hands, supporting of each other's weight, signified harmony between the two bodies. This negotiation was a negotiation between two Others on two levels. At one level, it was a corporeal encounter between two cultures, races and ethnicities. At yet another level, it was an encounter between two bodies trained in the two distinct movement styles of Indian classical Bharatanatyam and contemporary dance.

Ulf Hannerz argues that cosmopolitanism implies "the coexistence of cultures in the individual experience" (1990, 239). In the choreographies of Nova Bhattacharya and Natasha Bakht, the body becomes the site of embodying and performing this Hannerzian notion of "cosmopolitanism." Hannerz describes cosmopolitans as people who wish to actively engage and participate in the 'new' culture (1990). In a parallel notion, Stuart Hall posits that cosmopolitanism, as a behavior, requires individuals to draw upon a variety of discursive meanings, as well as to command multiple cultural vocabularies as a repertoire (Kendall, Woodward, and Skrbis 2009, 112). In the context of the dance world then, I argue that these Toronto choreographers, like Hannerz's cosmopolitans, choose to "actively engage" with the corporeal culture of the Other. Their bodies are trained in the discipline of Bharatanatyam, and because of their relationship of praxis with Bharatanatyam, the discipline of Bharatanatyam itself may be seen as "local" in relation to their bodies. Bakht and Bhattacharya both consciously venture beyond the repertoire and movement qualities of Bharatanatyam, and embrace, in form and underlying philosophies, characteristics of contemporary dance, thereby bringing in the movement of the Other culture into their own individual movement experience. Through their conscious choice of corporeal engagement with the movement vocabulary and philosophies of contemporary dance, as opposed to exclusive practice of a singular bodily discourse of Bharatanatyam dance, they may be viewed as symbolizing Stuart Hall's model of the cosmopolitan proficient in multiple vocabularies.

While Bakht and Bhattacharya perform primarily as solo artists, Hari Krishnan and Lata Pada have Toronto-based companies, namely "InDance" and "Sampradaya." Bakht and Bhattacharya have been commissioned to create works for other dance companies, such as Toronto Dance Theatre, and the Menaka Thakkar Dance Company; however, they most often work as solo artists, and it is often their own bodies that become the site of the performed negotiation and cosmopolitanism. On the other hand, Lata Pada and Hari Krishnan, with their company's productions, often open the choreographic space up, inviting dancers of other disciplines and backgrounds to engage with their movement aesthetic.

Lata Pada's *Shunya* premiered in 2008 at the Fleck Dance Theatre in Toronto. "Shunya," in Sanskrit, has multiple meanings, meaning nothingness, infinity, and also the number zero, which, as Lata Pada states in the program notes for the subsequent performance at the Contemporary Choreography conference (2009), was one of the starting points for the work. In the programme notes, Pada speaks of how her mathematician grandfather told her about how the concept of zero traveled from ancient India to China, Persia and beyond and how the motif of zero could signify both emptiness, as well as fullness of space (2009).

The cast features seven dancers, including two male and five female dancers, and three musicians. The dancers are dressed in ballooning black pants, and short sleeved, colored tops. Through the piece, the dancers shift back and forth from movement vocabularies and using their kinespheric space both in accordance with, and outside the norms of Bharatanatyam. They proceed from the grounded *puramandi* position of Bharatanatyam, to suddenly arch back into a plank position supported by one arm, in a movement dynamic rarely seen in Bharatanatyam. This shift of balance and center of gravity is sudden and unexpected, much like Natasha Bakht's transitions between the Bharatanatyam and contemporary vocabularies. The dancers proceed to Bharatanatyam lunge-like position (*aleeda*). Here, we might say that the lunge is used in the context of Bharatanatyam movement, with a set of other recognizable bodily movement characteristics that signify Bharatanatyam. For example, the hand is kept in *the pataka hasta* gesture, and the movement is controlled, as in a Bharatanatyam performance. The dancers proceed to execute recognizable phrases from the Bharatanatyam movement lexicon. A hand in executing a *mudra* is placed on the shoulder when the other arm suddenly engages in a free-flow swing, completely disengaging the viewer's association with Bharatanatyam for the moment.

Another section from the piece features a duet between a Kathak dancer and one of Sampradaya's Bharatanatyam dancers. The movements in this *pas de deux*, in the literal sense of the word, are somewhat reminiscent of contact improvisation, involving the giving of weight and working with each other's weight and centers of gravity. The Bharatanatyam dancer then proceeds into a lunge with her arms raised, and the male partner takes the opportunity to lift her and put her back down. She then takes the classical Bharatanatyam arm position, opening her arms out wide, and holding her palms in the stylized position. As her male partner lifts her, the Bharatanatyam dancer positions her feet in the *aramandi* position in the air, continuing to hold her arms in the stylized position. The female dancer runs away from her male partner in a brief, pedestrian run, and then is caught by him, and they both strike a recognizable pose from the Bharatanatyam lexicon in union. Their experience is a marked departure from the partnering experience in Indian classical dance, in which physical contact, if present, is significantly less, and lifting does not occur. Instead, in these moments, the dancers conceptually inhabit an experience similar to that of the traditional balletic pas de deux. Susan Leigh Foster claims that it was during the period of the Romantic ballet that divergent movement vocabularies for male and female dancers developed, prior to which, the pas de deux in ballet had mainly entailed the male and female dancers dancing alongside each other, or traveled in mirror opposition (1996). Romantic ballet's pas de deux, the legacy of which continued to be performed in eras afterward, involved the male dancer "supporting, guiding and manipulating the female dancer as she balanced delicately and suspensefully in fully extended shapes" (Foster 1996, 4). In the aforementioned duet section in Pada's *Shunya*, as in ballet, the female dancer is lifted and manipulated, even as she retains her feet and arms in positions of the Bharatanatyam lexicon. Here, a syncretism of movement vocabularies may be traced, with the contact and lift-based partnering of ballet and the hand and foot positioning of Bharatanatyam.

Kobena Mercer, in discussing syncretic elements in everyday life among people of the African diaspora, articulates that "creolization" of language in the African diaspora is a powerful syncretic element which appropriates aspects from the "master codes of dominant culture and creolizes them" (Mercer 2007, 255). The term "appropriation," which Mercer uses to describe syncretisation in the diaspora, does not imply a sense of mastery but rather, the insertion of elements of the Other. The dialogic is at work in these creative projects, but, as I will discuss presently, this dialogic can be associated more with the Hannerzian competent cosmopolitan, rather than Mercer's notion of creolization.

The piece is a space where different cultures, ethnicities and dance backgrounds encounter each other. Joining three regular Sampradaya company are the artists Johanna Anthuber, a Bharatanatyam artist from Germany who has trained extensively in Bharatanatyam and contemporary techniques; traditional Kathak dancer Anuj Mishra from India; U.K.-based dance artists Aakash Odedra, who has trained in both Bharatanatyam and Kathak forms; and Toronto-based Kathak dancer Reshmi Chetram. The music is also a collaboration between Praveen D Rao, who is also the composer, and Ernie Tollar and Maryem Tollar. The musicians perform live onstage.

Sampradaya's production *B2* (b-squared) is a collaboration between involves Sampradaya Dance Company and Toronto-based ballet company Ballet Jörgen. Britain-based choreographer Mavin Khoo was commissioned for this choreography by Pada and Bengt Jörgen, the Artistic Director of Ballet Jörgen. Ballet dancers and Bharatanatyam dancers dance alongside each other in this production. They are dressed alike, in white fabric tied as "dhotis" around their legs, and fitted white shirts. The distinguishing marker in the costuming is the footwear—the female ballet dancers wear pointe shoes while the Bharatanatyam dancers dance barefoot. They do not wear the ankle bells (*ghungroos*) as in traditional Bharatanatyam, and this, Pada pointed out at the Choreographic Dialogues at the York University Dance Department, upon an audience member's questioning, was due to Khoo's choreographic choice (Anderson). The ballet dancers in the piece often involved danced on pointe, with their hands in *mudras*. These two choreographed elements may be considered paradigmatic representatives of their respective dance traditions; pointe shoes and pointework remain emblematic of the ballet tradition, and the codified *mudra* gestures remain emblematic of the revived Indian classical dances. The choreography thus features a juxtaposition of the two movement disciplines onto the individual bodily experience.

Choreographically, *B2* features a departure from the choreographic approach in traditional Indian classical dances: in *B2*, abstraction, as opposed to mimetic representation, is used even in sections which feature lyrics. Traditionally, in the presence of lyrics, classical Indian dance is choreographed to interpret them. One of the sections of the piece is a musical interpretation of a Sanskrit verse "Bhaja Govindam," which is an ode to the god Krishna. In the choreography of this ode, the ballet dancers and Bharatanatyam dancers dance together, both executing form-dominated movements, as opposed to mimetic, expressive phrases, in their respective traditions, in unison.

Johanna Anthuber, currently based in Germany, performs a Bharatanatyam-based component alongside the dancers of Pada's Toronto-based company Sampradaya in *B2*. At the Choreographic Dialogue, upon the screening of a short excerpt from the work, an audience member asked Pada if the Caucasian dancer who danced alongside the South Asian dancers (referring to Johanna Anthuber) had also trained in Bharatanatyam extensively. Pada explained that in this production of the company, Anthuber danced exclusively as a Bharatanatyam dancer. This confusion in identities can perhaps, be seen embodying the larger play of identities in the collaborative work itself. This casting challenges the perceived alliance of identity between the dancer's body and the dance discipline she practices. Pada not only enables her dancers to express, through their corporeality, cosmopolitanism, but also opens up doors for other dancers to engage in this corporeal cosmopolitanism in her company's work.

Like Pada's work, in much of Krishnan's choreographic work, we find a similar cosmopolitan space, where the cultural and danced Other is invited to experience and engage with the cultural and danced Self. Krishnan's dancers come from diverse ethnic backgrounds, such as Chinese, Japanese, Indian, and Caucasian. Krishnan's *Red* (2008) features the dancer Hiroshi Miyamoto in a solo performance of Bharatanatyam-based movement. The choice of casting Miyamoto, a dancer of Japanese origin, in a piece exhibiting technical virtuosity in an Indian classical dance form, symbolizes the opening up of the choreographic space as a playground for cosmopolitanism. Thus their choreographic work can be seen as a site where cosmopolitanism is nurtured, as the space where the body of the cultural or disciplinary Other is drawn into one's familiar movement experience.

In Krishnan's *Bollywood Hopscotch* (2004), also performed at the 2009 festival, the dancers move between squares of light. The sound score consists of rhythmic phrases (*jathis*) of Bharatanatyam interspersed with fractions of "*Piya Tu Ab to Aja*," an iconic Bollywood song from the movie *Caravaan* (1971). In this section, the dancers parody the larger-than-life portrayals in Bollywood cinema; a female dancer loosens her hair, swings her head around, and a male dancer mimics the slow-motion run, evoking the dramatic run of the lead male characters in numerous Bollywood films from the 1960s to the 2000s. However, the male dancer's run here is in a jerky, robotic motion, remaining a commentary on, as opposed to direct quotation of the Bollywood dance movment. In the Bharatanatyam *jathi* section, the dancers execute Bharatanatyam movement phrases, and percussive footwork. The dancers move erratically through the space and between the squares of colored light. The colored lighting is at times reminiscent of the nightclub setting of the original song in the film.

Here, Krishnan, using a recognizable, iconic Bollywood song, brings out humor by displaying the contrast in aesthetics between the Bharatanatyam movement and the movement patterns that have often been used in choreographies of Bollywood musical films, perhaps also pointing to the difference in these two very distinct dance genres that non-South-Asian spectators and individuals often conflate with each other. The sudden switches between the genres, and the over-the-top parodying of iconic movements associated with Bollywood musicals serves to deconstruct the performance of "Bollywood dance," in which bodies are exoticized and displayed for audience consumption within South Asia, the diasporic South Asian community, as well as the larger North American milieu. His manner of doing so is almost tongue-in-cheek, and elicits a few giggles of recognition from the audience. His dancers are dressed in a variety of costuming—from tights and tops to midriff bearing short tops and shorts. As characteristic of many of his works, *Bollywood Hopscotch* comprises of a mixed-ethnicity cast, whose members also come from different movement backgrounds, in addition to having trained with Krishnan in Bharatanatyam.

Albright, in *Choreographing Difference*, reminds us of Butler's theory of identity as being continually in flux; and points out that this opens up the possibility of identity as being unstable and constantly re-enacted. She discusses how Montreal-based Congolese-Canadian performer Zab Baboungou evades categorization into popular perceptions of African dance through using sustained movement, as opposed to movement which parallels the percussive accents of the drums, which, Albright suggests, is usually characteristic of African dance (Albright 1997, 23). Through her movement onstage, Albright argues that Moboungou is able to resist this commodifying gaze (Albright 1997, 27), suggesting that through its "somatic identity," written into the movement itself, dance has the potential to dissolve boundaries of binary categories such as self-other, nature-culture and private-public (Albright 1997, 27), and thereby, can potentially be a transformative medium. Albright points out to the possibility of the somatic identity performed onstage may present a different identity than the identities of race and culture inscribed on the body of the performer. Perhaps we might apply this disjuncture also to the case of the work of Nova Bhattacharya and Natasha Bakht. In their choreographies, the body becomes the site where the Bharatanatyam dance background encounters the aesthetics and movements from contemporary dance and contact improvisation, and thereby disrupt the reading of their identities as static, and relegated to the confines of a Bharatanatyam dancer. In the productions of Lata Pada and Hari Krishnan, the multi-ethnic casts, through their corporeal Hannerzian cosmopolitanism, challenge and transgress the associations of ethnic identities with dancing identities.

THE DIALOGIC *PAS DE DEUX*: THEORIZING THE WORK OF TORONTO'S BHARATANATYAM-TRAINED CHOREOGRAPHERS

William Safran asserts that diasporic individuals and communities often retain a collective memory of the homeland, and of a collective longing for return to the homeland (Safran 1991, 83). He also mentions that envisioning of a utopic homeland versus a dystopia which characterizes their lived experience is more an "eschatological concept" (Safran 1991, 94), and that the existence of this myth of return to the homeland in the diasporic imagination is not necessarily based on an actual vision of physical return (Safran 1991, 94). Rajan and Sharma assert that theorists of traditional diaspora such as Safran had described the diaspora as fixed and stable entities (Rajan and Sharma 2006, 2), and in counter to this notion, they coin the term "new cosmopolitanism," to describe the behavior of individuals, including diasporic individuals, who "blur the edges of home and abroad by continuously moving physically, culturally, and socially" (Rajan and Sharma 2006, 2).

Even as Safran later states that these characteristics of "diasporic identity" do not necessarily pertain to the Indian diaspora, which has sometimes emerged as the dominant minority in some locations (Safran 1991, 89), his reading of the diaspora as a collective is inherently an essentialized one, signifying the very mode of identity reading that Stuart Hall warns us against. Hall problematizes the notion of identity as a fixed construct, and instead, advocates for identity to be perceived as being perpetually in "production," never complete but always in process. He asserts that the diasporic experience is defined not by an idea of "purity," but "by a conception of *identity* which lives with and through, not despite, difference; by hybridity" (Hall 1990, 235). In addition, Safran's reading of the diasporic identity as defined by a relation to the "motherland" as a collective overlooks factors such as generation. Among the four choreographers whose works I analyze here, Natasha Bakht and Nova Bhattacharya were born in Canada, and are thus the second generation South Asian immigrants. In the light of Hall's notion of the identity as continually being shaped and reshaped, one sees that the choreographies become a space in which this "process" of identity formulation is physically embodied. The dancers' transitions between movement vocabularies become physical manifestations of this "process" of identity formulation, and due to their existence as public performance, these choreographies become spaces where this process may be viewed.

Hannerz theorizes cosmopolitanism as a state of mind while Kendall, Woodland and Skrbis view cosmopolitanism as a "behavioural repertoire" (Kendall, Woodland, and Skrbis 2009, 1). The theorization of cosmopolitanism as a behavioral practice, crystallized as "intellectual and aesthetic openness toward divergent cultural experiences" (Hannerz 1990, 239) underlies the theorization of the work of the four Toronto choreographers whose works I engage with in this study. Using Bharatanatyam as their corporeal point of reference, they waltz with the aesthetics of contemporary dance techniques in their solos, or open the choreographic space up in their dance companies to engage in intercultural dialogue.

Uttara Asha Coorlawala, in her influential dissertation "Classical and contemporary Indian dance: Overview, Criteria and a Choreographic Analysis," proposes three categories of innovative Indian choreographers. Her first group consists of choreographers who distance themselves from traditional techniques, even while being informed by some of their aesthetics. In the second group, she places choreographers who work extensively with dancers who have trained in traditional techniques, and use these traditional techniques as points of reference and departure. In this group she places Chandralekha, Kumudini Lakhia, and Mrinalini Sarabhai. In her third group, the choreographers are invested in integrating "foreign influences" into their work. She suggests that these groupings need not be mutually exclusive, and that the work of choreographers may fit into more than one category (Coorlawala 1994, 217). I assert that among the four Toronto choreographers, the work of Natasha Bakht and Nova Bhattacharya most closely resembles Coorlawala's criteria for the third category, in which the choreographers consciously embrace "foreign" aesthetics and philosophies. Coorlawala's description of this third category is also reminiscent of the Hannerzian cosmopolitan, who willingly ventures beyond the "local" to embrace the "foreign" experience. In the solo works of Bakht and Bhattacharya, their own bodies are posited as the sites where this embrace of the Other occurs; they venture beyond their extensive Bharatanatyam training to experience elements of Contemporary and modern dance techniques. As choreographic pieces, their works present a dialogic relationship between the movements of Bharatanatyam, Contemporary, and Modern dance, and in the case of Bakht, also the Kalariyapattu martial art form.

Returning to Coorlawala's categories of Indian contemporary dance innovators, I argue that the work of Krishnan and Pada also fall under the third category in their inherent Hannerzian cosmopolitanism, and their ready embrace of the Other in terms of their venturing out beyond traditional Bharatanatyam narratives and themes, employment of movement from non-Bharatanatyam traditions, and use of multi-ethnic casts. It is also significant to note that Krishnan and Pada create pieces of traditional Bharatanatyam repertoire as well. As well, each of these four choreographers also fit into the second category, as their initial dance identities were formed through their Bharatanatyam experience.

Hannerz suggests that cosmopolitans may be connoisseurs or dilettantes, and that they may gain a competence in the artistic orientation of the Other (Hannerz 1990). Kendall, Woodland, and Srbis distinguish cosmopolitan behavior into categories such as "sampling," "immersive," and "reflexive" (2009). They indicate that of the three, the "immersive cosmopolitan" behavior is "deeper, more strategic, and desiring" in its engagement with the Other. They see this approach to cosmopolitanism as a conscious pattern of actions centered around "learning and cultivating engagements for the purpose of change, self-knowledge or improvement" (119). In the case of these Toronto choreographers, the competence develops from either direct immersion in the bodily techniques of non-Bharatanatyam forms, or through long histories of collaborative experiences with practitioners of Other disciplines. Bakht's work in the Contemporary movement stems partly in her work, training, and extensive touring with the Shobhana Jeyasinghe Dance Company in England, and also her collaborative work with Montreal-based Roger Sinha. Bhattacharya's work is also strongly informed by her long history of collaborative work with numerous Canadian Contemporary Dance artists such as Peggy Baker. Lata Pada, at the Choreographic Dialogues, stated that her dancers train in contemporary work as well, and that in addition to their ongoing core training in Bharatanatyam, they take workshops in a myriad of movement styles (Anderson). Hari Krishnan received modern and contemporary dance training at the Royal Winnipeg Ballet, School of Toronto Dance Theatre, and the Singapore Ballet Academy (Venkat). In addition, many of his dancers come from mixed movement backgrounds, often including strong contemporary dance backgrounds. In the case of each of these four choreographers, the engagement with the contemporary movement discipline has been through direct physical experience, in a manner similar to that of the Hannerzian competent cosmopolitan. The immersive cosmopolitan strategy articulated by Kendall, Woodland, and Skrbis is thus manifested in the corporeal encounter of these dancers in their direct physical engagement with the contemporary movement discipline.

It is through the choreographies created in contemporary contexts that the choreographers are able to embark upon a deeper personal investigation of their own questions and experiences. While most these choreographers also maintain their traditional Bharatanatyam repertoire, much of their choreographic emphasis is on the creation of works in a contemporary context. Through engaging with the Other, the choreographer himself or herself is able to find subjective agency. The cultural theorist Chris Weedon defines subjectivity as the conscious and unconscious thoughts and emotions of the individual, her sense of herself and her ways of understanding her relation to the world" (1998, 177). Tradition and traditional discourse itself ascribes the Bharatanatyam dancer its own partnership with the Other. The stories, themes, images, and motifs of the traditional Bharatanatyam dance often embody the experience of the *devadasis* or the temple dancers. By embodying or engaging with the corporeal and disciplinary Other then, these choreographers thus gain the agency to dance their quotidian selves. In the shifts of balance, movement quality, and centers of gravity, we see a foregrounding of the lived experience of the artist, of the delicate and precarious transitions between their diasporic Canadian identities, and their identities as people of South Asian origin, as opposed to the experience of mythical characters and the *devadasis*. Their contemporary works are marked by a distance from the figure of the *devadasi* and the mythic figures, and through this process, a distance, perhaps, from the homeland itself. Their embrace of their Others, both corporeal, personal and disciplinary, in their Canadian context, perhaps highlights an embrace of their lived Toronto experience.

CONCLUSION

The questions investigated by the Toronto Bharatanatyam choreographers are often deeply personal. The body, and the corporeal becomes the site where these negotiations, pushes, pulls, juxtapositions, and clashes are played out between the dancers and their counterpart dancer and media Others.

Natasha Bakht, Nova Bhattacharya, Hari Krishnan, and Lata Pada share the Bharatanatyam training as a point of departure in their work. Each of them is invested in engaging with movement vocabularies and philosophies of other dance forms, and in engaging with dancers from other movement and ethno-cultural backgrounds in their work. These performances are often part of larger, mainstream Canadian dance festivals where contemporary dance is greatly represented, and hence the spectatorship is also constituted greatly of Canadian contemporary dance audiences. Using the body/dancers' bodies as the sites of negotiation and manifestation of identities, these four choreographers often toy with the spectators' expectations of them as South Asian choreographers, and the expectations of engaging in cultural production which stays confined to essentialized notions of "Indian dance."

Through these kinetic relationships of textured corporality and metaphor, the dancing bodies of the choreographers themselves are brought into the liminal space between the boundaries of Self and the Other. This liminal space between the Self and the Other is the space where these dancers meet and interact, both corporeally and metaphorically. The gap between the edges of the dialectic thus becomes the dancing ground for these choreographers. It is in this dancing ground of liminality that the choreographers are able to bring their lived experiences into their creative work.

2

Neighboring in Strip City

Local Conflict and Spaces of Exotic Dance in Portland, Oregon

Moriah McSharry McGrath, Portland State University

Though exotic dance may be considered a fringe activity, it is probably the movement art most likely to be seen by Americans today.[1] Hundreds of thousands of exotic dancers perform in tens of thousands of strip clubs[2] across the country and the industry is rapidly expanding. Erotic dance, or striptease, teeters on the edge of respectability, normalized by its increasing appearance in mainstream cultural settings yet also retaining the stigma of a deviant activity.

A wide variety of social, political, and spatial processes contribute to the marginalization and normalization of exotic dance, many of them rooted in physical spaces. Perhaps the most obvious example of its spatial marginalization is the venue where exotic dance is performed: instead of the grand theaters and symphony halls that host élite dance forms, striptease occurs in strip clubs, ostensibly seedy bars that tend to be located in unappealing areas. Indeed, much of the spatial regulation of strip clubs and other sexually oriented businesses centers on minimizing its contact with "respectable" community activities, such as education, high-end shopping, and the domestic lives of nuclear families. The presence of a strip club—or any other business—confers meaning on the space surrounding it, and interactions with neighboring land uses (including users) influences what happens inside the strip club. Within the strip club, spatial factors also influence how dance is performed and how dancers experience their work. At each of these scales, there is contestation: tensions between policymakers, owners, neighbors, and dancers that play out in various spaces.

As such, a geographical exploration of striptease and the surrounding conflict can provide insight to these tensions and how they may be resolved, as well as to how they influence the dance form and the people who practice it. Insights about these place processes are necessary due to the ongoing expansion of the sex industry, which is reconfiguring the spaces of exotic dance and is likely to provoke conflict over spaces of striptease.

This chapter presents the findings of one such geographical exploration undertaken in Portland, Oregon—a city with a striptease scene that is large and diverse. Because the state's constitution effectively precludes zoning controls on sexually oriented businesses, Portland's many strip clubs are distributed throughout the city's neighborhoods, providing a rich variety of locational contexts to study. The study used a situational analysis (Clarke 2005) approach to study place processes that influence both striptease as a dance form and the experience of female exotic dancers who perform striptease.

The chapter begins by establishing the context for this exploration: introducing the strip club industry and research that has been conducted about it and then describing the study design. Next it presents findings about place influences on striptease in Portland at three different scales:

1. the city as a whole, including the spatial arrangement of strip clubs throughout Portland and the symbolic role that striptease plays in the city;
2. the neighborhood, evaluating how characteristics of strip clubs and surrounding areas influence the extent of conflict over the sexually oriented businesses; and
3. the individual strip club, focusing on how spatial conditions affect the performance of striptease by exotic dancers with particular attention to the unusual local institution of the neighborhood strip club.

Within and across each of these scales, interactions can support or undermine the perception of striptease as an art form. Exploring striptease at these scales builds on the knowledge produced by other researchers about striptease at the body and interpersonal (namely, dancer-customer) scale. One of the key findings is that the increased presence of strip clubs throughout the city, including in symbolically valuable locations like residential neighborhoods, has lessened the stigma associated with striptease. Ultimately, however, I conclude that the system under which the dance is presented reduces its legitimacy because the strip club business model centers compromises dancers' interests for the sake of customers' experience and club owners' profits.

STRIP CLUBS 101

American striptease has its roots in the burlesque shows of the early twentieth century, but the number of Americans who are watching and performing it has increased rapidly since the 1990s. A 1991 study (Weitzer 2000) found that 11 percent of Americans had been to a topless nightclub in the past year, and since that time the number of strip clubs has likely doubled (Liepe-Levinson 2002, estimates that number of clubs doubled between 1987 and 2002). There is no single consensus on the reasons behind this increased, but theories suggest a rapid sexualization of popular culture facilitated by evolving information and communication technologies (McNair 2002; Levy 2005) and new "postfeminist" expressions of women's sexuality

(Nally 2009). There are likely at least 3,600 strip clubs in the United States today (Bradley 2008), with an estimated 300,000 people working as exotic dancers (Jeffreys 2008)—a sharp increase over an estimated 68,000 dancers in 1997 and just 8,000 in 1960 (Forsyth and Deshotels 1997). By contrast, professional dance and choreography combined account for only 40,000 jobs in 2009; that sector is also growing more slowly than the economy as a whole (Bureau of Labor Statistics 2009).

Strip clubs are big business. By 1997, Americans spent "more money at strip clubs than at Broadway, off-Broadway, regional and non-profit theaters; at the opera, the ballet and jazz and classical music performances—combined" (Schlosser 1997, 44). In 2006, a morning talk show reported that American men spend about $15 billion annually on strip clubs, as compared to $4 billion on the "national pastime" of baseball (Jeffreys 2008).

What Does it Look Like?

In most American strip clubs, women perform for a predominantly male audience. These "exotic dancers," or "strippers," arrive on stage in skimpy costumes and remove items of clothing over the course of a dance routine performed to recorded music, usually for the duration of two or three songs. In many cases, the stage includes a floor-to-ceiling metal pole that the dancer may incorporate into her routine.

While dancers perform, customers place money ("tips") on the stage or into the dancer's garter belt. Dancers earn these tips in lieu of a wage, and often pay the club management a "stage fee" for each shift they work. After completing her stage set, the dancer may go backstage or circulate on the floor of the club. On the club floor, dancers may earn money by performing private dances for individual customers. Private dances may take place on or above customers' laps as they sit in chairs or on couches. Dancers may keep some or all of the money customers pay for these private dances and may earn a commission on drinks purchased by customers in their company.

. . . and does that really count as dancing?

There is an ongoing debate about whether strip club performances constitute artistic expression, economic exploitation, or something in between. Feminist scholars have struggled to analyze the power dynamics of stripping and other sex work, aligning in camps whose clashes were particularly bitter during the "sex wars" of the 1980s. The historical contours of these debates are covered in detail elsewhere (see, for example Sloan and Wahab 2000; Zatz 1997). Regardless of the stance one takes on these issues, striptease is one of the most easily recognizable dance forms in the United States: the silhouette of a female body dangling off a stripper pole, long hair flowing behind her is as familiar as the iconic shape of a ballerina.

Scholars of performance studies place stripping squarely within American dance history. Hanna defines dance as "purposeful, intentionally rhythmical, and culturally influenced sequences of nonverbal body movements" (1998, 44). Dance is comparable to a spoken language in that it has patterns of vocabulary, grammar, semantics, and pragmatics that are interpreted by viewers in a naturalistic manner (Hanna 1998). For example, some of the vocabulary of exotic dance includes hip gyrations and teasing manipulations of bra and bikini straps. There is a clear grammar in that dancers begin their routine fully costumed and proceed to remove items. The semantics of the dance are the intimation of the dancer's sexual availability. The pragmatics relate to the specific environment in which this dance is performed. The audience synthesizes these elements of communication into a sexual fantasy. The extensive and elaborate repertoire of exotic dancers is documented in Liepe-Levinson's (2002) *Strip Show*, which draws on research at strip clubs across the U.S.

Many classically trained dancers would not consider stripping to be dance, despite the fact that it incorporates the expressive elements discussed above. The pragmatics of exotic dance—for example, the fact that it occurs in bars and requires personal interaction with the spectator—prevent it from developing the same training system and elite organization that occurs with ballet and other types of dance (Hanna 1998). This is just one example of how place influences the social organization of striptease.

Hanna (2010) makes the point that striptease is just one of many dance forms that express ideas about sexuality. Further narrowing the perceived gap between striptease and dance, Hubbard (2012) notes that stylization of the body, a central characteristic of dance, is also at the heart of sex work (or erotic labor). Indeed, "sex itself may not even be the defining feature of prostitution in many instances given sex workers are effectively enacting and selling a performance," as do performing artists (Hubbard 2012, 36). Thus, there is a wide array of performances with sexual elements that are situated along a spectrum of social acceptability—that is, naked bodies in a modern dance piece in a theater are celebrated whereas naked bodies in brothels are considered unseemly.

Striptease has increasing cultural cachet in the U.S., as it grows more visible and socially acceptable (Brents and Sanders 2010). A burlesque revival has emerged, with theaters in some cities hosting performances that harken back to cabaret variety shows of the early twentieth century (Urish 2004). The most famous of these neo-burlesque performers is Dita von Teese, who has garnered corporate sponsorships and spots on couture runways. Stripper poles have made their way into *New Yorker* cartoons and even performances by teenybopper Miley Cyrus. Another recent trend is striptease classes for women hoping to strengthen their cardiovascular systems and/or romantic acumen (Regehr 2012; Whitehead and Kurz 2009).

WHAT DOES PLACE HAVE TO DO WITH IT?

There has been ample research about striptease, much of it touching directly or indirectly on geography. One strand (e.g., Shteir 2004; Glasscock 2003; Urish 2004; Ross 2009), has focused on how and where the dance form emerged. This literature includes geographical factors in its discussion of the evolution of the performance (and the regulation thereof) in different cities.

Another rich vein of analysis of striptease and space is the work on contemporary striptease employing social sciences approaches, much of it conducted by women who have worked as exotic dancers. These studies explore the bodily scale, describing dancers' uses and experiences of their bodies during performance (e.g., Barton and Hardesty 2010; Ferreday 2008; Forsyth and Deshotels 1997; Hanna 2010; Trautner 2005). Others study a different scale, concentrating on interactions that take place inside strip clubs among workers and customers (e.g., Egan 2004, 2006; Barton 2007; Bradley-Engen and Ulmer 2009; Brooks 2010a; Pasko 2002; Ronai 1989; Sanders 2004).

Yet strip clubs are situated in larger communities and dance of course reflects on larger culture(s); only more recently has research has delved into this multiplicity of factors that influence exotic dance (Wahab et al. 2011). The present study builds on this emerging field, responding to calls for research that illuminates the broader social context of strip clubs (Brooks 2010b) and that takes a geographical approach to "sexual-social activities" (Johnston and Longhurst 2010). For the most part, existing research on striptease—with the notable exception of Ross and Greenwell's (2005) illuminating analysis of the ways that a spatial hierarchy of venues in Vancouver, B.C. between 1945–1975 reinforced racial stratification—has considered place mainly as a backdrop. But place, especially for contentious activities, of which striptease is one, is a constitutive force for social activities (Marston 2003; Martin and Miller 2003). Thus, the present study builds upon our understanding of striptease by illuminating the conflicts over striptease in public and their influence on dance and dancers.

Strip Clubs as Spatial Problem

Strip clubs, where striptease is performed, are generally considered locally unwanted land uses, or LULU's (Popper 1981), and often become embattled spaces (Hubbard 2008, 2009). LULU's are resisted on the basis that they will decrease property values, negatively impact health, increase traffic, or make the neighborhood ugly, among other complaints (Schively 2007). In the case of sexually oriented businesses, additional objections include fears of increased crime or harm to the community's reputation through its association with this undesirable activity (Sides 2006; Maticka-Tyndale, Lewis, and Street 2005; Hubbard 2009). In many parts of the United States, conflicts over these LULU's are forestalled by land use policies that relegate sexually oriented businesses to industrial zones and other peripheral areas. These policies are a form of social reproduction that promulgates "bourgeois values which place a premium on discreet landscapes, clearly demarcated public and private zones, and eviscerated *representational spaces*" (Papayanis 2000, 348–349 [emphasis the author's, referencing Lefebvre]).

Hubbard and colleagues have done extensive research and theorizing about the relationships between place and sexual commerce (Coulmont and Hubbard 2010; Hubbard 2008, 2009; Hubbard, Matthews, and Scoular 2009; Hubbard et al. 2008), which provides an excellent foundation for thinking about how place influences striptease and how striptease influences places. Put very simply, this research has found that regulatory regimes stigmatize sexually oriented businesses and the locations where they operate. Striptease is not seen as a legitimate art form because the venues where it is performed are relegated to the margins, and these marginal areas are themselves stigmatized by the presence of the morally circumspect activity of sexual entertainment—threatening further degradation as a result of what Greenberg et al. (2008) call "neighborhood decline due to pariah land uses."

Hubbard and other U.K. researchers have also studied how informal social control (Hubbard and Sanders 2003; O'Neill et al. 2008; Scoular et al. 2007; Hubbard 1998a) affects conflict and stigma connected to sexual commerce, but this work has focused on street prostitution rather than striptease (in both the United States and the United Kingdom, the former is illegal and the latter permitted). Further, there is limited information on how these processes operate in a U.S. context and under different regulatory regimes. The present study builds on this knowledge by exploring a U.S. setting where informal non-zoning, non-licensing processes manage the location of strip clubs.

ABOUT THE STUDY

I use a situational analysis (Clarke 2005) approach to collecting and organizing the data. Situational analysis begins by defining a situation of interest—in this case, strip clubs in the context of Portland neighborhoods—and collecting and analyzing data about human and nonhuman factors that constitute the situation. Situational analysis is distinct from a case study methodology because it chooses a situation—or social problem—as the unit of analysis rather than a functional organizational unit (Yin 2003).

Because urban social phenomena cannot be understood in isolation, situational analysis is a promising tool for understanding how spatial change affects city life (Green-Rennis et al. in press) since it allows for analysis of interpersonal episodes and their embedding context (Mitchell 1983). Key aspects of situations include the *goals* of the key players, the elements of the social and behavioral *repertoires* of the players, the *roles* players fill, the *rules* governing interactions, the *skills* needed to fill the roles and follow the rules, the *difficulties* people face in carrying out their roles, the environmental *setting*, and the social and cultural *concepts* used to describe interactions (Argyle 1981). Like many other qualitative methods, situational analysis is well-suited to the study of processes because it allows analysts to explore reflexive or dialectical relationships between social and spatial levels reflexive without artificially partitioning them into discrete variables (Miles and Huberman 1994).

Strip City (the Study Setting)

Portland, Oregon, may not be known as a major arts city, but it does have a reputation for one type of dance: striptease. Historically, the anonymity and bustle of city life have created spaces where sexual minorities and sexually oriented businesses can exist with lessened opprobrium (Hubbard 2012), yet the high level of interaction between diverse populations also means that the expression of sexuality in urban public space often results in conflict (Knopp 1995). As the largest city in Oregon, Portland fills this role as hub of sexual cultures. Simultaneously, a "near iron-clad" (Green 2002) free speech clause in the state constitution effectively prohibits zoning controls that target sexually oriented businesses.

Portland has almost six hundred thousand residents and over fifty strip clubs. Many more populous cities have far fewer clubs and many more regulations about alcohol service, attire, and contact between customers and performers (Brunner 2006). Local folklore holds that Portland has the most strip clubs per capita of any U.S. city (Moore 2005), which was confirmed by my systematic review of the Portland's trade magazine for the sex industry (*Exotic*) and listings on "The Ultimate Strip Club List" website (http://www.tuscl.net). I found 7.2 strip clubs per 100,000 Portland residents in March 2012. By comparison, "Sin City" Las Vegas has the same population as Portland but just 26 strip clubs (4.5 per 100,000 residents). Clubs are also geographically diverse and found in every quadrant of the city (see figure 2.1), near homes, schools, places of worship, highway exit ramps, and industrial districts. Though this study addresses only clubs within the city limits, the diverse neighborhoods of the city vary in terms of physical and social conditions—ranging from a densely developed urban core to wooded residential neighborhoods with single-family homes as virtually the only land use.

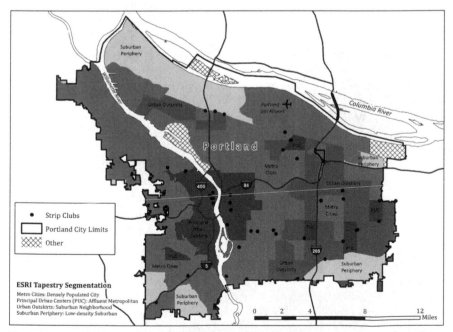

Figure 2.1. Distribution of Strip Clubs in Portland, Oregon
University of Minnesota Duluth Geospatial Analysis Center

Data Collection

Data collection included in-depth interviews, a review of media coverage and public documents, and field observations in neighborhoods throughout the city of Portland. Together, these diverse types of data create a picture of the social situation. In the presentation of the findings, interviewees have been given pseudonyms and their identifying details have been camouflaged. Pseudonyms are introduced in quotation marks the first time they appear. Quotations that do not mention an interviewee come from newspapers or publicly available documents.

Interviews

I interviewed forty-two people about their perspectives on strip clubs in Portland neighborhoods. While the study was about the city as a whole, I aimed to maximize the variety of perspectives I heard by focusing interview recruitment on three strip clubs that vary in age, size, and the type of neighborhood the club is located in. Because many interviewees had experience in multiple parts of the city and outside of the city, I heard about far more than these three clubs in the interviews.

I used different strategies to identify and invite different types of people to participate. Notably, I heard diverse ideas from the representatives of residential neighbors, despite the fact that for the sake of convenience I solicited this perspective through the officially recognized neighborhood associations, which sometimes pursue the interests of their individual participants more than addressing those of the whole populace.

For all interviewee types, I followed up at least two times after my initial interview invitation until the person declined to participate. I used e-mail, phone, and person visits to conduct follow-up.

Interviews ranged from 10–90 minutes and took place in homes, workplaces, and restaurants. Two of the dancer interviews were conducted over the phone because the dancers had moved out of town. At the end of each interview, I asked the participant for suggestions of other people to interview, and followed up on these. Interview recordings or notes were summarized into précis before analysis.

Other Data

This chapter also draws on local and national media coverage of the Portland's sex industry from 2005–2012, which shows how the issues have been represented in the popular imagination. Judicial decisions from relevant Oregon court cases and the text and pro/con statements for ballot measures proposing to further regulate the industry were used to understand the sociolegal framing of these issues. Finally, field observations at strip clubs between 2009 and 2011 provided an opportunity to evaluate the physical plant of strip clubs from an environmental psychology perspective, assessing their interaction with their surrounding neighborhoods.

Analysis

I employed analytical procedures developed by Clarke (2003, 2005), who describes her iteration of situational analysis as a toolkit for conducting grounded theory analysis "after the postmodern turn." Situational analysis shares grounded theory's process of ongoing comparison between data and interpretations (Cresswell 2003; Charmaz 2005), working through a variety of hypotheses in an effort to find the most reasonable explanations for the data (Clarke 2007). However, following Clarke, situational analysis is more focused on illuminating the complexity and multivocality of a situation rather than developing the kind of totalizing theory that is sought in traditional Straussian grounded theory. Key features of Clarke's method are mapping the situation, social worlds/arenas, and positions.

All data were imported the Atlas.ti qualitative analysis package (Muhr 2007), where coding was conducted. The discussion presented below is organized based on themes that emerged from this analysis.

SETTING THE STAGE: CITY SCALE

A combination of legal, economic, and social forces drive the extensive sex industry in Portland, making the city a place where striptease has flourished. Most notably, the Oregon state constitution effectively prohibits land use controls on sexually oriented businesses because it is one of two U.S. state constitutions that consider obscenity protected speech (Hawaii is the other). In the absence of zoning and other regulatory strictures, the location of strip clubs is determined by informal social and market processes. This section describes how these processes create space for striptease and how it is performed in Portland, including its role in the city's image.

Legal Context

A series of legal decisions has established a precedent that businesses and materials cannot be regulated on the basis of sexual content. In 1971, the Oregon legislature deregulated access to sexually explicit materials, and in 1982 the state Supreme Court established the precedent for obscenity as protected speech. Another decision in 1987 struck down a state obscenity ordinance. In the wake of these cases, municipalities including Portland attempted to craft ordinances that skirted the Constitution to limit clubs in number, location, and/or conduct; virtually all these efforts were have abandoned due to legal challenges. As the sex industry flourished, citizen-initiated attempts to alter the Constitution were put on the ballot in 1994, 1996, and 2000 but all failed to pass. Two additional Oregon Supreme Court decisions in favor of sexually oriented businesses in 2005 cemented the presence of the industry. These decisions affirmed the right of Oregon's sexually oriented businesses to locate in any area that is zoned commercial and municipalities' inability to enact controls on their hours of operation, alcohol service, or performers' attire.

Economic Context

Oregon's weak economy has also supported the industry's expansion. Spatially, sexually oriented businesses fill an economic niche in metropolitan development by occupying low-value spaces because their presence would not be tolerated in prime retail space (Cameron 2004; West and Orr 2007). Sexually oriented commerce tends to expand in times of economic restructuring (Tani 2002), and Oregon's economy has been especially weak in recent decades.

Interviews with owners of sexually oriented businesses and community leaders showed that the recent decline of the real estate industry has been a boon to sexually oriented businesses, which have been able to expand because property owners who would not ordinarily rent or sell their property to a sexually oriented business may no longer have the luxury of turning away a tenant that might be unpopular with neighbors.

Even when real estate costs are higher, opening a strip club is a low-risk investment in Oregon. Clubs do not need to get a license or pay any fees to have entertainers and obtaining a liquor license is easy and inexpensive. Existing bars can subsidize their operating costs by introducing exotic dancers because dancers pay fees to perform and share their tips with management, security staff, and bartenders.

Cultural Context

Portland's roots as a frontier town and more recent past as a politically progressive city contribute to the city's tolerance of the sex industry.

Portland in the nineteenth and early twentieth centuries is represented in local folklore as a freewheeling Wild West town of sailors and lumbermen, where many of the few women in town worked as prostitutes. The culture of the Portland region has a libertarian bent, resisting government regulation, particularly when it comes to individual conduct or the use of land. Organized religion plays a relatively small role in public life in Oregon (Killen and Silk 2004; Gallup 2012) and moral concerns about strip clubs are rarely raised. A "live and let live" approach is common, as embodied in the comment of a merchant whose business neighbors a strip club: "He's working retail as far as I'm concerned."

Mixing with this laissez-faire attitude is the emphatic embrace of expression and diversity that comes with the progressive consensus that has crystallized in the city since the 1970s. One exotic dancer who grew up on the area explains, "We're very colorful people, very accepting, a lot of artists, there's tattoos everywhere . . . I love it about Portland: it's just accepting, it's just like be who you want to be. We're all a bunch of hippies." With large gay, lesbian, and feminist communities, residents consider the city a sexually open place. For example, public nudity is legal in Portland, a fact that is most evident at the city's annual naked bike ride, which attracts many thousands of participants.

As a result, even people who dislike the idea of strip clubs defend their right to exist. A neighborhood leader who believes that strip clubs are connected to human trafficking sees this kind of response as the legacy of the days when many men left town to seek their fortune in the Gold Rush and lawlessness was the norm: "You see this history of progressiveness, like we had the first woman police officer ever. We also had the first Black-owned business on the west coast, and yet Black people couldn't come in to Downtown Portland. We have this contradiction in human value and devalue that's just weird and it runs in parallels to each other." From his perspective, Portlanders' belief in free expression overrides critical examination of how sexually oriented businesses function. A city employee explains, "pioneers who came out here to 'do their own thing' didn't want a lot of rules and regulations about things." A current-day business owner I interviewed takes this stance; he identifies as a libertarian and told me, "My beef is more with government intrusion than it is with Mistress Suzie!"

Others agree that the city gives a collective shrug of the shoulders to sexually oriented businesses. Said civil rights lawyer Charles F. Hinkle, "I don't really think that it really is a politically sensitive issue in Oregon. . . . There are enough voters in Oregon who like the free-speech clause interpreted as it has been and who have made that clear three different times" in referenda on regulating adult entertainment (Green 2002). Mainstream interests like Powell's Books and librarians' associations joined with sexually oriented establishments in speaking out against these measures. A city employee elaborated: "As Portlanders, we valuable individual liberty above community rights. Because of that we're more tolerant, not because we want it, but because [we] know the constitution. I may not like it, but you have a right to it."

As a result, strip clubs are part and parcel of Portland. Portland is proud of its famous strippers, such as rocker Courtney Love, who worked at Mary's, and Viva Las Vegas, who has immortalized the local scene in her memoir *Magic Gardens* (2009). There is an annual awards event honoring strippers.

Downtown's Mary's Club was "Portland's first topless," and its retro neon marquee is a landmark for locals and tourists alike (Cohen 2007). A downtown business owner recounted in our interview that in giving directions to customers, he has tried referencing a main street and a leading hotel, but mentioning Mary's Club always works best. The club's iconic cocktail waitress logo is a familiar sight on jackets and t-shirts around the city and Mary's was named one of the ten best strip clubs in the U.S. by *Men's Health* magazine (Gould 2005). Today the club is run by the third generation of the Keller family, and the marquee includes an epitaph for patriarch Roy, who died in 2006.

A rhapsodic *Travel + Leisure* article entitled "American Eden" (Austin 2007) described the situation with some bemusement, calling Portland an "idiosyncratic indie scene, where fair-trade cafés and strip clubs draw the same clientele . . . oddly enough, reasonable-looking young couples in the crowd are not an uncommon sight. Strip bars are as ordinary as the city's ubiquitous microbrew pubs, which are full of evolved frat boys in SNOB (Supporter of Native Oregon Beer) t-shirts."

TAKING THE STAGE: STRIPTEASE, PORTLAND-STYLE

This legal, economic, and social context has enabled the development of many venues in which striptease has evolved as a dance form. While the striptease conducted in Portland clubs is clearly the same activity as what happens in Las Vegas or New York clubs, Portland clubs have a local flavor. Because the clubs are found all over the city and very different types of spaces (ranging from small neighborhood bars to large suburban complexes), there is a wide spectrum of performance, including examples of innovation in the form.

Portland strippers don't always "look like strippers." Just as a certain body type is associated with ballet, there is a stereotypical stripper body: slim with large breasts (often silicone implants) and a small waist, with tanned white skin and long blonde hair. Women whose bodies do not meet this ideal often encounter discrimination in strip clubs (see, for example, Brooks 2001, 2010a, 2010b). Though Portland dancers do report instances of discrimination by club managers or customers based on their appearance, the city's clubs present a much wider spectrum of appearances than is seen in other cities.

While many clubs in the United States have historically banned dancers with tattoos or body piercings, several Portland clubs celebrate this look. These clubs have many dancers who are very thin, many with smaller breasts and hips, pale white skin, and/or sleeves or other large tattoo pieces. This more "goth" or "alternative" look was popularized by the Suicide Girls pinup website, which was launched in Portland. Even at more mainstream clubs in Portland, tattoos have become the norm.

Dancers' bodies are not the only alternative aspect of these performances. Some of Portland's best-known strippers are decidedly punk rock. With names like Malice and Rocket, they perform in multicolored Mohawks and leather jackets, accessorized with ripped fishnet tights and artillery belts. Eschewing the Top 40, these dancers perform to their personal favorite songs, which might include death metal or brooding atmospheric singers like Tom Waits. At several of Portland's smaller clubs, dancers select their music from a jukebox, giving the dancer a larger role in shaping the performance than is the case when the music is played by a DJ.

Portland is known for innovations in striptease and some routines are closer to performance art than boudoir fantasy. For example, Malice—who relocated to California—recently lamented in an interview with Portland stripper Kat (posted on the "Tits and Sass" blog on March 15, 2011) that even a toned-down version of a heavy metal number involving a nun costume, a gas mask, and a fake gun did not go over well in Los Angeles. Another legendary Portland strip club performance is the Devils Point club's weekly Stripperaoke night, where the strippers serve as backup dancers (and show-stealers) to customers onstage singing. Devils Point's strippers also offer weekly fire dancing performances.

In Portland, each club has its own style. Dancer "Fiona" described the experience of performing at her favorite Portland club, "It's a show, entertainment. They've got monkey bars on the ceiling, girls are swinging from the rafters. It's crazy, it's fun, the lighting is more complementary to the dancers." She contrasted it with another club, where "you have to be really good at the pole, it's more edgy, there's more tattoos, there's more of the rockstar punk [vibe]. You have to be more of an acrobat there." One owner described his club's style: "We're more on the burlesque side of entertainment. Most of the girls that work for me also spin around the pole and do crazy tricks and it's really entertaining. They don't just come out, prance around, and take their top off." The performance style in Portland clubs has been compared to Cirque du Soleil and other carnivalesque acts.

There is broad consensus—among interviewees, and as represented by local media—that strip club audiences in Portland include a wider swath of the population than they do in most other U.S. cities. The most obvious difference is the significant proportion of female patrons, which is notable given the fact that some strip clubs in other cities deny entry to unaccompanied women. Performing for this type of audience entails fostering more interaction between customers than would be the case with a typical strip club audience of solo men. Going to a strip club is socially acceptable in Portland: as many interviewees on all sides of the issue reported, "It's different here." These nontraditional audiences may be attracted to the clubs by their nontraditional performances and nontraditional locations—which can be near residential areas and business districts, making them familiar and easily accessible.

STRIP CLUBS IN THE NEIGHBORHOOD CONTEXT

Though strip clubs are part of Portland's image and many residents are proud of living in such an open-minded city, few embrace living next-door to strip clubs. While arts establishments and districts are often at the center of economic development plans (Strom 2003; Florida 2002), sites of sexual commerce like exotic dance are generally located in peripheral areas that reflect and reinforce negative stereotypes of these activities (Domosh 1999; Hubbard 1998b). When strip clubs appear in or encroach on more visible and valuable sites (either financially valuable, like a luxury property, or symbolically valuable, like a school or church), conflict usually ensues. The ability of strip clubs to exist without conflict establishes the status of the club on par with other nightlife establishments or performance venues.

Manifesting Conflict

The siting of new clubs has sometimes provoked outrage from neighbors, which they have expressed through strategies ranging from picketing clubs, lobbying the Oregon Liquor Control Commission to deny operator licenses, and negotiating stringent operating conditions with club owners. Residents' objections are most vociferous when clubs are located in residential areas, and especially if clubs are perceived as locating near schools or recreational facilities used by children.

For example, neighborhood leaders are currently fighting the expansion of the Casa Diablo strip club to a second location next to the Acropolis club at the edge of the desirable Sellwood neighborhood. Neighbors are unhappy about adding another strip club to the three already in the neighborhood, and are urging the Oregon Liquor Control Commission to deny the owner's license application because of the record of problems at the club's other outlet. Some of the same residents are engaged in a highly charged dispute with the owner of one club over the effects of noise in the parking lot, drunken customers leaving the club, and other negative impacts. They recently held a protest at the new club location, which was met with a counter protest by Casa Diablo staff and friends.

Another contentious site has been the Mynt club at the edge of the city's wealthy Laurelhurst neighborhood. The neighborhood association lobbied the Oregon Liquor Control Commission to deny the club's liquor license, ostensibly on the basis of the owner's mismanagement of a bar in another state. The information about the owner's background was unearthed by a neighborhood association member who likely drew on his training as a lawyer to conduct the research and present his findings to the media. The club still received a liquor licenses, but conditions were placed on its operations, such as a requirement that the owner be on the premises on weekend nights. The conditions imposed on the club's operations create a distinction between a strip tease (a problem land use) and other dance, because it is rare that arts establishments have such conditions imposed on their operations.

Infrequently, neighbor concerns have shut down a strip club or kept one from opening. One notable example is the Pink Marlin club in the Cully neighborhood, which has few amenities and a high concentration of immigrant and low-income residents. When the owner of several other sexually oriented businesses in the neighborhood applied for a liquor license for a new restaurant, residents and city employees were convinced he would open the restaurant and then add strippers. The neighborhood association approached him about completing a voluntary Good Neighbor Agreement, but negotiations were challenging and the applicant eventually withdrew the application. The neighborhood association's tenacity was central to the effectiveness of this strategy.

The fact that license restrictions are relatively rare helps establish the idea that strip clubs are normal businesses. A city employee who works with neighborhood groups expressed frustration with the fact that neighbors often had difficulty understanding the fact that this normalcy is codified in law. He told me,

"The neighbors are always upset . . . you know, instead of focusing on how to properly run a bar, what kind of security measures are you going to take, how are you gonna check ID, how are you going to ensure you don't have overservice, how are you gonna insure your lighting is good, what measures are you going to take into place that's gonna diminish the queuing outside so you don't have issues, the smoking impact, the concerns were: there's gonna be naked girls, and it's next to a school."

A club manager who has tried to work with neighbors also felt that residents' concerns were genuine but often misplaced: "They think that if a strip club goes up next to the [convenience store] all of a sudden there's pedophiles walking around trying to take their kids away. We all know that pedophiles would not come into a strip club. They would go to a library, where there's children. I've never heard of regulations put on those places."

Cultivating Coexistence

To many outsiders' surprise, some clubs have amicable relationships with their neighbors. Neighbors are more likely to tolerate (or even embrace) clubs when they are well established, have subtle signage, are responsive to neighborhood concerns, and support neighboring businesses.

While conflict is most common when clubs open, opposition usually wanes if few disruptions to neighborhood life occur after the opening. Most of the problems that do surface are typical of nightlife businesses: complaints about loud music and rowdy patrons that bother neighbors. Well-established strip clubs report few problems with neighbors.

Nelson, a city employee who works with neighborhood groups agreed, "Once you're established, it's not gonna change. People turn a blind eye to it unless the clubs change management and do something different in their format to draw attention to themselves." Timothy, an owner whose club is well received by neighbors, worked to avoid a rough entry to the community when he opened his club. He told me how they made incremental changes to a property that had been a bar for decades: "It was a very very easy gradual process of turning it into a strip club. I think it was to ease people into the fact that it wasn't their local dive bar anymore. It's their local dive *strip* bar. I think there was a lot of regulars, and I think if it just switched right away they would have been maybe turned off."

To some, strip clubs are neighborhood institutions. One club owner explains the role his business plays, "We get a lot of the neighborhood that comes in. On snow days we're packed because there's nothing else to do around there." From his perspective, the establishment is a cherished local bar; having strippers is almost secondary. A neighborhood leader explained how this influences her opinion of the club. She isn't bothered by its presence near her house because, "the people that go there . . . probably live in the neighborhood. It's not a place where people are traveling from the other side of town to come there. I don't know if I would feel differently if it were a regional draw. I think the distinction is 'our' strip club is a neighborhood place." She recognized that the dancers could be her neighbors, saying that she wouldn't be surprised if they lived nearby. She also noted that her neighborhood club hosted activities beyond striptease, such as live music, which made it feel welcoming to a broader audience. The integration of other artistic performances in the striptease venue also establishes the idea of exotic dance aligning with other arts.

Because location can be an important asset to a club, club owners may be genuinely concerned about their club's surroundings. Building reciprocity with neighbors further normalizes the club. According to a dancer, "I think a lot of the clubs that have been around for a long time have more of a stake in their community, so they feel like a shareholder in their community in that level." An owner explains how and why he resolves complaints:

I had one noise complaint one time from somebody who lived like a block away and they were complaining about one of our bartenders. They only complained once and I talked to 'em and I apologized. I'm always really really sincere about anybody that has any complaints about the bar. And I always try to solve whatever issue that they're having because that's the last thing you want, is your neighbors not wanting you there or a disgruntled neighbor. Any time that anybody starts to have a problem with you, and depending on how much free time they have on their hands, they can make it a real issue for your business.

Reciprocity helps build a club's stature in the neighborhood. One owner explains how he cultivates it:

We're definitely very friendly with all the businesses that are around there. . . . I went around and introduced myself to all the other neighbors and actually became really good friends with the [business] that's next door. And she ended up becoming a regular, and then she comes over and cooks [a holiday meal] for all the bar staff. And once a year, she lets us use her parking lot and we do a benefit. . . . I think it makes everybody feel good. I guess that's our little small contribution to the neighborhood.

In interviews, business people who reported knowing strip club staff as customers also unanimously reported being comfortable with the strip club's location nearby.

Keeping a Low Profile

Clubs also forestall conflict by being discreet in both appearance and activities outside of their club, which allows neighbors to treat them in an "out of sight, out of mind" manner. Because many of the concerns about strip clubs relate to changes they may cause to the neighborhood, it is easier for a club to contest this idea the less visible they are.

One dancer reports that because Portland's clubs aren't "in-your-face," they are not an overwhelming presence. Interviews with businesses neighboring one of the study's three focus clubs revealed that some didn't even know that the bar offered nude entertainment; not surprisingly, they also reported no problems resulting from the club's presence. Several merchants and neighborhood leaders who had experience working in neighborhoods where strip clubs were present suggested that if it was not possible to see inside the business from the street, minors were kept out of the club, and scanty attire stayed inside the club, there should be no problem for the neighbors. Some interviewees further commented that strip clubs are busiest at night, when most commercial establishments are closed and children are asleep.

One club manager contended that being discreet is part of establishing a more upscale "gentleman's club" atmosphere. He told me, "Our signs aren't offensive. They thought we were gonna have naked girls on it, XXX, Girls! Girls! Girls! As long as it didn't show nudity, we could put anything we wanted to. But we don't because we want to be a good neighbor." He continues: "We patrol the parking lot, we keep it clean, we make sure that we don't have any disturbances. . . . We never overserve, we cut people off if they're visibly intoxicated. We always offer cabs, we have a tow truck tow your car. We do what we can to make sure that what happens in here doesn't spill out to there. Legally and morally we have an obligation to make sure it doesn't happen. We really haven't had a lot of problems." Ostensibly, a gentlemen's club would be less troublesome to neighbors because it is not a sleazy establishment that threatens the neighborhood's identity as the domain of middle-class families.

There is at least one example of a strip club improving conditions in a neighborhood. As a city employee describes the opening of a new club in a commercial district: "Their security was very proactive and actually they started patrolling the area and really improved safety because before they were there in the night time there were a lot of issues because of [a facility in the neighborhood]—you saw a pick up in the drug trade too. So when the strip club showed up it actually made that little corner safer."

THE STRIP CLUB SITE

Conditions both in and outside of strip clubs can influence the character of dancers' performances and the dancers' experience of their work. Not surprisingly, the feature of club location that most influences dancers' experience is the type of neighborhood (residential vs. industrial, central vs. peripheral) the club is located in, because this affects their journey to work. Location can also affect the type of dance they perform: one very interesting finding of the present study is that Portland's peculiar institution of the neighborhood strip club offers a distinct performance experience for dancers. These variations are important not only because they affect the dance form but also because they affect the dancers' working conditions.

Finding One's Niche

Because there are so many strip clubs in Portland, dancers may end up performing in one or many niches. "Katherine" explains, "It's an amazing place to be a dancer. . . . You get a broad spectrum of options." Dancers I interviewed described trying out different clubs until they found one where they fit, illustrating distinctions between the styles of dance at different clubs. For example, Fiona described her favorite club as "more like pretty girls that are gentle," when compared to another place where "pounding your pelvis" to rock music was more typical. She considered both clubs well managed, but selected the former because it afforded the opportunity to do the type of dancing that interested her.

Dancer Terra considers club selection a matter of lifestyle. In our interview, she distinguised between city and suburban clubs and also among neighborhoods within the city. She expressed disdain for the suburbs and their denizens, describing dancing within the city of Portland as an escape from strip clubs populated by dancers who are all overly tanned with breast implants and teased blond hair and a landscape dominated by big box stores. As a multiracial woman, she felt at home working in Southeast Portland's neighborhood strip clubs. From her perspective, patrons in this bohemian part of town better appreciated her aesthetic (both physical appearance and personal style) than did people in other parts of the city. To elaborate, she explained that she rarely made much money when working in North Portland clubs where African American women and "thick" physiques are popular, or in working-class White neighborhoods where clubs were more "like biker bars." Another dancer, Mara, also decided to stay with clubs close to her home after trying out clubs all over town because she liked the sleepier character in her neighborhood, where dancing entailed a lot of conversation with customers as opposed to performing lapdances.

Clubs in centrally located, densely populated neighborhoods presented easier journeys to work for dancers. Short commutes and low transportation costs are prized by workers, and exotic dancers are no exception. Many dancers interviewed reported not owning a car during at least part of their dancing career; they either actively sought or simply benefited from working in Portland neighborhoods known for their walkability, bicycling infrastructure, and transit service. Portland's public transit system serves urban neighborhood business centers—and consequently, neighborhood strip clubs—much better than it does suburban areas that are home to the larger clubs. Since many dancers drink alcohol or use drugs while working, being in an area with a variety of transit options may also prevent incidents of driving under the influence.

Amenities near a club may also influence dancers' selection of workplace. Terra recalled the exhilaration of quitting time at her favorite neighborhood club, dancers streaming out into the fresh air, hopping on their bicycles to head to post-work adventures. The club's location in a lively neighborhood put it in close proximity to a variety of bars and other late-night destinations, making it a desirable place to work.

When asked to compare clubs in residential areas to clubs in industrial, downtown, or suburban areas, Xena declared, "I think neighborhood strip clubs tend to be more safe than other ones." Neighborhood clubs benefit from more "eyes on the street" (Jacobs 2002/1961) because they tend to be located near other businesses and residences and are often on streets with pedestrian and bicycle traffic as well as cars. Neighborhoods with strip clubs may also be safer because of increased police attention due to residents' fears of crime associated with the businesses (Edwards 2010).

The Neighborhood Strip Club

Portland is notable for its "mom-and-pop" strip clubs, run by small entrepreneurs and sometimes by families, such as the Keller clan that has presided over Downtown's Mary's Club since the 1960s. While the recent global expansion of the adult entertainment industry has spawned "big box" and chain clubs, such establishments remain uncommon in Portland. Many of the local clubs are not purpose-built but rather bars that added dancers after the free speech precedent was established (Sanchez 1997). These unusual neighborhood clubs merit special examination because their spatial configuration affects not only neighbors' perception but also how striptease is performed.

About half of Portland's strip clubs are in or near residential areas (sometimes right next to homes), while only a fifth are in industrial areas where large tracts of land might allow larger footprints. Figure 2.1 maps the city's strip clubs, including their relationship to neighborhood main streets, which are designated by the metropolitan planning organization. These are commercial districts nearby or integrated with housing, where small-scale businesses like cafés and hardware stores are located.

Virtually all of Portland's residential areas are dominated by single-family homes and low-rise buildings, a scale that dictates that neighborhood strip clubs be relatively small. Neighborhood strip clubs may be less than 1,000 square feet with a single stage. By contrast, Sapphire in Las Vegas is over 70,000 square feet (and boasts hundreds of dancers working each night). Even in New York's expensive real estate market, clubs top 10,000 square feet. The more intimate environment of small strip clubs affects how dancers work and their relationships with coworkers.

Neighborhood clubs differ from clubs in the Central Business District (located on the west bank of the Willamette River) or suburban areas in two major ways: they tend to be smaller and tend to be more spatially integrated into the communities that surround them. While there are certainly other influences on the work experience—most notably the club's management style—these two factors are generally positive influences on dancers' experiences. Dancers feel more appreciated as performers and as participants in the neighborhood.

Emphasis on Performance

Neighborhood clubs tend to be "stage" or "social" clubs, where dancers spend most of their shift onstage, rather than circulating through the crowd as is the practice at "hustle" clubs (for more on club typology, see Bradley-Engen 2009). With only two to three dancers working at a time, dancers spend a large portion of their shift performing onstage, accumulating tips left by audience members. Larger clubs may have scores of dancers working at once, so opportunities to be on stage are limited and dancers must solicit customers to purchase lapdances, performed at individual customers' seats for a fee.

Dancers at Portland's show clubs take pride in earning money for their stage performances, which they carefully choreograph and costume. This feeling of artistic expression is central to the job satisfaction of many dancers. For some dancers, working at a strip club is a way to earn money doing the same sort of creative performance that they are not compensated for as members of the local theater and music scene. Many dancers identify as natural performers and designers, and several told me about pursuing other careers in the arts. While dancers certainly like customers' tips and know that their physique is an important part of their earning power, their favorite customers are those who appreciate their style. Reporting on what she misses about Portland after moving to Los Angeles, dancer Malice explains, "I don't really get to put on a show down there like I do here. I can artistically express myself in Portland" ("Tits and Sass" blog, March 15, 2011).

Show clubs often foster more a more collaborative attitude toward skill building and earning among dancers. Xena explains:

> The smaller neighborhood clubs I think are really great because the girls look at it together. We'll all want everybody to make money. Work in a small club like that and everyone's like, "Yeah, hey, check out her. Isn't she cute? Isn't she great on the pole? Why don't you spend a few dollars on her and then you can come back and talk to me again?" But if you get out of those small little neighborhood clubs then it's gonna be so much more cutthroat.

At the smaller club, she sees herself as working with the other dancers to create a positive and lucrative environment for all of them. Hustle clubs work very differently: "I've worked in bigger clubs and I don't even know the girls' names I'm working with. They're all just a bunch of random bitches when it comes down to it." Smaller clubs often lack "VIP" areas or private rooms for one-on-one performances, so the dancers are also sharing one performance space with each other.

Strong personal relationships enhance dancers' sense of safety within the club. Dancer Fiona uses familial terms to describe the neighborhood club where she loved working. The manager was, "Somebody who wants to get to know you as a person and care[s] about you. While I was in school it was, 'How's school? What are you guys studying right now?' Just a close family relationship. And if you have any problems, you can go talk to them about a problem and not be afraid that you're gonna get fired." This concern extended to the events happening on the club floor: "Everybody feels like they're your older brother there. They've always got eyes on the back of their heads. They're always making sure you're okay." Ethnographic research conducted nationwide confirms that women tend to be happiest at these smaller clubs (Bradley-Engen 2009). Dancers I interviewed also told me about receiving more mentoring and support for learning how to dance in neighborhood clubs than in larger clubs.

Place Affinity

Though much of the literature on exotic dancers suggests that separating work and personal life is an important coping mechanism (Barton 2006; Sanders 2005;

Maticka-Tyndale et al. 2000), some Portland strippers have a strong sense of identification with the neighborhoods where they work.

Some dancers reported pride at making a contribution to the neighborhood where they worked. Xena explained, "Sometimes it provides a healthy environment for someone who just needs to get away from their everyday life who wants to have a little bit of fun. . . . It's a healthy way to do that if you do it right. I think that a good neighborhood strip club could really do it well. Some people they have perfectly healthy marriages, they have wonderful families and all they want is just a little bit of excitement on the side." Dancers emphasize the fact that their clientele includes couples, senior citizens, local business people, and veterans. Mara describes moments of being a health educator, therapist, and life coach while working as an exotic dancer. She reminds customers not to drink and drive, gives them a shoulder to cry on, and gives pep talks about staying sober.

Xena and Mara describe the clubs where they work as neighborhood resources, especially because they provide affordable entertainment in a city with a weak economy and high unemployment rate. These neighborhood clubs offer a performance that builds on ongoing relationships with customers rather than the cool remove of the gentlemen's club. This finding is notable given prior research finding that sex workers often feel excluded from the communities where they work, even when they patronize local businesses and live in the area (O'Neill et al. 2008).

Weighing Scale

These findings suggest that space and sexuality are key forces influencing exotic dance at a variety of scales. The notion of scale is controversial in geography, with some arguing that imposing ideas of scale on social systems is inherently hierarchical, imposing or reifying social structures and impairing our ability to see discern processes (Marston, Jones, and Woodward 2005) while others acknowledge these dangers but contend that when applied carefully, scale is still a useful organizing principle for understanding social arenas (Jonas 2006).

In the case of the present study, several well-defined scales proved to be important social structures influencing strip clubs. In some cases, these were scales of governance served to restrict the management of club siting. At the state level, the Oregon constitution and liquor control statutes preempted restrictions on strip clubs that entities at other scales wanted to enact. At the neighborhood scale, official neighborhood boundaries defined by the city determined what resources would be available to resolved problems (in the form of city staff). Other scales were less clearly delimited, functioning as social rather than administrative worlds. For example, though the study uses the city limits as its geographic parameter, discussion of the city's image in the public imagination does not necessarily hew to the boundaries of the incorporated territory. The meaning of "Portland" sometimes encompasses the entire metropolitan area or sometimes is much smaller, such as when an interviewee describes "how Portland is" based on a life where he or she has only experienced one small part of the city. Likewise, two neighbors' conceptions of "the neighborhood" may be very different based upon who they socialize with and which institutions they visit, yet the City of Portland has established very concrete neighborhood boundaries.

Though these scales are nested (i.e., neighborhoods are subdivisions of the city and each club falls conclusively within one neighborhood), their relevance to strip clubs is not necessarily hierarchical. At a given location or time, the role of a club in a neighborhood may be more important than the larger city context to the status of striptease. Indeed, scale interacts with other axes of organization, such as networks, mobility, place, and positionality (Leitner, Sheppard, and Sziarto 2008). So, I adopt scale as a heuristic framework but do not present it as a rigid linear structure through which all social processes follow the same path.

CONCLUSIONS: PLACE AND LEGITIMACY

Because the performance of dance is a cultural process that contributes to the development and maintenance of norms (Nash 2000), attitudes about and locations of striptease, strip clubs, and exotic dancers are continuously reconstituted in Portland's "sexscape" (Brennan 2004). Portland's experience with strip clubs shows that spatial diffusion of clubs can lessen the stigma of striptease, yet ongoing conflicts over clubs shows that striptease remains a contested form of dance.

While some interests in Portland remain troubled by the inability to zone strip clubs, the local currency of property rights, "live and let live," and sexual liberation arguments temper the stigma of exotic dance. In this regard, the city provides another example of an environment that offers some benefits to women performing sex work by normalizing (diffusing) rather than spatializating (concentrating) sexually oriented commerce (Maticka-Tyndale, Lewis, and Street 2005).

These dynamic processes of movement, space, and culture are embodied in the dancers who perform in clubs, which are in turn situated within neighborhoods and the city—each of these a scale of governance and social life. Because Portland is unencumbered by land use regulations on sexually oriented businesses, the sexscape is especially rich.

As consumer interest in exotic dance continues its rapid growth, spatialization may become untenable in cities where it has been the norm. The Portland case demonstrates that community response to spatial normalization has wider variation than has been documented in settings where the industry is more constrained. The insights from the city can be employed by urban planners trying to find a place for sexually oriented businesses, club owners who want to maximize profit by minimizing conflict, and—most important to readers of this book—dancers who are interested in expanding the art form of striptease.

Spatial Mainstreaming

To an extent, the geography of Portland's strip clubs disrupts the process of spatial marginalization, whereby governments and informal social processes relegate sex work to "circumscribed areas of the city, and then 'see' those areas through stereotypical images of red-light districts as dangerous and tantalizing places" (Domosh 1999, 431).

Being located in "respectable" neighborhoods confers a level of legitimacy to Portland strip clubs. When residents regularly see or pass by clubs, the sites become normalized, even if they are disliked. These locations also improve the respectability of dancers, since the location of sexually-oriented commerce reflects the social position of the people who engage in it and confers an identity on these people. Much of research on this phenomenon focuses on negative identities (Hubbard 1998a, 1998b), but Portland suggests that these processes work in both directions.

Several dancer interviewees told me they can't imagine dancing anywhere else. Xena reports, "I like it here in Portland. I don't think I could do it anywhere else. It's so normal here. You say you're a dancer here and people barely bat an eye. You go anywhere else and people are like, 'Oh, wow, crazy whore!' It's a big deal somewhere else."

Enduring Job Stigma

Yet the job satisfaction that many dancers shared with me masks structural barriers to economic empowerment and artistic expression as an exotic dancer. Even in the Portland case shows that, even when clubs are reasonably well tolerated, gender systems contribute to constrained labor opportunities for women—including informal workplaces with no occupational health oversight.

Many of the dancers I interviewed shrugged off the idea that their occupation was the product of an exploitative gender system, emphasizing instead the personal choice exercised and the flexibility afforded by their work arrangement. I struggled to reconcile my belief that these dancers are the experts on their own lives with the nagging suspicion that if there were better choices available they might choose different work that provides a steadier income stream, more stable work environment, and fringe benefits.

Halberstam (2005) offers some perspective on the value placed on flexibility in contemporary times. She contends that flexibility in gender, body, and identity are portrayed as empowering aspects of contemporary life, but that this flexibility serves to bolster the normative order (she focuses especially on heteronormativity) as people embrace individualism instead of resistance. She cites Lisa Duggan's description of "a new neoliberal sexual politics" and reminds the reader that "increased flexibility, as we now know, leads to increased opportunities for the exploitation of transnational corporations of cheap labor markets in Third World nations and in immigrant communities in the First World. The local and intersubjective forms of flexibility may be said to contribute to what Anna Tsing calls the 'charisma of globalization' by incorporating a seemingly radical ethic of flexibility into understandings of selfhood" (Halberstam 2005, 19).

While dancers and other artists around the world are used to scraping by on meager earnings, exotic dancers actually pay for the privilege of working. In Portland as in most of the United States, exotic dancers earn tips from customers but no wage from the clubs where they perform. While they may get grudging respect as artists, dancers are not legally considered employees, so they have no labor rights or fringe benefits like worker's compensation for injuries on the job. There are no state or local occupational health standards, despite the well documented physical and psychological hazards of the sex work (Bruckert 2002; Bruckert, Parent, and Robitaille 2003; Frenken and Sifaneck 1998; Barton 2006, 2007; Maticka-Tyndale et al. 2000; Chapkis 2000; Jeffreys 2008). These occupational hazards function of working conditions more so than the nature of the work itself (Spice 2007; Johnson 2006; Weitzer 2000).

The Future of Conflict and Coexistence

It is likely that conflict over sexual commerce will become an even larger challenge in urban environments over the next several years. While diverse sexual expression certainly exists beyond cities (Halberstam 2005; Shuttleton, Watt, and Phillips 2000; Johnston and Longhurst 2010), urban environments are a highly contentious venue for the interaction of sexuality and space. As Hubbard (2012) puts it,

> This is because cities are not just comings-together of people in the interests of social and economic reproduction; they are also sites of governance from which power is exercised through various apparatuses of the state. Cities are indeed host to the key institutions that have a vested interest in regulating sex as part of a project of maintaining social order: the police, local government, departments of planning and housing, the courts, hospitals, probation services, social services and so on. These institutions are rarely discrete or isolated, extending their reach from metropolitan centres out to the provinces and the countryside through *geographies*—as opposed to simply *geometries*—of power. (Howell 2009) [citation in the original] (xiv)

LESSONS FROM PORTLAND

The findings from this study contribute to the literature assessing the proliferation and stratification of the sex industry (Coulmont and Hubbard 2010; Maginn and Steinmetz 2011) and community responses to sexually oriented businesses (Edwards 2010), demonstrating that place processes contribute to perceptions of striptease and even the way that the dance is performed. The study also shows that increased tolerance of the industry does not necessarily improve dancers' stature, and that illegitimate business practices undermines exotic dance's legitimacy as an evolving art form.

Changes in the "adult entertainment" industry are proceeding rapidly (Brents and Sanders 2010), with adverse consequences dancers' well-being, especially those who are poor and/or women of color (Sanchez 1997; Bradley 2008; Brooks 2010b; Brents and Hausbeck 2010). While the sex industry grows increasing appealing and palatable to the middle class (Coulmont and Hubbard 2010), the industry's performers have become more vulnerable. Changing mores and a softening labor market led significantly lowered earnings due to an influx of underemployed women and eroded social barriers to nude dancing (Kay 2000).

Women in the sex industry continue to expose themselves to great risk because "the sexist and classist structure of non-sex industry jobs makes it difficult for women—particularly less educated and skilled women—to leave the industry" (Kay 2000, 49). These marginalized workers will continue to be concentrated in urban areas because the frisson of sexual commerce is valuable to the convention and tourism sector but is poorly tolerated in suburban areas (Sharp 2004). Cities present the opportunity connect exotic dancers' talents and expressive impulses to larger arts communities, but this potential is preempted by labor practices that delegitimate their work. Xena clamors for this sort of opportunity, explaining, "The naked human body is a beautiful thing; it should be exalted and respected. There should be more burlesque and more real performances." However, even at Portland's most innovative strip clubs, the "realness" of performance is compromised by the threats to performer well-being, which include economic and interpersonal volatility as well as political invisibility.

ACKNOWLEDGMENTS

I am grateful to the editors, the anonymous reviewers, and the Portland State Urban Studies Writing Interest Group for their feedback on earlier versions of this manuscript.

NOTES

1. Throughout this chapter, I use the terms striptease, exotic dance, and stripping interchangeably. Likewise, I use both stripper and exotic dancer to identify the people who perform this dance.

2. Strip clubs are venues where live dancers perform nude or partially nude. While there are some strip clubs that feature male dancers or both male and female performers, the vast majority of strip clubs in the U.S. feature only female dancers. The level of food and alcohol service as well as conduct permitted between performers and customers varies among states.

3

One Foot Inside the Circle

Contemporary Dance of Los Angeles Steps Outside Postmodernism and into Neo-Modernism-with-a-Twist

Teresa Heiland

Los Angeles (LA), an urban conurbation known as the City of Angels, is a national and international agglomeration of business, trade, culture, education, entertainment, fashion, media, science, technology, and tourism. It is considered the entertainment capital of the world for its television, motion picture, recorded music, and video game industries, and this sector of employment is known as The Industry. The performing arts play a major role in Los Angeles' cultural identity with over 1,000 musical, theater, dance, and performing groups (Smart Travel Info 2011). Surprisingly, even though LA has long been a center for innovative modern dance, LA has a reputation for not being supportive of theatrical concert dance, or, in other words, dance as art. In 1977 dance biographer Larry Warren expressed that "[Lester Horton's home base of LA] was regarded as a bush-league city, notorious for its lack of serious art" (1977, ix). Three thousand miles away from the capital of the modern dance world, it was assumed that nothing original or important could come out of LA. It has long been assumed that modern dancers must simply be emulating the work of more serious artists in East Coast cities where real art making happens. This attitude prevails: in 2004, San Francisco Herald dance critic Rachel Howard stated, "Southern California is not known as a hospitable locale to dance, and that alone makes [Stephanie Gilliland's contemporary dance company] TONGUE a success story" (2004). Time and time again, writers refer to the lack of serious art, and in the case of theatrical dance, a lack of an established West Coast style. Both the geographic and cultural contexts of the West and the art forms created in LA are predicated by relationships between rugged individualism, conquering of horizontal, far-reaching space, and invention. LA is home to people from more than 140 countries speaking 224 different identified languages (Elocution Solution 2011). With that range of diversity, individualism, and a terrain covering 468.67 square miles, an LA dance tradition would seem a misnomer. Is it even desirable to have a modern dance tradition in LA? A world dance tradition, a commercial dance tradition, or even a fusion tradition allowing for constant experimentation might be more fitting aims. When LA dance is criticized for not having a modern dance tradition, people are stating the obvious: many outsiders do not understand the values and goals within the so-called dance traditions of LA Simply put, LA dancers call the current continuum of theatrical modern dance "contemporary."

Contemporary dance is a name given to a broad genre of late twentieth and twenty-first century dance forms. Ballet, modern dance, hip hop, salsa, jazz, breaking, acrobatics, and so forth are amalgamated into a multi-purpose art form that speaks to many audiences. Rather than being a hybrid of fixed dance techniques, contemporary dance is more about a concept of hybridizing systems and methods originating from modern and postmodern dance. In a highly commercial city such as LA, dance transforms depending on the venue, purpose, and audience. Because LA is a gateway city, with easy access to the rest of the nation and the world, contemporary dance evolves and assimilates continuously. In LA, dance techniques seem to be far less sacrosanct than in older cities, and dancers are quick to value new skills and approaches to moving with little regard for the genre from which these modes of moving have sprung. While this practice seems blatantly opportunistic, it is actually reflective of code-switching, a mode of communication between people who live in communities where multiple languages are spoken. The concept applies to dancers in LA who switch back and forth between dance styles with assurance and engagement so that styles can merge and diverge as dancers need to communicate across and within domains. In LA, dancers have access to diverse learning and performing opportunities. Dancers who focus on ballet might also extend their skills and be good at performing other forms such as hip hop, aerial dance, tango, or breaking. Because of the sprawling nature of LA, there is no central hub of dance that makes it easy for dancers to be grounded, connected, or located. The relationships they have made between each other and their city-without-a-center create a web of dance at the peripheral margins of LA via the highways, the internet, the mobile phone, and the Dance Resource Center.[1] An LA dancer's geography is, thus, fluid. The people who live and work to create and perform dance make up the dance geography. They thrive in many corners of LA creating one performance opportunity after another by establishing their audience base, critical network, students, and their following.

In this chapter, I propose to uncloak the lifeworld of contemporary dance choreographers of LA. by analyzing interviews of key choreographers (see appendix for sample interview questions), exploring dance critics' reviews of their work, and analyzing urban theory about the postmodern structure of the city of LA. Using a grounded theory method, I coded and thematized the most salient features of interviews and reviews, and subsequently I cross-referenced these constructs with theories from history, sociology, economics, anthropology, and pop culture to better understand the relationships contemporary LA choreographers have with their city. I present this knowledge by weaving qualitative data and theory. From the perspective of contemporary dance of LA, I explore Bourdieu's concepts of *habitus* and *field*[2] in relation to dance as a hybrid product of cultures and LA as a unique post-postmodern city.

In the April 2000 issue of *Dance Magazine*, noted dance photojournalist Rose Eichenbaum questioned the fecundity of LA in terms of dance asking, "How could a city that nurtured the likes of Ruth St. Denis, Ted Shawn, Martha Graham, Lester Horton, Carmen de Lavallade, Alvin Ailey, Bella Lewitzky, Agnes de Mille, and Twyla Tharp, [among others,] fall flat on its face in creating a modern dance tradition of its own?" (2000, 68). Due to space restrictions, I will not provide a detailed historical overview of important dancers having emerged from LA, but instead I will explore a particular contemporary branch of the modern dance family tree. Writers have captured the essence of various historical dance figures born of LA, but the cultural milieu of theatrical dance and the emergent theatrical dance forms of this city have gone nearly undocumented outside of local dance reviews. For example, Angelinos are often told that they are not real artists until they have presented their work outside of LA, as if dances made in LA are not worthy of attention (Johnston 2009). When choreographers present outside LA, they claim they usually gain more respect if they do not reveal their home city. Admitting connections to LA could incite derision due to a perceived lack of serious commitment to art making. Given these perceptions, how might LA choreographers ever break down the stereotype about the dance of LA as not having a cultural identity of its own? Dance is not the only art form of LA that seems to be misunderstood. In 1971, when reacting to attitudes about LA architecture being devoid of cultural and artistic merit, architectural critic Reyner Banham stated that LA is inherently different and should be understood on its own terms (1971). Michael Dear, leading exponent of the Los Angeles School of Urbanism, asserts that "Banham's celebration of LA landscapes served to legitimize the study of Los Angeles, and to temporarily neutralize [. . .] the propensity of East Coast media and scholars to chart with mock amazement the eccentricities of their West Coast counterparts" (2003, 397). One factor that seems problematic for dance to be understood for its own merits is that LA does not have a strong central core of activity.

LOS ANGELES ON ITS OWN TERMS

In 1998, Michael J. Dear and Steven Flusty argued for the existence of a distinct LA School of Urbanism in order to discuss LA on its own terms because the lauded Chicago School of Urbanism, which asserts that modern cities are concentrated and revolve around a central core, does not apply to LA. The LA School is a mutable group of theorists from diverse backgrounds that aims to establish theories about how LA, and similar postmodern cities, are inherently different from modern cities that conform to the model of the Chicago School (Dear and Flusty 2000). Charles Jencks (1993) stated that the periphery of LA is often the center, and Michael Dear (2003) argued that its cultural environment places its margins at its core.

Contemporary dance of LA was actually born of a post-postmodern era that evolved a bit differently in LA than it did in other cities. Dance theorist and teacher of release technique Mary O'Donnell Fulkerson ("A Time Seeking its Name" n.d) suggests we should grant a more appropriate name for the era of contemporary dance in general, because the term contemporary says very little about what people are actually doing. She asserts that the title Ethical Reformation better represents this era of multiplicity and complexity, with its renewed interest in providing meaning for audiences. Contemporary choreographers are maintaining the postmodern freedom to adopt and accumulate many approaches to dancing and dance making, but importance is now being given to the modernist concern of having a point of view and responsibility to the audience. While Fulkerson speaks generally about contemporary dance, she describes what LA choreographers and critics have been arguing since the late 1980s, and what the Los Angeles School has been asserting about art of LA since the 1970s. It seems that LA launched head on into post-postmodern contemporary dance due to contending with these factors: lack of dance tradition, dispersed urban layout, and strong influence of the culture of the Hollywood industry. The geography of LA has power over its people and the advent of technology has sped up the process of post-postmodernism, offering Angelino dancers ways to conquer the difficulties this postmodern city poses while making the virtual margins, such as the laptop, the car, and the mobile devices, ever more central. When the margins are the center, something interesting happens.

To gain insight into the work, struggles, and inspirations of contemporary LA choreographers, I gathered names of choreographers that local dance educators described as the most representative of contemporary dance choreographers of LA. They are choreographers that work in what is called the hyperdance aesthetic, which I will elaborate upon throughout this chapter. Of the ten choreographers recommended, eight volunteered to be interviewed. Choreographer's names are used with permission.

I learned from the choreographers that their city-without-a-center offers many opportunities for studying, performing, and sharing dances, yet, as contemporary choreographer Bradley Michaud (2008) asserts "There is little patronage for ongoing dance company maintenance and development here."[3] It is widely known that managing the finances of a theatrical dance company in any city requires entrepreneurship and dedication, but starting a dance company in LA presents challenges that are due to its sprawling geographical layout and complex yet loose social network. In actuality, concert dance exists all over LA. It is presented in small venues by many grassroots organizations and self-funded choreographers that often pay to have their work produced so they can share their art. Critic Sasha Anawalt describes how embedded dance is in the LA community: "[It is] a city where dance riddles the inner sanctums of churches, temples, community centers, clubs, gymnasiums and zocalos, to say nothing of the nearly 280 legit performance spaces in mainstream theaters, large, mid-sized and small" (Sasha Anawalt Blog 2008). Anawalt's list signals the depth and breadth of committed choreographers in LA. The Dance

Resource Center's account of spaces shows there are 121 indoor performing venues, four outdoor venues, forty-five dance studios, thirteen universities with dance departments, and at least four visual art galleries that have presented dance (Southern California Dance Map 2011). Dancers and dance venues are ubiquitous, but while independence and entrepreneurship are keys to starting a company, pragmatics and continuous financial ingenuity are required for survival. Eichenbaum explains that "maintaining contemporary modern dance companies in [LA] and filling concert halls has been like pulling teeth" (2000, 68). She refers to the lack of a cultural center and separate communities connected by streets and freeways traversing vast distances. Eichenbaum discusses Donald McKayle's struggle with relocating from New York to LA. McKayle, honored as one of America's First 100 Irreplaceable Dance Treasures by the Dance Heritage Coalition of the Library of Congress, revealed that his company only survived three years in LA due to what he calls the city's obsession with moving pictures rather than observing live bodies in motion. Eichenbaum emphasizes that the "Hollywood machine dominates the LA psyche, drawing the focus away from art forms such as modern dance" (2000, 68). Choreographer and teacher Karen Goodman muses over her insights and experiences with several generations of theatrical dance in LA:

The gravitational pull of light, space, geography and Hollywood [. . .] Sun, air and vista radiate endless possibility in this iconographic land of promise—yet, are also its Siren's song. Sundays in the [dance] studio or at the beach? Audiences in the theater or at the movies? That remains the ongoing challenge for a dance artist in Southern California: to craft meaningful and magical work that meets the brilliance of this magical place. . . . And despite the long shadows that Hollywood luminescence can cast, live performance has benefitted from the wealth of dancers and collaborators in music and design who work in The Industry as well. (The Dance History Project of Southern California, 2012)

LA has served as a proving ground for modern dance, jazz, ballet, world dance, social dance, breaking, commercial dance, hip hop, and the list goes on. LA dancers work at being eclectic in order to gain potential for employment. This need for eclecticism may well have been what has kept traditional modern dance forms from taking hold in LA (2000). The modern dance traditions of much of the twentieth century required devotion to a central technique, not 25 different types. Dancers that are virtuosic in multiple dance forms and styles, from ballet to breaking, are more likely to be successful in The Industry, as they can be hired for a wider variety of jobs.

When dancers experience and acquire new styles and techniques from other cultures and assimilate those forms into their own dancing to the point that the purpose and origin of the original dance form can no longer be recalled, sociologist, anthropologist, and philosopher Pierre Bourdieu calls this act of adoption and assimilation *habitus*. Habitus, which occurs readily in the multicultural dance world of LA, is a mental structure or scheme through which people deal with their social worlds. Bourdieu (1980) calls the places or social domains from whence we borrow these dance influences the *field*. LA is a giant field providing many diverse dance forms. The concepts of habitus and field complement each other in that habitus is the social activity people engage in and the field is the social network within which that activity occurs. A social network consists of a variety of semi-autonomous fields such as art, religion, politics, business, and higher education. Bourdieu is particularly concerned with how powerful positions within a field can wreak havoc on less dominant players in the network—in the case of LA, dominant being the Entertainment Industry and non-dominant being the theatrical dance choreographers. People struggle for dominance within both cultural and social-class fields while aiming to establish what is important to them, such as what constitutes high culture and taste. Post-structuralist philosopher Judith Butler (1997) makes this connection even clearer when she states that the most important of the social domains of the field is the economic marketplace, which tends to be where entertainment dance in LA drives virtuosity and diversity in dance.

ENTERTAINMENT JUGGERNAUT

Bonnie Oda, a Martha Graham dancer who established the Los Angeles Dance Theatre in 1978 and co-founded the American Repertory Dance Company, stated that "LA, probably more than any other place, has a spirit of openness and adventure, with no preconceptions about what things should be like. This is very much in keeping with the soul of modern dance" (Oda in Eichenbaum, 68). While this statement may have been true for modern and postmodern dancers of LA, one key aspect seems to have changed. The trends in dance styles used by contemporary dance choreographers and The Industry require male and female dancers to be both competitive and willing to consistently take stuntman-like risks requiring strong, fast, and daring movements. Choreographer Jacob "Kujo" Lyons explains how this focus in central to his company, "We have this hybrid style of ballet and very technical break dance with an insanely hard body-to-body partnering style, and now we're experimenting with explosive forms of partnering that are a lot more dangerous" (2008).

To stay relevant and competitive in a city that is driven by entertainment production, choreographers and dancers must be up-to-date with the latest skills, dance styles, and looks. Television, movies, dance competitions, and technology drive dancers to stay current with what brings financial success. LA dancers compete for jobs in a community that values computer-generated renditions of impossible human feats and larger than life experiences.

Furthermore, researchers Paige Edley and Ginger Bihn attest that in Hollywood

[f]emale dancers' bodies are objectified and commodified [. . .] in order to sell tickets and souvenirs. [. . .] Dancers' bodies are not constructed as a whole person but as a physical body. [. . .] Living in a culture pervasive with self-scrutiny due to pressure from images and messages from the media is a reality of the technological age in which we live. [. . .] Living in LA, the center of the cult of slenderness and the entertain-

ment conglomerate of the world, could likely mean that dancers are under even more pressure. (2005, 220–221)[4]

The entertainment industry challenges LA theatrical dancers to choreograph and perform for audiences that often have an aesthetic education guided by Hollywood spectacle. Consequently, dance techniques in LA push the extremes, and physical risk-taking is a part of training, auditioning, and performing. LA is a city of hyper-dance and hyper-athleticism, which fuel the aims of the dancers that I interviewed for this study. Collectively, they expressed that they wish to dance in a way that mimics what gymnasts, martial artists, ballerinas, silk aerial artists, ballet dancers, circus performers, and stunt doubles do.

Because choreographers such as Hassan Christopher, Laura Gorenstein-Miller, Jacques Heim, Jacob "Kujo" Lyons, and Kitty McNamee are cross-pollinating dance styles to gain diversity in their expressivity, dance forms are becoming blended together to form technically formidable, yet ironically less diverse dance forms. Dancers train with the postmodern philosophy that all genres and forms are up for grabs, but they are also driven to master multiple techniques and skills to take on any blend of genres needed at a moment's notice. Edward Soja asserts that LA is "one of the most informative palimpsests and paradigms of 20th-century urban development and popular consciousness" (1986, 248), and the postmodern traditions of the late twentieth century are being fueled now by technology and cultural borrowing, creating a pastiche of movement styles. Younger dancers have been born into the epitome of the postmodernism aesthetic of popularization, which brings the hunger and drive for competition. Dancers still consider dance to be an art, but they are aware that they—and their audiences—are less responsive to subtleties found in some earlier classical modern dance genres. Viewers seem to have to be challenged and even conquered for live dance performances to compete for attention in LA, likely because audiences are educated more by the media than by attending the theatre. The audiences, too, are inundated with the commercial dance culture of film and television, and sitting in a theatre watching the gradual development of a twenty-minute dance piece is far less familiar.

In 2000, Algerian born French economist and scholar Jacques Attali commented,

> High culture, too, could very well be crushed by the entertainment juggernaut [of Hollywood.] Enter endless permutations of American neologisms that mark "show biz" in all aspects of life, edutainment, infotainment, train-o-tainment. At this rate, Hollywood hyper culture could secure political, industrial, and strategic control for the US over every other civilization on Earth. (2000, 644)

Attali argues that the arts and culture held in highest esteem around the world could eventually be influenced by the pervasive Hollywood Industry. In LA, some dancers perform in both the theatrical and commercial dance genres. The Industry typically pays better than contemporary theatrical dance companies, therefore some dancers that prefer to perform concert dance will cross over and work in

The Industry. Some choreographers manage to work successfully in both venues, although contemporary choreographer McNamee admits that she had to sacrifice creativity to work in The Industry. She eventually developed her approach to making it in LA by getting herself an agent and by blending commercial and theatrical dance in evening-length concert dances that work well in large, prestigious, LA venues (McNamee in Harkness 2003).

Success in dance, at least in Europe and on the East Coast of the United States, has long been defined by being a ballet dancer. With the lack of a consistently successful ballet company in LA, little girls who grow up taking dance lessons in LA. typically aspire to be successful in Hollywood. Their teachers and directors groom them for corporate dance auditions. Dancers in LA are lured into the hype of Hollywood and industrial dance shows, even when they do not realize they are lured to value them. The powerful enticement of Hollywood offers young dancers an artificial euphoria related to the acceptance of aiming to be the perfect, objectifiable performer for advertising—where she will be performing for the male gaze.

In a research study on LA dancers, Heiland, Murray, and Edley (2008) interviewed a contemporary LA dancer named Julie who talked about negotiating two contrasting representations of success for a female dancer. She said she can either seek validation that she is a beautiful dancer and deserving of the audience members' gaze, thus placing a premium on visual experience over kinesthetic empathy[5] or she can resist the desire to display her gorgeous legs for entertainment's sake and, instead, share inner aesthetic impulses made manifest through the rhythmic, dynamic expression of the whole body. Julie recognized that the contemporary genre of dance in LA offers her a wider palette of intellectual, emotional, and physical expression and experimentation than commercial dance. The extreme physicality, a key theme in contemporary dance, affirms for LA dancers that they can achieve movements that appear daring and risky, but that do not objectify the body.

Contemporary choreographer Michaud, who grew up doing ballet, tap, jazz, commercial dance, and Irish step dancing before studying at University of California, LA and dancing with Stephanie Gilliland, stated, "I think [many contemporary dancers of LA] probably crave what I crave, which is a true full-body experience with dance" (2008). How beautiful dancers appear is not emphasized in contemporary dance; central to contemporary dancers' success is how focused and biomechanically supported their dancing is and how willing and able they are to perform daring moves. Lyons (2008) stated that contemporary dance of LA is known to be fierce, challenging, and scary—and fiercer, more challenging, and scarier than anywhere else—requiring 100 percent of a dancer's attention in order to have success because it requires power, flow, and complex, daring trajectories through space. Theatre and dance historian Roger Copeland says that dancers that grew up in the late twentieth century have returned to aesthetic approaches important to early modern dancers, yet rejected by postmodernists such as the need to provide kinesthesia, choreographic empathy, physicality, and sensuality.[6] He asserts that a return to these elements in a new way is allowing for a choreographic dismantling of the voyeuristic gaze, and it now addresses the female spectator (Copeland 1990). LA contemporary dance engages extreme kinesthesia without valorizing the male gaze. This unleashing seems to bar entrance of the hegemonic factors of Hollywood into the space where contemporary dance theatre occurs. Kinesthesia *is* the tacit subject of much of contemporary dance of LA, and both men and women are performing challenging feats that entice kinesthetic responses from audiences.

Alain Berthoz, director of the Laboratory of Physiology of Perception and Action at the College de France, expresses that perception stimulates action and that with the discovery of mirror neurons in the cortex, we now know that these neurons fire when a subject performs an action or when a subject sees an action being performed. When we watch someone moving, motor circuits in the brain are activated that do not result in our movement, but we rehearse and experience that rehearsed mental movement (2000). Dance historian Susan Leigh Foster explains that long-standing features of our cultural, as well as physical, environment inform the way that we perceive the world. She addresses the notion that living in a world filled with digital technologies is restructuring the baseline experiences we have of our world. The level of constant stimulation and interruption increasing for all humans creates "networked bod[ies] made possible by new digital technologies similarly hooked into environments both immediate and distant" (2011, 125). It seems possible that Angelinos, who spend great amounts of time hyper focused on social media, technology, and driving in LA traffic, might experience live theatrical performances differently than audiences in cities that have a core center. Research into this hypothesis could prove enlightening.

Gorenstein-Miller has found a way to thrive before an LA audience. She explains, "There is no exact formula for success [in LA]. You have to forge your own road" (Gorenstein-Miller in Sussman 1998, 60). Choreographers in every city might say the same thing, but in LA the power of commercial entertainment industries must be negotiated. She brings a new attitude to how to survive by blending her own contemporary dance style with ballet and lyrical dance for her company Helios.[7] She choreographs for both the commercial and theatrical dance genres expressing that this dual approach creates no conflicts for her. Whether one chooses to put one foot in both circles or not, one must be wise to the fact that dancers vying to perform in LA companies must be groomed differently, with an edge to competitiveness, directness, and ability to push established boundaries. These requirements change the way one moves, thinks, performs, and evokes.

DANCE RESOURCE CENTER

A study by sociologist of the arts Volker Kirchberg (1995) showed that across the nation, 70 percent of the people who attend the ballet also attend modern dance performances. While ballet and modern dance have long been considered to be dance forms cognoscenti attend in many American cities, other theatrical dance forms have tended to be more abundant in LA, such as world dance forms, jazz, folk dance, commercial dance, and street dance. Kirchberg's thirteen-year study on American financial support for the arts revealed that LA had to be omitted from the study because LA's corporate structures consist of many companies already in the business of making money from entertainment and culture, hence they are sometimes less committed than other corporations to supporting non-profit arts organizations (1995, 317). Researchers decided it was far too complicated to examine LA's financial support of the arts due to LA being an entertainment megalopolis. One can only imagine the possible level of financial support dance companies might receive if LA were not a city that commodified dance.

In many cities modern dance companies have tended to survive on low budgets, so this struggle is not specific to LA, but Michaud asserted that LA choreographers must extend themselves even further so their companies can survive. A longstanding, committed audience base is hard to find and maintain in this city of distractions, plus shows run only a few days at a time and few critics are available to write about performances. Michaud (2008) stated, "The hard part [of producing in LA] is that it's so off the radar [for prospective financial supporters]." He described the level of support:

> It always comes down to money. To self-produce costs about $5,000 to $15,000, and to raise those funds, even if they have to come out of your own pocket once a year—I mean, it breaks your bank. The D[ance] R[esource] C[enter] helps dancers stay connected, but their focus is not on helping choreographers find ways to sustain individual companies and pay our dancers, which is what actually needs to happen to build that system up. (Michaud 2008)

Because of the protean nature of dance in LA and the desire to create a hub for dance, the Dance Resource Center of Greater Los Angeles was created in 1987 to provide support services for community-based dance activities and to maintain connections between choreographers, teachers, students, and audience members through a virtual network of news flashes, listings, and advertisements that feature all genres of dance. The organization assists with public relations, grant writing, and concert promotion, but, even with the help of the Dance Resource Center, the LA dance community is larger and more diverse than can be assisted. In addition to the more than 100 nonprofit dance companies in LA County, there are numerous unincorporated dance companies and groups, presenters, commercial studios, university dance departments, teachers, and thousands of students, working dancers (theatrical and commercial), and dance audience members. The Dance Resource Center provides the connection, assistance, and information to know, build, and strengthen the vast and varied community of those interested in dance (Mission and History n.d.). Interestingly, with all this growth, dance in LA is still seen as *less-than* by outsiders, due to its lack of a tradition.

Longtime Los Angeles Times dance critic Lewis Segal—when discussing a lack of a ballet tradition—tended to think that not having a strong corporate support for ballet was generally a good thing for LA choreographers' creative individuality (2006). If corporate funders are not dictating what should be done with their money, then artists can be freer to express themselves. He argued that the world of classical ballet was not evolving with the times in which we live, and that other dance forms speak to people better today.

How *do* LA dance companies survive? It turns out that support tends to come from the people, not as much from corporations as it might in other cities. In a 2010 study of corporate giving, researchers David Card, Kevin Hallock, and Enrico Moretti (2010) learned that the number of corporate headquarters in a city or region reflects charitable giving to non-profit organizations in that city or region. Researchers noted that from 1989–2002, the number of corporate headquarters and public contributions to non-profits such as hospitals and arts organizations dropped in LA and Chicago as corporations moved their headquarters out of those cities. San Jose, San Francisco, and Houston experienced corporate headquarter growth and increased giving while LA experienced losses. As much as Segal believes that a city without a long history of strong ballet companies is beneficial for artists' independent creativity because they are not beholden to large financial conglomerates, not having a culture that is consistently eager "to go to the ballet" does create stumbling blocks for choreographers seeking audiences and funders. It is, perhaps, more common to find an audience watching hip hop and breaking competitions, yet this is what makes the LA dance community unique.

HYBRIDS AND HYPERDANCE

The hip hop dance culture, with its scratching turntable techniques, rappers' gutsy performances, and dancers' creative breaks, evolved into a distinct style around the world, and this style has deeply entered contemporary dance of LA (George 2005, 14). Music and culture critic Nelson George explains that breaking began in New York City with African Americans that were dancing mostly upright doing moves inspired by James Brown, Michael Jackson, and dancing shown on the Chicago-based TV show *Soul Train* (2005, 15). *Soul Train* imported dance styles of locking and popping[8] from LA and, subsequently, Hollywood exposed them through low budget movies (George 2005, 133). During the 1980s, Dalton Higgins, author of *Hip Hop World*, stated that the overexposure crippled the genre because it became a fad, so it went underground. By the 1990s, it had regenerated as breaking throughout Europe, South America, and Asia with competitions in 33 countries. Artistry increased and Korean b-boys[9] brought more athleticism to windmills and head spins (Higgins 2009, 44). Breaking and hip hop had split entirely. Hip hop became a sexy, tough, upright, grounded style of movement. Meanwhile, breaking no longer expressed messages of hip hop, and it had entered the competition realm. The commercial film industry objectified hip hop and breaking, so dancers engaged themselves in its field. It assimilated into other dance forms via dancers' embodiment, became part of the theatrical dancer's habitus, and suddenly hip hop and breaking were part of theatrical dance, albeit rearranged and not readily recognizable.

When discussing these inchoate dance forms emerging out of hip hop, Halifu Osumare, scholar of African American and African studies, calls this phenomenon hip hop's two-pronged bodily text (2002, 38). She stated that, "[Judith] Butler's use of Bourdieu's 'habitus and field' is a compelling model through which to view the processes by which global hip hop youths construct their performed identities" (Osumare 2002, 39). I suggest these concepts are also applicable to those who adopt hip hop and various other dance forms into their own dance culture. For example, the "processes, tendencies, and attitudes" author and dance critic Brenda Dixon Gottschild describes as coming from an Africanist performance practice seem to exist in hip hop, b-boy dance, and contemporary dance of LA (2000, 12–16).[10] The risk-taking involved in contemporary dance of LA likely grew from that of breaking that sprung from hip hop. Writer and director of musical theatre Thomas DeFrantz states, "the elaborate spins, balances, flips, contortions, and freezes performed by break-dancers required extreme agility and coordination. Real physical danger surrounded movements. [. . .] The competitive roots of break dancing encouraged sensational movements" (2004, 75). DeFrantz asserts that hip hop allowed a black diaspora to begin, so hip hop and breaking are no longer a distinctly black practice. Instead, a black cultural practice had become a popular practice found in many dance forms. Aspects of this dance form, such as risk-taking, were assimilated into contemporary dance of LA and are no longer a direct invention of the black diaspora. Dance principles specific to contemporary dance of LA are a commingling of concepts from existing cultures melded with values found in competitive dance, sports, and martial arts. The overall theme of these dance forms is that extreme effort is a badge of honor. While contemporary choreographers do not aim to explicitly perform Africanist aesthetics, an Africanist aesthetic is imbedded in the movement. While the Africanist aesthetic helped shape contemporary hyperdance of LA, it does not seem to carry or set racial boundaries. Post-Colonial theorist Stuart Hall attests,

> America has always had a series of ethnicities, and consequently, the construction of ethnic hierarchies has always defined its cultural politics. And, of course, silenced and unacknowledged, the fact of American popular culture itself, which has always contained within it, whether silenced or not, black American popular vernacular traditions. [. . .] American mainstream popular culture has always involved certain traditions that could only be attributed to black cultural vernacular traditions. (1993, 105)

Contemporary dance, while it is a hybrid and has roots in vernacular traditions, is likely still more prevalent in the lives of dancers who can gain access to formal education rather than learning in the streets, although television and the internet have become ready teachers for those without access to formal dance education.

It is interesting to note that seven of the ten choreographers suggested as key figures to be interviewed for this study are white and college educated, and those same seven are male. While African Americans, Asians, and those of other ethnicities do

engage in contemporary dance, it seems the majority of the choreographers presenting their contemporary dance choreography in LA tend to be white males. Although
contemporary dance has blended concert dance forms with street dance, and it is not
defined by boundaries of race, it is bounded by opportunity, which is tied to money
and power. It is also unbounded by social and entertainment media, thus allowing
the Africanist Aesthetic to be enmeshed in every American dancer's embodiment.
The dance culture of hybridization is even more deeply part of LA and is influenced
by the vast terrain and powerful hub of The Industry pulling at every highway,
billboard, and large and small screen. The negotiation dancers engage in with the
entertainment industry opens up these new spaces of contestation that make LA a
prime ground for supporting these hybrid forms such as contemporary dance.

It is compelling to glance back at philosophical discussions among dance critics
about contemporary dance of LA. Donna Sternberg addresses a March 6, 1994 review of hyperdance by Segal titled, "The Edge of Dance." Sternberg states,

> Trends come and go. Ten years ago [in 1984,] Mary Jane Eisenberg's form of dance,
> termed "hyper realism," was in vogue. Now it's "Hyperdance." [. . .] In an art form in
> which your body is literally your instrument, I wonder how long the proponents of
> Hyperdance will be able to push their bodies to the limit. Hyperdance may burn itself
> out because there won't be anyone left to do it [, . .] a fitting tribute of the times. (91)

Having raw emotions and raggedness around the edges is part of the skill of expressing the virtuosity of the intent, meaning, and purpose of contemporary dance of
LA. If the influences of the diversity, Hollywood, commercialism, sun, sand, surf,
mountains, and vast terrain with ubiquitous highways continue to instill energies
into LA's inhabitants—and I imagine it will—then dancing will respond in kind.
What will evolve is the life force and curiosity people bring to a city, like their embodiment through movement.

Hyperdance has evolved and is now called contemporary dance, although there
is no single form or genre. It is a staple underlying philosophy of dance training in
LA. Since Segal spoke about hyperdance in 1994, the technique has been codified
to certain degrees and established as contemporary modern, contemporary jazz,
contemporary hip hop, and so on. The boundaries between the forms depend on
who is teaching, choreographing, or dancing. These contemporary techniques are
taught by instructors much the way modern dance and jazz were taught by their
respective proponents throughout history, but lines between these contemporary
categories are blurred depending on the respective divergent, convergent, and
systematic applications of the habitus of the teacher. While the term hyperdance
signifies more about the technique than the term contemporary alone does, dancers in LA know what to expect when a dance class is called contemporary—they
expect to experience hyperdance elements.

The words dancers and dance critics have used to describe contemporary dance of
LA parallel the themes that Jencks, Dear, and Flusty describe about living in cities
without centers: being off center; being off balance; being inverted; moving through

spirals, designs, and trajectories in relationship to gravity; using release, tension, and power; hyper-athleticism; hyper-physicality; speed; free-flowing; impactful; risk-oriented; egalitarian partnering; forceful trajectories; shifting directionality; alternate surfaces of weight support; awareness of a reticulating matrix around oneself; melding martial arts, sports, physical fitness; spatial ingenuity; and constantly testing one's stamina.[11] These are the basic elements of what was once called hyperdance, but can still be seen in contemporary LA dance today.

Kinesthetic Empathy

Bourdieu states, "The body believes in what it plays at: it weeps if it mines grief. It does not represent what it performs, it does not memorize the past, it enacts the past, bringing it back to life" (1980, 73). He speaks of the relationship between the belief and the body, what dancers might call the emoting body. Choreographers have described contemporary dance as a return to movement for movement's sake (to let the movement speak for itself). They are using the body to convey emotion through the movement, which is a clear shift toward kinesthetic empathy and away from previous goal of a non-emotive movement. Now movement for movement's sake extends movement capacities of the body to access emotional states that incite kinesthetic empathy from the audience. In this way, movement for movement's sake is at work to provide audiences with affective sensation. By captivating audiences kinesthetically, choreographers connect with audiences in the fullest ways possible both physically and affectively.

Roland Barthes, French philosopher and literary theorist, notes that since the advent of the surrealistic period of arranging objects irrationally, we no longer have authors who work alone as geniuses creating works of literature or other artworks. The term author has become obsolete because we now combine pre-existing texts, techniques, and artworks in new ways. We now have what Barthes calls scriptors, whose power comes with relating pre-existing texts—or, in this case, pre-existing dance techniques and technologies—in new ways that relate to current subject matter, issues of dominance, habitus and field, and states of human conditions. The choreographer as scriptor is continuously being born and reborn while reengaging one's habitus with the ever-evolving field, which consists of internet technology, virtual sharing of ideas, and multiliteracies of a more accessible world. For Barthes, the death of the author is the birth of the reader, but with the pressure to be the best reader, or gatherer of ideas, is the pressure to be the most skilled with creating new movement configurations (1977). The habitus and field of LA contemporary dance drives choreographers to work diligently to ensure that audiences are given as much to see and feel as possible, bridging the postmodern aesthetic of stimulating to the point of manipulation with a modernist desire to create a sense of meaning, a point of view. This complexity results in a habitus of dance works that take on a purposeful direction and have something of importance to say, while still being pushed to an extreme of emotional density.

This thorough and intense commitment signals an inherent distrust of audiences, as if viewers are incapable of meeting performers halfway. This approach to sharing seems wise in LA, where audiences are not easily amassed and inculcated into theatrical dance cultures. It is as if a report were issued stating that an LA audience might not be ready for experiencing physical subtlety and nuance. Is the *dasein* (the act of being in the average everydayness of the current fast paced, electronically plugged in society) so numbing that audiences need to be shaken to their visceral senses (Heidegger 1962)? The philosophies within the habitus of contemporary dance of LA seem to point to this need. While it is widely known that the glitz, glam, and bigger-is-better values were born of LA, the intensity of hyperdance seems to have originated in New York City and then was made even larger by LA choreographers. New York City choreographer and dare devil dancer Elizabeth Streb seems to have given birth to the form, developed it, and her progeny disseminated it. Streb is most widely known, beginning in 1979, for introducing ideals of pure athleticism as art to New York City. She focused on "concrete physical concerns that are particular to movement, such as velocity, force, and palpable risk. [. . .] She would rather display effects of gravity, than camouflage them" (Media, Wesleyan University Press and the Academic, n.d.). Nancy Reynolds and Malcolm McCormick state,

> Much of her work concentrated on velocity and simulating the thrilling sensation of risk she associates with downhill skiing and motorcycling. [. . .] The dancers [. . .] interacting with one another and following exchanges of verbal cues, swung from tables, leapt off platforms, and hurled themselves against padded walls or mattresses. Once in motion, they were trained to follow a movement's natural trajectory to the brink of real danger. (2003, 624)

When describing Streb's solo, Reynolds and McCormick detail the key element of her work that has been propagated into almost every corner of contemporary dance of LA: "The brisk pace and eccentricity of what was occurring tended to preclude associative idea: the medium—sheer physicality—was sufficient message" (2003, 624). How did this style become so interwoven in the LA habitus? Streb never trained dancers in Southern California.

Roots from Inside and Outside Los Angeles

Mehmet Sander, a Turkish choreographer with a style similar to Streb's, had studied briefly with her before settling in LA in the late 1980s for graduate study in dance at California State University, Long Beach. Sander shared and exchanged ideas through his choreography and teaching while he remained in LA (Perlmutter 1995). Sander's style converged with the technique of Stephanie Gilliland, another robust, risk-taking LA choreographer that was trained classically in Horton/Lewitzky technique by Fred Strickler. From 1967–1975 Strickler performed with Bella Lewitzky, who had danced with Horton from 1934–1950, at which point she started her independent career that shaped the foundation of much of the technical modern dance tradition of Southern California (Strickler 2012). The energies of Sander, Gilliland, and the dancers of her company, formed a vortex of new relationships with gravity, flow, weight, and space that changed the face of theatrical dance in LA. At this point, an intense new way of moving was emerging when LA choreographer Gilliland danced and worked with Sander and their colleagues. It was Gilliland's work with these techniques that integrated the hyperdance movement concepts deeply into the dance community over a period of about thirty years. She had set many works on dance companies before starting her own company, TONGUE, which performed from 1997–2004. In 1994, Segal (1994) said that the central members of the style burgeoned by Streb were considered to be Jacques Heim, Stephanie Gilliland, Joel Christensen, Franklin Guevara, Mehmet Sander, and Lori DuPeron.[12] Gilliland's company members, Holly Johnston, Bradley Michaud, and Patrick Damon Rago went on to spread the movement style through their teaching and their own dance companies. Johnston (2009) stated that there are a few contemporary dance performers that represent the ideal skills needed for contemporary dance of LA, most notably Rago, who has exceptional ability to undulate seamlessly through all three planes while traveling upside down, sideways, and backward, hovering as if floating in water. See Rago in figure 3.1. Also of note is the director of Oni Dance, Maria

Figure 3.1.   Performance of *Four Inches to the Left* at SOLA Contemporary Dance Festival, James Armstrong Theatre, Torrance, California, 2003, by Palindrome artistic director and choreographer Patrick Damon Rago.
Photographer: Keith Weng © 2003. Used by permission.

Gillespie, who opts to bring sensuality to risk taking and Keith Johnson, who entered the LA aesthetic when he transplanted from New York having had a successful career in contemporary dance in New York City.

LA serves literally as a hotbed for dance techniques that emerged from the aesthetics of Denishawn, Horton, Lewitzky, and Hollywood and those brought to LA from New York, Chicago, Europe, Eurasia, and Asia. These techniques flourished in the community becoming melded, augmented, and intensified emotionally to compete with the siren song of the geography of LA. See the visceral emotion of Johnston's company, Ledges and Bones Dance Project, in figure 3.2. While in LA, Sander further developed what Los Angeles Times journalist Donna Perlmutter calls, his "part circus, part gymnastics, part performance art, part killing field" ways of moving that "draw upon principles of physics and architecture [. . .] that are flesh and bone and thus damageable" (1995, 78). Originally from France, Heim relocated to LA to study for his M.F.A. in choreography at California Institute of the Arts. He contributed greatly to contemporary dance by exploring ways of creating spectacle with human movement in relation to manmade structures. With his background in European dance theater and exploring moving on, in, and around architectural constructions, he was brewing some extreme approaches of his own that, while more

Figure 3.2. *Evidence* [embedded], created November 2006, performed at the Diavolo, Los Angeles, California. Artistic director and choreographer: Holly Johnston. Dancers left to right: Sarri Sanchez and Arletta Anderson.

Photographer: Andrei Andreev © 2006. Used by permission.

commercial in approach, fueled a similar desire among dancers to give and engage in challenges as actively and intensively as possible.

The audience responses to Heim's Diavolo Dance Theatre shed light on how a contemporary dance company of LA can successfully serve a mainstream audience. While not a native of LA, Heim brought his LA-friendly, diverse theater, film, and dance experiences with him. By presenting works that require gymnastic-like dance skills coordinated neatly with moving set pieces, his large-scale projects offer arts audiences, including families, movement theater about humans relating to unstable environments—such as earthquake laden LA. Diavolo packages itself to appeal to proscenium theatre audiences and those that prefer the commercialism of Hollywood and Las Vegas. Heim created pieces with a jungle gym functioning as a city and projection screens, ramps, and platforms to show a relationship between people and architecture. See Diavolo dancers negotiating with Heim's elaborate sets in figure 3.3. Heim said, "I feel really trapped living [in LA], going from point to point in my car, so I wanted to a do a piece that is confined" that makes eight people deal with that feeling of being trapped. Showing the difficultly and strenuousness of these movements reveals human honesty (Segal 1994, 8). Heim and Hollywood share a symbiotic relationship that symbolizes what a successful dance company looks like and what artists do to make art and survive in LA. The epitome of post-postmodernism, in the case of Diavolo, is to create highly agreeable, sociable, family friendly art that is designed to join and unite communities during performances and

Figure 3.3.   Diavolo Dance Theater performing *Trajectoire*. Artistic director and choreographer Jacques Heim.
Photographer: Elazar C. Harel © 2005. Used by permission.

accompanying workshops. In LA, this post-postmodern way of finding voice in LA seems practical, perhaps wise, but this work, to me, seems closer to postmodernism than the post-postmodernism of the Gilliland progeny because the focus on human-precision-as-spectacle distances audiences from the humans performing it.

Most of the choreographers who work and teach in the style of hyperdance once danced and studied with Gilliland, her progeny, or with Heim. Segal said the name hyperdance came about because advocates "praise[d] it for its hyper-physical, hyper-kinetic intensity, while its detractors [said,] it's mostly hype" (Segal 1994, 8). Segal went on to explain that the LA form of hyperphysical dance is different from that evolving in other places. He noted that LA choreographers typically avoid portraying social themes or dramatizing human relationships. The focus is instead on "objects, architecture, and extending the physical limits of dancing" (1994, 8). While this trend continues, relationships are now clearly more important in contemporary dance of the twenty-first century.

CHARACTERISTICS OF THE CONTEMPORARY DANCE FIELD

LA audiences are familiar with emergent fusion dance forms, world dance, and non-proscenium performance events. The comfortable climate of LA tends to bring people out of doors, where street dance flourishes, and sometimes becomes reinvented as new dance forms. Habitus in these street-based performances might blend breaking, hip hop, circus arts, tai chi, ballet, mime, aerial, or gymnastics. When choreographers are appreciated for creative merging of styles and forms, new dance forms bring new aesthetic rules and these merge into local culture (Peterson 2010). The guidelines for shaping emerging dance forms are nascent, and the rules for judging their level of success can be less clear than with long-established dance forms. What is valuable, good, and worth supporting can be less clear for those who do not live in and become informed by the field and the ever-shifting habitus of LA. When asked about key characteristics of the social aspects, or field, of contemporary choreographers of LA, choreographers expressed three aspects of building a world for themselves: (1) supporting a community of dancers that are creating dance works, (2) existing and establishing themselves in a city that has minimal support structures for theatrical dance in terms of funding sources, and (3) working with new forms of publicity such as the internet. I also asked choreographers to describe what contemporary dance of LA is or signifies for them, where it has evolved from, and to where it might be going. The answers point toward the emotive. They addressed thirteen aspects of contemporary dance that relate to living in LA: (1) extending movement capacities of the human body, (2) engaging extremes in kinesthesia or kinesthetic empathy, (3) present-ing emotion through movement, (4) maintaining autonomy and individualism, (5) engaging in reticulating matrices in space, (6) exploring power in trajectories at high, middle, and low levels, (7) performing hyper movement, (8) sharing weight on various body surfaces, (9) intermixing movement genres, (10) challenging the audience-performer boundaries, (12) employing technology or structures in the performance space, and (13) using nontraditional performance spaces.[13]

LA contemporary choreographers argue that they want audiences to experience the movement, not to think about what is happening on stage. They are not interested in having their works deconstructed because the role of the dancing body is to make people feel what the dancers are expressing through the movement. There is no power in gender in this work, no power in representation, and no power in story, narration, or metaphor. By channeling the power to the performative, hegemony is lost on contemporary dance. This form of contemporary dance that is fighting and thriving in LA is the ultimate rebellion from the hegemony of Hollywood, as much as it is, ironically, married to it because the choreographers that make the work live and breathe adjacent to this culture. Critic Rebecca Joly, of *LA Yoga Ayurveda and Health Magazine*, described Michaud's dance as an "explosive, techno-infused display of grace and athleticism [. . .] dancers leapt, fell and flew [. . .] blurring the line between body and machine" 2007, 12). Choreographers adopt their need for power from Hollywood, their willingness to be in the moment in rebellion to it, their incredible lust for speed and aggression to be heard while they perform next to it. Hegemony exerts its power even as these choreographers strive to release its bonds. When writing about Michaud's performance in *Supercedure* on April 21, 2007, Segal stated,

> It's not quite snuff dance, but it's on the way . . . The fury could be directed at a community that marginalizes the art—makes it a struggle to exist here as a dancer, choreographer, company leader. Or it could be aimed at the body itself: ruled only for a time by, and inevitably slated to betray, the perfect control that exists at this moment. (E–8)

Figure 3.4 shows Michaud's company Method Contemporary Dance, which is recognized as dancing some of the fiercest choreography in LA.

Contemporary dance of LA rarely if ever shows the human being shaping and controlling the space. Often the dancer is flung, fighting, or reacting to what seems an invisible force within the space. There is a method of phrasing in contemporary dance of LA, especially in Michaud's and Johnston's work, that uses attention to space, force, and time in a way that reveals urgency, desperation, being affected by something or someone, or reacting to the something in the space around them. Dancers often begin with direct visual attention into space, then build momentum until they whirl, careen, dive, or even impact with space having released all visual relationship with the world or others. Dancers finally come to a point of rest with a calm, fixed gaze into space awaiting the catalyst for the next phrase. While the flinging, fighting, and reacting to space has influences from the Streb, Sander, and Heim, it also emerged from the street dances of breaking and hip hop that proliferate in LA dance studios, clubs, music videos, and on the streets. Contemporary dance of LA owes much of its upside-down-ness and risk-taking to the appropriation of LA street dance and club dance and the cultural manufacture of dance

Figure 3.4. Method Contemporary Dance performing *fuh-q* performed at Diavolo, Los Angeles, California. Artistic director and choreographer Bradley Michaud. Dancers left to right: Sidnie Charnaw, Nicole Cox, Jay Bartley, Jessica Harper, Bradley Michaud. Photographer: Carol Peterson © 2010. Used by permission.

forms that serve to fuel The Industry. Hybridizing is thought most often to begin with a dominant culture appropriating a minority or sub-culture, but there are no minorities in LA. Dear explains,

> Los Angeles, like all cities, is unique, but in one way it may typify the world city of the future: There are only minorities. No single ethnic group, nor way of life, nor industrial sector, dominates the scene. Pluralism has gone further here than in any other city in the world and for this reason it may well characterize the global megalopolis of the future. (2003, 499)

Some dancers grow up dancing street dances, and they bring their knowledge and experience of street dance idioms to theatrical dance. Jacob "Kujo" Lyons, who literally learned to battle in b-boy competitions long before he learned about theatrical dance, creates his own blended dance forms.

NEO-MODERNISM-WITH-A-TWIST

Lyons (2008) puts one foot inside the breaking competition circle (speed, acrobatics, being upside down, spinning on his head, winning) and the other foot inside the circle of neo-modern dance (sustainment, form, shape, line, meaning, purpose, relationship, story). He does so to access a wider audience, to express a wider range of concepts within his breaking competitions, and to bring a challenging acrobatic dance form into theatrical dance. He hybridizes the athleticism of breaking with the expressive possibilities of theatrical dance and ballet, thus creating a contemporary dance idiom that is similar to, but different from, the main group of contemporary dance choreographers. Imagine breaking, but with the traditional break poses shifting into sustained, slowly evolving linear forms moving into partnering—a new twist on neo-modernism. See Lyons's company, Lux Aeterna, in figure 3.5. He explicitly hybridizes finding it necessary to bridge the boundaries that competition environments and proscenium theatre spaces seem to prescribe. Lyons (2008) revealed that at times the audiences of the b-boy/b-girl competitions have been confused about his use of sustainment during his breaking competitions, and theatrical dance audiences and critics express enjoyment and note the weaknesses inherent in his emergent hybridizing.

Figure 3.5. *Fiddling While Rome Burns*, 2009, Alex Theatre, Glendale, California, by Lux Aeterna. Artistic director and choreographer: Jacob "Kujo" Lyons. Dancers left to right: Jacob "Kujo" Lyons and Ben "Windu" Sayles.
Photographer: Tim Agler © 2009. Used by permission.

The dance of LA is inherently multicultural, and yet the critical outcomes of the works seem to be tethered to the venue—proscenium arch or b-boy circle. Lyons is eloquent about his need to cross boundaries while keeping a foot in each circle. The sharing and borrowing of skill sets between his techniques can be considered a neutral exchange rather than an appropriation because neither culture is a dominant or mainstream commercial culture. It could be said that all contemporary dance choreographers of LA are stepping into new circles, and circles within circles, as contemporary dance continues to evolve, exchange ideas, and blend approaches to expressivity through movement. Human interaction and cultural assimilation from one non-dominant culture into another non-dominant culture supports the ongoing evolution of contemporary dance of LA.

A return to spatial awareness in combination with the movement patterning of release technique with increased levels of force and time essentially invites dance back to a modern approach to space, but with all the movement choices and virtuosity that release technique and the street dances of LA bring to the idiom. The gender neutrality of the 1960s and 1970s, which used a lighter, more free-flowing approach to androgynous movement, lives on in contemporary dance, but instead of embodying the indulging side of the continuum of energy choices, contemporary choreographers have shifted to using a strong force with speed. To remain androgynous in contemporary dance of LA requires that women perform skills that may well be more suitable to a stronger, more masculine physique. Contemporary female dancers, born into the era of competition dance, embrace these challenges with vigor. Androgyny in contemporary dance means that dance retains the inner spatial pulls and shaping of release technique and adopts the use of strong force, being upside down, flinging through the air, and blending neo-modernist postures of classical ballet and modern dance with characteristic moves from breaking.

It is well known that Hollywood sees bodies as commodities, so dancers in LA tend to feel compelled to master as many skills as they can to be prepared for serving and getting paid. Breaking, hip hop style video dance, ballet, and commercial jazz are all forms that dancers in LA explore at one time or another. The practice of these mediums as messages, whether acrobatic, sexualized, spectacle, groovy, powerful, or elegant, provide the sediment for human expressivity. The embodied consolidation of these mastered dance forms cannot be denied, and they create the bedrock for what theatrical dancers work with to achieve their myriad of goals in a city that is ruled by the Hollywood machine. The outcome is the embodiment of pure physicality and powerful athleticism required to capture the imaginations of an already overstimulated culture that has had less experience with theatrical venues and more with the proscenium arch of a movie theatre or a flat screen TV. Contemporary dancers of LA have created a technique that is an amalgamation of the qualities and movement patterns that they absorbed into their philosophies and approaches to moving; or in other words, their way of being has allowed various ways of moving that exist in their vast string of neighborhoods to be absorbed into their body-culture. This embodiment is directly related to the geography in which they struggle to survive and continue to express through their art.

By keeping one foot inside and the other outside the circle, LA contemporary dancers can be true to their own evolution as artists. Lyons (2008) admits that when he sees performances outside LA, he sees some similarities to what choreographers are doing in LA, but nowhere has he seen anyone perform contemporary dance skills with the valor and audaciousness required to do the choreography of contemporary dance of LA:

> In the break dance world, one of the things that you notice right away in terms of an East Coast and West Coast difference—the East Coast dancing is much more detailed, execution is properly done, and this keeps the dancing looking pretty nice. On the West Coast, we forgive a little bit of that in favor of some more virtuosity, a more difficult and bigger movement. Things aren't always quite so perfectly crisp as they might be on the East, and it's a typical thing in hip hop too. As I begin to learn more about this whole contemporary dance world, I'm seeing the same philosophies there too.

The long standing critique of LA dance has been that it is not up to par with that of New York City, as if LA should look to New York as its role model and try to evolve to be more like it, which is a Eurocentric aesthetic point of view from a modernist era. Arturo Escobar is an anthropologist who aims to make space for social theory about our post-post-modern world using alternative models that include understanding of globalization and difference and that do not conform to the European privileged experience (2009, 398). He aims to examine the politics of place, the study of networks, self-organization, and complexity of post-post-modern society. Looking from what Escobar calls a post-development stance, the dance of LA differs due to the decentralized structure of the city. The aesthetic viewpoint of artists as well as the viewpoints and needs of audiences is affected by living in a patchwork of cultural worldviews that reside alongside one another in a web of communities, highways, beaches, mountains, and postmodern influences of media and technology (Escobar 2006). This web or network of LA formed in a postmodern way without a central core and during a time when cities were designed with vast boulevards and cars in mind. From a post-development viewpoint, the dance of LA is perfectly where it needs to be in each moment, and it is made up of the community that evolves and shifts over time in relation to its people, its physical layout, and its virtual environment that defines the post-postmodern LA community. The imperatives of fragmentation have become the principal dynamic in postmodern cities like LA: the twenty-first century's emerging world cities are ground-zero loci in a communications-driven globalizing political economy (Dear 2003). Dance is clearly affected by this fragmentation.

Dear and Flusty (2000) use the term *keno capitalism* to describe the urban dynamics and spatial manifestations that have effected Angelinos, such as the emergence of few central hubs within a global economy and social polarization or large gaps between social classes or power relations, (those classes and relations include race, gender, religion, and ethnicity). Angelinos also experience a fragmentation of social, material, and intellectual life due to the challenges of the information age as cultural categories, spaces, and hybridizations dissolve identities. In LA, now that the city has taken form as a postmodern web of disparate neighborhoods and highways, city developers attempt to reshape sections to appear like modern cities that have a central hub in order to represent identity and tradition, or to attain a sense of power (Dear 2003). Dear asserts that LA is a palimpsest of earlier place-based centers of communication that continue to influence emerging forms of communication in postmodernity, and while postmodern cities do not have a center, postmodern forms of communication recreate the concept of center of the city, albeit not a true center (2003). Hall's words from 1993 ring true for choreographers negotiating theatrical dance in LA in the twenty-first century, "This decentering or displacement opens up new spaces of contestation and affects a momentous shift in the high culture of popular culture relations, thus presenting us with a strategic and important opportunity for intervention in the popular cultural field" (1993, 105). It is because of this continuing negotiation across geographic space that the dance forms of LA remain in flux. Because contemporary dance of LA has roots in an Africanist aesthetic, Hall's description of the African diaspora seems important to recite in honor of the rich dance heritage that is celebrated in so many ways in theatrical dance, in jazz dance, in breaking, in hip hop, and all of the hybrid contemporary dance forms.

> Always these forms are the product of partial synchronization, of engagement across cultural boundaries, of the confluence of more than one cultural tradition, of the negotiations of dominant and subordinate positions, of the subterranean strategies of recoding and transcoding, of critical signification, of signifying. Always these forms are impure, to some degree hybridized from a vernacular base. (Hall 1993, 110)

Those contemporary choreographers of LA that aim to make art and be innovative, but not give in to The Industry, have been adopting the diasporic aesthetic offered by the Africanist presence—and all the other cultures having physically or virtually visited LA—thereby merging and hybridizing the forms available to them. The Hollywood soundstage and The Industry is a space of contestation of cultures being appropriated, and the approaches to theatrical dance by contemporary choreographers reflect the power in this struggle to explore new realities and resist old hegemonies. When critics assert that LA has been unsuccessful at supporting a dance tradition, they are not looking through the lenses that allow them to understand the form and function of neo-modern contemporary dance in the postmodern city of LA. Yes, keeping a dance company going in LA is indeed difficult; however, the artistry in the choreography is evolving with the fragmented and global-oriented nature of LA along with a powerful twist of anti-hegemony that one would not likely find in other cities. Experiencing contemporary dance of LA on its own terms is essential for being able to really receive it.

NOTES

1. Founded in 1987 in response to the need for a centralized dance information network in Los Angeles, the Dance Resource Center of Greater Los Angeles is a service organization for dance with a mission to support community-based professional dance activity by providing its members access to information, resources, and services; and to promote the visibility of Greater Los Angeles dance on local, state, and national levels.

2. *Habitus* refers to the way in which an individual's instinctive sense of what might be achieved is structured into a pattern of behavior, forming, in Pierre Bourdieu's own words, "an acquired system of generative schemes objectively adjusted to the particular conditions in which it is constituted." *Field* refers to an environment in which people employ economic, cultural, social, and symbolic powers. See Pierre Bourdieu, *Outline of a Theory of Practice*, (Cambridge: Cambridge University Press, 1977), 95.

3. Bradley Michaud's assessment matches recent research. According to a 2006 study of wages of twenty-seven creative arts occupations in New York City and Los Angeles, economists Michael Dolfman, Richard Holden, and Solidelle Fortier Wasser (2007) discovered that NYC dance companies ranked the second highest of all the arts for total earnings ($31,651,873 in 2006), and LA dance companies ranked the lowest of all twenty-seven arts ($503,375 in 2006). It is clear that the NYC community supports its dance companies better than LA does, although this study did not state the number of dance companies or dancers working in each city. It is interesting to note that while wages earned by dance companies in NYC increased from $26,251,947 to $31,651,873 from 1990 to 2006 (actually a decrease when accounting for inflation), in LA the wages for dance companies dropped from $1,476,658 in 1990 to a mere $503,375. It is interesting to note that while the wages of the LA film industry grew from $765,106,673 to $2,475,194,512, the NYC film industry wages remained relatively stable from 1990 to 2006. So, as the wages for the LA film industry have swelled, the dance company wages have collapsed, and meanwhile the wages of the film and dance companies of NYC have remained constant. For more information, see: Michael L. Dolfman, Richard J. Hodlen, and Solidelle Fortier Wasser, "The Economic Impact of the Creative Arts Industries: New York and Los Angeles," *Monthly Labor Review*, October 2007: 21–34.

4. For a discussion of self-scrutiny and objectification of women, see Paige Edley and Ginger Bihn's, "Corporeality and Discipline of the Performing Body: Representations of International Ballet Companies," in *Intercultural Communication and Creative Practice: Dance, Music and Women's Cultural Identity*, edited by Laura Lengel, (Westport, CT: Praeger, 2005), 213–228. For an exploration of a group of LA college aged dancers, see pages 259–260 in Teresa Heiland, Paige Edley, and Darrin Murray's, "Body Image of Dance in Los Angeles: The Cult of Slenderness and Media Influence Among Dance Students," *Research in Dance Education* New York: Routledge 9, no 3 November (2008): 257–275.

5. Kinesthetic empathy—the concept that while watching dancers move, observers experience the movement empathically—is a subject undergoing psychological research. Scientists believe there are areas of the brain that link action observation with empathic responses (Calvo-Merino, Jola and Haggard 2008; Hagendoorn 2004; Gazzola, Aziz-Zadeh, and Keysers 2006; Keysers and Gazzolas 2009; Pichon, de Gelder, and Grezes 2008). Dancers and dance audiences have long spoken about this phenomenon (Daly 1992; Foster 2011; Martin 1939), but science is still working to understand what occurs in the brain to bring about these experiences (Brown, Martinez, and Parsons 2005; Calvo-Merino, Grèzes, Glaser, Passingham, and Haggard 2006; Cross, Hamilton, and Grafton 2006).

6. For a thorough history and detailed analysis of concepts about kinesthesia and choreographic empathy, see Susan Leigh Foster, *Choreographing Empathy: Kinesthesia in Performance*

(New York: Routledge, 2011) and Alain Berthoz, *The Brain's Sense of Movement* (Cambridge, MA: Harvard University Press, 2000).

7. Lyrical dance is a fusion of ballet and jazz dance styles. Through lyrical dance, performers aim to illustrate meaning and emotion communicated by a song and, hence, aim to interpret the accompanying music in an emotionally expressive way. Lyrical is an extension of long-established dance forms; hence, dancers might label a dance form based on its most prevalent featured genre, for example, lyrical ballet, lyrical jazz, lyrical modern, contemporary lyrical, lyrical hip hop, and so on. Though the label lyrical was first applied to dance expressing to jazz music, it is commonly danced to music of any style, including hip hop, rock, swing, pop, or classical.

8. Locking and popping are two of the original funk style street dances that came out of California during the 1960s–1970s. Locking is based on the concept of locking movements, which basically means freezing from a fast movement and locking in a certain position, holding that position for a short while and then continuing in the same speed as before. Popping is based on the technique of quickly contracting and relaxing muscles to cause a jerk in the dancer's body, referred to as a pop or a hit, which is done continuously to the rhythm of a song in combination with various movements and poses.

9. The term b-boy comes from b-boying, or breaking, and is a style of street dance orginating in 1970s New York City hip hop culture. The dance form evolved from being a street dance to being a competitive dance around the world. Movements are performed in a space with audience members on all sides of the performer. Dancers perform fast spins, flips, and maneuvers based on four primary elements: top rock, down rock, power moves, and freezes. B-boying was originally danced to hip hop music and the term comes from poses that were held during the break beats in the music.

10. The scope and length of this article does not allow room to elaborate on the movement analysis of contemporary dance using Laban Movement Analysis; however, Brenda Dixon Gottschild (2000) has provided the characteristics of Africanist aesthetics in dance and these can be used to summarize qualities found in the movement. The aspects that are most clearly identifiable in contemporary dance in LA are: embracing the conflict (a precept of contrariety, or an encounter of opposites); high-affect juxtaposition (mood, attitude, or movement breaks that omit transitions and connective links); ephebism (power, vitality, flexibility, drive, and attach that recognizes feeling as sensation, rather than emotion); and the aesthetic of the cool (an attitude that combines composure with vitality).

11. These principles were gathered from various reviews in newspapers and magazines and from interviews with LA contemporary dance choreographers Holly Johnston, (director of Ledges and Bones) interviews by author, audio recordings, Los Angeles, CA., January 17, 2009 and October 12, 2011; Bradley Michaud (director of Method Contemporary Dance) interview by author, audio recording, December 16, 2008, Santa Monica, CA.; and Patrick Damon Rago (director of Palindrome Dance Theatre) interview by author, audio recording, January 21, 2009, Los Angeles, CA.

12. Jacques Heim created his commercially successful dance company Diavolo Dance Theater in 1992. In "'Foreign Bodies': Life on the edge; Music, sculpture and dance meld in the stunning Diavolo piece," *Los Angeles Times*, September 6, 2007, E–5, erstwhile critic Lewis Segal states in 2007 that Heim's approach to contemporary dance theatre is built around hyperdance, but compared to other contemporary choreographers, he employs his technique in marketable, large, theatrical productions that tour the world and draw large crowds (E-5).

13. This list of interests was gathered from various reviews in newspapers and magazines and from interviews with LA contemporary dance choreographers Johnston, Lyons, Michaud, and Rago.

4

Some Dance to Remember

The Emotional Politics of Marginality, Reinvention, Embodied Memory, and All That (Cape) Jazz

Tamara M. Johnson

I first experienced Cape Jazz dancing in September 2006 when jazz instructors Clyde (41) and his wife Amy (29) took me to the Galaxy in the Rylands/Athlone neighborhood of Cape Town, South Africa. Although we were attending one of the famous Galaxy traditions, the Saturday Sundowner, Clyde and Amy picked me up in the city center long after the sun descended behind Signal Hill and the sky was blushing various shades of purple. Clyde raced down the N2, careened around corners in the back streets of Athlone, and dropped Amy and me at the curb in front of the Galaxy so that we would get past the bouncers in dark suits and through the doors before 7 pm to avoid the R40 (approximately $6) cover charge imposed on patrons at (and after) 7 pm sharp. I followed Amy through an environment of steel and neon until we settled ourselves at high tables between the bar and the dance floor. Clyde found us later and supplied us with some Appletizer, a quintessentially South African non-alcoholic beverage, while we waited for the band to finish setting up. There were not many people in the club—a handful of people sitting in tables around the dance floor or chatting with the bartender—and although recorded music was pumping loudly, preventing polite conversation, no one was dancing. I am not sure how long we sat there with the air conditioner blasting to match the cold décor and the ice clanking in my glass, but it felt as though I sat shivering for about an hour before the club began to fill and one couple felt sufficiently moved by the music to get onto the dance floor. I then got my first taste of Cape jazz. I was surprised to notice that Cape jazz is not always danced to what I consider to be jazz music. That evening, I heard songs by Stevie Wonder, Nora Jones, and Luther Vandross. I even heard a fast tempo version of the Brazilian classic "Mas Que Nada." I spent most of my time watching that evening, trying to pick up the steps by observation. Cape jazz couples, linked at the hands, twirled, twisted, and dipped their way around the dance floor. The swirling lights ricocheted off the sparkle in sequined blouses and skirts. Some couples executed fast spins and dips, while others have developed a smoother style. I left Galaxy that night intrigued, but a bit confused as to what Cape jazz actually is and what it means to its practitioners.

While I received a variety of responses to my questions about Cape Jazz dancing and how it evolved, there is a general consensus that "jazzing" involves a mixture of dance styles that emphasize an embodied response to a feeling inspired by the music rather than to a structured turn pattern or a specific count. The syncretic nature of Cape jazz—the woven-together-ness of its multiple movement histories spanning several continents and time periods—makes pinning its "origin" to a particular place and time an impossible task. Nevertheless, multiple Cape jazz "origin" stories have emerged among dancers. The most common origin story describes jazzing as a form of cultural expression that developed within a self-identified coloured[1] community on the Cape Flats on the outskirts of Cape Town's city center. Cape jazz dancers most often adamantly define jazzing as a quintessentially local practice, yet at certain moments, global music and movement influences from Latin America, the Caribbean, Europe, and the United States feature prominently in the "origin" story of Cape jazz. These contradictions reveal the shifting and dynamic meanings of "global" and "local" or "foreign" and "familiar" as well as the ways in which these concepts are produced relationally, and implemented by jazz practitioners in response to perceived threats and judgments. The intricately woven global and local narratives and meanings associated with jazzing reflect the dance's role in the formation of coloured identity and collective embodied memory, and expose the dynamic possibilities of social transformation in Cape Town.

Of course, concepts of "global" and "local" rarely represent rigid and encapsulated processes. The argument that global and local processes are entangled and interdependent is not new; there is an extensive literature on the process of "glocalization" (Swyngedouw 2004). In this chapter, I am arguing, however, that there is a strategy and an emotional politics to ways in which these terms are used by dancers to describe Cape jazz. Through the embodied practices of Cape jazz, emotional politics cultivate collective memory among participants and defend this memory from "outside" forces operating on the dance floors of Cape Town's jazz clubs. In the process of defining "colouredness" through jazzing, notions of the global are viscous.

Arun Saldanha uses the term viscosity to describe the ways in which race, not only as a social construct, but as a phenotypic materiality can result in the coagulation of bodies; the ways in which bodies "stick" to not only to each other, but also to the particular spaces "through certain behaviours and physical and cultural conditions" (2006a, 173–174). Race's spatiality, Saldanha argues, "is not one of grids or self/other dialectics, but one of viscosity, bodies gradually becoming sticky and clustering into aggregates" (2006b, 10). Viscosity describes the not-liquid-yet-not-solid state of matter in which a substance flows slowly across surfaces and through space, pooling and thickening in areas, gathering for a moment, then oozing on leaving some sticky residual reminder of its presence. Viscosity implies a seemingly predictable pattern of movement, yet a slight change in surface friction can cause a change in direction of movement. At times, a viscous substance is seemingly frozen in place, but, with heat, movement resumes.

I apply Saldanha's theorization of viscosity to the concepts of "global" and "local." For Saldanha, race is "constantly morphing" and not defined by inflexibility or rigidity. I argue that concepts of global and local are applied with expediency to describe Cape jazz as a form of cultural expression. Examining the ways in which these concepts are applied to Cape jazz as a social dance practice reveals the emotional politics involved in establishing a common narrative and collective memory of the coloured experience in Cape Town. These emotional politics also involve negotiating entanglements of memory, movement, and meaning through dance. Dance is not only movement across a floor, but it can be a set of patterns, movements, and connections that help people locate themselves relationally in the world. Viscous conceptualizations of the "global" flow uneasily through Cape jazz narratives, pooling around discussions of stylistic influence. Viscous notions of the global also ooze alongside local histories of marginality and isolation, then, with heated confrontation, notions of global become more unpredictable and estranged from the story of Cape jazz, moving off in a different direction, but always leaving residual storylines as evidence of its influence.

Cape Town has always been a city of global flows and influence. Yet in the not-so-distant past, many residents were isolated from global connections: non-white populations were forcibly removed from their homes, and spatially marginalized in segregation areas often on the outskirts of cities, televisions were banned in South Africa until 1976, and cultural and sports embargos were imposed on South Africa to express disapproval of the apartheid regime. For many residents, global access continues to sit in uneasy tension with forced localization.

In Cape Town, the scars of apartheid are not only still visible on the urban built landscape and in socio-spatial patterns of movement, but are also concealed in the memories of many of the city's inhabitants. Emotive experiences with the past are revealed and relived in the actions and embodied practices of the present. Through social dance practices, shifting entanglements with conceptualizations of global and local are worked out in everyday encounters on the dance floor. These encounters speak to the broader emotional politics of social transformation and reinvention in Cape Town. This chapter examines the emotional politics of embodied collective memory as expressed through shifting attachments to notions of global and local in Cape jazz practices.

EMBODIED MEMORY, EMOTIONAL POLITICS, AND THE CONSTRUCTION OF NARRATIVE

To understand Cape jazz dancing as it is defined and practiced in Cape Town today, one must examine the role of memory in the movements, interactions, and narratives of Cape jazz dancers. The following section explores the theoretical connections between collective memory and emotional politics as manifested through embodied practices. Geographers and other scholars have long recognized the relationship between landscape, memory, and meaning (see Hayden 1995; Alderman 2003; Till 2005; Mills 2010). Just as places shape and become repositories for memories, memories are formed as "bodily experiences of being in and moving through space" (Johnson and Pratt 2009). Memories of dispossession are not only linked to sites like District Six in Cape Town, or recorded and filed away in archives, but also embodied (carried and transmitted) in dance practices.

Building from the work of French sociologist Pierre Nora, Diana Taylor (2003) describes the repertoire as an enactment of embodied memory through gestures, movement, vocalizations, and performances. The repertoire, she acknowledges, is considered to be "ephemeral, nonreproducible knowledge" requiring one's participation in the production and reproduction of knowledge by "being there," during the transmission of knowledge (20). The embodied acts of the repertoire are ever-present, and "reconstitute themselves, transmitting communal memories, histories, and values from one group/generation to the next. Embodied and performed acts generate, record, and transmit knowledge" (21). Taylor goes on to argue that traditions from the past are "stored in the body" and then "transmitted 'live'" thus "experienced as present" (24). For Taylor, the relationship between the repertoire and the traditional archive, which Taylor describes as "supposedly enduring materials" like documents, videos, letters, maps, and bones, is not binary (19). Instead, the repertoire complements the traditional archive, and works with it to expand knowledge (22, 24). Cape jazz dancing serves as a repertoire such that memories are "stored in the body" and transmitted among dancers. Taylor describes a "transmission" of knowledge and traditions; I argue that emotions associated with memory and meanings are also transmitted along lines of affect in dance spaces, binding dancers in an affective experience.

In what geographer Keith Woodward (2007) has termed "the emotive turn" in Anglo-American geography, geographers have recently emphasized the importance of affect and emotion when studying the relationship between the body and place. Geographic studies dealing with affect have emerged, in part, in an engagement with Nigel Thrift's work on non-representational theory. Thrift's Non-Representational Theory opens possibilities for an examination of practices, "corporeal routines," and examinations of the body regarding pre-cognition, affect, and the sensual, challenging the hegemony of cognitive and visual epistemologies. Thrift describes affect as "a form of thinking, often indirect and non-reflective true, but thinking all the same. And, similarly, all manner of the spaces which they generate must be thought of in the same way, as means of thinking and as thought in action. Affect is a different kind of intelligence about the world, but it is intelligence nonetheless" (2008, 187). The "most immediate and intimately felt geography is the body," the site of affective transmission, "emotional experience," and expression (Davidson and Milligan 2004, 523). Brian Massumi describes affect as a "felt but impersonal, visceral but not neatly corporeal, force of intensive relationality (2002)." In this chapter, I discuss affect as a non-conscious, unarticulated feeling transmitted between bodies and across spaces; an "intensity" that, as Mike Featherstone (2010) describes, resonates "below the threshold of articulated meaning" (199). It is a feeling that inspires an embodied response. In interviews and casual conversations, dancers often described the "vibe" of a particular place. In these exchanges, vibe describes a feeling or energy transmitted between and among people and through space. The affective confluence of bodies in motion, energy (generated, in part, by attitudes and movement), sound, and light creates vibrations, a vibe that attaches sentiment to place and influences the dancing experience. Emotions are recognized, expressed, or represented forces working within and upon a body also inspire actions and reactions. Affect is not confined within the body; it relies upon a circulation among and interactions with other bodies.

The body, as the most personal geography, is a site of memory and meaning shaped through affective rendering. Memory, according to Adrian Parr (2008) does not simply "happen to a body, it subsists throughout it" (1). Giorgio Hadi Curti (2008) argues that memory, emotion and affect are inextricably inter-related forces operating through the body and they must be analyzed and understood together. The body is "a force which actively re-creates remembering and forgetting through its capacity to affect and be affected" (8). Because memory subsists throughout the body, he argues, memory and emotion always work together and are inseparable from experience. The body, Brian Massumi contends, is defined primarily by its capacity to move and its capacity to feel (2002, 1). Memory works through the body in conjunction with affect and emotion to inspire action/movement. I argue that it is also possible that movement such as dance works through the body to inspire emotion.

Cape jazz dancing is movement and memory and emotion generated through the body and transmitted to other bodies along lines of affect. In interactions between jazzing bodies, experiences are shared and memories are reproduced in multiple ways: in the way the enjoyment of a certain song is felt through a dancer's embrace, in the familiar twist of a signature move, in an exchanged smile or a knowing wink among old friends, or in a quick conversation about 'that one time when . . .'

For Curti, the mutually reflexive nature of emotion and memory within the body contributes to the recognition of individual collective selves and the formation of identity, including its indelible connections to place. The transmission of emotion and memory through affective register, thus, impels for and their roles in the formation of collective memory. Collective memory is "an expression and active binding force of group identity" (Hoelscher and Alderman 2004). Maurice Halbwachs (1992 [1941]) argues that groups of "believers" construct places of meaning and memorial significance, grounding feelings and memories that would otherwise be transient (Allen and Brown 2011). This process of collective commemoration builds symbolic significance around particular material forms (such as statues, shrines, monuments, or street names) and embodied activities (rituals, performances, or parades) that can "immobilize" and preserve common recollections of past events for a certain group of people (Allen and Brown 2011; Wachtel 1986). The body, then, becomes a significant site of collective memory formation and communication. Karen Till (1999) describes social memory (broadly defined to include collective, cultural, and public memory) as an ongoing process in which social groups 'map' their myths of self onto and through a place and time."

Of course, the link between collective memory and historical accuracy is tenuous because memory is haunted by forgetting and is therefore subject to manipulation and coercion, but also to resistance, negotiation, and counter-memory. The process of shaping collective memory is a political one. Karen Till (2005) argues that places of memory have historical meaning and constitute social and power relationships beyond the monumental sites of significant events. Places of memory are therefore "spatial and social contexts of events, activities, and peoples" (291). I argue that it is the affective and affective and emotional ties that make the politics of memory so salient, and it is the emotional politics of collective memory that is behind intense struggles over spaces of belonging.

South Africa's re-entry into a global financial and cultural economy post-apartheid, and the current context of shifting political, social, and spatial transformation, and nation-building creates a sense of urgency to the process of remembering (and forgetting) the past. The emotional politics of collective memory raises the important questions: What should be remembered? How are events, people, and places commemorated? What is allowed to be forgotten? Who decides? The formation of collective memory is often constructed or heavily influenced by the agendas of powerful or dominant members of the group, thus collective memory is never fixed and predictable but is often contested (Hoelscher and Alderman 2004).

Cape jazz, as an embodied activity, has taken place in a variety of venues and across a variety of spaces and time periods in Cape Town. Cape jazz dancers have a wide range of experiences with and memories associated with the dance, yet overtime, participants have constructed a collective Cape jazz narrative from a combination of memories, perceptions, and experiences. For many Cape jazz dancers, the emotive, intimate spaces of cape jazz dancing have generated a sense of community and a space of belonging—forming an 'inside' for protection and escape from an 'outside' sense of uncertainty and marginality (both during apartheid and in the post-apartheid era). As I demonstrate with Cape jazz, often it is agitation from outside the realm of the familiar that inspires the creation, protection, and re-articulation of collective memory, and the viscous attachments to concepts of global and local. I examine social dance practices to understand the ways in which the affective and emotional politics of embodied collective memory interact with notions of "global" and "local" among dancers in Cape Town.

I define my methodological approach as critical performance ethnography in which I examine the interconnectedness and spatiality of body, emotion, space, and event while recognizing and narrating my role as an active participant, being influenced by and influencing the situations and people involved in this research project (see Hart 2006; Madison and Hamera 2000). I participated in the nightlife practices of my informants and followed them not only through the city, but also onto the dance floor. Because I shared emotive moments and movement with dancers, my body became an undeniable part of the scene. I was an active member of the Cape jazz and salsa scenes in Cape Town from August to January of 2006, and from April 2009 to May 2011. I conducted forty-two semi-structured, in-depth interviews with club owners, dance instructors, participants, musicians, and DJs. Additionally, for over two years I engaged in casual conversations, listened to Cape jazz narratives, and conducted archival research. I was also a semi-professional salsa dancer, performer, and salsa event organizer. I performed with most of the salsa dance companies in Cape Town as well as several of the local salsa musicians. I taught workshops and private lessons in Cape Town, directed an all-female salsa dance company, and choreographed routines with prominent dancers in the scene. This level of active participation allowed me not only to observe the emotional aspects of people and events but to participate fully in them. People have expressed feelings about actions or events to me in casual conversation on the dance floor that they would not repeat in a recorded interview. In addition to being expressed verbally, emotions such as frustration, excitement, and disappointment can be read through the body and are often subtly expressed through gestures, eye contact, posture, and in the lead and follow of social dancing.

HISTORY OF CAPE JAZZ: THE POLITICS AND COMPLEXITIES OF JAZZING AS "GLOBAL" OR "LOCAL"

The contemporary Cape jazz dance practice forms a rich and complex tapestry that involves the history of Cape Town itself. Cape jazz dancers describe the movement of jazz as a mixture, a blending of Cape Town dances and rhythms dating back to the times of slavery. Several Cape jazz musicians also point to this blending of local rhythms as integral to the development of Cape jazz music. They also refer to Cape Town's position as a port city on the Atlantic coast since the seventeenth century, and its ability to attract the global flows of goods, labor, and cultural practices as part of the reason for the rich blending of influences that inspired Cape jazz music. Cape Town, as Steve, owner of one of the top Cape jazz clubs in Cape Town explains, "is the center point of the world"; a "melting pot" for races and cultures since its inception. Jazz in Cape Town is the result of local musicians blending musical elements common to American jazz, Latin dance music, and urban South African music. In this chapter, I am not suggesting that Cape jazz is a global music and dance form that became local; it has always locally realized.

The following historical examination will focus on three important aspects in the development of Cape jazz narrative. First, I explore the relationship between experiences and perceptions of social marginalization and the construction of a coloured identity. Second, I briefly highlight policies and memories of spatial marginalization of the coloured population and the development of the Cape Flats. Third, I explain the linkages between Cape jazz dancing and the emotional politics of coloured social and spatial identity in Cape Town. I then emphasize the viscous ways in which global and local are utilized by Cape jazz dancers in the historical construction of this narrative.

Social Marginalization

A Cape jazz dancer once joked with me that the coloured population originated nine months after Jan van Riebeeck's expedition arrived in the Cape in 1652. What he meant, of course, is that he associates colouredness with the product of sexual interactions between European settlers and indigenous Khoi and San peoples. In fact, the historical development of coloured identification in the Cape is complex and fascinating and is, of course, shaped by the rich and complicated pattern of social, political, and economic interactions in the Cape and in South Africa more broadly. What I offer here is a brief discussion of the ways in which coloured identity has been, and continues to be conceptualized and contested in order to establish a foundation for the contested meanings and negotiated spaces of Cape jazz dancing.

The social constructionist view of coloured identity popular among scholars believes in the agency of individuals to form their own complex and multifaceted identities. Scholars understand identity formation to be an ongoing, dynamic process in which coloured identities are relational, forged in particular social and historical contexts (Erasmus and Pieterse 1997). Of course, just because scholars recognize the socially constructed nature of colouredness does not mean that everyone I interviewed spoke in those terms. I discuss the political and social roots of feelings of collective marginality among members of the coloured population in Cape Town historically, but I am in no way suggesting that every person ascribes to this understanding of colouredness. There are countless ways in which people define themselves, remember the past, and envision the future.

The history of slavery in the Cape plays an important role in the early designation of Cape Town as a melting pot resulting, in part, from the global flows of labor into the city. Slavery in the Cape Colony was established in the mid-seventeenth century, and slaves were imported from such places as Angola, Mozambique, Malaysia, Indonesia, and Madagascar to service the needs of the new colony. Although abolished in 1838, slavery established social relations and hierarchies that remained intact long after the practice ended, and concepts of race, color, and status linked to these social relations are still embedded in Cape Town's social fabric today. This blending of culture and status is the foundation of a coloured identity that persists today and is continuously evolving. Among cape jazz participants I interviewed for this project, Cape jazz dancing is tied closely to narratives of colouredness as they have developed in Cape Town.

In colonial Cape Town, society was stratified based on notions of social respectability and status with racial categorization emerging much later (Ruiters 2006, 119). 'Miscegenation' was a component of Cape Town's "special tradition" of "racial mixing" that dates back to the 1600s (Bickford-Smith 1995, 67). Between Jan van

Riebeeck's arrival in 1652 and the abolition of the slave trade in 1808, approximately 63,000–65,000 slaves were brought to the Cape (Martin 2000a). In early Cape society, local officials "turned a blind eye" to (often exploitative) sexual relationships between European settlers and women of color because it allowed white employees a sexual outlet without the need to import and support European women (Ahluwalia and Zegeye 2003, 258). However, with creeping color prejudice in the late 1600s, legal marriages between European settlers and the non-white population occurred less frequently, and non-marital interracial sexual relationships frequently occurred in the form of "institutionalized concubinage" between slave owners and enslaved women, or between white laborers and women of colour working in brothels in town (ibid, 69). Interracial sexual activity occurring as master-slave concubinage or casual sexual interactions between white men and women of color implied relationships of white power and were not viewed as threatening to the perceived superior social status of white men. In contrast, intermarriage implied social equality and was therefore condemned (van den Berghe 1960).

By the beginning of apartheid policies, "blood mixing" was viewed as a "vile and debasing practice" that would result in the "degeneration and loss of moral values of poor whites in the cities" (van den Berghe 1960, 70; Erasmus 2001, 10.) Government officials insisted that racial mixing threatened public morality. After 1948, it was imperative to the racial and spatial philosophies of the apartheid government and to the enforcement of race-based segregation that the state develop a system for establishing clear, "common sense" boundaries between state-defined racial groups, particularly between coloured and white groups (Ruiters 2006 citing Posel 2004).

Scholars of the development of coloured identity discuss the ambiguous and ambivalent positioning of colouredness during apartheid where it operated very much within the legal ideological confines of the system. Conceptualizations of coloured identity were often perceived as not only not acting against the state, but also often viewed as complacent or even complicit (see Martin 2000a; Erasmus 2001). The coloured population was granted certain "privileges" and escaped certain regulations to which the black population was subjected: the coloured population did not have to carry passbooks, often had better access to housing, education, and employment opportunities, and were not held to the same strict liquor licensing laws. Likewise, coloured Labor Preference legislation protected coloured jobs in relation to African workers effecting not only socioeconomic status of coloured workers, but influenced migration and residential patterns as well. Also, the enforcement of the Group Areas Act in the mid-1960s, members of the coloured population were allowed to live in cities in order to be closer to factories, unlike black laborers (Ruiters 2006).

In describing her formative experiences and her own path to self-discovery, Erasmus discusses the sentiments of respectability and shame that are closely linked to her middle-class class coloured experience (2001). According to Erasmus, in her youth she was taught to understand that as a coloured person, she was "less than white" but "better than black" (emphasis in original, 2). She recalls that "the humiliation of being 'less than white' made being 'better than black' a very fragile position to occupy" (2). Because colouredness was associated with miscegenation, Erasmus admits that implicated in this identity were concepts of impurity, illegitimacy, immorality, and untrustworthiness all of which lead to feelings of shame (Erasmus citing Wicomb 1998). Martin (2000a) suggests that it was not uncommon for members of the white community to view the coloured population as "objects of an absolute scorn expressed . . . [in] insults and stereotypes" (106). According to Erasmus, the struggle for respectability caused her significant anxiety and discomfort. Apartheid labels and ruling class mentality have labeled colouredness as inferior and in-between, making it difficult to recognize coloured on its own terms (Erasmus).

Spatial Marginalization

Social and spatial marginalization plays an interconnected role in the development of a Cape coloured identity. In conducting this research, a common origin story emerged, linking the development of jazzing to the experience of forced removal, displacement, and subsequent spatial marginalization. The emotional politics of forced removal is closely tied to the history of District Six.

After the abolition of slavery in 1838, government compensation to recently freed slaves was used to build row houses and streets near the harbor for settlement (Potluri 2004). In addition to former slaves, immigrants arriving in Cape Town often settled in the area that became known as District Six, creating a culturally heterogeneous area which later became a threat to the ideology of the apartheid state (ibid. 2004, 11).

The development of the Cape Flats, located in a low-lying area of drift-sand and spare vegetation situated between Table Mountain and Hottentot Holland mountain range, serves as an important counter-balance the District Six neighborhood. For the early part of Cape Town's history, the environmental conditions on the Cape Flats were inhospitable to farming and inaccessible for transportation and communications thus creating a formidable geographic barrier to urban expansion (Joint Town Planning Committee of the Cape and Stellenbosch: Outline Development Plan for the Cape Flats 1969, 37, 38). The early 1800s saw the first attempts on the part of the Forestry Department to stabilize the sandy soils, resulting in the establishment of small farms and a network of local wagon paths which later became Modderdam, Klipfontein, Duinefontein, and Lansdowne roads. The construction of hard roads in the 1840s and the construction of railway lines in the 1860s laid the foundation for the subsequent "radial urban pattern formed by the southern suburbs and northern municipalities" (ibid, 38–39).

From the 1920s, the Cape Flats experienced intensified urban expansion, a response, in part, to the increase in demand for developable land for low-income population groups relocated from the city center. Forced removals to the Cape Flats began as early as 1920 and were often presented as a philanthropic endeavor to promote health and welfare or good neighborliness. The "sanitation syndrome" in the decade following an outbreak of the Spanish flu was the primary impetus for the removal of poor residents from slums in the center of Cape Town (Dumbrell 1998, 13). Municipal officials believed that the majority of the coloured population resided in unsanitary and overcrowded slum conditions in areas like District Six. They believed these areas should be cleared in order to improve the city's public health crisis. In September 1926, the Mayor's office replied to concerns about the health conditions in Cape Town's inner city slums by announcing that the City Council's Housing Policy for coloured citizens included opening up "healthy" areas like Athlone for residential purposes in order to relieve the "congestion in the slum centre" (Western Cape Archives, 3/CT 4/1/5/579).

In spite of local government's development of "coloured" public housing estates on the Cape Flats for lower income families, and the existence of a few wealthy neighborhoods segregated by class and prejudice, almost one-third of the Cape Town population continued to live in racially and culturally mixed areas prior to World War II, making Cape Town the least segregated city in South Africa (Wilkinson 2000; Besteman 2008). The Minister of the Interior introduced the Group Areas bill to Parliament in 1950 by arguing that "[i]f you reduce the number of points of contact [between people in different racial categories] to the minimum, you reduce the possibility of friction . . . the result of putting people of different races together is to cause racial trouble" (quoted in Trotter 2006, 6). Under the Group Areas Act, between 1957 and 1985, approximately one hundred fifty thousand people in the Cape Town area were forcibly removed from their homes in areas such as District Six, Claremont, and Tramway and relocated to dwellings in declared "coloured Areas" on the Cape Flats. This process eventually reorganized Cape Town into the most segregated city in the country (Trotter 2006; Besteman 2008). Scholars suggest that was the trauma of forced removal and segregation that began in earnest in the 1960s that spurred the development of a more cohesive sense of a collective coloured identity (see Adhikari 2009; Trotter 2006).

Proclamation 43 of the Group Areas Act declared District Six a white area, and the first forced removal of residents began in 1968. Between 1968 and 1982, approximately sixty thousand people were evicted from District Six alone and relocated to the Cape Flats, and the entire area (with the exception of a couple of places of worship) was destroyed (ibid. 2004). Many monuments, museums, and memoirs are dedicated to the experience of forced removal from District Six; some argue that the area has become romanticized in collective popular memory. The area is often narrated as a place of "tolerance and mutual respect of difference" or a place "where race was transcended," standing like an oasis in stark contrast to the realities of apartheid South Africa (Ahluwalia and Zegeye 2003, 262). For former residents of District Six, a "deep sense of injustice" resulting from forced removals and a separation from the past drives identity construction (Beyers 2009, 83). District Six exists in popular memory not only as a site of struggle and loss, but, perhaps more forcefully, as an area known for its rich cultural heritage, and for the vibrancy of everyday life. The former District Six neighborhood is often considered by jazz enthusiasts to be the home of a music and dance culture that fostered the development of jazz.

CAPE JAZZ DANCING AND SOCIAL AND SPATIAL IDENTITY

From a history rooted in slavery, emancipation, and oppression at the Cape, two musical traditions important to the development of Cape jazz emerged: the distinctive ghoema rhythm, and the development of dance hall traditions among members of the coloured population. The rhythm known as ghoema (also spelled ghomma) was central to performance culture during slavery and is still commonly referred to as the heartbeat of Cape Town (Layne 1995; Willis Personal Interview 2010). According to Steve, Cape Town musicians like Robbie Jansen, Abdullah Ibrahim, Mac Mckenzie, and Jonathon Butler infused jazz with ghoema rhythms (personal interview). After emancipation, British influence led to the development of two traditions of coloured social dancing in the Cape: a high-status dress ball or "social"; the second is an Anglo-Afrikaans style of square-dancing, which Coplan suggests is still performed in coloured communities in Cape Town today (2008). As musicians performed in country dances, formal balls, seaside taverns, and dancehalls, coloured artisans were at the forefront in creating a popular Western Cape performance culture that would be nurtured over the next 250 years (Coplan 2008). After they were emancipated, formerly enslaved musicians formed dance bands that became popular among all segments of nineteenth century Cape Town society (Martin, 2000b). Dance halls became important aspects of social and political life in the Cape, and they played an important role in the development of a class of coloured musician whose reputation spread with the migration of coloured laborers throughout the country (Layne 1995; Coplan 2008).

Perhaps inspired by similar local histories of slavery and oppression through the present, the influence of black American music on Capetonian cultural expression did not begin (or end) with what is now known as Cape Jazz. Historian Valmont Layne points to the formation of significant musical, literary, and intellectual trans-Atlantic connections between black South Africa and black America in the early twentieth century. According to Coplan, American jazz music has been more influential and more accepted in South Africa than in any other country in the world (2008, 178).

Profoundly influenced by the overseas success of its black American equivalent, the development of the jazz band tradition in urban South Africa exploded from the 1920s onward, with coloured musicians in Cape Town among the first to develop the western-style dance bands that monopolized the dance circuit by the 1930s (Layne 1995; Miller 2007). For this reason, since the 1930s, "dance music was often seen and understood by its contemporary practitioners and audiences as a performance style unique to coloureds" (Layne 1995, 11). According to Layne, dance music has been featured prominently in the everyday social life of Cape Town's coloured townships since the 1920s, where amateur bands played important roles in the development of local musical traditions and in the formation of a community identity. Most musicians began their careers performing in the Cape Carnival parades through the streets for the New Year, for Christmas bands, in the Star Bioscope, as well as in dance halls in District Six, the neighborhood that would later be bulldozed by the apartheid government, on regular weekends. Bands, Layne argues, formed the cornerstone of activities surrounding the use of community spaces in coloured communities all over the city.

By the 1940s, the fusion of marabi,[2] American jazz, swing, and jitterbug—even Latin American rumba and conga—inspired the creation of a jazz style that is uniquely South African. According to Coplan, jazz's roots as a black American form of expression rooted in African heritage that is "modern but not white" inspired the musical articulation of an African urban identity (2008, 158). Likewise, its international status gave jazz a certain prestige, sophistication in its cosmopolitanism. In fact, "jazz became part of struggle against cultural isolation and segregation and expressed aspirations of majority of urban Africans" (Coplan 2008, 17).

In Cape Town, responses to jazz were initially ambivalent. Jazz was viewed as a moral threat to proper comportment by some of the city's elite of all ethnic backgrounds. However, jazz gained ascendancy as it became associated with glamorous American big bands and Hollywood films. Much of the exposure to American jazz music came from the cinema. Movie theaters served as social gathering places and were the only spaces that allowed relative freedom of social (and romantic) interaction for members of the Cape coloured community in the 1940s and 1950s. For working-class communities, a trip to the cinema provided "windows onto the outside world" (Muller 2004). During an interview, jazz practitioner Vincent Kolbe remembers being paid by bandleaders to view the newest films and memorize lyrics and music so that the latest American music could be played the following Saturday night at social dances for the coloured community. Kolbe underscores the importance of leisure time for politically oppressed coloured working class populations in the postwar period: "I mean all people, no matter what color you are or where you live you fantasize on the weekend about being a princess for the night" (Muller 2004, 79). With this connection to film and glamorous images, jazz in Cape Town became chic among mainly middle class and professional coloured audiences interested in the fashion and lifestyle associated with jazz (Layne 1995).

Jazz clubs were becoming increasingly popular in the mid-1950s and early-1960s when apartheid legislation was less enforced than in other South African urban centers, and jazz still found a few safe havens (Coplan 2008). At its height, the jazz scene was focused around the white city center and areas such as Woodstock, where jazz had an integrating function, challenging apartheid policies by bringing together people of all backgrounds interested in the performance of good music (Miller 2007).

From the early 1960s, jazz music was becoming increasingly popular yet difficult to pursue as an art form, as the racial mixing that occurred among jazz participants became increasingly problematic for the apartheid state. According to influential jazz vocalist Sathima Benjamin, the character of Cape Town changed dramatically for people of color from 1950 to 1962: "It was no longer the Mother City evoking a profound sense of place and home; it was a place of exclusion, fragmentation, transgression, and boundaries" (Muller 2004, 67). State enforcement of the Immorality Act,[3] the Group Areas Act,[4] and the Separate Amenities Act[5] played a critical role in the transformation and destruction of jazz communities. The state suppressed all performances that catered to mixed audiences, and jazz performance became a "dangerous activity, monitored and raided by security forces" (Muller 2004, 102). Pass laws and curfews made it difficult for black musicians to perform outside of townships, and they often became targets for the police.

By 1964, the jazz scene in Cape Town was slowly dying (Rasmussen 2001). Apartheid practices drove many jazz artists such as Hugh Masekela, Abdullah Ibrahim, and Sathima Benjamin into exile. The jazz musicians who remained in the city continued to play, but they witnessed the destruction of their cultural environment, and the music scene was dramatically altered (Coplan 2008; Rasmussen 2001).

As people were forcibly removed from areas like District Six, an area that was considered to be the hub of jazz activity in the 1950s and 1960s, and as liquor laws began to relax for coloured Group Areas in the 1960s and 1970s, allowing for more establishments to sell alcohol and clubs for jazz dancing to proliferate on the Cape Flats. Trevor 56, founder of the studio Danz Afrika, traces the movement/migration of Cape Jazz dancing from places like District Six to the "townships" (lower-income areas of the Cape Flats such as Hanover Park, Bontithwuel, and Lavender Hill) where jazzing emerged as a direct result of forced removals and relocation: "When people moved from District 6, jazz was attached to it. Everybody was forced to move and you get your Bonithuel, Helderveld, Hanover Park, Lavender Hill—all of those people were pushed there. And those people wanted to jazz" (Personal Interview 2010). According to Trevor, the people forcibly removed to these locations carried the practice of jazz dancing with them. Trevor then alludes to a diffusion of Cape Jazz dancing that was not only spatial, but occurred along the lines of social class and status as well:

> [T]hat feeling spread to all of the nicer coloured areas: . . . Lansdowne, Wynberg, the nicer parts of Athlone . . . it spread there as well. So it became a coloured thing and not just a township thing. It was nice that the so-called upper-crust people came to do it and identified with it so it was not just the poors.

Of course, curfews imposed on black South Africans during apartheid affected them not only in their homes and residential areas during the night, but also excluded them from all amenities during the night. Not only were black South Africans prohibited from attending jazz sessions in neighboring coloured communities, but, as Tony explains, white Captonians would very rarely travel to the Cape Flats at night. And a clause of the General Law Amendment Act of 1968 enabled the Minister of Justice to prohibit the sale of liquor for on-site consumption to members of the coloured and Asian population groups in a white group area (SAIRR 1984), thus, jazz clubs in white areas of the city centre would have had almost no coloured patrons. Trevor states, "Remember, we couldn't go to white clubs. So we had to have our own clubs where we had to identify with jazz. . . . Because all the clubs in town were for whites." Therefore, Cape Jazz dancing developed almost exclusively in isolation within the coloured communities of Cape Town, with the heart of the jazz club scene on the Cape Flats.

Sensuality and immorality attached to racial mixing was viewed as "dangerous" to the apartheid philosophy. This ideology contributed to the development of Cape jazz in isolation. In October 1975, Mr. Isaacs, the owner of the Jazz Tomb Social Club located in Athlone, applied to the Department of Community Development for a permit to authorize white guests to attend sessions at his club to increase exposure for talented jazz bands (Western Cape Archives CDC 385, 32/1/4400/177). The Department of Community Development rejected the Jazz Tomb's permit, stating that in agreement with the local police department, issuing a permit to "a coloured social club, specializing in jazz music and with dancing, would not be advisable" (ibid.). During the 1970s, similar permit applications were filed by the Beverly Hotel and the Gold Finger Lounge in Athlone. These permits were granted on the explicit basis that white invitees would not be permitted to dance and, in some cases (Western Cape Archives KAB CDC 384 32/1/4400/122 and Western Cape Archives KAB CDC 383 32/1/4400/67).

Feelings of isolation were imposed by state, but also, once imposed, this sense of isolation also created a safe haven sought out by jazz dancers. Cape Jazz dancers indicate that dancing, for them, served as an escape from the stress, burden, humiliation, marginalization, and oppression of apartheid. In the nightclub, Steve remembers,

> You would go and you would be in a world where there are no restrictions; you lost yourself in the music. . . . Some clubs you'd dance from 8pm-1am, but some clubs you'd go in at 8pm and stay right through 'til 6 in the morning. All night long. But in was about the music. And I think people went there to escape from this frustration of not being able to integrate.

Trevor says that "we [members of the coloured Cape jazz community] danced our way" through the struggles of apartheid. When you dance, you are in your own vibe, your own world—you forget all those things. It was a form of escapism." Clyde explains that for those four or five hours, inside the cocoon of music and behind the closed doors of the windowless club, one could forget about what was happening outside (See figure 4.1).

In the midst of forced removals and isolation, some musicians in the 1970s and 1980s began to embrace the sophisticated sounds of jazz artists such as Miles Davis, John Coltrane, and Charley Parker, which exposed Cape Town musicians to a "whole new world" of musical style that was not only about rhythm and the basics of jazz, but jazz became an art form that required hours of study and practice (Jamal, Personal Interview 2010). It was at this moment during this period of exploration, suggests Jamal, that jazz music for "listening" began to develop on a different level to that of jazz music for "dancing."

Until the 1970s and 1980s, people were dancing to Cape Jazz music. However, in the early 1980s, jazz musicians in Cape Town began to focus more on improvisation

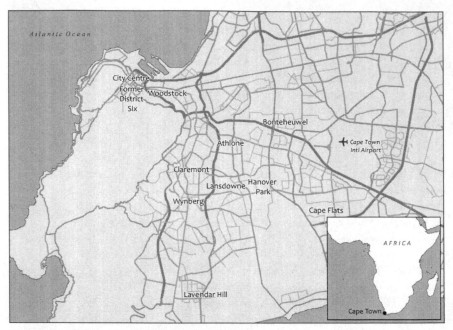

Figure 4.1. Map of Cape Town, South Africa
Data Sources: DIVA-GIS and ESRI. Map created by University of Minnesota Duluth Geospatial Analysis Center

and experimentation with rhythm and melody, a project that caused their music to become too far removed from the danceable beat that the public enjoyed. The music became more about education and less about entertainment. As musicians became more passionate about this particular style of jazz, bands became increasingly less popular with Cape Jazz dancers. "They just wanted the thing that they loved, the thing that made them dance" (Personal Interview, 2010). Dancers began seeking a style of jazz that resembled American Rhythm and Blues or Adult Contemporary. Jamal believes that as jazz bands became less popular with Cape Jazz dancers, the nightclub scene shifted away from live music and leaned more heavily on popular recorded music. This describes the music in the jazz club sundowner that I attended. This shift implies simultaneous processes of global flows and local development.

In recent years, the style of Cape Jazz danced in clubs has also been evolving. Dancers describe the subtle incorporation of body movements from dance styles such as tango, hip hop, and, most significantly, salsa (the relationship between salsa and jazz will be discussed extensively in the following chapters). Several jazz instructors have become dedicated participants in Cape Town's salsa scene and many Cape Jazz dancers have admitted in casual conversation to attending salsa venues to "steal with the eye" the intricate turn patterns common to salsa styles practiced in Cape Town. Dancers will then add their own "Cape Town flavor" to the moves. Trevor says that Cape Jazz today looks much like ballroom rumba, jive, and Cuban salsa blended together.

The Cape jazz narrative as expressed by dancers is primarily linked to experiences of spatial and social marginalization of members of the coloured population on the Cape Flats. Although notions of the "global" are vital to and ever-present in this narrative, the next section explores the current increasingly "local" trajectory of the Cape jazz narrative, particularly as dancers encounter and defend Cape jazz against salsa in Cape Town.

CAPE JAZZ: ISOLATED DEVELOPMENT ON THE CAPE FLATS

The Decline of Cape Jazz: Staking a Claim for the Local

In our first interview in 2009, Trevor told me that "[Cape] jazz [dancing] will never die." One year later, Trevor was less certain of the eternal nature of Cape jazz dancing. Several of the most dedicated practitioners are concerned about the apparent decline in enthusiasm and support for Cape Jazz dancing. Darren has noticed a significant decrease in number of dancers since 2005. Trevor traces the decline to around the year 2000 and claims that popular trends "from overseas" such as pop music, house, and old school have captivated the clubbing youth and are beginning to squeeze out Cape Jazz and Cape jazz enthusiasts. Clubbing, as DJ Robert points out, is an activity that tends to be more lucrative when targeting a younger population. As a musician and events promoter, Jamal recognizes the importance of separating his desire to hear jazz music and catering for a larger market with different musical interests. "At the end of the day you must give the people what they want to get the money to pay the rent" (Personal Interview 2010). Even Trevor, who frequently vocalizes his despair at the declining interest in jazz dancing admits that he cannot blame club owners for acting in their best financial interests, and that club owners are afraid to lose money by pursuing jazz music nights instead of hip hop or house music nights. DJ Robert admits that the jazz dancing population is aging, and clubbing has become less important to people: "Jazz, the fusion of funk that we tend to play here is not as in demand as it used to be a couple of years ago. . . . A lot of people that were coming to clubs [have] different demand on their lives. . . . We haven't found that new generation" (personal interview). Perhaps it is this sense among dancers that the practice of jazz dancing is in decline that ignites sentiments of loss and simultaneous motions to restore jazz; to memorialize it as evidence of coloured cultural expression. There is also an impulse to fiercely defend jazz from outside forces and influences.

I was invited into the jazz scene in 2006 by dancers I knew from the salsa scene who enjoyed both. Although I was warmly received by male dance partners, I picked up on tension and hesitancy regarding my salsa background through the comments and body movements of some partners. Despite the rhetoric among participants of social dance as a unifier and a facilitator of collective identity formation and belonging (see Johnson 2011), tensions exist both within and between salsa and cape jazz communities. These tensions are less over the specific movement vocabularies of each dance, but are instead indicative of overarching struggles over meaning, memory, and belonging.

Much of the tension between salsa and cape jazz practitioners stems from the ways that these two forms of cultural expression developed differently in Cape Town (see figure 4.2). Nightclubs featuring Cape jazz dancing are typically located in the suburbs, particularly those areas that are historically working class and professional coloured areas. The clubs that dancers most often discuss are concentrated in Athlone, Lansdowne, and Epping Industrial, although smaller jazz clubs exist all over the northern and southern suburbs, and in the Cape Flats. In contrast, the salsa scene in Cape Town formed relatively recently (in 2002), and is more heavily focused in the city centre. While several instructors teach classes in other parts of the city, the largest salsa schools, most of the performances, and the successful regular socials occur in town. The community of salsa dancers is relatively ethnically or racially diverse compared to other dance scenes in Cape Town, although, many participants mention a shortage of black South African salsa dancers in the scene. Participants in Cape Town's salsa scene are overwhelmingly middle-income people in their mid-twenties

Figure 4.2.   Night Club in Cape Town
Photographer: Tamara M. Johnson

Figure 4.3.   Salsa Dancers in Cape Town, South Africa
Photographer: Tamara M. Johnson

to mid-thirties with a heavy proportion of college students and professionals associated with the corporate world or academia.

The histories of both cape jazz and salsa movement have similar connections to swing and ballroom dance traditions. Cape jazz dancers emphasize the important influences that dance styles such as langarm,[6] the bob (similar in movement and flow to swing), and ballroom and Latin have had on jazzing movements. Likewise, some of salsa's movements have been inspired by swing and the Lindy Hop transferred in Harlem's hottest nightclubs, ballroom and Latin, the hustle, and Afro-Caribbean body movement and the traditional dances of Cuba. Cape jazz and salsa dances in Cape Town are similar in movement, but with the following important distinctions. According to several instructors of both jazz and salsa, the basic steps are similar, but the music is used differently. The Cape jazz basic step is described by Trevor as a continuous forward and backward movement that is similar to rhythmic walking. This basic step does not necessarily occur on a specific count in the music as salsa does, and also does not adhere strictly to a slot or circle floor pattern. Dancers maintain contact at the hands and rarely use standard dance hold. Salsa dancing, in contrast, often begins in dance hold, and steps and turn patterns align more strictly with the eight-counts of music. A woman dancing salsa (if she is following) takes her first step back with her right foot, then shifts her weight forward, and steps forward on her right foot for the third beat of the music. She then steps forward with her left foot on the fifth beat, shifts her weight back, then steps backward with her left foot on the seventh beat of the music. Jazz dancers do not pause in the basic step as salsa dancers do (the pattern describes salsa as it is most often danced in Cape Town has a pause on the 4th and the 8th beats). This pause in movement often gives the salsa follower (usually the female dance partner) time to style or to embellish her basic step with shoulder rolls, arm flares, and hip rotations. As a salsa dancer, I have noticed that, in order to follow a Cape jazz lead, I have to keep perpetual tension in my arms because I am not sure when my partner is going to lead turns. Likewise, I have noticed that jazz followers generally keep their legs straighter—the knees are less bent and the hips do not move as much as in salsa. There is also very little emphasis on shoulder shimmies and rolls as well as chest and torso isolations as with salsa. Turns in jazz dancing can be executed at any point in the music, whereas in salsa, certain turns are only led on specific counts. One jazz instructor explained that, when dancing with me, he recognized my salsa background because the tension in my body slacks in the middle of my basic step (I usually do a modified salsa basic to jazz music—I try to keep my legs straighter and to keep more tension in my arms—also, because my legs are stiffer, I tend to shuffle my feet more during jazz, whereas I have been trained to accentuate my foot steps and placement in a salsa basic). Because I relax my body, this instructor mentioned that if he had wanted to do a move in that pause, he could not have because I relaxed the muscle for a beat. The tension in a jazz follower's frame is always present.

As Bertram (33), a salsa instructor, notes, the borders between cape jazz and salsa dances in Cape Town have become very blurred where they were once very distinct. Several instructors are trying to fuse elements of cape jazz and salsa to reach a wider audience. Interestingly, the two dance companies focused on this endeavor are among three companies that are currently (and have been consistently) teaching in both the city centre and in the suburbs/on the Cape Flats. In order to make salsa movement more accessible to jazz dancers, Darren of Mfusion subtly mixes the two forms in his classes, often without his students realizing that he is blending the similar movement concepts. Clyde of Salsa Fusion Dance Company, who also blends elements of salsa and jazz styles admits that he encountered resistance from other jazz instructors to this approach. Clyde mentions that, because many dancers learn by watching other dancers, dance moves will be traded back and forth across the dance floor either through observation or direct connection and communication between bodies. According to an observant jazz musician, both styles appear to be mutating in Cape Town.

In spite—or perhaps because—of the similarities between jazz and salsa dance forms, a tense rivalry has developed between the two forms. Darren, one of the jazz instructors who teaches a fusion of jazz and salsa, claims that he has been dancing at salsa venues and has had salsa dancers tell him that salsa is better than jazz. Trevor believes that some salsa dancers "look down on us jazz people," protesting that "jazzing is our roots!" Amy of Salsa Fusion (formerly Jazz Fusion) is frustrated by what she describes as the "high and mighty" attitude of some salsa instructors who are intent on replacing jazz: "They keep saying they will make jazz die down. They can't do that because it is a culture and they don't understand that." A couple that teaches jazz in

Wynberg wanted to explore salsa classes, but felt unwelcome in classes led by two separate instructors. In both cases, they felt that salsa dancers were "stand-offish." Trevor expresses his dismay and disappointment at this behavior, insisting that "it is almost like these salsa people have this opinion that they are superior to anybody else. . . . The salsa community frowns upon the jazz dancing. . . . This is our culture! Don't take away our culture!" Trevor claims that it is this behavior that gives the salsa community a negative reputation in the eyes of many cape jazz dancers.

Bertram argues that the "in between world" of the coloured jazz community feels threatened by salsa as "something new to come into their environment" (Personal Interview 2009). Not only is salsa a relatively new dance style in Cape Town, it has also been imbued with certain meanings and value systems that position it in opposition to cape jazz: it has been described as foreign, "high class," and even white. Bertram claims that people in jazz clubs would say to him: "don't bring your white dance here" even though he tried to explain that the roots of salsa are not white. Bertram, himself a member of the coloured population, acknowledges that historically, members of the coloured community have "had to fight for everything that they wanted." He also recognizes that jazz is part of a "tradition" within the coloured community, but he is unimpressed by the reluctance to adapt to new dynamics and to adopt new influences. Darren explains that "salsa is international, Cape jazz is local. When something [like Cape jazz] is close to home, it doesn't easily adapt to what comes in from outside. So salsa comes in and nudges against jazz and if something nudges against you, you have a reaction back toward it." Darren laments that instead of each community being open to and curious about the other one, the resulting tension has created an unnecessary and unpleasant conflict over meaning and belonging.

The tensions that have emerged between jazz and salsa practitioners reflect meanings that have been attached to these dances and encounters with different visions and approaches to their urban experiences in Cape Town. Participation in these dance scenes can elucidate the ways memories are created through dance and the ways in which these memories are defended. Cape jazz, as cultural expression, serves as a counter-narrative to the shame that Zimitri Erasmus (2001) describes. Participants describe jazz as a validation of colouredness, as evidence of culture, and as way to write and commemorate a collective history of resilience. The dance floor is a site in which narratives of colouredness are shaped.

Cultural expression continues to be a way of navigating feeling of marginality; cultural expression is a method of asserting presence, demanding recognition, resisting invisibility, and defining oneself. Cultural expression is also often a complicated battleground of emotion, meaning, and status. Cape jazz inserts itself into this cultural sphere of self-fashioning. The overwhelming consensus on the part of Cape jazz practitioners is that Cape jazz dancing is unique to the coloured community in Cape Town, and emerged in the context of apartheid, segregation, forced removal, and marginality. Trevor succinctly explains the important of memory, belonging, and collective affective space:

Many times I used to be humiliated. It was frustrating in the sense that it's your country and you are not free in your own country. So this jazz thing, when it first came out, we protected that stuff—it was unique to Cape coloureds, to the Cape Flats. . . . It was something that belonged to us. It is a total, total Cape Flats coloured thing. . . . So it was a way of identifying ourselves on the dance floor. Being unique. Being us. We were referred to as being "whatnots" so the whatnots showed them that we also have a culture. We can also dance . . . "this is ours" and this is what the whites can't take away from us—our dance, our originality, this is what we do. . . . So I say that apartheid had a lot to do with the origination of jazz. (Personal Interview 2011)

The cultivation of collective memory is important to the development of Cape jazz not only as an expression of feelings of marginality but also of resilience. The experience of forced removal and subsequent segregation, while not shared by everyone living in neighborhoods in and around the Cape Flats, did create a dominant narrative of marginalization and survival among members of the coloured population that I interviewed for this project. Cape jazz dancing began to develop during this experience of displacement, resettlement, and reconstruction of new homes, communities, networks and lives. During these embodied exchanges through dance, a narrative is produced and re-produced: a commemorative narrative about a collective coloured experience and "appropriate" identity asserting distinctiveness and resistance to marginality.

In his research on dispossession and memory among former residents of District Six, Henry Trotter (2006) found that the deeply emotional and shared experiences of forced removals united people; these affective ties initiated a desire for people to narrate their common experiences. Narrating memory, Trotter argues, provides emotional, archival, aesthetic, social, and political resources for survivors of traumatic experiences. In reconceptualizing individual identities and social networks, both of which were damaged and disoriented post-displacement, the forcibly removed found solace in reminiscing about their pasts. Through nostalgic storytelling, people began to agree on how to appropriately remember the past. As Trotter illustrates, community identity is often forged through shaping and sharing memories of a common (traumatic) experience. These narratives of movement, change, marginalization, adaptation are passed down through generations. Carlton and Abdul know of their friends' and family's experiences with forced removal, just as they learned how to jazz from friends and relatives. Cape jazz dancing is an embodied expression of affections that emerged in and flow from a particular moment in space and time (i.e., working class and professional coloured/Cape Flats/Apartheid). Cape jazz dancing has become part of the fabric of the Cape Town experience, and meanings attached to jazz, although they change, are carried and communicated through the body along lines of affect, and transmitted between dancers on the dance floor.

There are a variety of schools now teaching Cape jazz dancing classes, and competition among them has been the impetus for defining and loosely codifying specific Cape jazz moves. Particularly with the threat from salsa, jazz instructors and avid dancers are quick to point out those new movements that are not jazz. Among some, there is a resistance to incorporating moves from other dance styles (particularly salsa). Therefore, Cape jazz as a dance is movement, yet it seems to be not only trapped in place as jazz clubs are only located in certain parts of Cape Town, but also trapped, through pressure and codification, in certain patterns of bodily movements. Yet, this resistance to incorporation is an effort in futility because the style of Cape jazz continues to evolve.

While there is a clear origin story that emerges for Cape jazz dancers—I do not want to present an over-simplified view of social interactions and zones of exclusion that operate within the jazz scene. The practice of attaching these meanings to Cape jazz dancing glosses over individual experiences, homogenizes differences, and obscures inconsistencies. The purpose of the origin story narrating Cape jazz as a cultural practice rooted in forced removal and marginalization, articulating the resilience of a working class coloured population is inspired by a desire to construct collective affective space. Cape jazz dancing serves as a repertoire such that memories are "stored in the body" and emotions associated with memory and meanings are transmitted among dancers. Particularly as Cape jazz dancers feel confronted and challenged by salsa dancers, and as jazz itself is in decline, the communication of meaning and memory through movement becomes an urgent, emotional project for dancers and instructors.

EMOTIONAL POLITICS AND
VISCOS APPROACHES TO THE GLOBAL

The always-global, always-local nature of Cape jazz dancing is ever-present in its evolving narrative. There are strategies and emotional politics to ways in which "global" and "local" terms are used by dancers to describe Cape jazz at various times and in various contexts. Through the embodied practices of Cape jazz, emotional politics cultivate collective memory among participants and defend this memory from "outside" forces operating on the dance floors of Cape Town's jazz clubs.

While closely associated with notions of cosmopolitanism, transculturation, and global flows, the sentiments attached to Cape jazz have shifted such that isolation has become a significant aspect of the Cape jazz narrative. But notions of the global also permeate contemporary descriptions of Cape jazz in interesting ways. On one hand, jazz in Cape Town has been associated with global influences in its formation: American minstrel, jazz, and Rhythm and Blues musical influences, Latin American rhythms, and body movements inspired by dance styles such as swing, ballroom, and salsa. Its association through glamorous Hollywood cinematic productions gave early jazz music and socials a cosmopolitan cache. On the other hand, Cape jazz dancing is increasingly being defined, at moments, against the "foreign," urban, and cosmopolitan profile of salsa in particular. Though jazz is often discussed in terms of its development in isolation on the Cape Flats, jazzing as a dance form is not a product of isolation. At moments in its story, jazz represents the flexibility, evolution, and movement of dance that inspires change. At other moments, there are temptations to codify jazz, to restrict its movements to particular, identifiable patterns, to fix it in the embodied memory of those who have danced jazz for years.

Cape jazz dancing, much like the city of Cape Town itself, has evolved as a product of global connections combined with local influences: American jazz and dance band music mingled with South American and Caribbean rhythms and combined with local ghoema beats to create the music that inspired the Cape jazz dance tradition, which, in turn, borrowed movement styles from langarm, ballroom, swing, and salsa. In spite of its complex, syncretic history, the common narrative constructed by practitioners, is one in which jazzing is often geographically and culturally fixed: Cape jazz is a form of cultural expression that developed on the Cape Flats and performed primarily by members of the coloured population. The story of jazz is tied closely to feelings of isolation and marginalization resulting from forced removal and remote relocation, apartheid restrictions on movement and mixing, and bans on inter-racial dancing and drinking. Some dancers welcomed the jazzing experience in popular nightclubs as a cocoon of isolation providing an escape from the humiliation and oppression of apartheid.

It is important to understand not only the processes and local implications of globalization, but also to explore the ways that notions of global and local are used by people in order to explain their place in the world. Identification with the concepts of global and local within the Cape Jazz scene expose emotional politics embedded in personal histories, urban policies, and the complicated processes of collective memory formation and articulations of belonging. A collective narrative is created and expressed through jazz dance practices. Just like the movements and patterns of the dancing body through space, these narratives of memory and identity are constantly evolving, demonstrating the ways that people see themselves in a changing world. Memory is not only our current recollection of the past; it evolves and is continuously recreated in the present, thus shaping the future (Bergson 1988; Jones 2005). Therefore, our relationships to past experiences are not static, but evolve over time much as dance movements evolve. I argue that concepts of global and local are also not static; Saldanha's theorization of viscosity accurately describes the expediency with which the concepts of "global" and "local" are applied to Cape jazz dancing by dancers themselves.

NOTES

1. Throughout this project, I often utilize racial terminology that was imposed on the South African population during apartheid: Indian, white, coloured (using the South African spelling, from the apartheid category that included those of mixed race, Khoisan, and South and Southeast Asian ancestry), and black South African. While I recognize that these terms are socially constructed and represent relationships of power rather than biological categories, they are still commonly used in everyday language in South Africa. People are, however, redefining themselves both within and outside of these terms.

2. Marabi—brief definition—relation to cape jazz—for more info see Ballentine. Marabi is a "cocktail" of local and imported musical styles that, when combined, creates a unique sound that became known as African or township jazz. Marabi developed in a particular socio-economic context—it was dependent on shebeen society in South Africa's townships.

Marabi, as it was danced, reflected this approach to life, placing few bodily "limits on variation and interpretation by individuals or couples" (Coplan 2008, 117). Because of its association with alcohol consumption and unabashed bodily movement, marabi came to symbolize low social status and immorality and was often criminalized by both white authorities and a black elite. It was in the best interest of the black and Coloured bourgeoisie to distance themselves socially from marabi culture; however, marabi music found its place in the hearts of African audiences who would never have attended a marabi party in a shebeen or dance hall (Coplan 2008).

Despite marabi's success as a genre, the South African government's attempts to control urban space and social life led to the destruction of the social and spatial context that fostered marabi as a cultural practice.

3. In 1927, the Hertzog government passed the Immorality Act outlawing sexual intercourse between Europeans and Africans.

4. The Group Areas Act declared that certain urban areas were to be designated for exclusive use of one particular racial group. It became compulsory for people to live in an area designated for their classification (White, Black/African, Coloured, or Indian/Asian), which was imposed from birth by the rigid Population Registration Act of 1950.

5. The Reservation of Separate Amenities Act of 1953 allowed for public facilities and transport to be reserved for particular race groups.

6. The late Cape Jazz musician Robbie Jansen discusses the influence of *langarm* dance music on the Cape jazz musical tradition: *langarm* "is a caricature by poor people of ballroom as we know it. The dance and the music of ballroom is strict and formal, whereas *langarm* is raggy and lose" (quoted in Miller 2007b, 1). Undoubtedly, Cape Jazz dancing loosely borrows some of the movement patterns and partner work tradition from ballroom, but takes the relaxed approach associated with *langarm*.

5

Social Dance as Social Space

Jonathan Skinner

When I dance, space and time cavort with me. When I dance, my feet cycle into the ground in new ways, propelling my body into spins. When I dance, I hear my heart echo the percussion in the music. When I dance, I love in front of me. When I dance, there is no other time, and I have made my space.

This chapter is about movement and the body, specifically migration and social dancing. Both involve the criteria of time and space and connect with the expression of social identity. It starts with an introduction to space, turns to the space of the dance, exemplifies the conditions of the social dancing migrant, and ends by considering the narrative of social dancing migrant. Throughout this examination of the meaning of social dance for the migrant in Belfast, Northern Ireland, there is the recognition that the dance is difficult to represent. A dance is a fleeting movement; a social dance, is typically understood to be an informal and temporary partnership, usually between the sexes and often for the duration of a song being played in the background. "Twelve minutes of love" is how Kapka Kassabova (2011) characterizes the two of three Argentine tango dances she might have with a stranger. These dances can turn dancers into temporary lovers, even if it is just in our headspace (Skinner 2009). It has the power to salve and satiate our selves: "I wouldn't mind even dying right now," an impassioned Silvio once told a salsa dancer visiting Dublin after what he considered to be the best dance of his life (Skinner 2010). Even without a partner, social dancing "precipitates an incredible longing" for the pleasures of the body (Gotfrit 1988, 123), to reconnect with the aches of desire and longing rather than the pains of old age. It is a time for contradiction, indepen-dance and transgression in a seemingly ordered, regulated and increasingly bureaucratic modern environment. Gotfrit (1988) enticingly describes this dancing as a "dancing back," a dance between regulation and resistance. In the partnered salsa context of this chapter, it is a "dancing back and forth" (Skinner 2008), a particular use of space to resonate with oneself and to dance across a number of divides—all felt through eight years of passionate dancing in Belfast and up to a year of comparative dancing in Sacramento, California, and heard about in over three hundred interviews.

DANCING ACROSS THE DIVIDE

"What's your name? What school did you go to?" The man is chatting up my dance partner who has just gone over to the bar for a pint of water. She is leaning on it watching the other dancers, aglow with a light sweat and the satisfaction of executing some of the moves and sequences we have practiced at her home earlier. This is where she enjoys herself and sometimes meets interesting men.

This one is interested. He is steering the opening conversation to find out what side of the divide she is on. Is she a Protestant or a Catholic? This is all revealed in her answers. An Irish name and an integrated school quickly tell him what he could not figure out from her dancing. He backs away, retiring, and we return to the dance floor, an impromptu space between pillars in an inner city pub.

Whilst the salsa music is playing, the salsa dancers have their salsa space. When it stops, or when it changes to a more audience-friendly rock/pop mix, we drift off the floor and start to line the sides of our socially constructed dance floor. We are at the Cat & Kennel on a Monday night, traditionally quiet for drinkers, but recently given a lease of life with a DJ'd Latin Club Nite. As a salsa night, it follows on from some lessons elsewhere in the city. It has had to move from several other venues once the hosts realized that the influx of dancers to the venue did not equate to a large rise in the sales of drinks.

The night proceeds with a regular formula. From half nine, the DJ and percussionist friend and co-worker set up speakers, drums, mixing desk, and many colored mirror balls and lights. They work quietly in a raised area of the bar that has been roped off by the staff. Some of the early dancers hover around, greet each other and take their places for the night. A growing pile of overcoats develops close to the DJ area. But, as yet, there is no salsa. The DJ will only play salsa tracks when he sees a potential dance audience. If it is a mixed crowd then he will alternate salsa with reggaeton urban sounds and pop. Until the mix in the audience develops, he sticks to contemporary rock and pop tracks. Whilst he scans the building audience for dancers, the single male dancers scan their crowd for recognizable female dancers they can dance with, or for beginners whom they can impress with their learned moves. The mistake of an evening is to lose an observation position and to be relegated to the back crowds where dancing is harder to negotiate, and self-consciousness begins to build. Another mistake is to not know where to place oneself prior to dancing. It is all too easy to have to stand next to someone you don't like, a rival or an enemy even, and to have to make polite conversation until the music drowns out such difficult necessities.

BELFAST AND THE GEOGRAPHY OF SPACE

This social dancing takes place in Belfast, a post-industrial city that has been riven by decades of sectarian troubles between Protestant and Catholic, Loyalist and Nationalist, each social-cum-religious group attempting to assert and control the space of the city and the province of Ulster. This history of violent colonization and decolonization of hearts and minds has eased with the 1998 Good Friday Agreement. Subsequently, there has been a slow but increasingly relaxed and mixed use of social leisure time and space in the city. This has especially been seen in the rise of social dancing. Whilst there has always been a strong ballroom social dancing tradition, with dance students carefully negotiating their journeys through blockaded streets, and enduring physical and oral probing to enter the security ring set up around the city centre in the heights of the Troubles, the last decade has seen a rise in the number of jive, swing and, in particular, salsa classes. The open, lively and youthful choreographed geography of a transnational dance scaffolded upon an exotic music complex appeals to university students, young professional people, and those in search of sexy fun, escapism, and perhaps even a new relationship (see Skinner 2007, Pietrobruno 2006).

In his commentary on Belfast's new leisure spaces, Alan Bairner (2006, 124–5) characterizes Belfast as one of the transitional cities, *fin de guerre* Belfast akin to post-socialist *fin de millénaire* Budapest, *fin de siècle* Vienna, interwar Berlin, post-revolutionary Paris. It is a renaissance city of sorts attracting international interest, partly before its gritty past is lost. "The Troubles put Belfast on the map!" one informant told me. It is the destination of choice for the edgy tourist seeking a darker than normal tourist experience (see Nagle 2012). He goes on to cite Dawe (2004, 207, cited in Bairner 2006, 133) who criticizes both the old and new branding of Belfast: "Belfast, more than many other European cities, has been stereotyped to death; its complex history in permafrost; its geo-cultural life as a port, haven, hell-hole, spectacle, dumbed down before the term was invented." Belfast is still an aggressive city, divided, abnormal, a wounded landscape of consumption rather than production, inhabited by a still a broadly white, Christian population "albeit separated by doctrinal differences" (Bairner 2006, 124), with middle-aged men enjoying the semi-risk free public spaces that would have been too dangerous in the 1970s and 1980s (see also Schnieder and Susser 2003, Lysaght 2005).

The Club night has been extensively advertised with posters about the bar, through a resident teacher who provides free introductory salsa and bachata lessons for all at the start of the evening, and via new social media, Facebook events in particular. It is a regular dance night. But it has changed recently in that it has become less of a pure salsa night, more Latin as in Latino/a. A lot of the salsa dancers now save themselves for other nights in the week. The salsa students don't come here any more to practice their moves learned previously or to watch the more experienced dancers in the hope of picking up tips and picking up occasional dances. Out of the forty or so dancers, only seven or eight come from the salsa classes, and out of those, only three or four are dancers who have been dancing there for a long time. The dance space, constructed socially and practically by dancers dancing and drinkers accommodating them, has shifted. The bass rhythmic grit and grime of Sean Paul have replaced the band medleys of Tito Puente. Africa is still evoked, but through Jamaica rather than Puerto Rico or the Dominican Republic. The dancing is more unschooled, raw, natural, improvised rather than choreographed and practiced. The straight lines and rigid torsos of LA line-style salsa have been replaced by a curving of contra-body motion. Partners no longer face each other with tension in the arms to lead, follow, catch and add torque to fast spins. The dancing is in group circles, in partnerships hugging and holding each other, enjoying the company and sensuality of the other person as much as the music, and sometime the dancing is back-to-front, moving together with a taste of raunch rather than a hint of sexiness.

The use of space has shifted from salsa to Latin. It has become a night of social identification rather than social escapism. The DJ dances in front of his audience of dancers, singing along with the songs, waving his hands in the air and talking to the crowd through the microphone. Sometimes he joins the percussionist. Occasionally both of them leave the makeshift DJ area to dance with some of the women—many of whom are single, and are singing the songs whilst working practiced moves in female group circles. The dancing is to be seen. It is also about letting off steam as a group. Here, on the Latin nights most are not Protestant or Catholic but immigrant living in Northern Ireland, adopting to the local lifestyles but needing some space to express one's birth identity. That space is claimed on the social dance floor.

In their collection *Everynight Life: Culture and Dance in Latin/o America*, Delgado and Muñoz (1997) draw together contributions assessing the "politics of location . . . re-imagining Latin America" (Delgado and Muñoz 1997, ix). This is from North America. The dance perspective gives it an extra-ordinary angle, highlighting difference rather than integration: queer tango, night-time salsa identities, latinness and AIDS sickness, up-side-down capoeira. These differences are highlighted in the body, embodied differences as pointed out by Desmond (1997, 33–64), and as evinced in the latin club in Belfast. For Desmond, we carry a lexicon of moves with our bodies. We use our bodies to enact social relations just as we create social space. Both are fashioned and refashioned in the movement of the body and in the trends and tides of transmission between Latin America and North America (Desmond 1997) and the Caribbean islands and North America (Skinner 2012). For Desmond, an upper-middle-class Anglo suburban couple dancing Latin dance styles is a safe and temporary action in a protected and bounded environment, more Anglo-Latin adventure with Euro-American carricaturizations on the Latin American emotional self—sensuous, passionate, heterorotic (Desmond 1997, 50; see also Laffey 1995).

The Gaellic version of Desmond's Anglo-Latins have been chased out of the Cat & Kennel in Belfast in favor of more commercial music and dancing. As they left, there were mutterings about how the DJ should play more pure music, referring to the classic band tracks from New York. The hardcore salsa dancers—as they liked to see themselves—didn't like the Cuban folk salsa or hiphop-inflected sounds. If they were particularly judgmental about the music and dancing, then they wanted the sound of the clave so that they could dance LA line style on 2—starting their footwork on the second beat of the bar rather than the first beat. For these now absent dancing bodies, the "participatory musical genre" (Febres 1997, 176) which characterizes that salsa had gone too ghetto.

Another Thursday night in the calendar and we aim for the Cat & Kennel after a tango practica in another pub up on the Falls Road, a dance practice session that some dancers will not go to because it is held in a pub, and in a Nationalist district in Belfast at that. I am with some new friends, some contemporary dancers and an Irish dancer trying out tango for variety. A busman's evening? At the Cat & Kennel there is no point in waiting for salsa music to come on to reclaim the dance floor. We dance as a circle, each accentuating our own specialisms. As the dance tracks develop, we extend our own individual activities to include each other, living, whirling, stepping, hip rotating in the moment. It is an impromptu amalgam taking shape and taking place. I find myself using my reach, my toe points, my bent back, all taking me out of my dance comfort space. The space is a circle rather than closed couples. We take turns stepping in.

Are we dancing out our identities? Is my identity changing as my body integrates and familiarizes itself with new moves? Certainly the moves are new, and flow from transnational movements brought by MTV, DVD, and Latin migrants. A romantic, and perhaps semiotic, interpretation of events is that this social dancing is, as Delgado and Muñoz (1997, 10) coin, a "rebellion of everynight life." This is the bodily writing of historical identity, a tension between the colonization, regulation, standardization, codification of movement, and creativity, resistance and improvisation in the human subject. This thesis is also articulated in analyses of gender and the dance (Gotfrit 1988) and the development of dance standards (Cresswell 2006a), in effect, as the human subject reacts to the impositions of western modernity and the capitalist employment regime. For salsa, the flows and development of the dance reveal an Anglicization as it becomes codified by dance teachers and dance examining bodies. This is the difference between street salsa and studio salsa, or mambo as it is distinguished. In one form, the attention is to precision and choreography learned and practiced. In the other, the attention is to passion, *sabor*, heart and control of an ever-changing dance floor environment. How, for example, can the pillar in the middle of the pub be played with and integrated into the dance: rolling off it, dodging behind it to play hide and seek with your partner, resting against it, kicking off it, lap-dancing into it. This is creativity in the dance coming from experience and from thriving in an uncontrolled dance environment. It is by no means pristine. The space opening out on the dance floor might be a danger coming from a drunk spilling his pint of Guinness. And the drunk might still be dancing nearby. In this environment, the back heels stay off the ground, reducing the studio-taught Cuban hip motion, but increasing the rapid change of direction in the street-style and avoiding Achilles injuries from other dancers.

And yet the salsa and club movements in the Cat & Kennel are not indicative of a Latin "bodily consciousness" (Delgado and Muñoz 1997, 14) or any West African motor-muscle memory (Hazzard-Gordon 1990) or complex memory of difference (Clark 1994). These are not deliberate counterhistories undertaken through conscious social dancings. Delgado and Muñoz (1997, 17) sum up their romantic dance position interpreting these actions as authentic instances when "[t]he diasporic dancing body becomes the vehicle for the articulation of culture under siege." For them, then, to continue, "[d]ance literally remembers cultural practices repressed over centuries of conflict." This would suggest that there is a radical agenda at play in our dancing leisure time. This politics of dance folds past histories and horrors such as slavery into present human movements: the rumba evincing the steps taken into the ground by slaves' shackled feet and, as Delgado and Muñoz (1997, 25) suggest, "the wild motion of the mambo [that] evokes abolition." Dancing salsa, for them, is an embodied and practiced consciousness, transnational in its sweep, Pan-Latin in its scope for identification. Needless to say, there is a difference between a metonymic commentary on human movement as actual romantic continuity with the past and more synecdoche interpretation of dance movements physically evoking a painful era (Langer 1953). My position is against the suggested claustrophobic inheritance of particular traditions, as the habitus of history, as I feel the romantics Delgado and Muñoz and others sometimes declare. I do not deny Desmond's softer position that "social identities are signaled, formed, and negotiated through bodily movement" (Desmond 1997, 33). But I add to this the performative. We perform the identity we socialize into and/or associate with. We enhance that performance with design: movement and dress. On occasions it is deliberate. Sometimes it is by accident. Often it is different. Always, it is imaginative (see Skinner 2010).

If movement is a social marker, a cultural text, then it needs to be given an imaginative reading. Dances do diffuse from person to person, group to group, region to region, country and continent to country and continent. In their adoption and adaptation hybrids develop which can be desexualized and codified such as the tango or the waltz, the jive or the salsa (Skinner 2012). These crossover brokerings can be seen in the waltz by Vernon and Irene Castle, in ballroom by Victor Silvester, and even in music from Elvis to Eminem. Generally, these shifts are from black to white, from poor to wealthy populations. Such refashioning stereotypes Latin American identity through the dance movements, exoticizes and commoditizes it. One can play at being Other in the dance studio but return to oneself at the end of the wild evening out. This is Desmond's characterization of the "Anglo-Latin" (Desmond 1997, 48). But conversely, one can also return to being oneself on the dance floor. The rub is knowing which is which. The authenticity of social dancing cannot be taken for granted, particularly when it is being framed and interpreted within a complex of black and Latino positionality, by detached academics who also identify as passionate practitioners and birth members of ethnic groups. As Lamothe (2008, 15) notes in her study of black identity in ethnography, detachment and solidarity are an uneasy mix to maintain.

Related studies of social dancing in clubs show different positions and attitudes toward identity and social relations. James Farrer (2002) investigated the rise in popularity of disco pub culture amongst the young in Shanghai, China. Relations there are for fun. They are places where the use of space is very visual with the playing and flirting, watching and waiting, "normalized [. . .] sexual voyeurism" even (Farrer 2002, 301). The dance nights were places for students to assume adult roles, to dress in aspirational clothes. These are fun places, deliberately culturally ambiguous so that identities can be altered, distant partnerships avoided and strangers courted with "an assumed intimacy, touching, joking, whispering in the ear, and pretending feelings that aren't 'real'" (Farrer 2002, 292). Farrer considers these relations to be trivial. They are night-time plays. They are features of an experimental plastic sexuality noted by sociologist Anthony Giddens (1992) in his commentary on the disjuncture between sexual relations and reproduction. In this late-Modern era, in which the narrative of the self has to be continually reworked, post-traditional young women now stress sexual experience as opposed to sexual innocence. These are the consequences of market reform for James Farrer, the anomie of late-modern city living for Anthony Giddens.

These positions are more intrinsic reactions to circumstances for Gracia Farrer (2004) who examined social ballroom dance parties in Tokyo, Japan, and Heike Wieschiolek (2003) who looked into salsa dancing in Hamburg, Germany. Both of these authors examine social dancing in the context of migration. Farrer looks to Chinese immigrant social dancing in Japan as a subculture: immigrants creating their own distinct leisure space to recuperate from the discriminations taking place around them. In other words, for Farrer, the social dancing was less of a play with identity but more a recuperation of identity, a retreat to build up ethnic identity networks, to gain acceptance, to recover individual identity and status damaged in migration. It is a space for solace and the self. Social dancing creates a social haven (Farrer 2004, 660) in Tokyo for the Chinese migrant. Further, Farrer (2004, 666) writes, "[i]n a dance party, even the most socially stigmatized people outside of the dance hall could have a moment of glamour within." Illegal Fujian immigrants, stigmatized even within the hierarchy of Chinese immigrants, were praised as skilled dancers at the dance events. This is "ethnically enclosed leisure," Farrer (2004, 671) declares. In Tokyo, the immigrant dance floor—a sanctuary where cameras are banned so that people can relax from the threat of deportation—became a space for practicing a form of belonging. In sum, "Chinese immigrants' dance hall practices [. . .] provide a space for immigrants to adopt individual strategies to maintain a continuity and consistency of personal identity and individual purpose" (Farrer 2004, 672). This ethnically constructed leisure space allowed participants to obviate the negative and emotional consequences of their migration. It became one of the few places where they could maintain their personal identities.

Wieschiolek makes a similar point in her study of the salsa dance scene in Hamburg and its relationship with the wider society. There, many of the dancers are living their diaspora with dance as the connection point back to the motherland. It is more than a mobile nostalgic lodestone. Teachers, dancers, or onlookers even, of Latin American origins are considered to have, as Wieschiolek (2003, 126) coins it, "ethnic competence," as in a self-appointed expertise from birth of rhythm by blood rather than by learning. This dance autochtony separates the German salsa students from the Latin American salsero or salsera whether or not the migrant danced back home, or dances in the salsa clubs that they socialize in in Germany. Wieschiolek suggests that this competence is acquired according to different cultural models of learning: the Latino or Latina has grown up in a particular embodied environment favoring and naturalizing body movements, attitudes and behaviors, whereas the Germans are attracted to the salsa complex for the exotic escapism it affords. The result is that the German students treat the salsa dancing skills as an educational exercise, studying and learning it in lessons before the dancing begins. The women have to learn to devolve their autonomy, and the men have to learn to lead their dance partners. All this tactile awkwardness is in marked contrast to the blood dancers who turn up and rely upon their machismo and their upbringing to shine on the dance floor.

Both cases of social dancing amongst migrants show how the use of space is linked to notions of identity lost in one moment and regained in another. These examples show a strained connection with reality, migrants holding onto a sense of self, migrants remaking themselves on and around the dance floor, and having it affirmed and reconstituted with their dance partners. The element of pretence, often associated with glamour (McMains 2006), can be temporary as in a release from the stresses of conforming to an alien lifestyle, maintaining different ways, to figuring out foreign conventions. This does not mean that there is no identity or a loss or attenuation, but can lead to an intensification.

Friday and Saturday night we do the double, two late nights of salsa dancing in two very different venues. The Empire is a Victorian music hall converted into a pub with bands, food, comedy acts, and a salsa lesson and general dancing each Friday night. It acts as a feeder for new dancers into lesson nights during the rest of the week. It can be random and chaotic as a dance floor, sometimes exquisite with a flow around and between the drunks and student party dancers forcing you to time your breaks, to not over-commit in any move so that you can accommodate the shifting space around you. Other nights, it can be a sleazy evening of guys hitting on girls, cheap drink, and a wall of cigarette smoke either outside, or once, before it got banned, inside and from the hands of lay dancers. You don't know which night you will come away with. Sebastian works the crowd and we start a dance off with our partners. We play to the watchers and we tease our partners with spins that end in extreme drops, and with delicate syncopations with the music. In the Empire, you create a crowd with your dancing; and make your space with your elbows and your style.

The Windsor is different as a venue, as a clientele, as a music and dance night. It is the upstairs bar and function room of a private tennis club in the city. Though it is an open evening for all who pay, you need to know about this monthly salsa event. Each night has a guest teacher and a guest DJ working with the salsa promoters.

They take care of the dance floor, a square in the middle of the room, sprung wood, a fast and slippery floor for dancing on. I love it for the spins. It is where only salsa dancers go. The women often dress up for the dancing, and the men work through their routines they have practiced and memorized. No one dances alone, no women dance together, and women only dance when they are invited to by their male leaders—though they can indicate that they are up for a dance by standing waiting around the dance floor, swaying to the music.

Pietrobruno (2006, 14–15) describes the association between hip movement and bloodline as a popular misconception. Certainly dancers grow up within their own "movement culture," thus acquiring a certain "dance vernacular," motion as their movement heritage. But this is subsequently expanded, adopted, integrated, especially so if the migrant turns to the salsa to assist in their self-representation in an alien environment. It becomes theirs. Pietrobruno makes these points about the glocalization of the dance in Montreal, Canada, its local reception. For all the change, hybridity, adoption and adaption, she tries to sustain the argument that it is a dance with a long historical tail to it coming out of an Afro-Cuban rumba complex. The global transmission of this dance—of a distinctive non-utilitarian movement system through space (Spencer 1985, 1)—still retains its emotive past: as she writes, "the Puerto Ricans adapted the rumba, changing it into salsa, the altered the grace note from an eighth note to a sixteenth note. [. . .] [S]alsa inherited the isolation of the foot [. . .] salsa perpetuates the hip isolations of rumba" (Pietrobruno 2006, 36). "As part of an oral tradition," Pietrobruno (2006, 206) adds that "this dance is not stored in documents but in the bodies and minds of its dancers." Its performative present, however, has become increasingly sexualized in Montreal by Montrealers of Latin or non-Latin descent who learn the dance in the clubs rather than at home or on the streets, and thus come to associate it within a different cultural context, commercial rather than spiritual. This is the mistake of viewing the dance externally, from the outside rather than from the inside. As an observing participant in Belfast, there is the same autoerotic and autoexotic practice taking place with migrants recreating and recapturing notions of their homeland, and playing and dancing into stereotypical national characteristics.

ANGELINA'S SOCIAL DANCING REACTIONS

Here, in Belfast, the transnational dancer meets the transitional city, performing versions of their selves on the dance floor in their everynight life. Angelina is Argentinean, a mother of three children married to an Irish man she met when he was working in Argentina. She came to Ireland with him, unaware of the dark sunless days, the rain, and the cultural differences between the two countries. Her double consciousness can mark her out as an Gaellic-Latin. I interviewed her after meeting her at one of the Cat & Kennel evenings. She goes there for a number of reasons from nostalgia to independence. She picked up the dance in Argentina at family parties and social gatherings. After a few months of dancing salsa in Belfast, she tried out the Windsor with some of her Spanish friends she goes out with. Her biographical account lends vivid testimony to the above discussion on the migrants' dance space. Whereas Angelina felt comfortable and at home in the pub, she felt intimidated by the Windsor: "I found the place extremely intimidating because like it was a closed place, people knew exactly how to dance." She even went so far as to describe the place as soulless because she felt that the dancers were *executing* the moves, demonstrating technique and skill, but without passion or much interaction. In her own words, "it wasn't a party," for her:

> *Respondent:* I just feel that the dance techniques are great, but there wasn't a sense of partying, there was a sense of I go with my partner and I dance with him and I may mingle a wee bit but it's only us and there's no, no real interaction. It wasn't a party. I think that is strange for me and that night there was a lot of technique, very controlled movements, lots of spinning around, but I don't think they were having fun, or trying to. I'm sure they were having fun but from the outside it was all very controlled, "let's see what I can do?" "I'll show you what I can do," and it was still very flat. I think it has to do with the culture. It has to do with the culture and not letting yourself loose and you know there's a lot of that in all the parties that are here. Everything's very controlled and very organized. Society is the same and I think it has to do with: "let's control the dance." "Let's get the technique right"; "I know the movements and it's fine."

For the South American migrant, there is a comfort about moving and music. This is not reflected in the Belfast salsa dance night where the movements are with deliberation and careful practice. These dance movements and dance environments Angelina found frustrating. The Latin club night was inclusive. All could make use of the space. The salsa dancers' night was exclusive, a disciplined form of leisure with informal constraints set in place. In fact, I ended up dancing with her vernacular style that was rotating around the body rather like a rock-n-roll jive to the salsa rhythms. She, and her friends, did not enjoy the night out, and it did nothing to affirm her Latin identity that she had hoped that it would do. She was even part embarrassed in front of her European friends for not being able to dance her dance.

"Dance wise," Angelina found the evening frustrating. She also articulated other frustrations beyond the physical, namely, the emotional and in terms of her personal identity maintenance. She recognizes that this dancing is just one of many things that sets her apart from her Northern Irish husband and neighbors. For Angelina, her identity is demarcated by her physical, cultural and linguistic sense of difference. And she sought to continue that.

> *Interviewer:* Is this dancing one way of maintaining your identity here?

> *Respondent:* It is my way to an identity. I do have an identity because I'm not from here and I work hard to not lose it. And it gives me a sense of belonging: you know, if we were dancing and if they did understand what the song was saying they would laugh their heads off so that gives you that extra click, you know. Well, I do belong to this.

For Angelina, the salsa night can and should be about dancing with the music. She likes to sing and move, karaoke dancing on the dance floor as opposed to the set choreographies by dancers who run through their dance patterns regardless of what is being played by the DJ or on the CD that is set and left to run. Angelina's dancing is not restricted to the dance floor. She dances around the kitchen with her children, part in reaction to the rejection and difference she feels as a migrant to Northern Ireland, and part to instruct her children in the ways and habits of life in her Argentina.

Respondent: It's my reaction of rejection because I thought how can you cut all the links with, you know, your country? So I listen to music from my country, but not only my country, in Spanish, not necessarily from Spain. I watch the news. I watch documentaries. I watch TV programs from Argentina for the kids as well and I drink our Mate tea which is our thing. And I have to work towards that and in terms of dancing: dancing is quite a huge part in my everyday life at home with the kids, we dance when cook or we listen to music. It's whatever I can get . . . I try to listen to music that I would naturally like back home and I want the kids to know about music.

Interviewer: So is it like throwing off a forced culture identity?

Respondent: I think it probably is, you know. Here I am. This is what I do. I know how to do it and I'm having fun—in your face. There are people in the Latin community here that just go for a good dance, and just get it out of their system.

Interviewer: So would you say a different connection to the music and to the body going on?

Respondent: I think there is, but I think there is a different connection with ourselves with everything in here I don't think that this society has the same relationship where the feelings and the body and the music and you know. . . . Here, everything has to be rearranged and for all Latin American people that is going to be a problem, always. That's why, whenever we find and meet people from other areas in Latin America, we just, the first thing we do is just play and you would become friends with people you'd never imagine you'd become friends with but that does happen and, of course, that's your identity. You're different in here. And you're different among yourselves as well but you share something. The language is fantastic! Imagine four countries speaking the same language with lots of variations. That's fantastic! So I am not surprised that dancing is so controlled and so organized and, my friend, she was saying that she could see them dancing and everything was very perfect—"you know they know how to do this" and "they know how to do that"—and then you look at them and they look like robots.

Poignantly, dancing is Angelina's "reaction to rejection." Angelina did not like to be drawn into why she stayed in Northern Ireland if she so wanted to return and felt so out of place and so wanted to return to her motherland. Even though her husband and children were not with us, it felt like a potential betrayal and so I was told jokingly that I was not allowed to ask that question. We moved on in this interview. Significantly, Angelina did admit that she felt that the longer she was in Northern Ireland, the more she felt and noticed the differences, from friends booking in to socialize with her rather than just call around unannounced, to the solitary nature of her family interactions in larger social gatherings here. She looked out for the transition in her children on the airplane ride to Argentina and was disappointed by their reaction, overcome and embarrassed by the warm and extroverted welcome by the extended family over there.

> *Respondent*: I think the longer you stay here, the more awkward it is to fit in, at least for me.
>
> *Interviwer*: Really?
>
> *Respondent*: Because then you can see the differences and you so see the way it is affecting you. But the longer you stay—at least that's what happened to me—the longer I stayed, I realized that the place and the people really didn't go with me at all . . . everyone is very controlled. There's no spontaneous things happening.

A mingling community chaos versus a controlled individualism, Angelina was disappointed by the dance night at the Windsor, but she enjoyed the hustle and bustle of the Empire and the Latin club nights at the Cat & Kennel. She "felt more at home in the chaos." It was dark in the Empire and you could dance with anyone however you liked. So it was not intimidating. She relaxed there. "It was like Argentina!" Angelina developed this point for both Argentina and Northern Ireland, suggesting that society is reflected on the dance floor. It is as though the physical space and the cultural space map over each other. She was also not the only migrant from South America who felt this.

> *Respondent*: Chaos! It is not only me! It's people that I've talked to not from here: what you see in society is translated on the dance floor and I think that's very clear. That's a very good picture of society . . . Argentina is a mess. It is very chaotic and there are no rules and I think we're not so restricted whereas here it is an island and you can see it. It needs an influx of people saying different things to change the place. It has remained an island for an awful long time.

Angelina drew equivalences between a place and a people: the dancing—or lack of—matched the people's behavior. She demonstrated Spencer's (1985) "society and the dance" thesis. She found Northern Ireland staid and predictable, calm and orderly. This was in marked opposition to the chaos of family and neighborhood she grew up with. This chaos stayed with her and she came to recognize it as a part of her identity when she saw how different she was from her Northern Irish friends, family and neighbors. She retained that chaos and cultivated it in her children such that they became able to switch and become naturally at home in either of the two different environments. She glimpsed her chaotic Argentina at the Empire and at the Cat & Kennel. In other words, these social dance leisure spaces took on emotional import for her as an immigrant. This nighttime danceland resonated with her sense of homeland. It was elusive, traces of a migrant's homeland through the turbulence of Friday nightlife in Belfast city.

SOCIAL DANCING SPACE REFIGURED

Geographer of relations, Doreen Massey (2005, 9) is attracted to space as "the product of interrelations." She reviews the concept in terms of its representation and philosophical notions and associations with time (Fabian), interiority and femininity (Irigaray), the immobility of the dead (Foucault), the constitution of difference (Derrida), relational politics (Latour). Massey (2005, 195) concludes her text with the comment that "sociability is to be configured" through space. Though conditional upon time (duration), it is through space that meeting occurs. As Massey develops, "[t]he spatial in its role of bringing distinct temporalities into new configurations sets off new social processes." Her work cites Fabian to critique a modernity under which space was conceptualized as a dividing line, a differentiating colonial developmental model associated with temporality. This "geography of modernity [is] a repression of the spatial, it is also a repression of the possibility of other temporalities," Massey (2005, 70) writes. This modernity is challenged and perhaps ended by the arrival of the margins at the center, by the influx of migrants to the old Imperial centers of power and industry, shipbuilding as in the case of Belfast. The postindustrial, postmodern new world (dis)order is one challenged by the proximity or disavowal of space. Massey suggests that the migrant is a figure from the past. Certainly in migration there is "an assertion of coevalness" (Massey 2005, 70), a cotemporality— a recognition space and a space for the realization of one's identity and imagination as an equal with the host.

In contemporary Belfast, the immigrant is the new cosmopolitan flaneur marked, according to Hannerz (1996), with the characteristics of savior-faire, cultural competence—at home in the long haul. The migrant is the figure for the future, as recognized by Angelina, necessary for the balancing of Belfast. They, along with the tourist, are taking the city forward in multiple simultaneities, breaking down traditional Loyalist-Nationalist divisions, creating—though often also overcoming—new racist and ethnic animosities (black, Asian, Romany). In their movements they fashion a new space, understood to be a-temporal, synchronic and depthless, for postmodernist Fredric Jameson (1991). For the migrant, they are just trying to be themselves. This can be reappropriated on the social dance floor, in the pub and the club especially.

Travel, with its spatial imperative, infuses the migrant. They are able to defuse on the dance floor. It is there that they allow their identities to catch up with their selves, a necessary self-narration in a world where technology has annihilated time and space differences (Harvey 1990) and where the global spatial imaginary takes on local import, quite literally. The leisure evenings are catch up times, the meeting of friends and strangers on the dance floor, one-off companionship without a past or a future. Such is the liquidity of urban living who laments such "mis-meetings" (Bauman 2000, 95). These are city spaces where sociality is touched upon and the masks of public living can be slipped momentarily away from the face. This is not a modernity of exile or diaspora. Nor are these spaces for refugees. These are Latin night spaces where the chaos—and what Huggan (2009, 146) describes as "ontological confusion" of travel—can be resolved and cultural memories restored. Or, more forcefully, it is in these night zones that there is a "nomadic metaphics" of mobility—from migrants, from dancers—that we see everyday resistance to the spatialization of domination (Cressey 2006, 47). Angelina and others become in their social dancing, perhaps showing too, the mobile—just as mobile as their bodies—and "only momentarily static" (Housee 1999, 140) nature of identity, working out who they are; becoming by "Being in an Other context" (Arshi et al. 1994, 231).

At the start of the social dance there is a negotiation of partnership. During the dance there is a movement back and forth, pushing and pulling the salsera into the leader's space, but also maintaining the space of the frame. There are boundaries, some of which are traversed, just like the nations traveled through. This chapter has focused on the social dance space and the migrants' imaginaries surrounding it. There are other spatial perspectives possible. Corsín Jiménez, for example, opens space out from its shackles with place, allowing in the social relationship by treating it as a capacity, as an extension on activated place. "Space is no longer 'out there,' but a condition or faculty—a capacity—of social relationships. It is what people do, not where they are," Corsín Jiménez (2003, 140) suggests. As such, this chapter, then, is more of a contribution to narrative examples of space being routinized and re-experienced if not brought under control by migrants creating home in a world of movement (Rapport and Dawson 1998, 6–7). Angelina from Argentina dances her home, plunging into the chaos. Where Rapport and Dawson (1998, 8) articulate exiles writing and ordering an intellectual home, or other migrants standardizing and routinizing their behaviors and exchanges, within this use of social space, there can also be comfort and solace in the disturbance of an over-scripted or overly ordered narrative.

6

Mediating the Other through Dance

Geopolitics, Social Ordering, and Meaning-Making in American and Improvisational Tribal Style Dance

Georgia Connover

The haunting sound of the ney flute floats through the air before it is joined by the syncopated beat of a doumbek and the raindrop-like cadence of a didgeridoo. The three instruments, of Persian, Southwest Asian and Australian lineage, intend to evoke unknown, exotic locations. As fair-goers stop to listen, and to wait before the performance stage for what promises to be a spectacle of music and dance, out of nowhere the metallic clang of finger cymbals pierces the air: 1,2,3 pause, 1,2,3 pause. The new rhythm adds to the mélange of sounds in a way that is both discordant and harmonious. The music is unfamiliar, yet orchestrated to produce a sense of time-lessness, as if to provide an auditory escape from ringing cell phones in the crowd, generators powering fry vats and air poppers, and other busy sounds of the modern world. In contrast to the fast-paced chaos of the fair, the music sells a different story, one that is distinctly romanticized . . . and overtly placed. The music resonates with Orientalist tropes as it connotes scenes familiar in the mind's eye from movies and videos—bazaars in Marrakech and camel trains in the Arabian Desert . . .

In the summer of 2005, I spent many months attending American Tribal Style (ATS) and Improvisational Tribal Style (ITS)—sometimes referred to collectively as Tribal Style belly dance—workshops and classes, dance conferences, and more than 100 performances across the United States. I also spent those enjoyable months doing what felt remarkably not like work, conducting formal interviews and dancing alongside, hanging out and informally conversing with dancers while reading as many books, magazines and websites about tribal belly dance as possible. As someone who spent my life dancing, it was a pleasure to leave behind university classrooms in order to immerse myself in performance and practice venues dedicated to this unfamiliar form. It was also a pleasure to take home the reams of transcripts, field notes and texts in order to study dance, not for its history or physiology—as

I had done in some of my undergraduate courses—but to examine its cultural and spatial assumptions. Using content and discourse analysis, I analyzed written texts to understand the historical trajectory of cabaret and tribal style dances. Analysis of field observations and interviews allowed me to make sense of the way traces of past discursive formations have articulated with modern tropes to continue to produce contemporary imagined geographies of the Orient.

During this period, I also followed one ITS group based in the U.S. desert south-west to its performances, practices, rehearsals, and social outings, occasionally even clumsily filling in for a missing member during a rehearsal. The troupe, admittedly, was selected for the very practical reason of its proximity to me at the time, but also because it was actively engaged in the local dance scene and with the wider tribal, belly dance world. The troupe had seven members, all of whom valorized the fluid-ity, the beauty and the strength of tribal style dance. These women, all Caucasian, some earning advanced degrees, one a stay-at-home mom and the others employed in middle-class jobs, looked to the dance to escape the normalcy of their daily lives and to spend time with their tribe of women. While it would have been satisfying to succumb to their narrative about the power, allure, and femininity of tribal dance, the underlying story that emerged was one of identity construction, the performance of geopolitical norms, and the production of imagined geographies through dancing bodies. It is this story that is critical, as it reveals spatial and gender hierarchies that persist in a time and place that is far from being post-racial or post-gender.

GEOPOLITICS, TEXTUALITY, AND DANCE

Because of developments in media technologies, individuals now have unprec-edented access to information about the world, making it increasingly possible to imagine what that world might be like. Indeed, much of what we know about distant lands and the people who inhabit them comes not from our direct experi-ence residing in those places, but constitutes an imaginative geography formed from various texts—books, movies, websites, music, dances—representing them (Berry, Kim, and Spigel 2010). This point is particularly salient when one considers that global images and narratives disseminated through texts are anything but objec-tive reflections of reality. Rather texts are *mediated*; they are technologies through which meanings, and all of the power relationships underpinning those meanings, are transferred and constructed (Lukinbeal and Craine 2009). Understanding texts as transferring meaning—and embedded systems of power relations—into new contexts of meaning-making, makes it possible to study how space is not only rep-resented, but also how it is *produced* through texts. Space is not a fixed, backdrop against which events unfold. Rather it is a process, continually in the making and re-making through material and discursive practices. And "no object, whether it be text, image, or space, is pregiven and representable in its full presence; rather, signs are contingently and multiply sutured to objects through the operation of social power" (Jones and Natter 1999, 242). Examining how space, texts and signs are sutured is a process of making elided power relations visible.

Derrida (1974) theorized that signifiers have meaning not because of what they signify, but because of differentiation, the process of distancing the signifier from what it is *not*. With this framework, it is possible to understand the social *process* of meaning-making or, as is salient here, of place-making, to be one of setting boundaries between what is given meaning and what belongs *outside* that meaning. According to Derrida, deconstruction is the work of examining signifiers, their constitutive outside, and the social processes through which settings-aside occur. Deconstructing texts, be they books, maps, landscapes, television shows, popular songs, or in the case of this work, dances, reveals social boundaries that are embedded within and produced through such texts (Harley 1988; Morrison 1992; Braun 2004; Duncan and Lambert 2004; Huq 2006). As such, deconstructive studies such as this one reveal a history and a context within which the process of differencing occurs, and through which shared meaning is created (Morrison 1992, Hall 1997).

For several decades, geographers have deconstructed texts in order to examine how the world is socially ordered, and then seemingly fixed into political, economic and social hierarchies through those texts (Harley 1989; Corbett 2000; Dittmer 2010). They have studied, for example, the discursive distinction between society and culture and how those distinctions configure space (Braun 2004), how places such as the home are given gendered meanings which reinforce public-masculine/private-feminine relations (Hayden 2002; Duncan and Lambert 2004), or how maps, by questioning territorial claims, reproduce dominant geopolitical discourses (Monmonier 1996; Crampton and Krygier 2006; Culcasi 2006; Perkins 2008; Wood, Fels, and Krygier 2010). Critical examinations of place representations in mediated texts, then, attempt to understand how signifying practices—those practices that produce meaning—order not just the word, but also the world.

It is only in the past twenty years that scholars have begun to examine dance as a mediated text, which like other texts can be understood to transfer and produce meaning (Brooks 1993; Desmond 1997; Goldberg 1997). And, like texts, dancing bodies are embedded within social contexts that structure the types of meanings they can convey (Bull 1997; McRobbie 1997; Martin 1998; Landzelius 2004). Uneven power relationships embedded within wider social discourses serve to frame dance practices at the same time that dance practices articulate with discourses to produce social orders, which then become so naturalized as to elide embedded power relations (Desmond 1997). In this capacity, the cultural practice of dance can, and should be studied as a deeply power-laden, social practice (Martin 1998). Geographers are only just beginning to engage with this work even though they have much to add. By intersecting critical deconstructive theories with the study of dance practices and the social ordering of space, geographers can theorize dancing bodies as part of an on-going process of meaning-making which serves to produce and reproduce power-laden imaginative geographies of the world (Said 1978; Desmond 1997; Landzelius 2004).

As the music plays on, evoking romanticized images of Bedouin caravans and tribal markets, the audience awaits the arrival of the dancers. The imaginative portrayal of a primitive, distant East is completed when a group of women, wearing wide, floor-length, earth-toned skirts, cropped and mirrored Indian-style choli tops and trible-esque coined and intricately tasseled hip scarves, enters from stage left. Sunlight glints off of burnished Afghanistani and Pakistani kuchi jewelry and highlights intricately tattooed and pierced bodies as the dancers yip, ululate and wind around the stage in a wide circle, finally breaking apart to form an arc along the back of the stage. The group moves slowly to the music with repetitive sequences of hip sways and chest circles. The moves are languid and fluid, the legs soft and the arms slightly bent. The focus is not on extensions and leaps but on grounded, torso and hip-based movements. The effect is one of fluidity and strength, as the dancers' uplifted torsos and focus on one another convey a sense of distance from the audience . . .

American Tribal Style is not *authentic* to anywhere. The dance is an ensemble of images, sounds and movements collected from pictures, videos, music, dances and movies about the non-Western world. It is fantasy, meant to eschew anything traditional while still celebrating its own history, putting emphasis on lineages of dancers. Innovation, and ownership of that innovation, is emphasized. Even the name given to the dance in the 1980s, American Tribal Style, is synonymous with the matriarch of Tribal Style Dance, Carolina Nericcio, and is meant to suggest a blending of temporal contexts: a juxtaposition of the progressive, modern West with a rooted, primitive, but absent East. ITS, which evolved out of ATS and likewise is performed by troupes around the world, has in many cases replaced most of the tribal-looking elements from ATS with bits from street genres such as hip hop, industrial, trance and other such artistic scenes. ITS, however, still retains the basic movement vocabularies and discursive codings of ATS. It has held onto the tribal moniker and invested it with new meaning in recognition of the dance's American lineage. According to the dancers who study and perform both ATS and ITS, the powerful, tough, real and overwhelmingly white, female bodies doing these dances are meant to be distinguishable from the pink, Barbie-doll like, idealized and sexualized female bodies performing that other, more rooted Oriental dance, belly dance.

In his seminal work on Orientalism, Edward Said (1978) pulled from Derrida in order to demonstrate how the East, or Orient, has been historically constructed as an outside other to the West. The resultant West/Orient ordering hierarchically fixes space into two discursive categories at the same time that the meaning of either category is constituted through its pairing with the Other. The incorporation of this binary into cultural practices, like Tribal Style dance, continuously reproduces and fixes into place the constructed Us/Other relationship, along with the power relations embedded within and elided through this spatial imaginary.

Furthermore, the binary is uneven because it works by defining a monolithic and dominant West by what it is not: an essentialized and marginalized East. Thus reductionist representations of Oriental people and/or dancers as indolent, ignorant, highly sexualized, rooted, or primitive are not about what the Orient really is, but rather are narratives that describe what the West is not (Said 1978; Buonaventura

1989). Rather than recognizing all places as fluid assemblages of social, material and spatial practices (Massey 2005), this trope represents Other places as essentially fixed in time and space while also hierarchically ordering the world around a valorized Western identity (Dittmer 2010). The essentialized Oriental *other*, then, is constitutive not only of an imaginative geography of Oriental people and places, but of the image of a complex, productive, innovative, rational, enlightened and modern western *us*. Furthermore, by setting aside the Oriental other and constructing a western identity based upon this increasingly vanishing other, it is possible to discursively construct a global, cultural hierarchy which valorizes Western ideals (Said 1978).

Tribal Style belly dance provides a unique lens for understanding the co-constitutive relationship between the West and East, the articulation of the material, spatial and the social, and how the dancing body works between social orders to mediate meaning. Both American Tribal Style and its offshoot Improvisational Tribal Style borrow costuming, music and movement elements from different, sometimes remote cultural worlds, while translating those borrowings through their own place-based filters (Buttimer 1976). Through their dance, ATS and ITS dancers write a protest of Western norms that serve to sexualize and objectify women, thus issuing a challenge to a western social order. This protest, however, is accomplished through the use of a West/Orient binary that erases Arab bodies from view while casting American women who do more traditional Oriental dance as sexualized and objectified.

BELLY DANCE AND THE VANISHING ARAB BODY

The name belly dance was coined by a 1893 Chicago World's Fair promoter, Sol Bloom. This was a time when it was scandalous to vocalize the names of one's body parts. Bloom had paid out of pocket to import a troupe of male and female Egyptian dancers to perform at the Fair's Midway Plaisance (Carlton 1995). When, night after night, theater seats remained empty, Bloom resorted to hyperbole and scandal so as not to lose money on his investment. He called a press conference, put his female dancers on display and named their dance after a body part, and a particularly scandalous one at that. The name stuck, and has even been adopted by people from Egypt, Turkey, Lebanon and elsewhere to describe their cultural dance form.

Because representations are materializations of social relations embedded within space (Jones and Natter 1999), Bloom's sexualizing of the dance was successful because it fit with Orientalist discourses already circulating about the depraved, Egyptian body. The fair occurred during a historical moment in the United States when representations of the Arab world were popular and upper classes would dress in elaborate costumes to host Oriental tea parties, buy titillating paintings of exotic harem girls painted by western artists but using scantily clad white women as models, and read the travel writings of western authors narrated using Orientalist tropes (Buonaventura 1989, Carlton 1995). Bloom's erotic sales pitch successfully filled empty seats by reinscribing the contemporary Orientalist narrative onto the bodies of his hired dancers. It not only reproduced the imagined West/Orient, rational/ sexual binary, it produced a new geographical imaginary. It was in this context—the Chicago World's Fair and the scientific fascination with the deviant Orient—that the term *belly dance* and dances of Southwest Asia were indelibly linked to one another and, more critically, were given highly sexualized meanings in U.S. contexts, meanings that continue to have salience even today (Salem 1995).

From the turn of the century into the 1920s, lower class performers began to use their shows to mock the supposedly refined and scientized sexuality of the upper classes. They created such hilarious and overtly lewd dances as the *hoochy cooch*, the *Vision of Salome* and other exaggerated and highly sexualized forms of belly dance to mock the bourgeoisie. Such performances, meant to reject the civilizing project of the elite, erased Arab bodies from the performance stage but continued to produce a fictionalized Orient, this one replete with harems, erotic dancing and sexually available girls clad in nothing but veils.

In the 1960s and 1970s, people who had migrated from the actual Orient to major cities in New York and California opened restaurants and nightclubs catering to their diasporic tastes. They hired American women who were willing to learn their native rhythms and steps and to perform in their ethnically mixed cabaret shows. As Oriental dances become increasingly popular and more women began to study them, some sought out southwest Asian women who could properly teach the dances from back home. Those who could, traveled to North Africa and Southwest Asia to witness these dances as they were performed in their different places of origin, and then shared what they learned by setting up American schools for belly dance. Some dancers instituted a social movement to re-present the context of this dance in terms of its meanings in the East and to cull out the imaginative representations of a monolithic, exotic, sexual Orient. Some dancers even started efforts to protest the very *belly dance* name (Morocco 1985). But for a large number of dancers, and generally for white audiences, belly dance—with name intact—retained its essentialized sexuality even without the same vulgarity.

> Under the ethos of sexual liberalism, and with the coming of consumer capitalism and new roles for women, American middle class men and women began taking on elements of sexuality—public expressions of passion and desire—which had formerly belonged to the sexual other. The working classes, African Americans, and sexual radicals like the Greenwich Village bohemians represented sexualities in real opposition to the White bourgeoisie, but throughout the nineteenth and early twentieth centuries, their differences had been projected onto Arabs, where they were expanded and magnified into a fantastic, imaginary sexuality. After sexual liberalism, the Arab world continued to provide a venue for imagining sexual and gender roles, but *Arabs* themselves, that is *Arab* bodies, became increasingly invisible. In their place were Americans (or Europeans) who had integrated elements of *Arab* body and sexuality into their own bodies (Salem 1995, 246).

Through the articulation of belly dance with the new sexual liberalism, the dance was largely recast into a form of ritual celebration of the *sensual* female body, a gendered distinction that has carried forward into contemporary cabaret and tribal styles of dance (Salem 1995). For example, in *Belly Dance* (2004), Australian dancer Keti Sharif describes the belly dance as soft, beautiful, and feminine (Sharif 2004). She goes on to write that "the women of the Middle East, to whom this dance belongs, use it to celebrate their bodies and to communicate a powerful message bequeathed them by their ancestors. They remind us that beyond the confines of society, this is a dance for the spirit" (Sharif 2004, 4). The magazine *Tribal* includes articles on meditation and spirituality alongside letters from readers about the femininity of belly dancing (Mandy 2006). Carolena Nericcio and others make repeated reference to the dance being done by females, as in this quote from the FatChanceBellyDance website. "Imagine this: there was a time in history, a long time ago, when the bounce and sway of a woman's hips was considered so beautiful that they set it to music and made a dance out of it" (Nericcio 2007). In an interview, tribal dancer, Faye,[1] celebrated the dance as a

> form of movement that really takes advantage of how our bodies are built and how we are shaped. We are curvy and we are soft and we are round. We have these curves and shapes and forms on our bodies and the way our hips move is different (from men's). You know, we have hips and it's, is just really takes advantage of how our bodies are constructed. Our bodies are perfectly made for belly dance (Interview, June 2007).

These curves and forms that Faye constructs as unique to the female form discursively produce a category of dance that is both natural and instinctively connected to the female body (Goldberg 1997). This natural body is one that cannot help but be sensual and even erotic when belly dancing. "It is very erotic and sensual, but that is not its purpose. It is not meant to be, you know. It's more coming into your own body and being a woman. It's very feminine. And women are sensual and women are erotic and that's the nature of things" (Interview, June 2007).

> *In unison, the arc of white, female dancers along the back of the stage performs slow, mesmerizing movements originating from the chest and hips. These movements are accented with snake-like arm waves and flamenco-styled wrist circles. Unexpectedly, three women break free from the arc and make their way forward into a tight triangle. Unlike the background dancers, who move using only a few repetitive movements, the downstage trio incorporates more varied steps. One dancer makes her way to the front of the triangle as the group performs, in unison, hip lifts and twists, chest drops and circles, torso twists and undulations, wrist circles and military like pivot turns. When she is ready, the point dancer relinquishes her lead position by forcing the other two women into a tight circle. Around they go until another dancer steps forward to the front of the triangle. As the drum beats and a reedy, recorder-like mizmar wails on, the trio fades back into the chorus to be replaced by a duo, and later another trio and so on until the music fades away and the dancers settle into a final pose . . .*

Even though the basic movements are done by men and women in Southwest Asia, and it is common to see a man jump up to join a belly dancer during her performance, and to publicly sway his hips or shake his shoulders—as Arab women are unlikely to perform such movements in a mixed-gendered space—the narrative about belly dance being a dance performed by women for women is one that seems to pervade much of the popular literature on the form. Goldberg calls this a return to the *distinctive body*, a body that for women is curving, undulating and circular but that for men is vigorous, mechanical and strong (Goldberg 1997). The narrative of naturally feminine belly dance movements, then, produces new ways for Caucasian women to find pleasure in their gendered bodies, but also genders the dance and erases the male Arab body from view.

TRIBAL DANCE AND THE RE-IMAGINED ARAB BODY

It is here that the story of ATS begins, in the 1970s, a time when feminists were working to destabilize a dominant, patriarchal social order and had adopted belly dance as a project of bodily reclamation. In a magazine dedicated to Tribal Style Dance, Frascella (2003) writes that so-called cabaret dancers typically fit a western beauty ideal. They were usually thin with long flowing hair, and dressed in midriff-baring costumes that sparkled and shone. Dance student, Masha Archer began taking classes within this climate of female sexual reclamation, but objected to the belly dancing bodies that other feminists embraced. From Archer's perspective, to be hired, the American belly dancer had to meet a Western beauty ideal and, as such, was objectified for her looks rather than appreciated for her dancing ability (Frascella 2003). Archer objected to this presumably sexualized belly dancer, a distinctly Orientalist discourse. But, in challenging this spatial discourse, she produced another imagined geography, that of the primitive Orient.

The West has constructed an imaginative geography of tribal people as not governed by the rational need to control their bodies. Instead, the dances of primitivized others are often characterized for their bodily mastery, not their artistry, or they are described in terms of their pelvic movements, signifying an underlying sexuality (Kealiinohomoku 1969). Reading the work of Kealiinohomoku, it is possible to understand how these sorts of essentializing narratives about the primitive other create a constitutive outside to proper western dance. Embedded within these textual representations of primitive dance is the prevailing message that the other form of dance is not white and that white people's dances by contrast are artistic and refined. Discourses that primitivize others also frequently sexualize them. This imagined sexuality, however is not the controlled, moralistic sexuality of the West. It is, rather, constructed as something more natural (Brooks 1993). Because primitives are seen as closer to, and therefore more connected to nature, they cannot help their sexuality. At the same time, they do not attempt to control it, and it oozes out in their cultural practices, especially their dances. In this way, the dances of primitivized others get coded in a way that is highly sexual (Martin 1998). Using this trope of the naturally sexual Oriental, Archer re-worked the dance, reinscribing it onto more natural female bodies. Archer's dance project was one of social consciousness, as she sought to downplay what she translated as a heightened objectification of cabaret belly dancers. Archer's project, however, resorted to more "traditionally rooted modes of negotiating nature and the body" (Pitts-Taylor 2003).

Archer took dance classes for only a short time before breaking off to form a dance troupe of her own. In the first, comprehensive popular work on Tribal dance, the *Tribal Bible,* Carolena Nericcio describes Archer as "an artist who happened to dance for awhile" (Djoumahna 2003, 18). According to the *Tribal Bible* author Kajira Djoumahna, because Archer had studied for only a short time, she had little foundation in choreography and dance. So she drew more on her artistic background than on dance practice to redesign everything about belly dance, from the music to the movements and the costumes. For example, Archer replaced the glamorous cabaret style top, which she thought exposed too much of a dancer's breasts with a coined bra that was to be worn *over* a choli—the cropped, short sleeved, top worn under Indian saris. Instead of slit skirts, which revealed a dancer's legs, Archer dressed her troupe in wide, loose pantaloons, gathered at the ankle and waist. Additionally, dancers wore a fringed shawl tied around the hips and over her pantaloons. Hair too was covered. Archer designed a sort of turban that swathed the head and thus made it impossible to determine the length or color of a dancer's hair (Djoumahna 2003; Frascella 2003).

In terms of movement, Archer sought to remove *looser* movements that she believed unnecessarily sexualized the body. In the 1970s, female choreographers were moving away from the idea of the female on display and were redefining the female dancing body as *geometrical* or *architectural,* as a mechanical body devoid of sex, with dances that usually concentrated movement away from the *sexual* pelvis (Goldberg 1997). This signification of the desexualized body as uplifted and controlled (and more masculine) pulled directly from Victorian discourses about the proper rational body, one that signifies its propriety through controlled, rigid movements (Buonaventura 1989). While it was not possible for Archer to eliminate pelvic moves from a torso-based dance, nor would she considering that she was drawing off of feminist tropes about naturally female movements, she did train her dancers to keep their torsos more uplifted and their movements smaller and more *controlled* (Djoumahna 2003). For Archer, adding architecture through a properly rigid torso signified the dancer's power and control of, rather than submission to, the audience's gaze (Frascella 2003). It reproduced notions of the structured, de-sexualized body by adopting rationalized and masculinized postures, even while executing movements that were distinctly gendered female.

Floorwork, too, was problematized by Archer. Once done in the cabarets of Cairo, Istanbul and Lebanon, floor routines were also performed by American dancers. During a typical cabaret show, a dancer would balance a prop such as a cane, tray, or candelabra while lying or kneeling on the floor and executing a series of hip, ribcage and torso movements. These performances were meant to signal the dancer's skill and control. Archer, however, completely removed floorwork from her repertoire because she believed that it allowed audiences to look down upon her dancers. Keeping the dancer on her feet was said to retain her position of equal power to her audiences (Djoumahna 2003; Frascella 2003).

Archer also reformed the dance format in order to eliminate star dancers. She regularly attended restaurant and nightclub performances but was remonstrative of what she called the *challenge-style*, referring to the solo nature of the performances and the way in which each dancer seemingly tried to out-perform the others. To stop any perceived competitiveness between dancers, Archer required her students to work together as a group. Archer did not choreograph, nor did she count. Instead she encouraged her students to move artistically with the music. To work together, they had to look at and work with one another rather than the audience, enforcing cooperation between dancers and fostering sort of distance between the dancer and the viewer. If the dancer depended upon her *tribe* in order to perform, then she then could not care about the audience or how she is rated by that audience (Djoumahna 2003).

Archer's dancers, in their *harem* pants and turbans, performing small, controlled hip sways and lifted chest circles, articulated a purposefully ethnic look with an American sense of power. Archer replaced the individual with the tribe, loose movements with controlled, and revealing costumes with tribal garb. In each case, she translated images of the East through primitivizing discourses from the West. She pulled from pictures of the Orient, performances by cabaret dancers, and embodied discourses about proper movements to create a new, dancing body; one that refused objectification and sexualization but which did so through performing a tribalized and fictionalized outside other.

In 1987, Archer moved from California to New York to pursue what became a successful career in jewelry and clothing design. In the resulting absence, Carolena Nericcio, a student of Archer's from the age of fourteen, decided to found her own troupe. According to published interviews, when Nericcio first began teaching, she thought what she was doing was belly dance. The more she researched the dance as part of her role as instructor, the more she realized that Archer's style was fantastical. Rather than feel a need to study traditional belly dance as her contemporaries were doing, Nericcio took a different tack. She used the opportunity to relieve herself of the need to preserve any sort of authentic dance practice, and began to build upon the fantasy base (Djoumahna 2003; Frascella 2003).

In *Tribal Bible*, Nericcio is quoted as saying she always viewed Archer as a powerful person who taught her that women do not have to be "quiet, pretty and feminine" and that "power and presence are more important than being pretty" (Djoumahna 2003, 15). Nericcio has attempted to convey that same sense of power, defined as inherent in the natural, female body, to her own troupe, as evidenced by this statement in an instructional DVD produced and popularly distributed by Barnes & Noble Books.

How did we go from honoring the natural shape and substance of a woman's body to seeing it as something imperfect? Nature created us perfectly—an incredible system of nerves, muscle, bone, and blood, all interwoven in such a way that an impulse from the brain can make a hip bounce or an eyelash flutter. The modern culture in which we live has no interest in the original perfection of the body. We seem to have lost our respect for nature and its infinite wisdom of balance (Nericcio 2004).

For Nericcio, performing a fantasized dance of the East allows for the return to a supposedly balanced, female body, a body that has been lost to the modern, western world. This othering trope, of a more naturalized East that respects bodily wisdom, carries through ATS and has been passed along into ITS.

In addition to carrying forward the discourse of a more primitive, Arab other, Nericcio also retained the tribal feel, while adding new elements to Archer's basic ethnic design. For example, Nericcio added a 10-yard skirt and a fabric hip belt made with earth-toned dyes and adorned with large yarn tassels like those used to decorate camels and horses. To provide more space for displaying the large North African, Afghanistani and Pakistani jewelry collections of her dancers, she increased the size of the turban (Djoumahna 2003; Frascella 2003). She further adapted the movements and added subtle cues to help dancers lead and follow one another (see figure 6.1).

Figure 6.1.   Belly Dancers in Procession
Photographer: Georgia Connover

Nericcio also continued the process of rationalizing the dance. Cabaret movements usually did not have names. Nericcio started naming the movements and combinations, using fantastical terms such as the Arabic hip twist, the Gawazee (after pre-1920s Egyptian dancers) and the Basic Egyptian. She also added a 4/4 count (Nericcio n.d.; Stants 2006), a count which did not fit much of the classical music with its 1/4 tones, syncopated beats and unfamiliar 9/8, 7/8 and other such rhythms. In hindsight, Nericcio describes the process as one of, "diluting the cabaret movement to make it broader and a lot more repetitive" (Djoumahna 2003, 26). It was also, however, a process of formalizing, and rationalizing, the dance, of creating a new form that discursively removed it from its primitive, more natural, less architectural roots.

Interestingly, under Nericcio, body modifications become symbolic of the dance. The articulation of body art and dance results from and is constitutive of the non-normative discourses embedded within the style. When she started teaching, Nericcio did not advertise; all promotion was word-of-mouth. Her classes attracted mostly people from the alternative scene in San Francisco, people who were interested in belly dance but who did not fit the look of a belly dancer (Djoumahna 2003; Nericcio 2007). According to Nericcio, "they could have any type of body type, or any hairstyle. We've had hairstyles and body types and piercings of all kinds" (Djoumahna 2003, 19). Bailee, a Tribal Style dancer extensively trained in ATS, is heavily tattooed and has stretched lobes and multiple ear piercings. She explains that Nericcio and the women who followed her all had body modifications.

> Carolena was tattooed when she started doing it already. . . . Paulette from Gypsy Caravan was in a punk rock band. Married a guy from a punk rock band . . . was a real alternative person. Jill Parker was heavily tattooed from the get go. So I think that, the royalty of ATS—which tribal fusion grew out of—were these women who, most of them, were already alternative. That's how they ended up there (Interview, June 2007).

Nericcio's troupe started performing at tattoo shows and conventions and became well known within the tattoo community. While body art was not part of the tribal project under Archer, it was the case that the tattoos showed well in the costumes and could be constructed to complement the dance while also signifying alterity, and have consequently become part of the dance aesthetic. Tattoos often cover the entire side of a dancer's torso, stretching down below her hip line and up across her shoulder; holes in the earlobes may be stretched to accommodate clunky earrings carved from bone or wood. In any case, the tattoo and piercing is taken further than is considered normative (see figure 6.2).

To create a dancing body that challenged modern expectations for a woman's perfect, and objectified, physique, Nericcio and her dancers articulated imaginative geographies of tribal peoples in the Middle East and North Africa with tattooed, pierced, and rigidly controlled Western bodies. Reinscribing primitive, natural, ethnic bodies onto their own non-normative bodies made it possible to create a dancing body that is naturally sexual, but not eroticized, and to thereby reject what

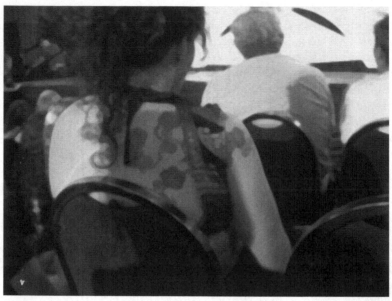

Figure 6.2. Tattoos on Belly Dancer
Photographer: Georgia Connover

they saw as artificial displays of beauty. Body modifications furthered this challenge by marking these dancers bodies as not simply non-normative, but distinctly and purposefully deviant.

When asked to describe what makes ATS different from other genres of belly dance, Nericcio and many dancers with whom I spoke said it is as much about the attitude of power and subversiveness as it is about the aesthetic presentation (Nericcio 2007). They also widely cited a different, but related trope: the family-like loyalty of the female tribe. The focus of the dance, they said, is each other and not the audience. This is largely claimed to stem from the improvisational format of both ATS and ITS. The dances are not choreographed even though the dancers appear to move as if they are one. Prior to a performance, dancers spend hours practicing sequences and formations in addition to subtle bodily cues hidden within those sequences and formations. Using a sort of call-and-response format, the dancer who happens into the lead position in any given formation, uses the rehearsed cues to notify the rest of the group what to do next. No one performer stays in the lead. Rather, the group alternates who leads and who must follow. The result is a dynamic performance that is so seamless it is unlikely the audience realizes what it is watching is not choreographed. It is also a performance in which no one woman controls the outcome. Rather everyone shares that privilege and responsibility. It is this practice that is embodied in the dance and signified by the referent *tribal*.

The tribal nomenclature is one that had begun to circulate to describe Archer and Nericcio's unusual form of belly dance. The term *California Tribal* was first used derisively by some cabaret dancers to critique its tribal appearance and reliance on a primitive, constitutive other (Morocco 1985). The name stuck, however, and was taken up by tribal dancers who reinscribed it to suggest an ideal of a distinctly female, group solidarity against an objectifying public. Its use discursively linked female bonding and strength with the clan structure of a tribe. In so doing, it romanticized what it means to be a female living a tribal lifestyle. It also determined who could properly perform as a tribe. Women, and particularly transgressive, Caucasian women were constructed as having the most appropriate bodies for performing these Orientalist ideas.

As Nericcio's dance became more formalized and popular, it came to be called American Tribal Style Bellydance [*sic*]. In using this phrasing, dancers incorporated the contested *tribal* terminology with the word *American* to explain the dance's provenance. The name is putatively to signify the dance's lineage. Although what they do differs significantly from belly dance, tribal dancers today continue to use this nomenclature because it signifies not a traditional dance of Southwest Asia, but they argue, an American creation, just as the name belly dance is. And for her performance group, Nericcio chose the now iconic name, *FatChanceBellyDance*. Her explanation for the name resonates with all of the problematic discourses of gender, sexuality, and objectivity embedded within the ATS genre.

> There's that story about when I (Nericcio) was young and dumb, I would tell men I was a belly dancer and they would ask for a "private" show. I would think *Fat Chance*! I told my friend Jim Murdoch, who's a clown, with a rather subtle, outgoing sense of humor, and he said, *Oh, Fat Chance Belly Dance*! I just knew I wanted it! (Djoumahna 2003,18)

Even today, the shortened *FatChance* is synonymous with ATS and with power, natural sensuality and "the strength and beauty of women" (Atkin 2006). Markedly, both Arabs and men were, and still are, absent from ATS and its distinctly gendered construction.

FROM CELEBRATING THE NATURAL FEMININE TO VALORIZING FEMALE INNOVATION

The ATS project of empowering dancers through de-sexualizing the dance is one that has carried forward into what can loosely be called Improvisational Tribal Style dance. Despite appearances to the contrary, ITS dancers generally have some grounding in ATS and may still perform American Tribal Style movements. It is also possible to see ATS borrowing elements from ITS. ITS is difficult to describe as it is a style that purposefully defies categorization and has many variants and offshoots, all which fall under the collective moniker *tribal* to acknowledge the ATS lineage. Tribal Style dancers emerged out of ATS troupes, but pushed the theme of innovation further. Following this modernist trope, Tribal dancers have placed themselves on the cutting edge of performance and continuously pull from developments in dance and art to inspire new fusion performances, incorporating more modern elements such as industrial music, leather costume pieces, pop and locking moves, and 1920s flapper-inspired costuming into the mix. Many groups continue to use the group improvisational format. Others, however, perform choreographies or semi-structured dances and some individuals have established themselves as solo artists (see figure 6.3). What binds this style, what gives it its identity, then, is not its look, or the music, or the movements, although tribal dancers do influence one another's aesthetic creating a loosely cohesive look. Instead, what defines this genre is its fluidity. Tribal dance is a project of exploring new territory, of innovating, and of drawing from the rich world of art that is increasingly made available through mediated texts.

Improvisational Tribal Style, which was the particular focus of my fieldwork, is a group improvisational format that articulates the trope of group solidarity and tribalness with more contemporary discourses about innovation and change. Cabaret styles of belly dance are not traditional in the sense that this, or any cultural object, can be a historically stable creation (Bhabha 1994). Indeed, cabaret "is a melting pot of expressive Oriental dance" that draws from Flamenco, classical Indian dance,

Figure 6.3.   Belly Dancing Solo
Photographer: Georgia Connover

Persian dances and from the United States (Sharif 2004, 84). Dancers in Southwest Asia, where the dance originates, like those in the United States, continue to explore and fuse new movements, musical styles and costuming elements into their dances, and often have their own dance lineages, which are reflected in their personal styles. Despite stylistic differences between places and dancers, there do seem to be trends, which like fashion come in and out of style.

Despite this fluidity, tribal dancers largely characterize cabaret forms in monolithic terms. Kealiinohomoku (1969) was one of the first anthropologists to recognize the way that ethnic dance and discourses about ethnicity and primitivity often get collapsed onto one another. As such, the dances of ethnic Others are not understood to be complex, nuanced, and evolving, but rather are represented as essentialized and stuck in an imaginary past. Tribal dancers repeat this trope, recognizing cabaret dance as rich in tradition, but rooted to its past. Once dancer I interviewed even took issue with the *authenticity snobs*, a term I also heard in casual conversation. In the interview, Cloe said that tribal dancers do not feel disdain for more traditional forms. Rather, they have the utmost respect for anyone who studies a particular style and "really does the research and is following the way it is done over there, then it is great in a way as preservation. I am fine with that, as long as they also respect that it is important to also have innovation" (Interview, June 2007). All the dancers I interviewed reiterated this innovative/rooted binary, telling stories about respect for preserving a traditional past while also disparaging what they see as the attitude that the dance must remain fixed in time. "I don't care much for the authenticity snobs because, one, often they aren't as authentic as they think they are and, two, they are really using it as a crutch to feel self-important" (Interview, June 2007). The theme of innovation is a reflexive project of, according to Cloe, crossing boundaries and those cabaret dancers who do not appreciate innovation, in contrast, remain mired in a traditional and bounded past.

The Orient has historically been constructed in such a way as to suggest that not only is it primitive, but it is stuck in its primitivity, suggesting Orientals are incapable of change. "It shares with magic and with mythology the self-containing, self-reinforcing character of a closed system, in which objects are what they are *because* what they are, for once, for all time, for ontological reasons that no empirical material can either dislodge or alter" (Said 1978, 70). The ITS narrative of the traditional Oriental dancer abandons the overtly primitivized ATS other, only to replace it with an Other that is still rooted in a closed system. Through this process, the Other is dehistoricized, depoliticized and fixed in time and space (Bhabha 1994).

In contrast to this discursively fixed Other, as it is inscribed onto the body of Caucasian cabaret belly dancers, ITS dancers perform their modernity by constantly striving to innovate, by borrowing from other genres. For example, dancers clothe themselves in costumes that pull elements from belly dance, such as bared midriffs and belts and ties to embellish the hips, but their costumes may also contain punk, gothic (see figure 6.4) and/or street elements.

Figure 6.4. Goth/Punk Style Belly Dancing Dress
Photographer: Georgia Connover

Some ITS styles are even self-described as gothic, or urban, or Asian fusion. Props may include elongated, Thai "claws" that fit over the tips of the dancer's fingers, Chinese fans, fire poi balls, or fabric bat wings. The music borrows frequently from rock and heavy metal, industrial, Bollywood, Aboriginal, Japanese kabuki, steam punk, jug band and Bedouin musical styles. Adornments may include burnished, *kuchi* jewelry from Afghanistan or Pakistan, fingerless gloves, fishnet arm covers, and elaborately decorated headdresses with shells, jewels, feathers, and Geisha-like hair sticks (figure 6.5).

Rather than skirts, dancers often wear pants with flares. Or costumes may be fashioned after Kimonos, with tied fabric belts and Asian inspired prints. Or, dancers may wear hooded, cropped sweatshirts, with short skirts layered over leggings, resembling styles from hip hop or crew dancers. Or costumes may borrow feathered head bands, fringed costumes and musical stylings from the roaring 1920s. With their fusion of modern and primitive, foreign and familiar, distant and near, dancers embody modern ideas about creativity as a signifier of modernity.

Figure 6.5.   Complex Hairstyle on Belly Dancer
Photographer: Georgia Connover

This last point is additionally significant because it reproduces a western trope about progress that has, embedded within it, a hidden power imbalance regarding who deserves credit for knowledge production (Brush and Stanbinsky 1996). As the Oriental other is increasingly erased from view, so is that Other's ownership of his dance. The American lineage of Tribal Style dance is passed along from one dancer to another, and was brought up in article after article that I read. The dancers I interviewed all spoke of their dance instructors, and those instructor's instructors. Moves, too, were credited. Whenever a new move or combination was taught at any of the workshops I attended, the woman or troupe that created and named that movement was acknowledged. The tribal dancer, in contrast to the ever more invisible Other, continuously celebrates the creativity that modernity permits, while making western ownership of the dance visible. By decontextualizing and stabilizing the absent identity of the Oriental other, the ITS dancer permanently provides an invisible, but fixed constitutive outside from which to construct her own, progressively modern dance identity. Moreover, she further invests herself and divests that Other from creative ownership of the dance itself.

ITS AND IT'S RE-SEXUALIZED OTHER

In addition to perpetuating the erasure of Arab bodies from belly dance, ITS dancers are producing a new, overtly sexual belly dancer. This can be seen in the movements and costumes, and in the venues in which tribal dancers may perform. Because they reject traditional forms of dance, tribal dancers do not tend to perform in more traditional venues such as restaurants or hookah lounges, which are blatantly ethnic. Indeed, the ITS dancers I interviewed were unsure that they would be warmly received in these spaces:

> (In the venues in which ITS dancers perform) you aren't going to find those Middle Eastern men of high status . . . it (Tribal Style dance) will bother them. It is probably the younger generation of guys that is hanging out, you know. And they don't care; if you are wearing fishnet, they are like cool. If they happen to hear something with a Middle Eastern beat, they are like, what's that? Opposed to the men that are more established, that are more traditional. They wouldn't be in that venue. (Eva, Interview, June 2007)

Like cabaret dancers, ITS dancers do perform at street fairs and community festivals, but they also dance in what Eva referred to as less "traditional" and "glamorous" spaces, like nightclubs and bars, places where cabaret dancers do not generally perform. According to Eva, for a cabaret dancer to perform in a club or bar, "it would have to be a high-class bar . . . not like we do" (Interview, June 2007).

In contrast to the feminist cabaret and the ATS dancers who attempted to recast belly dance as a non-sexual, folk dance or as a dance that embraces a woman's sensual, but not sexual, self, some ITS dancers are now performing in venues that are openly sexual. For example, I watched one performance during the intermission of a festival featuring one-act plays that focus on or include lesbian, bi-sexual, and transgendered actors and themes. I have also watched many ITS performances that were followed by a drag or burlesque act, or I have seen tribal styles dancers using sexually suggestive signifiers such as crawling on the stage, making beckoning gestures toward the audience, and wearing corsets or costuming associated with the Cancan (a dance that was designed to titillate the audience by providing glimpses of the dancer's legs and crotch while she high kicks). The group I followed danced at venues that included not only late-night clubs, but also circus-sideshow themed performances and, critically here, drag shows and fetish balls focused on bondage and other sexually deviant practices.

The re-connection of sexuality and belly dance, a connection that feminists and ATS dancers attempted to sever, is embedded in modern narratives about the sexually liberated woman. This new version of the sexually liberated, belly dancing woman, however, is made possible through the rational, refined, and masculine characteristics of Tribal Style dance. During one interview, Dahlia said that it is precisely because ITS is so grounded and powerful that a troupe can push the boundaries constructed between belly dance and sexuality. In several of the interviews, dancers said they had eliminated the flirty, bouncy, and more feminized movements of cabaret dance and replaced them with movements meant to perform strength and control. "All the (tribal) women look so strong and so like, we are going to kick your ass if you even come near us" (Interview, June 2007). "Just the look of ATS," said Cloe, "is very grounded and powerful and like, you know, you mess with me and I will beat you up, powerful" (Interview, June 2007).

With Enlightenment thinking came a valorization of rationalism, which was further equated with masculinity, modernity and culture. The constitutive other to this rational male was the natural female who, like the primitive, could not help nor escape her irrationality (Foucault 1978; Bell and Valentine 1995; Wolff 1997). Modern narratives that link naturalness to femininity may materially allow women to reclaim their bodies, but they discursively reproduce a hegemonic patriarchal system that valorizes the male as cultured and rational and the female as other (Haraway 1991; Butler 2006). Women, and especially belly dancing women, who act and dance like women are constructed as being unable escape their subjectivity and their fixed status as desired objects. In contrast, by reinscribing masculinity onto their bodies, tribal dancers perform an Enlightenment discourse that men are in control of their sexuality and how that sexuality is consumed (Bell and Valentine 1995). This discursive reproduction of a rational-male/natural-female binary was repeated in the literature and is a theme I heard discussed several times between dancers. This paring served to credit the original ATS dancers for their ability to eliminate the overt, objectifying sexuality inherent to Oriental dance, thereby enabling later tribal dancers to re-introduce a more controlled, challenging and thus libratory form of sexuality.

> When FatChance came out, that was in the seventies or the eighties when women were trying to say we are not sexual objects, you know, and now we kind of are. We are reverting a little bit I think. But the women are a lot stronger in their sense now . . . but now I think they (FatChance) did that for us. They proved that women were not just sexual objects so now we can be safe and put it out there. (Interview, June 2007)

The dancers in the troupe I interviewed all said they feel as if they do not have to deny their sexuality and, in contrast to the cabaret world where the sexuality is imposed upon women through the male gaze, they can reclaim their sexuality and publicly celebrate it. By eliminating more primitive and objectifying forms of sexuality, and by adding signifiers of strength and control to the dance, the problematized, objectified sexuality has been discursively stripped out, allowing dancers to add a new, overt sexuality back in—when and where they choose.

EXIT STAGE LEFT

Throughout the history of belly dance in the United States, the Arab Other has been constructed as a way to produce a refined, modern, rational American body.

Early western constructions of belly dance relied on the trope of the exotic, sexualized other and, in so doing, placed belly dance as a dance of the Orient. When belly dancers first performed in the United States, at the 1893 Chicago Worlds Fair, they were eroticized for their curving bodily movements and exotic dress. Working class entertainers wishing to mock bourgeois hypocrisy, seized onto the Arab images, which the upper classes consumed vociferously but claimed to study academically, and translated them to highlight their vulgarity (Salem 1995). In the 1960s and 1970s era of reclaimed female sexuality, feminists re-imagined belly dance as a way to celebrate women's powers.

The tribal style dance project, which emerged from this context, is steeped in Orientalist power relations. It is a reflexive response to a dance hierarchy that sets western dance forms and western beauty ideals above the dances and bodies of outside Others. Contrary to their titles, ATS and ITS bellydance depart dramatically from *belly dance*, sometimes bearing very little resemblance to the form that serves as a foundation. The name is meant, instead, to signify a blending of aesthetics from the East and the West and to challenge the centering of contemporary dance politics in the West.

Tribal style is consciously and admittedly pure fantasy. Everything about a tribal style performance is mélange, an incoherent coming together of Western imaginaries with sounds, costumes, and movements from Persian, Indian, and Arab and other "primitive" cultural contexts, and that are fused onto an inescapably marked Western body (Bell and Valentine 1995). ATS and ITS dancers articulate the spatial, the social and the artistic in order to purposefully write a challenge to power-laden, uneven constructions that valorize the idealized, thin, beautiful, and objectified female body. Yet Tribal Style dancers perform their transgressiveness by reproducing an imagined geography wherein the Arab body vanishes, and an Orientalist body re-emerges. In this way, Tribal Style dance remains mired in geopolitical constructions of a primitive and feminized Oriental other.

Borrowed elements are not assembled in a "free-wheeling anything goes eclecticism or hyperrelativism" that serves only to challenge the complexity of modern society (Soja 1996, 81). What is borrowed and how those borrowings are translated into a scripted whole is embedded in a complex, power-laden cultural milieu. Part and parcel in this milieu is a powerful but imaginative geography that divides the world into a West and rest binary (Said 1978). If studies of cultural geography help to build awareness of taken-for-granted values, attitudes, and behaviors, then studying the taken-for-granted values embedded within dance practices—especially forms such as ATS and ITS which are premised on borrowing from other cultural worlds to challenge normative values at home—will help to make sense of contemporary imaginative geographies which filter what is borrowed, how it is borrowed, and how it is performed (Desmond 1997). Such work can also provide insights into popular tropes that continue to produce imaginative and deeply politicized geographies of the world (Derrida 1974; Dittmer 2010).

The dancers join hands and bow, as a troupe, before they exit together. Brightly colored baskets and mirrored drums litter the now empty stage. As the last bars of music fade into the breeze, a dancer calls out to the audience with a loud ululation. The cry seems to recall an Oriental Other, even as that Other disappears from view.

NOTE

1. Dancer's names are pseudonyms.

7

Mimetic Moves

Dance and Learning to Learn in Northwest Alaska

Matthew Kurtz

Kotzebue is an Iñupiaq Eskimo community on the arctic coast of Alaska.[1] In 1946, it became the first "Eskimo village" in the Arctic to be marketed by the airlines as a tourist destination, an arrangement that continued until 2004. In the absence of a road system, the community is the hub of an air taxi network serving the Northwest Arctic Borough, which covers an area larger than Maine or Scotland. Nearly half of the borough's residents live in Kotzebue, whose population was tallied at 3,201 people in the last census (U.S. Census 2010). The majority claim Iñupiaq Eskimo heritage, the culture indigenous to northwest Alaska. The public sector and the world's largest zinc mine are the major employers in the area. Since paid employment is not abundant, hunting and fishing often put food on the table. Heavy goods and fuel are barged into Kotzebue during the three months when the sea is ice-free, at the same time that 565,000 tons of zinc ore are shipped out from a port to the north.[2] The airport at the south end of town is therefore a busy one. It accommodates the air taxi network, the cargo planes that bring groceries into the region, and the Boeing 737 passenger jets whose landings mark the daily rhythms of life in Kotzebue.

It was on one such jet, in an afternoon in September 1998, that I made my first arrival in the community. I was on a pre-packaged three-day tour of northwest Alaska, following an itinerary that had been used for over fifty years. The package featured an Iñupiaq dance performance at the end of the day. I was especially looking forward to the Iñupiaq dance: I had taken training in modern dance and choreography a decade earlier (along with some preparatory ballet and jazz dance classes) and on this September day, I idly wondered to what extent Iñupiaq dance would show itself to be a fundamentally different medium. Such thoughts were interrupted as I joined eleven other tourists in the airline building at the south end of town—"not a bad number for the end of the season," we were told. Two were from Austria and the rest, retirees from the lower forty-eight states. I was the only tourist from Alaska. A bus carried us two short blocks to a white tent near the beach. Inside, we took our seats on folding metal chairs. Three teenagers then began to tell us about items on a table: rope made of seal skin, masks from whalebone, and furs. Two of our speakers, wearing locally made kuspuks or dresses, pronounced their Iñupiaq names. The third said his English name was Charlie.[3] He joked about mosquitoes in town, then watched us all with a smile while saying that his favorite food was "just the normal stuff"—whale fat, seal, pizza, and hamburgers. I think we all laughed.

In this chapter, I want to examine the mimetic performance of Inupiaq dances and the dance of mimetic performances in northwest Alaska. Walter Benjamin once defined mimesis as "the gift of producing similarities—for example, in dances, whose oldest function this was—and therefore also the gift of recognizing them" (1978, 333). He suggested that, among all creatures, humans had the highest capacity for mimesis. There it had led to the realization that, since the original action had been constructed, it could also be re-constructed. Benjamin's critical insight, however, was to recognize that this gift of seeing resemblances had itself been re-constructed, changing over time and space. Writing in 1933, he argued that mimesis had a history, that it was a socially constructed learning technique: it was the nature that cultures used, in different ways, to produce second-nature (Taussig 1993). In what follows, I hope to give flesh to Benjamin's insight, to better understand the poignancy of the Iñupiaq dance performances and the extent to which they may stand as figures for a rather different learning formation in northwest Alaska.

Empirically, I will focus on the practices through which dance performances and the business of dance have been produced as exhibitions in northwest Alaska. This will help to illustrate some significant differences between three conceptual configurations that I introduce in the analysis:

1) exhibitions of cultural practice;
2) cultural practices of exhibition; and
3) enactments of calculable space.

Methodologically, I use the first configuration in the next section. It forms the framework with which I outline the social and spatial contexts in which Iñupiaq dances were performed in recent decades. I use the second and third conceptual formations in the chapter's subsequent sections, and they bear an affinity with the non-representational theories of Nigel Thrift in geography. Like Benjamin, Thrift has argued that people are "imitative animals," that "human beings subconsciously mirror each other's actions in a constant iterative ballet of not-quite duplication" (2008, 85–86). Moreover, in his early installations of non-representational theory, Thrift chose to focus on dance for his main illustrations (1997, 2000).[4] Indeed, since then, studies of dance in geography often launch from citations and critiques of Thrift's 1997 essay (e.g., Nash 2000; Revill 2004; Lorimer 2005; Cresswell 2006b; McCormack 2008).

Nonetheless, my reasons for citing Thrift's work are theoretical rather than topical. My principal argument is methodological in nature. I suggest that, to learn about dance in different contexts, and to do so in progressive ways, geographers may need to "learn to learn from below" (Spivak 2008). This may require the extension of our methodological registers, to say the least, so as not to foreclose our analytical and pedagogic practices. In this chapter, my methodological devices—the three conceptual formations above—are drawn from Thrift's work. We share an interest in practice, conceived as performative presentations and as mutable concatenations of corporeal routine and technology that are just stable enough to apparently reproduce themselves (Thrift 2007). Like Thrift, I am persuaded by arguments in contemporary social theory, like those of Benjamin, that "practices constitute our sense of the real" (Thrift 1996, 7). Thus the chapter may resemble Thrift's non-representational theory in its animations.

Nonetheless, similarities come with differences. I believe two are notable. First, I hope to add more historiographic sensitivity to Thrift's experimental forms of writing. Second, by playing at the northern margin of North America, my work reaches further afield than Thrift has tended to look in his explorations of the transmutations of experience within capitalism. That said, my aim is like that of Colls (2012) in relation to non-representational theory: I do not wish to repeat a disavowal of Thrift's work, still less to endorse it by imitation, but rather "to embrace a mode of generous critique that involves 'an openness to others that not only precedes and establishes communal relations but constitutes the self as open to otherness'" (Diprose 2002, 4).

The rest of the chapter is delivered in four sections. The first sketches the start of packaged tourism and the exhibition of cultural practices in northwest Alaska after 1945. The years marked a shift in management, from control by outside operators into the hands of the local community. Elsewhere I have analyzed the significance of more self-determination in the tour's management (Kurtz 2010). Here, my purpose is to contextualize the dance performance through a historical account of the tour and its participants. The next section explores two distinct cultural practices of exhibition. I suggest that Iñupiaq dancers may have been engaging in cultural practices of exhibition in the past—that is, conducting a playful exercise in mimesis—whereas many observers clearly fashioned the dances as the converse: an artful exhibition of cultural practices. However, to draw this contrast may overstate differences between the epistemologies and pedagogies of Iñupiaq performers and those of their metropolitan audience. Accordingly, I try to temper the contrast in the third section, which explores the business of dance in Kotzebue. I argue that its practices of accounting are also mimetic performances, practices that helped some residents become calculating subjects working on behalf of their community. In the fourth section, I discuss the hazards of non-representational theory, and I suggest that tracing the ways in which past practices are recuperated and transformed in more distant sites may offer a means to build more suturing pedagogies. I revisit Charlie's performance in the conclusion.

EXHIBITIONS OF CULTURAL PRACTICE:
TOURISM IN KOTZEBUE

In May 1946, the Seattle Times ran a headline to announce that "the first planeload of tourists ever to visit the Bering Coast" had arrived in Nome, Alaska. A group from Alaska's largest city had chartered a plane and "took part in the wild stomping dances the Eskimos put on for them" in Nome. With unconcealed conceit, the Anchorage Daily Times reported that a "program of spectator sports" was arranged, "with the Anchorage people the spectators and the Eskimos indulging in strenuous exercise." The Iñupiaq dances had served as an exhibit, it seems, for the metropolitan audience to observe. A more sedate item in the Nome Nugget indicated that the group landed briefly in Kotzebue on their trip back to Anchorage.

The following week, Wien Airlines (a regional carrier based in Fairbanks) announced a new Excursion Tour Department under the direction of Charles West, a travel agent and former military pilot. For $50, customers could purchase an "Arctic Circle Flight" on a scheduled flight to one of the various villages that Wien served in northern Alaska, returning on the same day.[5] West soon convinced his employers to offer a weekend trip for "flightseeing Alaska," to depart on June 9, 1946. Having advertised that "Refreshing Pepsi-Cola" would be served in flight, West left the Fairbanks airport with ten passengers bound for Kotzebue, Alaska. There, as he recalled, "Our small band walked through the village and down the beach. We saw fish drying on the racks, admired sled dogs tied to their primitive kennels, studied a Beluga whale dragged up on shore. For visitors from interior Alaska who had never seen how the coastal peoples lived, it was a fascinating experience" (West 1985, 33). The Sunday excursions continued through the summer as the budding entrepreneur promoted the trip on the radio. "One of my prime spots for posting notices," he noted, "was in construction-site latrines." In 1946, the U.S. military was building up its bases in Alaska, and Fairbanks "overflowed with thousands of construction workers [with] time to spare" (West 1985, 34).

A boomtown it was. The census would soon show Fairbanks had tripled its population over the decade, with more than 18,000 people by 1950. Anchorage would see an eight-fold increase, with 31,000 civilians by the end of the decade. Both had become the sites of major military bases during World War II and the Cold War. Before the war, Fairbanks had not been very distinct from Alaska's smaller communities like Nome (or even Kotzebue, with just 372 people) for any journalists who were familiar with larger cities like Seattle. But after the war, with thousands of people and ongoing construction, this was no longer the case. Fairbanks and Anchorage had become the heart of what would be called 'urban Alaska' (predominantly white colonial metropoles) while, on the other side of a racialized divide, the smaller indigenous communities would soon be called 'rural Alaska' (Kurtz 2006). There, at the other end of Wien Airlines' excursion, the changes in Kotzebue wrought be military construction would have also been visible to those ten tourists in 1946. The Civilian Aeronautics Administration had already built communication towers at the north end of town, and the Army had improved the airfield, extending Kotebue's landing strip to 1,800 feet.

These changes solidified a number of trends that had begun to mark the settlement as the major modern transportation hub for Alaska's northwest region. Archaeological excavations begun during the war found sites around Kotzebue that had been occupied six hundred years ago. Oral histories report that, in the early 1800s, almost two hundred people lived in the immediate vicinity of Kotzebue (called Qikiktagruk), so that the combined communities in that locale constituted what was perhaps "the richest and most powerful village in Northwest Alaska" (Burch 1998, 204; VanStone 1955). Before the first Europeans had stepped foot in the region, an annual trade fair was taking place every summer at Sisualik, ten miles northwest of Qikiktagruk across the bay. Situated near the mouths of three major rivers, the fair brought a thousand people from northwest Alaska and across the Bering Strait together to engage in festivities and the business of trade. After the western arctic caribou herd was decimated in the 1880s, the site for trading moved from Sisualik, where sandbars prevented deep-water boats from visiting, to the shores around Qikiktagruk where coastal waters were deeper and where commercial whalers and other vessels were by then known to visit, trade, and recruit labor (Burch 1977). Once again, Qikiktagruk had become an international port of call and a powerful village in the region.

Thus when the first missionaries arrived in the region in 1897, they settled near Qikiktagruk. They named the place Kotzebue, after a German explorer who approached the area in 1816. With assistance from local leaders, the missionaries started Quaker church groups and schools in upriver villages (Burch 1975, 1994). The first permanent trade post was established a few years after. By 1910 the census recorded 193 people in Kotzebue. By 1950 it had increased to 623, mostly due to rural migration from a region whose overall population remained stable (U.S. Census 1913, 1952; Burch 1998). With the help of military contracts, Wien Airlines had established weekly service to Kotzebue by the war's end. Bush pilots then offered chartered service from Kotzebue to the smaller villages (Smith 1966). The importance of the trade fair and the exchange of indigenous goods were in decline, but Kotzebue had remained a central hub for long-distance travelers and for the movement of goods and people around the region.

By the summer of 1947, the enterprising pilot and tour manager at Wien Airlines had started his own business in Fairbanks: Arctic Alaska Travel Service. Before the summer started, West hired two young pilots, Celia Hunter and Virginia Hill. They had been weathered into Kotzebue while making a cargo delivery in February 1947 and had attended an Iñupiaq dance festival at the time. Their enthusiasm about sharing their experience helped to convince the entrepreneur to charter an idle cargo plane for a weekend trip to Kotzebue and Nome. Under the auspices of the travel service, Hunter and Hill conducted four tours that summer. Guests witnessed the display of local cultural practices as they rode in a skin-boat, participated in a blanket toss, and watched dances. The tours continued, and by the summer of 1950, Wien

Airlines had purchased a three-story structure on Kotzebue's shoreline—the Wien Roadhouse—for guest accommodations.[6]

Widespread advertising brought these developments into broader networks of circulation. By 1950, West had opened a branch office in Anchorage, placed ads in The Milepost, promoted the tour with cruise-ship companies and national airlines, and distributed information to others in the tourism business (West 1985). As a result, the tourists were no longer just construction workers from Fairbanks. In June 1950, for instance, Kotzebue's Mukluk Telegraph reported that all seven guests at the Wien Roadhouse were seeing Alaska for the first time (Joiner 1950). By 1954, the package tour to the arctic village had been the subject of illustrated, multi-page articles in Sunset and Travel magazines, as well as in the Seattle Times pictorial section.[7]

These promotions were accompanied by structural changes that standardized the tours. This too was lauded in travel magazine articles—the uniformity of "a pitcher and a wash basin" in every hotel room; the "planned" entertainment; the regularity of price for room and travel; and the comparability of things seen against expectations learned elsewhere. One travel writer noted that there were "no igloos . . . but almost everything else jibed: kayaks, oomiaks, fur-trimmed parkas" (Spring 1953). Yet a local journalist parodied such predictability (see textbox 7.1).

The author, Gene Joiner, was an independent bush pilot and the publisher-editor of an irregular, short-lived, and scurrilous newspaper in Kotzebue titled Mukluk Telegraph. The note was likely a parody of a press release by Wien Airlines, issued soon after taking over the ground operations. It illustrates how predictable the tour had become by 1951. The tour's standardization had allowed Joiner to narrate the experience from the perspective of an anonymous third person (yet another 'tourist'

TEXTBOX 7.1
"Arctic Expeditions for All" (Joiner 1951)

"Wien Alaska Airlines is offering the tourist an opportunity to explore, in comfort and luxury, the real home of the Eskimo, the land of the Midnight Sun. One can now travel over the land described by the adventurous explorers on the lecture platforms. Thanks to their generous government mail subsidies, Wiens have now been able to purchase modern airliners and . . . the airline-owned hotel, where planned entertainment such as skin boat rides, whale hunts, and full-dress Eskimo dances, are offered nightly for the modern explorer's enjoyment. Met at the plane by one of the airlines many friendly hostesses, the tourist is given a guided tour around the town, and an opportunity to meet bona fide Eskimos, to photograph a world visited only by the most rugged adventurers, ride in comfort in the airline bus, where less fortunate visitors have left bloody trails from their frozen feet. After leaving Kotzebue with a fresh, smartly uniformed crew, the airliners continue west to the furthermost western point in our hemisphere. . . . The memorable tour is then completed by a flight in the midnight sun back to Fairbanks, where he receives a Wien 'Arctic Circle Certificate' to prove to the folks back home that he has really crossed the Circle."

like myself), in contrast to the first-person narratives often used by earlier travel writers. If his historiographic performance worked well among his scandalous headlines, Joiner's classed, gendered, and racialized position also helped. As petit bourgeoisie, he was deriding what he saw as collusion between larger regional air carriers and the federal government with their "generous" subsidies. Referring to the tourist as "the Arctic explorer," his note played on the masculinity associated with exploration and its concerns about traveling "in comfort and luxury." And as a white, well-educated colonial, the local writer could make fun of the excesses of white metropolitan wealth—riding "where less fortunate visitors have left bloody trails from their frozen feet"—at the same time that he was lampooning the process of popularization that had opened such opportunities largely to white middle-class men and women— "Arctic Expeditions for All."

To paraphrase Walter Benjamin (1969), this process of popularization can be understood as the work of travel in an age of mechanical reproduction. In lieu of an incomparable journey to witness something unique, the experience of travel in the industrial age had turned into tourism: journeys designed for standardization and reproducibility.[8] In Kotzebue, this came with scheduled transit, the standardized fare served upon arrival (e.g., "Refreshing Pepsi-Cola"), a guided walk down the beach, a skin-boat ride (depending on weather), and a nightly "Eskimo dance." Indeed, the standardization set many "bona fide Eskimos" apart, since the diverse Iñupiat in the village—very few of whom were employed by the airline—were well placed to meet and challenge the standard expectations that visitors held in regard to people native to the region.

Transformations in the budding tourism industry were accompanied by changes in perception among its middle-class travelers as well. Various technologies had facilitated an increased sense of social distance, short-circuiting opportunities for contact and interplay between people that had long been a staple among visitors to Qikiktagruk. Larger ocean-going passenger vessels had isolated earlier travelers from much extended engagement with people in Alaska's indigenous communities, for instance, but air travel sharpened the discontinuity. Planes permitted villages to be seen as a discrete entity from above. They also quickened the contrasts, allowing a city to be experienced and a village to be gazed upon within hours of one another. World fairs and the advent of motion pictures pushed this perceptual shift further (Benjamin 1969), readily letting places be consumed as if they were commodities or spectacles. By the 1950s, tourists could see rural villages in Alaska—then more than ever—"as anachronistic elements of a landscape that was passively viewed, without direct contact" (Braun 2002, 220; Harris 1997).

Yet the viability of the tour did not come without serendipitous complicities of geography. Seven years after Chuck West brought his first group of tourists to Kotzebue, Wien Air hired Chester Seveck, an Iñupiaq from Point Hope. Seveck had worked for years as a herder for the Government Reindeer Service. In 1953, he began to greet visitors and to "herd the tourists" as they disembarked from the plane in Kotzebue. The airline and a new Alaska tourism coalition paid Seveck and his spouse, Helen, to undertake tours through the United States and Europe in the winter, promoting tourism to Alaska at numerous travel fairs and on nationally syndicated TV shows (Seveck 1973). Around the same time, political leaders in the Territory were starting a major media campaign for statehood. By the end of the decade, its advocates had garnered lead articles about Alaska in national media: *The Nation* and *National Geographic*, later in the *New York Times*, *Life*, and *Time* magazine (Naske 1973). Alaska was thus in the spotlight across the United States in the 1950s. In many cases, the media photos held that spotlight on Kotzebue, one of the few destinations north of the Arctic Circle that travel writers could reach via commercial airlines, and where journalists found the Sevecks all ready—in body and in form—for an already familiar dance and the expected tour of a "real Eskimo village."

National media attention brought an increasing number of visitors to Kotzebue in the 1950s and 1960s. But as the new State of Alaska began to select its real estate, it also posed a threat to the subsistence livelihoods of Alaska's indigenous people. By 1966, a statewide movement had begun to press Native land claims. This would have a direct impact on those who participated in the dances. To settle the land claims, Congress created twelve regional Native corporations. Among them was NANA, a Native corporation based in Kotzebue and owned by 4,000 Iñupiat shareholders in the northwest arctic region. NANA built a new hotel and a museum in Kotzebue for the tourists and by 1980, their numbers had climbed to 10,000 tourists per season. After Chester Seveck passed away in 1988, the Seattle-based tour operator filed for bankruptcy, at which point NANA acquired the ground tour and turned it into a training opportunity for local teenagers. For the next fifteen years, young shareholders in the Native corporation, like Charlie, gained the chance to work with elders, interact with tourists, and practice Iñupiaq traditions like dance, even while the tour's structure remained much as it had been fifty years earlier.

Let me review. In the preceding pages, I have outlined the development of tourism as the context in which cultural practices (like dance) were put on exhibit in postwar Kotzebue, Alaska. I summarized how one businessman mobilized some local Iñupiaq practices, arranged them for display before the eyes of tourists, and later set their exhibit on tour. Yet my narrative was also engaged in this maneuver: I sketched the cultural practices of an entrepreneur (his advertising strategies, tour arrangements, and use of new technologies) in order to exhibit these practices to a reader's gaze. The narrative extended a number of invitations: to watch the development of package tourism in Kotzebue; to mark the new transportation technologies that made it possible; to notice the changes in perception that shaped the experience; and to observe the historical contingencies that colluded with its success in this place and time. My analysis, in short, has operated as an exhibit, rendering the practices of an entrepreneur more visible to distant readers.

In the next section, my goal is to disturb an epistemology that presumes to know through observation, one that imagines the social world as a vast 'exhibition of practices' that can be examined like items in a museum or on a list. My focus is the Iñupiaq dance performances. My approach is more experimental, and my method is to explore an epistemology that imagines the social world as tumultuous 'practices of exhibition' and interplay. I contrast these epistemologies using a crude opposition about the assumptions that likely informed the way that the Iñupiat performers and metropolitan visitors each understood the dances. The opposition serves largely as a pedagogic device, one that distinguishes 'exhibitions of practice' from its converse, varied 'practices of exhibition.' I suggest the latter is a more productive analytical register.

CULTURAL PRACTICES OF EXHIBITION: IÑUPIAQ DANCE

When Chuck West started the Sunday excursions in the summer of 1946, his customers saw no Iñupiaq dances around Kotzebue. He started to think about arranging such dances in autumn when he joined the Governor of Alaska on a visit to Kotzebue, where several Iñupiat residents performed a dance in the governor's honor.[9] But he had become concerned that Iñupiat residents "were shy and timid about performing their dances for strangers," so he provided ice cream for everyone as an enticement (West 1985). Those dances remained sporadic until Chester Seveck was salaried as an "Eskimo tour guide" in 1953 (Smith 1989).

Attention to the historiography of Iñupiaq dance (those moments when writers like West inscribe a particular reading on the past) can open up a space in which to examine the frames that metropolitan authors bring to bear on the performance. For instance, if West thought the Iñupiat had been shy in the past about dancing, others reported a different disposition. In one of the first recorded encounters near Kotzebue, a British officer reported,

> I was received in a more friendly manner even than the day before. [An Iñupiat group] led us to a small piece of rising ground near their tents, where we sat down upon broad planks. . . . The whole village then assembled, better dressed than they had been on our first visit, and ranged themselves in a semicircle in front of us, preparatory to an exhibition of one of their dances, which merits description as it was the best of the kind that we saw (Beechey 1831, 394–395).

Beechey then devoted over three hundred words to the performance. A U.S naval officer was invited fifty-eight years later to see several dancers perform at the annual trade fair, where a "crowd [of] about twelve hundred natives . . . allowed us to pass through to a spot favorable for observation" (Healy 1889, 72). But the Quaker missionaries banned Iñupiaq dances in 1900. By all historical accounts, the ban was effective until the 1930s, when a Catholic church was built and Iñupiat families from other denominations, like Chester Seveck, moved to Kotzebue (Smith 1966).

Other scholars have written about the religious politics of dance in Kotzebue (Smith 1989, Burch 1994). What they leave unremarked is the repetitiveness with which Iñupiaq dance was framed as an exhibition in earlier historical accounts. Beechey, for instance, uses this very term in his account above. Mary Barrer, a journalist who contributed to Travel magazine in 1954 after taking the packaged tour, was equally explicit:

> One of the most fascinating aspects of the trip is the exhibition of native dancing. This exotic ritual is performed to the saturnine beat of skin tom toms. As six men pound the drums, others chant tunes while dancers form a line on the floor. . . . Each motion is representative of an event and the dances portray experiences from the life in the villages or of the family. Some are triumphant demonstrations of a successful hunt, while others somberly depict a great tragedy (Barber 1954, 42).

Harry Franck shared his own observations in 1937 in a Kotzebue roadhouse as follows:

> Natives sat on the floor in an ever-thickening circle against the walls, the musicians [or drummers] forming one end of the ellipse. . . . Dancers posture, feet wide apart, knees bent, jump about stiff-legged, raising their arms and stiffening their muscles in an attitude of defiance and defense. They stomp and cavort as if imitating an angry reindeer . . . The men seemed always to be involved in some mighty struggle in their dancing: hunting the whale, the walrus, fighting crunching ice and raging seas. Women, on the contrary, floated about the room with rhythmic grace, their arms alone telling the story (Franck 1939, 230–231).

With such longstanding spatial arrangements between the audience and the performers, why should the word exhibition spark any curiosity or doubt? Why question its use? I believe we should be circumspect about what the dances may have been exhibiting. The observers above presume the performances were an exhibition of Native culture. Their histories assume this was its function. Dance performers put skill and grace on display, and the performances were then re-presented, elsewhere, as signifying an experience or struggle—like a "whale hunt" (see figure 7.1)—in their lives or in the lives of their predecessors. Such histories suggests the Iñupiaq dances played out like a metropolitan museum exhibit, where objects on display can be mobilized to represent something somewhere else—an activity or, more broadly, a culture.

Hence we should examine the role of exhibitions in the lives of metropolitan travelers who wrote our published histories of Iñupiaq dance. The central fact is not that exhibits, world fairs, museums, arcades, and department stores had become popular in advanced capitalist societies. The key fact is that the living world was being rendered up as an exhibit, the display of people as if they were commodities. Middle Eastern visitors in Europe, for instance, found Parisians "a curious people, with an uncontainable eagerness to stand and stare." One such visitor devoted many pages "to the Parisian phenomenon of le spectacle, a word for which [that] author knew of no Arabic equivalent." The accounts described these spectacles in Europe at length, "the curious crowds of spectators, the organization of panoramas and perspectives, the arrangement of natives in mock colonial villages" (Mitchell 1992, 293; cf. Gregory 1995).

Figure 7.1. A photograph in National Geographic Magazine, June 1956 issue, captioned "Dancing to Drum Rhythm, An Eskimo Tells the Story of a Whale Hunt" (Grosvenor 1956, 772–773).

What was more, the accounts of many travel writers—in Kotzebue and elsewhere—focused largely on moments that were already arranged like exhibits. With such displays, knowledge had come to be understood in a peculiar way, premised on an epistemology in which a representation or signifier could be compared to what it represented (reality) to determine its accuracy. Dances were presented in travelers' accounts as if they were exhibits that always represented something else: an actual whale hunt, the indigenous culture, or some ontological reality that one could also know more directly. As a representation, dances mirrored and dramatized an off-stage reality.

But evidence suggests that Iñupiaq practices have often been premised upon a different epistemology. Many anthropologists now argue that in Yupik Eskimo societies (Morrow 1990; Fienup-Riordan 1994), Inuit culture (Briggs 1991) and Iñupiaq communities (Bodenhorn 1997; McNabb 1985), meaning may be considered indeterminate or simply withheld. In these cultural formations, interpreters suggest that representations are not thought to mirror a clear-cut reality. Rather, judgments allow for other interpretations. Pedagogy with young people involves posing practical problems that encourage thoughtful and active experimentation instead of lectures that yield a single 'correct' answer. Identity is assumed to be unstable, making it undependable, but also ripe for adaptation. A tent can be turned into a sled, a knife can be made out of saw blade, or an Iñupiaq dancer can become a White person (naluagmiut). The key was adaptability. As Arnakak (2000, 11) suggests, Iñupiaq culture might best be defined by "qanuqtuurunnaaniq, or the concept of being resourceful to solve problems."

The Iñupiaq language engages an epistemology premised on adaptation. In Iñupiaq, one can distinguish between two styles of teaching with the words ilisayuq and isummaksaiyuq. Both mean 'to teach,' but ilisayuq is used to refer to a formal educational style like that which teachers from metropolitan North America often employed. The root, ilit-, means 'learning' and ilisayuq means to lecture, to invite students to memorize, to practice or summarize correct answers by drill, to cause learning. In contrast, the root for isummaksaiyuq is isuma, which means thought or reason, and a common translation of isummaksaiyuq is 'to cause thought.' Isummaksaiyuq is to encourage a student to observe, to play or experiment with something, to find ways to adapt it, to give careful thought to a problem (Briggs 1998). In Iñupiaq, it was useful to clearly distinguish between these two pedagogic styles: to help someone become educated or learned (ilisayuq) on the one hand, and on the other, to help them become observant and thoughtful (isummaksaiyuq).

These cryptic observations require elaboration, so as to clearly articulate how a mimetic performance, like an Iñupiaq dance, could engage in something other than the representation of something else. Briggs's (1998) ethnographic work on Inuit child-rearing techniques is illustrative in this regard. She shows how parents in a remote camp on Baffin Island often used a particular "genre of behavior" to socialize children: the construction of charged dilemmas, dramatization, and acting in ways that are otherwise proscribed for adults (e.g., "loud, aggressive, intrusive"). She argues that this is done to encourage a child to play out how they might want to act in a given situation. It gives children a safe opportunity to experiment with a repertoire of bodily actions, practices, identities, and roles. It helps them learn about the potential consequences of certain actions and how they can solve a problem by acting differently. Brigg's primary example is the socialization of a three-year-old, whose budding self-awareness was cultivated as her relatives challenged her to consider the affective benefits and costs of acting like a (thoughtless) baby. As the camp's residents teased her about her baby-ness, she was encouraged to give careful thought (isuma) to the choices that they let her make regarding her behavior.

Briggs glosses these scenarios and dramas as play. She believes that they are a constitutive element in everyday Inuit practices. Rather than scolding children, enforcing rules or boundaries that limit their behavior and autonomy, she argues that play is repeatedly exemplified as a proper (Inuit) way to handle conflicts and difficult situations: "at least, pretend to be playing" or joking. She reasons that play engages children in a lively and creative range of mimetic behavior that, as Katz has noted, is distinct from mimicry. This is because mimetic practices are "not simply the ability to both see resemblances and create similarities between things, but the flash of insight made or read off of that process that impels a moment of invention . . . [and] a realization that the original"—the putatively 'real' practice that play imitates—"is also made up: not a fiction, but a performance" (Katz 2004, 98). Play is not trivialized as opposite to the 'serious' business of life. For Briggs, these playful practices of imitation, exploration and socialization in the camp help to create "a habit of living with dilemmas" with humor, confidence, and attentive care. They are the "means by which Inuit children acquire both an active awareness that the world is constituted of problems to be solved and the ability to discover those problems, to observe them actively and [attentively], and to analyze the implications for themselves" (Briggs 1991, 271).

Such a context is suggestive. It implies that Iñupiaq dances might be better understood as playful practices of exhibition and mimetic behaviour. It suggests the dances need not only be seen as artful representations of extraordinary events or everyday practices. Iñupiaq dancing could also serve as an engagement, a mimetic experiment which toys with a subject and an audience through interplay. Thomas Johnston, an ethno-musicologist, has written about Iñupiaq dance along these lines. For him, its forms and functions reflect varied social structures across the Arctic. He historicizes Iñupiaq dance as a longstanding "conciliatory mechanism" and a "useful lubricant for easing tension" in small communities. Johnston argues that the "'diplomatic immunity' afforded by its enactment of social criticism served as a face-saving device which avoided the trauma of dysfunctional confrontation" (Johnston 1990, 196). With satire and humor, dancers could exert subtle pressure to ameliorate hostilities and promote what he called a "stable ambiguity" among the people present, with no clearly innocent or guilty parties (Johnston 1978).

Yet my objective is not to write an ethnography of Iñupiaq dance nor to explain its functions. Rather, my purpose here is to disturb an epistemology premised upon the line between on-stage 'exhibitions' and the off-stage practices that they were said to represent—and to do so by raising another possibility. In northwest Alaska, dance may have been one of many cultural practices of exhibition and play, part of a formation that continually worked at building a repertoire of tactically useful actions and behaviors, through what Benjamin called a mimetic "compulsion to become the Other": an angry reindeer, a foolish or successful hunter, or a White (naluagmiut) visitor. As Taussig (1993, 33) argues, the recognition of resemblances is not entirely a cerebral matter. It is an "object-prone exercise in differentiated space" where people "become and behave like something else," where others confirm the performance with playful mimesis of their own.

In Kotzebue, however, wires may have gotten crossed when the tourists repeatedly failed to join in the play. Many different archival photographs suggest the visitors largely remained unpretending tourists, standing on the sidelines, watching, smiling, and taking photos. In doing so, they may have encouraged the Iñupiaq performers to become more like their naluagmiut visitors, compelling the dancers to explain their moves in the familiar language of representation—as an artistic display of an event or an exhibit of traditional cultural practices in the community. It would likely have been far more difficult to explain Iñupiaq dance as a complex cultural practice of exhibition and teasing, of collective mimesis and play.

Again, let me review. Over the last few pages, I drew a distinction between the "exhibition of cultural practices" and "cultural practices of exhibition," associating each with different cultural epistemologies. I used oppositions to flesh out each framework, delineating the habituations of metropolitan and Iñupiaq modes of engagement and learning which, I suggested, informed the way that the Iñupiat residents and their metropolitan visitors may have experienced dance in Kotzebue. Yet there is a major problem. The distinctions obscure the incorporation of Iñupiaq practices into capitalism's exhibits of culture, into its world of enchanted commodities through ubiquitous devices, like those massive "wish-book" known as the Sears catalogue that appeared in Iñupiaq homes long ago (Burch 1975; Warbelow 1990). To temper the contrast, and to better explore the affinities, I will shift focus—from dance performances, to the business practices within which Iñupiaq dancers were held accountable in recent years.

ENACTMENTS OF CALCULABLE SPACE: THE BUSINESS OF IÑUPIAQ DANCE

When Charlie presented himself to our group, he was working for an enterprise called Tour Arctic. Established in 1988, Tour Arctic was a subsidiary of NANA, the Native corporation based in Kotzebue. Charlie was a shareholder as well, one of the 10,200 Iñupiat who owned NANA. At that time, the company controlled $167 million in assets, employing about 10 percent of its shareholders. The corporation's early success came from oil-company contracts elsewhere. By fiscal year 2000, NANA was making profits of $6.8 million from producer services, $7.0 million from natural resources income, $7.8 million from securities, $3.3 million from various hotels in Alaska, and $1.3 million from its zinc-mine services (NANA 2003). So Tour Arctic was just one of NANA's smaller operations, generating a net-loss of $192,300 that year.

NANA was created in 1972 as a result of the land claims movement and the Alaska Native Claims Settlement Act. The law allocated a billion dollars and 68,000 square miles of land to Native ownership. Its most remarkable feature was a corporate approach. Instead of reimbursing tribes or individuals for lands lost, the settlement transferred assets to new Native corporations. The 76,500 people who the federal government recognized as "Alaska Natives" would become shareholders, owners of these new business corporations. The corporate approach was a highly creative mimetic adaptation which was first proposed in 1968 by the Alaska Land Claims Task Force, whose chair was an Iñupiaq activist from Kotzebue. Its drafting committee members were leaders of Alaska Native organizations. This is not to argue that corporate neoliberalism among the Iñupiat developed entirely as a result of indigenous agency. In part, it was a response to other constraints: the committee hoped to reduce the role of federal government among Alaska Native people, later supporting this corporate approach with the catchphrase, "In the white man's society, we need white man's tools" (Arnold 1978, 153).

Within historical accounts, it is also important to note that the creation of Native corporations gained popularity and force in the halls of Congress. There, the nation's elect had been mobilized within an assemblage that invoked adaptive 'entrepreneurial' firms and people in Alaska, each endowed with autonomy within a corporate market economy. Congress circulated the normative supposition that people are best governed through their freedom to choose, that Alaska Natives should be encouraged "to understand and enact their lives in terms of choice" (Rose 1999, 87). Yet such an obligation to choose (between doctors, job-training programs, or NANA board candidates for instance) marks a specific kind of governance rather than its absence. Thus the pertinent question is a descriptive one: how the most radical device for social engineering in the land claims settlement—its corporate form—re-organized the shape of governance and "the terrain in which choice as such is possible" (Scott 1995, 194).

With Native corporations, that terrain was restructured around the practices of financial calculation. Business models had been increasingly applied to hospitals, universities, and non-profits, each of which were "obliged to organize their activities as if they were little businesses" where everyday activities were to be "recoded in a new vocabulary of incomes, allocations, costs, savings, even profits" (Rose 1999, 151). Received theoretical approaches would likely examine this profusion from the basis of pre-constituted subjects: in the agency of individuals or in the structure of interests promoting the use of financial calculation. But some of geography's recent theoretical innovations would describe its emergence as a proliferation of effects born out of meticulous, object-laden techniques like accounting. Instead of writing up its practices and devices as aids to corporate neoliberalism or capitalism, such practices are seen as a fundamental part of capitalism's experimental ordering, inadvertently working their way into the substrate of experience, and continuously re-constituting a sense of what is significant (Thrift 2005).

In Alaska, their effect was the production of new calculable spaces as the background of expectation in small communities like Kotzebue. Calculable spaces are the natural habitat of those who work for an enterprise or organization. They are the domains that come into existence in a regime of calculation and economic visibility (Hopwood 1987). Calculable spaces form a background that, while rarely questioned, tracks and activates hands and minds. They form part of what Thrift (2008, 67) calls the "'embodied unconscious,' a set of basic exfoliations of the body" through which time and space are crafted from moment to moment. Examples include "the 'division' that a manager controls, the 'cost center' that one is responsible for, and the 'budget' that the individual administers" (Miller 1992, 75). Their appeal resides in the fact that calculable spaces do not necessarily correspond to physical locales. Therefore ways of linking individuals and activities that cut across geographical and physical boundaries can be established. Responsibilities can be instituted or transformed without making changes to the spatial distribution of individuals, machinery, or offices. Rather than physical attributes, the creation of calculable spaces requires only a representation of the space about which calculations are to be made and a technology capable of generating calculations of that space. And comparisons can then be made between spaces of a similar type. Thus 'Return on Investment' allows the performance of the managers of different divisions within a company to be evaluated and compared. 'Standard costs' as they feed into the budgetary process allow the monitoring of the performance of a product line (Miller 1992, 77).

To a novice, the calculations can be tedious and awkward, far from simple. When care for an elder in the family, for instance, is folded into an account at the Kotzebue Senior Center, the new rules, procedures, and forms can be overwhelming. Hours spent looking for summer help can be subsumed on the books of NANA Temporary Services, but that requires a job description and various estimates. Time used for Iñupiaq dance training can be recorded on a ledger for Tour Arctic. The device at once tracks and constitutes the company's expenses, but it requires the acclimatization of new time-keeping routines. Once habituated, the remarkable spaces that these habits call forth—like Tour Arctic—become second-nature as the background of experience.

The proliferation of calculable spaces can be attributed to the diffusion of new technologies of accounting—bills, receipts, fund numbers, spreadsheets, the bottom line—all of which arrived in northwest Alaska in recent decades. This should not imply that accounting practices in general were new to the region. For centuries, the huge trade fair at Sisualik had been a site of calculation as river and coastal people negotiated exchanges (Bockstoce 2009). In the twentieth century, Iñupiat became acquainted with the power that local naluagmiut business owners held—entrepreneurs who arrived with capital assets and no visible obligations to share their wealth with extended family members. And since airline and barge companies had employed Iñupiat women and men, managing small incomes were longstanding (though uneven) practices in the community.

If money management and canny trade were old-hat, managerial accounting was new. It had emerged in the early twentieth century in attempts to control costs in the First World War (Loft 1994). It was then that statistical notions of 'standard costing' had been developed, against which the actual costs incurred by an employee could be compared through analyses of variance (Loft 1986, Chatfield 1974). The techniques and presumptions did not go unchallenged (Johnson and Kaplan 1987; Fleischman and Tyson 1999), yet managerial accounting had made it feasible "to attach norms and standards of behaviour to every individual within the firm. Efficiency could be individualized and rendered visible" (Miller and O'Leary 1989, 101). The effect extended the reach of supervision beyond the space of a whaling vessel or merchant store (where prohibition and force could be exercised) to a field of possibility, constrained instead by the time and money allotted to an employee to complete the work for which they were responsible (Miller 1992).

Financial calculation did not facilitate the emergence of corporate forms all on its own in this part of the continent. Other devices, techniques, and practices were used as well, each fabricating a company like Tour Arctic as an intelligible entity and a calculable space. They included the registration of a corporate charter with the state; the artful invention of a logo; the making of organizational charts, mapping various levels of authority and realms of responsibility; the standard use of business cards and letterhead; the making of iconographic images through an interplay of dance performances and photographic technologies; the production of brochures that harnessed those images; regular negotiations for a few inches of advertisement in newspapers and magazines, and so on. The choreography of these presentations and artifacts then began to hail the new enterprise, whose Native owners were socialized into its presence through meetings, newsletters, and the recitation of job titles. These gave ongoing shape to a new calculable space.

The habits and devices in Kotzebue were far from mere imitations of metropolitan business practices. As Thrift notes (2008), adaptation and improvisation are necessary for the successful repetition. Through a series of mimetic moves, the Iñupiat executives at NANA had adapted the techniques of accounting to create a new calculable space, which reached well beyond Kotzebue. From the date that Tour Arctic was established until it was closed some sixteen years later, its director worked out of an office in Anchorage, a city five hundred miles south. There, its advertising staff had access to various support services for promoting the tours. Accounting extended the reach of its director to the operational staff, who worked in Kotzebue: the ground tour manager, guides, drivers, and young dancers like Charlie. Their activities circulated between NANA's museum (where the dances were performed), a fish camp or tent on the shoreline, a hill-top road for sight-seeing, and the NANA-owned Nullagvik Hotel, where tourists were regularly deposited and withdrawn on the following day.

Likewise, its transactions circulated through NANA's financial accounts, where its subjects were constituted as assets and liabilities, so ordered through arrangements of numbers on a page. Indeed, to enact a calculable space was in part to engage in a series of mathematical maneuvers: first, the reduction of a group of activities and artifacts to a set of figures, measuring value and cash flow volumes; second, their comparison against and relation to other figures, each the result of translating activities or things into numbers; third, their management from a distance with the continuous re-allocation of assets and labour through directives and bank orders; and lastly, their distillation to a single number annually, 'the bottom-line,' presented as profit or loss. The figure was constructed each year in NANA's Annual Report and presented to shareholders throughout the Northwest Arctic Borough, where the practices of accounting obliged each such owner to act in view of the company's bottom line.

With small returns on equity that are endemic to the tourism sector, Tour Arctic made little money. Indeed, in its final years, the local enterprise appeared as a loss: ($44,230) and ($52,643). Until 2004, when the cost of replacing an aging museum facility overwhelmed the diminishing revenues of a declining tourism market, Tour

Arctic had been visible as a financially marginal measure. Yet it was easily seen as a minor cost in relation to NANA's profits, listed elsewhere on the same page of the annual report. The printed list is an old cultural technology, but its effect should not be understated. When Tour Arctic was exhibited in a list of profits—for example, $5.5 million for government contracts in FY 2003, $4.2 million for hotel operations—NANA's Board could agree on a decision, annually, that Tour Arctic was a worthwhile loss, and for three reasons: Tour Arctic presented a legitimating image of NANA to the public as a cultural entity; it generated jobs and training opportunities for young shareholders in Kotzebue; and the development of local human capital was calculated to be a relatively small expense.

The last point is not a small one. Surveys and other devices had shown high unemployment rates in Kotzebue for years, especially for young adults, and by the 1980s, the rates of suicide had become particularly alarming (Maniilaq Association 1985). In response, NANA's leaders had decided to create jobs—to cultivate opportunities in the community that others could choose to perform and explore—by supporting less solvent local business ventures with the company's profitable investments elsewhere. Such a "human resources development" approach helped Tour Arctic's parent company gain recognition as the most successful Native corporation in Alaska (Gaffney 1982). Recent theoretical perspectives would also highlight the practices of accounting, those performances through which some residents became early leaders by turning themselves into calculating subjects, the Iñupiat women and men at NANA who created jobs for young shareholders in the region, even when it meant reporting apparent 'losses' on the corporation's financial statements.

Perhaps that dance of business practices is best understood as a playful engagement in mimetic adaptation and creativity—to behave and become like something else as circumstance suggests. In such a case, managerial accounting was enlisted into the repertoire of the cultural practices of exhibition, at the same time that the mimetic performance of a corporate model in Kotzebue created a new space, a calculable space, for engagement and learning.

DISCUSSION: EXTENDING OPENNESS, EXTENDING THRIFT

The three sections above were a series of mimetic moves, animated by the creative mimetic pedagogies that I have been learning through my work with Iñupiaq people. My analysis of dance and the business of dance drew, nonetheless, on Thrift's nonrepresentational theory (or style) in geography. His approach "locates the weight of social being in the act itself, as a gesture of physicality rather than a representative code" (Gagen 2004, 423). His work strives to elucidate the "conditions of intelligibility" for the terms of experience, which only works in relation to an embodied, material embeddedness (Thrift 1996, 2007). To this end, Thrift has been "concerned to characterize many elements of the world as a part of thinking, thus diversifying what is thought of as thought" (Thrift 2004, 89). Such elements and characterizations have changed over the course of Thrift's career. For instance, my first section mirrored his early concerns with the historical geographies of consciousness and technological assemblages like transportation (Thrift 1988, 1996). The section on the practices of exhibition in Kotzebue played off his later interests in elusive embodied experimentations and his call for a non-representationalist style (Thrift 1997, 2000), while the last section, on the production of new calculable spaces, paralleled Thrift's more recent fascinations with new managerial practices and the broader genealogies of background, where "the number tends to cast the world reciprocally in its image as entities are increasingly made in forms that are countable" (Thrift 2007, 96; cf. 2005).

To better understand non-representationalist theory, it helps to historically situate this body of work. It emerged as part of an "evolving articulation of various branches of poststructuralist thinking and writing within human geography" (Wylie 2010, 103). In the 1980s, 'new' cultural geographers and feminist geographers started to use poststructuralism to analyze discourses, texts, and landscapes as key sites through which identity was constructed. Non-representational theory surfaced in Thrift's work in the 1990s, attending to bodily performances and practices as the "precognitive" dimension of subject formation. The work widened an engagement with poststructuralist theory in the discipline, opening up spaces in which to explore the ways that knowledge and experience were constituted through embodied routines and gestures.

In recent years, disciplinary reviews of non-representational theory have tended to recollect more differences than continuities. The retrospective critiques have noted a number of losses and foreclosures in non-representational theory, including a healthy wariness of abstraction (Nash 2000); mindfulness of the effects of differences by gender, age, 'race' and dis/ability (Jacobs and Nash 2003); caution about the aura of authenticity (Revill 2004); attention to consolidations of power through 'experience' (Saldanha 2005); and not least, greater historical sensitivities (Tolia-Kelly 2006). My reading of these engagements is that, more than entirely necessary, they have collectively played into pervasive relations of opposition in the discipline, tending to repeatedly "generate defensive self-representations or gestures of counter critique" (Grosz, cited in Colls 2012, 440). Like Colls, I believe that form of critique has been inclined to "hinder the possibility of productive engagement with non-representational geographies" (2012, 440). To work toward more collaborative forms of critique, one might try to extend Thrift's project with exercises that reach toward those aspects of poststructuralism that were lost in non-representational theory. These would neither be disavowals of his work, nor endorsements by imitation and alignment, but rather, creative mimetic extensions of similarity and difference.

As Tolia-Kelly (2006) notes, historical sensitivity was a crucial aspect of poststructuralism that was lost. That sensitivity is not easily grafted onto Thrift's recent focus on newness and the furtive ways that socio-material relations are now being re-made with new toy technologies (2005), R&D strategies (2007), or behavioral finance strategies (2008). Nor is recuperating a greater historical sensitivity an

easy task within a framework that highlights the social world as a forever indeterminate "practical achievement" that can just as easily fail at every moment, "an
ordering" that never rests (Anderson 2009, 504). Yet it should be noted that the
historiographic elements (the practices of social memory that enliven the writing,
materiality, and reading of history) are also embodied performances. They proceed
through recollection, forgetfulness, durable routines, and destruction. They invite
attention to the ruptures and recuperations in the play of social memory (Kurtz
2006). In such moments, many pasts are folded into the present. In geography,
this observation has informed studies of photographs (Rose 2000), museums (Till
2005), and testimony (Harrison 2010). The preceding account of Iñupiaq dance,
with its attention to ways in which different aspects of the past may have been
de-activated and re-activated in the practices of exhibition, gestured toward such a
more-than-representational historiography.

If historical sensitivity presents one dimension in which non-representational
theory could be extended with care, another is to reach further afield geographically. While Thrift acknowledges both the necessity and promise of drawing from
"cross-cultural comparisons" (2007, 173), his own work has largely been exercised
in Euro-American societies.[10] Moreover, comparison itself has a problematic legacy.[11]
As Robinson (2011, 126) notes, "comparativism—the ability to cast one's eye across
a range of disparate cases and consider them equivalent for analytical purposes—is
itself a profoundly colonial inheritance." It risks recuperating the Eurocentrism that
seeks to know the 'other,' that presumes it is always possible to access a different
society (Kuokannen 2008), or that concludes an understanding of difference is undesirable. For western academics, responsible practices in postcolonial work involve
both "recognizing the limits of what we can hear" and "an openness and vulnerability
to that which most resists European thought: those aspects of the 'other' that are not
shared," that are simply withheld (Noxolo et al. 2012, 424).

It follows that extending non-representational theory further afield is better
envisioned as "learning to learn from below" (Spivak 2008). Simply to learn from
below is an old recipe. It often leaves privilege untouched, with the lines for social
mobility removed. This is because "learning from the subaltern requires a prior step:
learning to learn—or clearing the way for an ethical relation with the subaltern" (An-
dreotti 2007, 76). This prior step extends the ethos of openness embedded in non-
representational theory, further opening us "to a generous sensibility, one that might
be capable of re-enlivening our affective engagements with others and fostering a
heightened sense for what might be possible" (Popke 2009, 83). It involves learning
from the uncomfortable refusal of engagements that we imagine to be responsible,
as well as recognizing that we are limited in what we can hear and understand, as
Noxolo et al. (2012) argue. But it also involves remaining focused on the subaltern
as educators—young and old—who may wish to teach us how to be more accessible teachers, more receptive students, or better human beings. Thus the purpose of
reaching further afield is not to produce more knowledge about knowledge, but to
patiently and persistently engage in what Spivak (2008) calls a suturing pedagogy.

CONCLUSION

We must work to make these other pasts come . . . it is not even "learning about cultures." This is imagining yourself, really letting yourself be imagined (experience that impossibility) without guarantees, by and in another culture (Spivak 2003, 52).

When Charlie shared his list of favorite foods—whale fat, seal, hamburgers, and pizza—I wondered if he was playing with his audience in the tent. He had articulated a list of apparently comparable items, a practice that was all too familiar. In that list, he provided an even number, two that his audience would probably associate with Iñupiat people, two with Anglo-American teenagers living elsewhere. But these associations may mark a rather naluagmiut epistemology, one that makes several assumptions: that meanings are usually straightforward and certain; that its categories are unambiguous; and following from this, that essentially the same activities are revitalized, the same performances are replayed, again and again. However, Charlie may have been letting us choose (in good Iñupiaq fashion?) which category we thought he should belong to—a young Iñupiaq adult or a typical American teenager. Perhaps he was even letting us choose whether those two categories were separate ("either/or") or overlapping ("both/and").[12] To me, Charlie's list was a parody of received notions of culture and ethnicity, problematic categories that I find myself using anyway. Moreover, his list seemed to be a playful tactic to get me to think, to encourage me to learn (isummaksaiyuq). From my experience in Kotzebue, this now strikes me—paradoxically, given my suspicion of cultural or ethnic categories—as a rather Iñupiaq thing to do.

It was getting late in the day and Charlie's list had led my stomach to grumbling. But dinner was not next on our agenda. Instead, we tourists were taken to NANA's museum. Upon entering, I saw a diorama whose image had become familiar from Tour Arctic's brochures: two Iñupiat wax figures stood in a life-size skin-boat, near taxidermy and sculptures of the sea life in the Kotzebue Sound. We were soon directed to the auditorium seats for a dance performance. Our entourage said very little about each dance other than its name. While the performance could be photographed, the bodily enthusiasm that the young dancers shared was not readily represented on paper. And with time, their dance performances started to stand as figures for a fairly different learning formation in Kotzebue, less so as another corporeal medium of expression comparable to modern or jazz dance. They were active mimetic engagements with others. Charlie asked us to join him in the last dance—a suturing pedagogy, and an invitation to unsettle the categories that define who are the performers and who is the audience.

NOTES

1. The paper benefited immeasurably from the suggestions of eight generous readers outside of Kotzebue: Jean Briggs, Henry Buller, Verdie Craig, Elizabeth Gagen, Oluf Kulke,

Adam Pine, Kim Walker, and an anonymous reviewer. Comments after its presentation to the geography departments at Open University and Queen's University (Ontario) were also enormously helpful. I remain responsible for all its flaws.

2. See "Red Dog Mine" at http://www.nana.com (accessed September 3, 2011); for a synopsis of the regional economy and employment, see Shanks (2009).

3. "Charlie" is not his actual English name. I use a pseudonym to protect his identity.

4. Thrift uses the general topic of dance as a way of "illustrating" non-representational theory, for at least three reasons. First, it challenges the privilege of meaning. Second, it offers a chance to engage with theories of the body and "ambulant theorizing." Third, dance studies have produced a rich archive of experiments in performance art (see Thrift 2000, 137–141).

5. *Fairbanks Daily News-Miner* (1946, 3); see also Wien Airlines' advertisements as early as April 30, 1946 in the Fairbanks newspaper.

6. Author's interview with Virginia (Hill) Wood and Celia Hunter, October 2, 2000. Wood and Hunter reported that, along with one friend, they were "about the only white people" to attend the Iñupiaq festival at the schoolhouse in Kotzebue. On the hotel's conversion, see West (1985). Wood reported that she completed the conversion in August of 1949.

7. For instance, Spring and Spring (1953), Spring (1953), and Barber (1954).

8. One need not use Benjamin to theorize tourism, since there is an extensive literature about tourism in the social sciences. Early theorists include Stephen Britton and Rob Shields in geography, John Urry in sociology, and Valene Smith in anthropology. Indeed, Valene Smith's contributions were based on her fieldwork in Kotzebue. Yet to reach responsibly into this literature would go well beyond the scope of the chapter, at the same time that the mimetic faculty has been largely left untheorized in such work about tourism.

9. Author's interview with George Rogers, July 5, 2000. For a note about the governor's visit, see also the *Nome Nugget*, September 18, 1946.

10. Thrift's recent work (e.g., 2009) may be indicative of an increasing number of exceptions.

11. There is now an emerging body of work in geography that is rethinking spatial and cultural comparison as a colonial and postcolonial methodology. That literature includes Larner and LeHeron (2002), Robinson (2006, 2011), McFarlane (2006, 2010), Jazeel and McFarlane (2007), McCann (2010), and Raghuram (2011).

12. I am indebted to Jean Briggs for raising the latter possibility.

8

Dance, Architecture, and Space in the Making

Frances Bronet

Beating a Path, a storefront interactive dance installation based on a set of moving platforms, and *SpillOut*—a 40 foot long, 12 foot high, 2.5 foot wide, climbing, dancing and performing wall of elastic bands in a cylindrical drum building, are part of a series of full-scale built investigations examining reciprocal relationships between movement and space, opening up the possibility of transcending predictable enclosures and responding to actual movement of bodies.

THE CONCEPT OF SPACE IN THE MAKING

Many architectural designers of renown develop spatial envelopes that have great formal identity but are either independent of the way that people move in and around them or force particular kinds of movement patterns in what we call *ready-made space*. In *Beating a Path* and *SpillOut*, we challenge this framework by setting up installations to respond in time with dancers. Here we construct or evolve space—what we call *space in the making*, generated by the movements of action artists. These temporary projects act as pilots for long-standing space for ordinary inhabitation.

In these two projects, dancers and architects offer an alternative to ready-made space. The idea of *space in the making* borrows from Bruno Latour's concept of ready-made science versus science in the making (Latour 1987). Latour asks whether the profile of an experiment and its outcome will change based on its context. In our situation, context (in this case, inhabitants) has an opportunity to actually transform space.

The concept of *space in the making* sets up a model for designing where we would not have a ready-made design (predetermined set of drawings), a ready-made procedure for assembly, or a ready-made model for occupancy. This means that any physical construction would not be based on a preconceived or generic idea about the context, the project, the occupants, or else. In a *space in the making* model, the designers work intimately with the situation at hand and the design emerges from the full-scale and particular situation of the site. These conditions include the acts of the designers, the physical and cultural context, and the interactions with the users throughout the process from conception to occupancy.

Both *Beating a Path* and *SpillOut* demonstrate the *extreme possibility of designing and occupying in movement* or creating through the making, where the space of construction and of inhabitation cannot be fully determined without movement, without face-to-face interaction.

Through a set of simultaneously emerging installations and corresponding choreographies, we explore how design in movement can motivate new ways of liberative building and inhabiting, ones that challenge the hegemony of design in ready-made space. In an influential example, Gary Snyder compares the boundary of the current State of California to the natural boundaries of the bioregions that California comprises (Snyder 1990). Snyder addresses the arbitrary and/or time-specific quality of political authority as opposed to the non-arbitrary quality of the natural authority of the biogeography. When the political process of making a boundary comes to an end, the resulting space of jurisdiction is fixed, treating everyone uniformly, having little to do with who you are or what you do (Bronet and Schumacher 1999).

Space in the making affords chance experiences that encourage fluid reciprocity between space and movement. The boundaries are not fixed. The projects set up ambiguous liminal conditions allowing variable commitments with multiple and often non-predictable ways of occupation. This does not diminish the responsibility of the architect to not design a framework, it does not mean anything goes, nor big gym-like spaces without any constraints celebrated. There is still a formal final proposal; however, two conditions must be met. One: the space of the project must emerge concurrently from the specific context—the way the dancers move, the container in which any elements are placed, while both the space and the dance iteratively unfold, and two: even in the final performance, possibilities of how each audience member can view or understand the whole will be different.

BEATING A PATH AND *SPILLOUT* AS SPACES IN THE MAKING

In both *Beating a Path* and *SpillOut*, the projects began with placing found objects in the space of rehearsal. The dancers would play and create action movement skits with these objects—a 15-inch diameter, 8-foot-long sewer pipe with a piece of plywood precariously perched, a small scaffolding structure stitched with spandex strips. It doesn't matter what we started with. In *Beating a Path* and *SpillOut*, these tests of watching how any armatures could be morphed with the movement became the basis of the final structures. Early trials of *Beating a Path* showed how movement and space were dependent on each other. Images 1 and 2 illustrate this process of dependence for *Beating a Path*. As figure 8.1 shows, discovering physical elements that could be *played* was critical to the unfolding of the project.

Figure 8.1.   Interdependent Movement and Space in *Beating a Path*
Photographer: Gary D. Gold. Used by permission

One goal of the performance installation was to demonstrate how movement affected space, which included recording movement in the storefront and having it be reflected by the changing of the enclosure, the form and the quality of space. Where there was no repetition of movement, the space would revert to its original shape. In one very obvious marking, this occurred through wall prints at the windows, where the dancers repeatedly rubbed their heels against the surface. One or two iterations left a faint trace; hundreds turned the trace into a gouge. In the field of ropes, the dancer's body pushed the ropes aside; in the moment of the dancer's departure the ropes went back to what seemed to be their initial place. Over time, the repeated pushing apart of the ropes moved their original knotting, and the field of ropes began to adjust to the specifics of the body engaging it. As figure 8.2 shows, then, the vertical surface of spandex registered the body in the moment. Without the pressure of the dancer, the material fundamentally reverted back to its taut first condition. The rolling platforms operated in the most extreme way. When the dancers moved the platforms, they pushed into the standing audience. The spectators had to be conscious of where the platforms were and when; the onus was on the audience to move out of the way, otherwise they would get hit. The audience was a part of the performance. Space was made by the audience moving. There were tense moments. When the dancers ran in one direction on the rolling glass floors, they were part of Newton's Third Law of Physics: to every action there is always an equal and opposite reaction; hence the performers move in one direction and the floors move in the opposite direction. That means an audience intently watching as the dancers run away from them might miss that the floor is on a collision course with their shins.

The remaining images in this paper illustrate the installation *Spill Out*, and its efforts to further illustrate the reciprocity of fixed architectural space and human dance

Figure 8.2.   Dancers Playing with Movable Physical Elements in *Beating a Path*
Photographer: Gary D. Gold. Used by permission

movements. For example, in *SpillOut*, the elastic wall may have been too taut or too loose with strands too far apart or too close. The dancers' engagement with the elements in full scale in real time gave the designers clear signs of what had to change. In every iteration, the physical frameworks changed as the dancers became more familiar with the elements, and as the elements became more tuned to the bodies of both the performers and the body of each emerging phrase. The goal was to have an installation that was both architecturally rigorous and stunning while allowing the dancers to have a myriad of ways to perform and to be viewed, both inspired and supported by the installation.

Figure 8.3 shows the original spatial configuration of *SpillOut*. It was a 40-foot-long, 12-foot high, 2.5-foot-wide steel scaffold-like structure, covered with thousands of spandex strips. As the dancers illuminated the difficulties and limitations of the materials, scale of spaces, and opportunities to engage the structure in multiple ways, the onus was on the architects to evolve the structure. The project evolved from a small wall covered in rubber bands, a surface doomed to snap, catch on skin, and deteriorate over time in light—all conditions that could have been the foundation of a powerful performance, but less likely to survive the normative demands of rehearsal overuse. As the dancers illuminated the difficulties and limitations of the materials, scale of spaces, as well as the opportunities to engage the structure in multiple ways, the charge of the architects was to reciprocally evolve the structure.

Figure 8.4 shows the final *SpillOut* structure that was made of reconfigured scaffolding. Working intimately with the dancers helped evolve a safe construction. For example, the connectors of the struts had to be padded, the floor had to be wide enough to move but not too close to the spandex to impede movement—all so that the dancers didn't get hurt on the assembly nor stop the most ambitious movement.

Figure 8.3. Original Spatial Configuration of *SpillOut*
Photographer: Gary D. Gold. Used by permission

Figure 8.4. Final Spatial Configuration of *SpillOut*
Photographer: Gary D. Gold. Used by permission

Inside the structure, there is a visceral sense of containment. However the elastic surface and the location of the lighting can transform this inner world to one seamlessly
connected to the outside or to one that feels totally separated from the arena, based
on both the action of the dancers and the condition of the lighting.

The final evolution of the project revealed a number of ways to see, use and experience the performance/installation. The wall itself could be seen as solid when lit from
outside and the dancers rendered invisible, as figure 8.5 shows. Here, *SpillOut* was
sited in a nineteenth century red brick Gasholder building, 100 feet in diameter, 50
feet high. From a distance with peripheral lighting, the spandex wall structure appears
almost solid. It could be translucent when the lighting was from above and diffuse;
it could be totally transparent when lit from within making the dancers fully visible.

Demonstrated by figure 8.6, the configuration of the structure allowed for both
framing the body and also for the dancers to transgress vertical boundaries.

The opportunity of having the structure be read as one whole frame, as a series of
divided frames, or as overlaps of the two scenarios offered multiple ways of engaging
the work. With the light from within, the spandex almost vanishes, and the dancers are
fully visible. For the choreographer, this was key; most dance companies do not want
their compositions visually impeded. Much negotiation occurred around how much of
the human bodies were visible and how much they were intrinsically part of the architectural landscape. The consistency and spacing of the ribbons of spandex allowed for
the body to be seen as a full figure, or as one cast in shadows, as shown in figure 8.7.

Figure 8.5. *SpillOut* in Nineteenth Century Gasholder Building
Photographer: Gary D. Gold. Used by permission

Figure 8.6. Dancers Transgressing Vertical Boundaries in *SpillOut*
Photographer: Gary D. Gold. Used by permission

Figure 8.7. Dancer Cast in Shadows in *SpillOut* Performance
Photographer: Gary D. Gold. Used by permission

The structure could appear as muscular where the floors, knuckles of the connecting rods, and steel bars flexed; or appear thin and planar with no depth at all, presenting the dancers as scaling a veneer. The surface could appear impenetrable, or totally operable as the dancers pulled the strands apart, to be fully visible or to create varying degrees of apertures.

As figure 8.8 shows, the spandex could be pulled apart, stretched for the dancers to emerge or retreat.

Over a long period of time, the spandex became plastic, losing some of its elasticity, and the dance itself had to shift, accommodating the material changes. The dancers must always be aware of how their bodies are interacting with the materials to take advantage of the fluctuations, both subtle and dramatic. When the bodies acted as a set, the figures can be seen as individual forms as well as shapes creating a scene, an arrangement of phrases that are both abstract and figural (See figure 8.9).

The dancers could be in and out, penetrating the surface with ease, pushing the bands apart. They could appear closed out or trapped inside, depending on the light. Figures 8.10 and 8.11 show that depending on the source of the lighting, the bodies are either partially obstructed by the spandex or they are seen as fully woven into the spandex.

And even when sealed inside, the light thrown from one end of the wall could create a complete and distinct set of performances from cast shadows on the cylindrical interior surface of the Gasholder House.

Figure 8.8. Stretchable Spandex Bands in *SpillOut* Configuration
Photographer: Gary D. Gold. Used by permission

Figure 8.9.   Lighting Arrangement Makes Dancers Abstract Figures in *SpillOut*
Photographer: Gary D. Gold. Used by permission

Figure 8.10. Different Lighting Arrangement in *SpillOut*

Photographer: Gary D. Gold. Used by permission

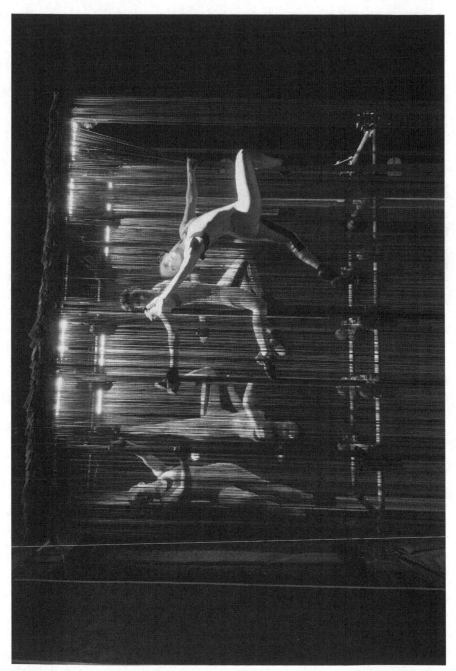

Figure 8.11.   Another Lighting Arragement in *SpillOut*
Photographer: Gary D. Gold. Used by permission

Figure 8.12.   Shadow Display of Dancers in *SpillOut*
Photographer: Gary D. Gold. Used by permission

Figure 8.12 shows that the performance had an entire set of compositions emerging on the walls of the Gasholder House. Ultimately, the viewer could see the work multiple times and have a completely different experience each time. One viewing may be concentrated only on the building shadows, another could engage sections of the spandex wall, another that (sitting far enough back) could see the entire scaffold, or there could be combinations of all of these. It is unlikely that anyone could actually get it all at once. This is, indeed, the point—as a *space in the making* as opposed to ready-made space, nothing could be read at once; both the dancers and the audience had multiple modes of experiencing the performance. The lighting of the show, the space and the mode of construction were all critical to the making of the project. In figure 8.13, the wall is almost opaque and the eye moves readily to the wall shadows. Figure 8.14 shows how the spectator is pulled between the power of the performance in and on the wall, and the shadows sharing space with the vestigial stair of the Gasholder. The dancers had the opportunity to use their own projections for another way to use their own bodies and establish phrases that had both two-dimensional and three-dimensional components.

Figure 8.13.   Another Shadow Display of Dancers in *SpillOut*
Photographer: Gary D. Gold. Used by permission

Figure 8.14.   Multidimensional Display of Dancers in *SpillOut*
Photographer: Gary D. Gold. Used by permission

DANCEABILITY AS A SPACE IN THE MAKING

Beating a Path and *SpillOut* have propelled another investigation, working with *DanceAbility*, a mixed abilities dance company. This new project pushes the same fundamental principles of *space in the making*. People with disabilities generally participate less in cultural and physical activities. We can project that the constraints of the physical environments contribute to this; and that there is an opportunity for architecture to celebrate the uniqueness of people with and without perceived disabilities. Given that current architectural and design norms prescribe and limit our actions for all people, including for people with disabilities, how do we both challenge the constraints while also deeply engaging the body and making it continuous with the space itself? Architecture and design students and practitioners have limited exposure to both designing for unpredictable movement, creating space that unfolds, as well as experiencing the needs and possibilities of people with disabilities. As figures 8.15 and 8.16 show, *DanceAbility* addresses issues around movement and space with mixed abilities groups. The project begins with the found objects of crutches and wheelchairs as the basis for inserting new elements and corresponding movements. Multiple iterations starting with these initial sketches will generate the production.

Figure 8.15. *DanceAbility* **Performace with Participant in Wheelchair**
Photographer: Gil Grossi. Used by permission

Figure 8.16. *DanceAbility* **Performance with Participants of Various Abilities**
Photographer: Gil Grossi. Used by permission

By working with people who already confront normative understandings of movement, this project continues the examination of how movement can influence space creation, taking what might be seen as an extreme movement condition to understand that *all* occupants should be able to participate in the making of architectural space.

9

At Home in Motion

Networks, Nodes, and Navigation the Varied Flight Paths of Bird Brain Dance

Katrinka Somdahl-Sands

> Dancing is a sifting through, a gleaning,
> a search for that glint that binds us to a moment of recognition.
> Dancing is a visible language of hidden meanings,
> biting at the heels of what is knowable.
>
> —Monson 2011

The subject of this chapter is a navigational dance project performed by Bird Brain Dance in the fall of 2002. Over the course of this dance project, choreographer Jennifer Monson and her company literally followed the migration pattern of tagged ospreys as they flew south from Maine to Venezuela. The migratory tours of *Bird Brain Dance* were an attempt to link the dance world to art and science, illuminating linkages "between the natural world's fragile, delicate strength and the creative process" (Monson 2011). Each performance event began with a sensory workshop to help the audiences become mindful of their present moment, followed by the improvisational performance itself, and each event concluded with a discussion amongst the performers and audience members about their mutual experience. Ms. Monson used the idea of location to ground her work in the bodily realities of those present. Locations in this dance project were the source material for improvisational movement during each performance. A location was founded on the unique physicality of a performance site, which acted as inspiration leading to non-literal movement impulses. Location was a way for the performers to acclimatize quickly to their ever-transitioning environments. As an artistic project the focus was on helping her performers and audience members experience their environments differently and become comfortable in the translation of experience to interpretation.

Using data from interviews, video recordings and the performer's online journals to illustrate their embodied understanding of transition, I will show how Ms. Monson created a deep sense of place, a home, in their moving bodies. The embodied locations created during the series of performances are contrasted to an analysis of non-places, specifically understandings of the spaces of migration and travel. Auge and others argue that while in transition we miss the meaning of place, we pass over it (1995). Yet *Bird Brain Dance* is showing how one can be at home in the transition, how all of the places passed through become integrated into ourselves across space and time. Monson does this by making explicit, conscious, and visible the relationship between the affect and experience of non-representational theory and the representation of those affects/experiences that can be communicated to others. In particular I am interested in how this is accomplished *on the move* (Cresswell 2006a). In this chapter I will show how movement and mobility can show us things that are harder to see when stationary. I argue in fact, that like the migrating birds, human bodies are also inherently the repositories of their previous points of interaction, up to and including the present moment. The structure of the article will detail (1) the project itself, (2) the building of a sensual sense of location, (3) the implications of a mobile performance, and (4) how these things can be conveyed when *on the move*.

BIRD BRAIN DANCE

Bird Brain Dance is an experimental dance troupe led by choreographer Jennifer Monson.[1] During the fall of 2002, Ms. Monson, three dancers, a videographer, a tour manager, and I participated and documented the Osprey Tour.[2] This dance performance began in August of 2002 and continued through October. The Osprey Tour was the second of four navigational tours following the migratory pathways of birds and grey whales on their journeys across northern and southern hemispheres. These animals are links between continents and ecosystems. Their migration creates webs of interaction that are material, delicate, and infinitely complex. In fact, some small birds have more contact with more parts of the Earth than most of us will have in a lifetime. The particular tour I documented followed Ospreys (also known as sea hawks) on their journey from Maine down the Eastern seaboard, through Miami, Cuba, and finally Venezuela. Unfortunately, I was unable to continue the tour past Florida. The tour may have officially begun in August of 2002 at an estuary in Maine, however the actual process of creating the tour began long before that. Ms. Monson wrote dozens of grants,[3] hired a tour programmer/organizer, and determined the route and dancers. Overall, there were four migratory tours undertaken by Bird Brain, each tour provided approximately thirty free outdoor performances and included both a formal and informal educational component. This tour was then just a series of 30 dances. Many of the performances also included a panel discussion afterward[4] that included artists, scientists, leaders of arts centers and environmental organizations along its 3000-mile route.

During the Osprey Tour the individual performance events all followed the same structure. Ms. Monson would introduce herself, her troupe, and her mission.

Then she would lead a short sensory workshop to ground the spectators in their immediate surroundings. At the conclusion of the workshop the performance itself would begin. The dancing was a combination of choreographed material, improvisational scores, and inspiration in the moment. The final portion of each event was an open discussion between the performers and the audience members about the proceeding shared experiences. The migratory tours of Bird Brain Dance were an attempt to link the dance world with the terrain of wildlife refuges, aquariums, state and national parks, and urban streetscapes in order to reach the variety of audiences who frequent these habitats.

Each performance of Bird Brain included a brief introductory workshop on navigation and sensory perception that helps prepare the audience to experience the performance (Monson 2011). The workshops were intended to lead the audience to connect with their own navigational skills and to relate our skills to those of animals, helping the audience become more aware of their environment. The performers also hoped to use movement and dance to teach school students about bird navigation and physiology by showing the audiences how the birds navigate and how we as humans also navigate over distances. Ms. Monson wanted to use the interconnectedness of migratory bird habitats as a metaphor for how our own communities are linked (2011). As the company followed the southward migration of ospreys from their nesting sites in Maine along the Eastern seaboard through Cuba through to their winter homes in Venezuela, they saw themselves as weaving together a community across continents, ecosystems, and cultures that "will support and provoke a dialogue about the symbiotic, contradictory, and confrontational relationships between art, technology, environment, power and place" (Weisz 2008).

September 6, 2002
Prospect Park
Journal Posted by Jennifer[5]

I started at an over-grown ditch by the lake. A mallard duck was snuffling its bill in the moss/algae in the pond. I wondered for a minute who was watching who. Behind me were some kids on bikes. I could feel their curious gaze. I felt their willingness to look at something weird—to enjoy it. I started building my dance, expressing something about my feeling of space. The sensation of the duck's bill in the water as center of the moment, rippling out to my own body; then to the gaze of the boys on the bikes; the trees beyond them; the streets of Brooklyn beyond the park; Long Island, Staten Island, Manhattan, the plane above and the dome of the sky and then beyond that. My body felt like a quicksilver cipher, reflecting off so many energetic sensations and thoughts. . . . This event fulfilled my vision of BIRD BRAIN in so many ways. I loved our audience that came from the bird world, the dance world, the queer world and the neighborhood. . . . I really enjoyed the dancing and felt connected to our environment, our audience and the clarity of the movement. [During] the panel discussion . . . Peter Mott . . . mentioned that migrating birds often recruit local birds to join the migration and he asked our audience if they noticed our recruitment. We were spontaneously joined by some of the kids on bikes in the middle of the performance. That made us all very happy.

NODES: SITE-SPECIFIC DANCING

Performance is a particular set of "cultural presentations that have recognizable the-atrical components: Namely, framing devices that alert the audience, spectators or participants to the reflexive structure of what is staged" (Kershaw 1992, 15). Dance is a form of (generally) non-vocal performance in which the body moving through space is the medium of the art. "Dancers' bodies not only shape space, but their actions energize and give meaning to the spaces in which they perform" (Somdahl-Sands 2007, 16). Watching dance creates a kinesthetic response in the audience that produces a kind of physical consciousness of both the performers and spectators bod-ies. Dance historian Elizabeth Dempster explained the corporeal relationship of the body to space within modern dance stating that "the modern dancer's body registers the play of opposing forces, falling and recovering, contracting and releasing. It is a body defined through a series of dynamic alterations, subject to both movements of surrender and movements of resistance" (1995, 28). However, the emotional and symbolic aspects of dance performances are also important since in this art the body is explicitly used as the site where social and psychological, spatial and rhythmic con-flicts are enacted. The physical and symbolic aspects of the art can be seen in most dance performances. Dancers luxuriate in the physicality of the body, while directing focus to the meaning created by the dancer's body moving in space.

Bird Brain Dance uses nature, exploration, and everyday spaces to bring dance to people who would probably not see it, or certainly wouldn't see it in the spaces they performed in—streets, nature preserves, city parks, or school yards. Site-specific dances take a particular place as the inspiration and setting for the performance. Through reading a site, physically, sensually, intellectually, and emotionally, the choreographer is "able to provide a performative translation of place that heightens our awareness of our surroundings" (Kloetzel and Pavlik 2010, 2). A site-specific choreographer, in this instance Jennifer Monson, does not want her audience to just see a local place, but to actually engage with it in a new way. The goal is a physical exchange between the audience and the place where the audience is sensitized to local contexts; to "replace indifference with interest . . . [and even] compel us to experi-ence space in novel ways" (ibid., 3). Site-specific work does not give easy answers to what a site means. Bird Brain Dance pushes boundaries with their subtle emphasis on wonders of natural world that allows their audience to "discover layers in the place and place/human-place interface" (ibid., 5). Kloetzel and Pavlik (2010, 6–7) describe how site-specific dances share a focus on *attending to place* which includes two aspects: attention and tending. Attention to place is about drawing the attention *to* the place, so that both the audience and performers are more cognizant of exactly where they are. The second aspect of attending to place is creating a connection *with* the place, which implies a kind of stewardship or tending of that place. Attending to a place in their schema is also active, attending requires a focus on the process of working with people and place over time and not just looking at the final product.

Site-specific dance performances articulate the properties, qualities, and meanings produced at the nexus between the event and its location. Site specific performances require reflection from the beholder as the assumptions about the place for art are often called into question. When Jennifer took her work to the state parks in Maine or into the streets of the East Village, New York City, the performers and audience members alike confronted their efforts 'to locate or place' the dance when the proscenium theater frames was not present. Instead of surroundings being presumed to be a blank slate, we explicitly look for meaning in those surroundings. Thus a key to understanding a site-specific piece is the location itself. Exploring one's location was actually the foundational score for the Osprey Tour. Location in this context, as a score, refers to the process of keying into your sensory awareness of a site, triggering a unique response to that 'location.' This deep awareness of the place is the spark inspiring movement. This score allows for good (non-verbal) communication between dancers as they each become apart of the others location. This locational score also creates a very intimate response to the audience. As a part of the environment they too become part of the stimulus for the performance.

The performer, Alejandra Martorell, wrote in an online journal about how she interpreted an early location on the tour and what she yearned to experience in future performance locations.

August 28, 2002
Performance Notes: Province Lands Visitor Center
Journal Posted by Alejandra

The gravel was hard but I enjoyed giving weight into it and feeling the roughness on my skin. . . . I was mostly focused on the architecture and the visual input of the place: the shadows of the auditorium's benches, the benches themselves, the lines of clouds in the sky, the gravel, the grass on the edge, the shrubs, the short wooden fence that marked the walking and bicycling paths. . . . I felt the attention of the audience very clearly, and liked the inversion we created where people were sitting on benches but looking back to the rear of the auditorium. . . . My arms are always very prominent in the movement initiation as well as gesturing. I yearn for a more grounded and integrated feeling of my body when I dance. I think of Jennifer's dancing and how the earth seems to come through her legs, into and out of her belly, her whole torso and out through her limbs.

One of the reasons public performance is so successful in its ability to attend to place (Kloetzel and Pavlik 2010) is that performance is a direct form of experience. The experience of watching or performing in a site-specific work is sensuous, qualitative, immediate, intuitive, and non-cognitive. It is a "direct qualitative experience that is characteristically non-discursive and hence non-rational" (Berleant 1970, 119). A dance performance is thus able to express meanings not usually accessible through words. Dance uses rhythm, bodies, and movement to create a kinesthetic response in the audience. Dance *affects* us. Dance critic Marcia Siegel writes that the experience of observing dance is fundamentally intuitive, visceral, and preverbal. Only later do we bring words, categories, systems to rationalize what we've experienced. If a dance doesn't suggest meaning by its performance, no amount of intellectualizing can put meaning into it (Siegel 1988, 30).

This is why dance is so attractive to writers utilizing non-representational theory. Dance is experienced by both performers and spectators through the body and through the senses. We watch the dancers' bodies move, listen to their breath, and can sometimes even feel the vibrations as they roll to the floor. The senses give us our world, which we then create into organized understandings. Some senses can be labeled proximate while others are distant. The proximate senses yield the world closest to us, including our own bodies. The position and movements of our bodies produce proprioception or kinesthesia, somatic awareness of the basic dimensions of space. The other proximate senses are touch, sensitivity to changes in temperature, taste, and smell. Hearing and sight are the senses that make the world out there; they are the distant senses. Yet despite being initially experienced through the distant senses of hearing and sight, dance triggers responses in our proximate senses that are often difficult for audience members to describe. Morgan Thorson, one of the performers, attempted to describe how the interaction of her senses and the landscapes of the performances were influencing her sense of self.

August 31, 2002
Boardwalk Beach
Journal Posted by Morgan

From here we go anywhere. The landscape is coddling us now. The silence wraps us in a benevolent embrace, pushing us into the future and bringing the not so distant past with us. Those authentic movements, those shiny duets, are accumulating in my bones like sand falling through a narrow hourglass. The environment has . . . framed us each, just now in a grandiose picture. We flatter one another, and the landscape . . . I take notice of small creatures, I bend and bow to their flattering gaze. . . . While my mind jumps from memory to intellectual reflection, I can still hear . . . the rhythms of the waves, the clucking of the birds, the lapping of the tidal pool. I can't escape my desire to dive in, to catch my eye in the glint of the sun bouncing off the water; dappled shimmering surface of gold, silver reflecting a fiery warmth.

Morgan is writing about place as sensation. What are the sensations of the place you are in right now? As you read, feel your weight in your chair. Notice the small shifts of pressure on your body as you sit. Now listen for something very close to you, perhaps your own breathing or your clothes rustling or even your hands brushing against the pages of this book. Now take a moment and listen for something far away. What is it and how far away do you think it is? How do you know? Can you orient yourself in space, in the room you are in, in relation to what you see or what you hear? Could you close your eyes and navigate to the door? Where is your home from here?

These perceptual exercises are a small portion of the sensory and perceptual workshop Monson would conduct before every performance. In the workshop she also has the participants move toward each other with their eyes closed, or towards a sound from the environment, she also asks them to pay attention to the feel of the air on their bodies as they move in spirals. What she (and I) did with these activities is "alienate" (to use Brecht's term) you to your habitual approaches by requesting that you step out of them. In an academic book, you usually are not addressed directly, nor are you expected to DO anything. Your usual job is to sit, read, and hopefully understand. You are rarely aware of your surroundings (or your bodies for that matter) unless it somehow disrupts your ability to perform your task of reading and comprehending the text.

Ms. Monson believed that these sensory workshops before the performances were important because it created a frame for the dancing. Ms. Monson was aware that many people do not have any experience with experimental dance and thus lack a reference point to interpret what they were watching during a performance. Another site-specific choreographer, Ann Carlson, summed up this idea when referring to her own work: "I think it would have helped to have an intermediary activity that would have broken down and/or explained a little bit of what you were doing. You know the space between pedestrian behavior and abstracted movement" (Kloetzel and Pavlik 2010, 110). This is particularly important in site work where the majority of theater conventions telling the audience how to orient their experience may be absent.

During the workshops Ms. Monson could see her audiences begin to relate to their environments with their senses not just their minds; their "bodies soften," and how they "interacted with each other softer" (2011). At the end of the workshop she would often ask them to look at movement in the environment, sometimes this statement would be the transition to the performance itself. Ms. Monson liked that this transition to performing would allow the audience to see us as a part of nature. As a part of nature there are no aesthetic criteria to judge the dance. The movement is thus a vehicle for engaging in the ideas. It confuses the boundaries between nature and the world (Monson 2011). The movement stemming from sensation breaks expectations and creates/shows an intimacy with the environment. The workshops allowed the audience to travel this circle of sensation, to interpretation, to action with the performance. The audiences were small, 10–30 people and so the performers could almost interact with all of them one on one. After the performances, audience members would come up to the performers and say, "I've never seen anyone move like that." They were seeing new things that the body can do. What the Bird Brain performances were doing was dislocating people from their habits to relocate them somewhere else—in their own bodies. In essence using performance to try and build a valuing for other forms of intelligence.

The response among the audience to the dancing is one of affect. While it is unlikely that the audience member had truly never seen anyone *move like that*, what had changed was his or her appraisal of that bodily action. The movement looked completely different after being taught how to appreciate the internal experience of the senses and then taking those senses into movement, which is an external representation of experience. Derek McCormack describes this realization as "becom[ing] responsive to different surfaces of attention rather than seeking to go behind or beyond them" (2003, 493). The act of truly witnessing the dance answers Dewsbury's call to "stop separating the world out into meaningful representations on the one hand and ephemeral sensations on the other, and to become attentive instead to truths folded into the fabric of the world itself" (2003, 1908). The space of the performance folds the performers, the audience and the locations together to build a sense of belonging, to feel in place even as they move through the site.

NAVIGATION: MOVING THROUGH PLACE

The difficulty with relocating the audience, and the performers, in the fleshy reality of sensation is that "the implications of thinking through the corporeal are not as straightforward as might be imagined"(Latham and McCormack 2004, 705). This is not least because "when a body is in motion, it does not coincide with itself. It coincides with its own transition: its own variation" (Massumi 2002, 5). A body in motion, performing or not, can never be exactly reproduced, so there can be no fixity of meaning, it can be strived for but never achieved. Consequently a dance performance is an experiment that may go off in unforeseen directions. Dance is an experiment in the seamless integration of the experiential and the referential (Dewsbury 2003). "It is one way of understanding the nature of your attention as you are engaged within a practice. And yet something more takes place" (ibid., 1918).

September 21, 2002
Navigation, Hawk Mountain Sanctuary
Journal Posted by Jennifer

I realize how vigorously I am navigating my external and internal worlds and desires conceptually, kinetically and emotionally. Today as I prepared to start the performance I didn't know how to orient myself. . . . I wasn't sure how to begin. . . . [A] simple and generous introduction . . . was needed to allow me to make my odd, shy transition from person to dancer. What is that transition? What is the difference between me as person and as dancer? Because [the] introduction of the dance as interpretive of osprey behaviors and because I was feeling the layers of process embedded in my body I felt like the transition had to do with an animal's keen awareness. I became more watchful, more intent, more conscious of each movement—it's effect on the landscape, on me, on the space between me and the audience. The thing about being a person is that most movement has a task at hand—drawing the binoculars up to your eyes to spot a bird, reaching out to catch your balance or to unbutton your coat. That's true of animals as well, catch the thermal up, dive towards food, preen a feather. There is a directness and efficiency to each action. Yet my dancing is about sensation, opening up pores, eyes, nostrils to sensual input in order to respond with movement driven by my imagination. I navigate the world between representation, abstraction and sensation. Is it less representative to look up at the architecture of the branches in the trees and have that trigger me to splay out my limbs in angular, crooked movement, or to feel the wind take my arms into a swaying swirling wind current, than to stick out my arms and imagine soaring like an osprey? My mind and body ran rampant with literal images today as I swerved between the immediacy of responding to the humidity, . . . the hard ground and rocks, the image of osprey and the sensation of movement transitioning me up the trail towards Javier and on to Alejandra and Morgan.

Understanding all movement as a kind of performance produces situated relationships between performer and place, suggesting a geographically and historically located practical knowledge (Edensor 2000). Embodied movement has been discussed within geography (Cresswell 2004; Thrift 2004; Adey, Budd and Hubbard 2007; Bissell 2009), but walking creates a particular form of a sense of place (Adams 2001). Edensor argues that "walking articulates a relationship between pedestrian and place, a relationship which is a complex imbrications of the material organization and shape of the landscape, its symbolic meaning, and the ongoing sensual perception and experience of moving through space" (2000, 82). Moving through space as a pedestrian (or as a dancer) is conducive to a reflexivity brought about by the sensual body and it's multiple senses.

Moving through a place by one's own power facilitates being involved with the place through all of the senses sight, hearing, touch, smell, kinetic, movement/work of muscles and taste, so the sense of place developed is based on these senses. "In peripatetic place-experience lies the basis of a special kind of knowledge of the world and one's place in it. . . . it is a more profound mode of experiencing place" (Adams 2001, 188–89, see also Casey 2001). One particular kind of moving described by Adams as "light peripatetic" is a kind of ritual where one "attunes oneself bodily and mentally with the universe and especially with nature" (2001, 193). To be attuned to one's environment one has to be both sensitive to it, and then to harmonize with one's surroundings. This is another way of explaining the locational score utilized by Bird Brain during the Osprey Tour. Moving through an area while attuned to it produces a heightened sensitivity to the environment as well as a heightened sense of self as could be seen in Morgan Thorson's journal entry from above. As the surroundings unfold all around the mover it is not a dominating vision, rather it is a multi-sensory experience intertwining person and place.

September 13, 2002
Transitions
Journal Posted by Jennifer

As Robin and I headed down the Garden State Parkway in bumper-to-bumper traffic, I couldn't help but slow down. Physically moving through space slowly, yet mentally my brain was still racing with the multi-tasking and anxiety of NY. I could feel the familiarity of being on the highway. There is a certain way that time seems to hold still in the car. . . . I am absorbing and processing my internal experiences as the outside world flashes by. I am realizing now how essential that time is. Even though I hate driving, I hate sitting for hours, I hate gas stations and service centers. I don't like the transition from the car to tent. Even though both are made out of something like plastic and they both offer shelter and comfort in their own way. I like how my tent makes me feel the immediacy of the elements. It amplifies the sound of the rain and the wind. It magnifies the heat of the sun. The car insulates me from the elements. We listen to the radio . . . so I am connected to the world in a more long distance way. In my tent I am connected more intimately with dirt and air and bugs and plants. . . . the liminal moments in the day when I suddenly pay attention to the details of a raindrop running down my cheek, the leaves turning red early because of the drought down the east coast, a thick orange stripped caterpillar pulling its corpulent body across the hard, tan sand scattered with acorns.

Urban movement is constricted and often restricts sensual experiences of place (Boddy 1992; Davis 1999). De Certeau describes how walking is tacitly used by urban pedestrians to create "spaces of enunciation" (1984, 98), paths of fleeting creative inscription, as they attempt to avoid the constraints on movement in cities. However, even the tactical walking/movement of these pedestrians is often unreflexive and simply habitual practice. Thus the audiences who would attend a Bird Brain performance are likely de-sensitized to their environment. Prior to the sensory workshop they are likely not in tune with their surroundings in a light peripatetic way. Through the attending to place by Bird Brain, the audience becomes in tune to the place of the performance. Lippard describes the longing for connection to place that we lose in our urban environments as "the lure of the local . . . the pull of place that operates on all of us, exposing our politics and our spiritual legacies. It is the geographical component of the psychological need to belong somewhere, one antidote to a prevailing alienation" (Lippard 1997, 7). Yet this quote makes assumptions about how one should cure alienation from nature, the body, and the city. The assumption is that as humans we have a psychological need to belong somewhere and that somewhere is place based, the local.

However, in the discussions about place and an alienated non-place, place is formed through shared language, local references, and the "unformulated rules of living know-how, . . . where one's location or position is known, whereas non-place is produced by passing over place" (Kaye 2000, 9). Non-place has two distinct and complimentary realities: the first is spaces formed in relation to certain ends (transport, commerce, leisure), and two, the relations people have with their spaces. The first is about a projection forward, and individual's relationship to moving on (a commitment to a later future place); the second is about the relationship of moving, a mobility that suppresses the differences of place. Yet even if every Dairy Queen in every small town looks the same, the meaning imbued into it by the local inhabitants is unique to those inhabitants (Relph 1976). It's the migrants, tourists, and non-locals who would see that locale as a non-place. This is what Auge (1995) is alluding to in his discussion of non-place that it is in transition that we miss the meaning of place, we pass over it. Urban space is increasingly organized to facilitate directional movement by both pedestrians and vehicles reducing points of entry and exit and minimizing distractions. Such designs, instead of being "relational, historical and concerned with identity" (ibid., 107–8) produce realms of 'transit' as opposed to 'dwelling,' sites of 'interchange' rather than a meeting place or 'crossroads.' Non-place is created through dis-placement. Thus it is stability that is placed; while movement leads to non-place.

Nevertheless Bird Brain is explicitly trying to counter this idea of non-place through traveling. They are not negating place as they migrate, but by alienating people from their normal modes of identifying the place a new sense of place is created. What Bird Brain is doing is trying to show how one can be at home in the transition, how all of the places passed through can become a place. Entomologist Hugh Dingle suggests, "migration is specialized behavior especially evolved for the displacement of the individual in space" (Monson 2011). This could just as easily be a definition of dance. "As dancers/improvisers, we tune and hone our skills of navigation in order to move through the moment of creation with acute sensitivity to our surroundings, cultivating our senses to be prepared for the unpredictable and unexpected" (ibid.).

Cresswell showed how people on the move can be deemed to be out of place (2006a). The dancers of Bird Brain are matter out of place, but on purpose. We in the west are very distrustful of those constantly on the move with no place to call home (Cresswell 1996, 2006). We do not have nomadic traditions and we fear them, no more so than the myth of the placeless Gypsy (Kabachnik 2010). The image of a nomad, Roma, or vagrant is the opposite of the in tune and attended light peripatetic wanderer, it is a mover as outcast, excluded from society (Adams 2001, Cresswell 2001). When place is "seen as a mere fixed location" it will "deny place to those who are not sedentary" (Kabachnik 2010, 199). Home is the place that often constructed as the foundation of the self, the space of identity and yet is also constructed as immobile—a fixed location (Bachelard 1994).

Home is a loaded term. According to Heidegger (1971), home is associated with dwelling, and is the key location in which a spiritual unity is found between humans and things. Home for Bachelard is a dwelling, but it is also a symbol of shelter, security, pleasure, and the storehouse of memories (1994). Bachelard argues that the childhood home is the ideal: "it begins enclosed, protected, all warm in the bosom of the house" (ibid., 7). To Bachelard, when we think of home, "we travel to the land of Motionless Childhood, motionless the way Immemorial things are." (ibid., 6). We of course know that the domestic domicile is not so simple. It can be a place of violence, work, and social construction or segregation of people according to gender, class, race, and age. This is so because "[h]omes are not about inclusions and wide open arms as much as they are about places carved out of closed doors, closed borders, and screening apparatuses" (George 1996, 19). I believe this particular understanding of home is reflective of an understanding of identity as bounded and separated—by our bodies, our communities, our nation-states (Blunt and

Dowling 2006). Our identities are attached to these boundaries and the separations they create, whereas to cross these boundaries (by being a hobo, refugee, or even a transsexual) is to transgress social expectations of who we are supposed to be. Stasis perceives change as corrupt and migrants unsettle the settled. But does the orthodoxy of identity in place serve us? Does the definition of home need coordinates? Can anyone think about a static conception of place or home anymore?

But home (bounded or not) is still the ideal. And our bodies (bounded or not) are our homes. It is in our bodies that we feel and dwell. And so the question Monson was asking with her performances was, what happens if we take that home, our bodies, and move? Home is important to the mobile, such as the Roma, it is the place near kin (Kabachnik 2010). This is a home-place based on our corporeality and on the connections across space and time, what Ms. Monson would call snail trails embedded within lines of connectivity, webs, and grids that cross our arbitrarily assigned notions of here and there and us and them. Like the migrating birds, human bodies are also inherently the repositories of their previous points of interaction, up to and including the present moment.

September 5, 2002
Urban Migration: Patagonia to the River Project
Journal Posted by Jennifer

The next store over was a kind of chacha shop with feather boas and sunglasses and hats. I knelt down next to a woman sitting on a chair in front of the shop. I needed a little rest and the energy on that part of the block was call for more interaction. She asked me where I was from and a tumult of answers came tumbling to the tip of my tongue—the Patagonia Store; Wells, Maine; Massachusetts; Brooklyn; California; the world of experimental dance? What does that map look like? Then she asked where I was going and the same thing happened—to the Hudson River; Cuba; Venezuela; the integrated world of art and conservation? How would an Osprey answer the question? The NE nesting grounds? Latin America? The journey in between? I keep talking about finding home in movement and I felt that way dancing through the streets, relaxed, nervous, resting, bored, interacting on private and public levels. Then I asked the woman where she was from originally and she said Russia and my mind made both a geographic and cultural map. I tried to place each of us on the map together—like those big city information maps with a big red dot and arrow that says, *you are here.*

NETWORKS: THE MOBILITY OF PLACE

Positionality is the foundation of subject identity in space (Grosz 1995). But location and *dis*location are crucial to understanding the social relationships that underlie our multiple and shifting identities through space (McDowell 1999). Performance, in general, and dance, in particular, can privilege certain dimensions of experience so that their dynamics and mechanisms can be better understood. Dance performances are able to illuminate the unstable and sensuous notions of place that are often obscured in the processes of everyday life. For instance, "here" is a "moment of encounter" not a fixed site (Amin and Thrift 2002). Massey contends that places, like here, are "not so much bounded areas as open and porous networks of social relations" (1994, 121). The spaces of our lives are an act of becoming. Places are relational, produced and reproduced through human practices. Places may be a location that is infused with meaning, but it is also clearly about connections.

Everyday life has so many dimensions that much of what we experience is taken for granted and ignored. It is made up of recurrent human and material practices, daily rhythms, and of course our embodiment. Our everyday lives are the "intermesh between flesh and stone, humans and non-humans, fixtures and flows, emotions and practices" (Amin and Thrift 2002, 9). Mobility is a foundational piece of everyday life, to the point that it is ontologically prior to actually moving. In a panel on the meaning of mobility Hayden Lorimer stated that "mobility can be the continual flux of sitting still" (Merriman et al. 2008, 206). Cresswell continued this thought by discussing how "[a]s a discipline we fall back on things that seem more fixed, even in the most fluid interpretation of them. We fall back on boundaries, and material structures, spaces and places" (ibid., 206). So how can we think about material structures, our recurrent practices, and daily rhythms as mobile even if they appear still?

The locations of Bird Brain's performances may appear still, but are in truth rife with movement. They are founded on the physicality of a place but that inspiration led to nonliteral bodily translation. The whole point of location as a score was to look at the moment of transition. What are quick transitions, slow transitions, can you live and feel *at home* in transitions? Can our identities and our 'home' always be located even while in motion? Traveling with the work is very different than doing a piece in one place. In one place the work accretes layer upon layer in the space. This does not, cannot happen, on the move. The acclimatization must happen much more quickly, as it does with birds when migrating. But what Bird Brain Dance showed their audiences, by their workshops and performances, was that quick acclimatization is not only possible, but that everyone could do it. We all have sensing bodies, and those bodies are our homes.

October 11, 2002
Miami River Inn
Journal Posted by Jennifer

> I can still feel the hugeness of the sky above me even as I feel pushed down into this asphalt urban landscape. I feel a kaleidoscope of images. I want to keep them all moving in front of me. I don't want to lose the preciseness of each experience. I want to order each one here and turn the dial to see the next.

Artists and choreographers have the ability to show their audiences questions they might not have thought to ask themselves as social life can be temporarily reordered during a performance. Bird Brain shows how the body is the means through which we experience and can feel the connections present in the world.

The performer's "body takes shape through its interactions with other objects, bodies and landscapes. . . . [O]ur physical body and sensations are understood to be on the move, interconnected with other bodies and contexts. This means our sense of embodiment is dependant on how our body is put to use" (Macpherson 2010). The interactions of bodies, sensations, intellectualizations, and actions "weave together a community across continents, ecosystems and cultures that are created through mobility" (Monson 2011).

AT HOME IN MOTION

When questioned by one of the dancers on the tour why there were so few people at the performances, Ms. Monson stated that she didn't really care. She was drawing a line of energy with movement and bodies. They completed the journey. They tied the continents together like the birds. As a dancer she believed she had to start there and let the reverberations, energetic and spiritual, move out from that place. I'd like to end with a description of what it feels like to be at home and in motion.

October 31, 2002
The body's cloudy gardens
Journal Posted by Javier

I write from the green that floods my eyes. My breath is graceful, soft, easy. In these last days of the tour I'm living in the clouds, and I am not just saying this. Venezuela's Rancho Grande sits within a great forest. Trees, orchids, insects, birds with psychedelic plumage, and other animals inhabit the clouds of this biological reserve. When the thin wet veil envelopes all this greenery, the rhythm and speed of time run out. Sight becomes foggy and the silence that was already present becomes overwhelming. You see in a whole different way. The private senses of the self are altered perceiving other realities. Disorganized but coherent, my body moves unregulated. The gesture here is decoded, it has no meaning and at the same time it can mean everything. Ordinary movement now exists under different premises, and a strange pleasure fits between skin and meat, between bones and blood. I inquire, I search the particular pleasure that I carry and I am happy to find myself dancing and driven by the unknown. I am many fragments. . . . My heart is pumping and my lungs expand. I feel like I will never be tired, and I attribute it to the hazy and humid air that I breathe. . . . I do not know where I have left the harsh criticism and the body as subject and the study of the postmodern. I do know that a strange pleasure reigns in me, and I acknowledge that in me inhabits a different and absolute happiness that tells me I'm alive in new ways. And I can travel like a bird in the mist sensing my own routes. So, like in a bird corridor, sensations and emotions migrate through my body and I recognize some of them as physical . . . I . . . learned and continue to learn to observe with my senses. I translate with my body that which I have collected via the senses and thus create within and outside of me a new environment or Landscape. I have visited, altered, created many Landscapes throughout this migratory route.

NOTES

1. Jennifer Monson has been pursuing an original approach to experimental dance forms in New York City since 1983 when she graduated from Sarah Lawrence College. In that time, she has created a wide body of work that incorporates well-developed collaborative relationships with many artists including Zeena Parkins, John Jasperse, Yvonne Meier, and David Zambrano. Her solo work has been presented at many venues in the United States, Australia, Europe, Latin America, and Tanzania. Her project, Bird Brain, has been awarded two Rockefeller Foundation MAP Grants (2000 and 2003), a New York Foundation on the Arts (NYFA) BUILD Grant (2000), Creative Capital Foundation Grant (including second round competitive funding, 1999–2001), Geraldine R. Dodge Foundation grant, New England LEF Foundation grant, and Altria Inc. grants. The Bird Brain: Ducks and Geese Migration has also received an NPN Community Fund grant for documentation and evaluation. The three Bird Brain Migrations each provided approximately thirty free outdoor performances from Mexico to Canada and from Maine, through Cuba to Venezuela and from Texas to Canada. In the Ducks and Geese Migration school children in four cities participated in the educational component and in Bird Brain Flocking dances (Monson 2011).

2. Choreographer/Dancer: Jennifer Monson. Dancers: Alejandra Martorell (Puerto Rico), Javier Cardona (Puerto Rico), Morgon Thorson (Minneapolis, MN). Tour Director: Barbara Bryon. Videographer: Robin Vachal.

3. The tour was funded in part by Creative Capital Foundation, Jerome Foundation, New England LEF Foundation, Phillip Morris Companies Inc., Rockefeller Foundation MAP grant, Foundation for Contemporary Performance Arts, The New York Foundation for the Arts TechTAP, and BUILD programs, the New York Foundation for the Arts, and Individual contributions sponsored the dance. Scientists supporting the project include Mark Martell at the Raptor Center and the University of Minnesota and Keith Bildstein at Hawk Mountain Sanctuary, Pennsylvania. Individual performances and sites had other donors and partners, for instance in Miami Bird Brain partnered with Tigertail productions and thus collaborated with Miami Museum of Science (where they had a performance and panel), Spring Garden civic Association, the Trust for Public Land, City of Miami Parks and Recreation, Jose Marti Park, Miami River Commission, Everglades National Parks (Monson 2011).

4. Panel discussions with local scientists, conservationists, and artists followed most of the performances. The audience had the opportunity to discuss issues of migration, navigation and conservation on both a local and global level. Bird Brain worked with local partners to identify panelists in the community that were interested in exploring and discussing these issues.

Tour 2 panelists included June Ficker, Wells Reserve, ME; Karen McElmurry, Managing Director, Center for Wildlife, ME; Don Hudson, President, The Chewonki Foundation, ME; Sue Haley, Supervisor, Salt Pond Visitor Center, MA; Peter Mott, NYC Audubon, NY; Rebekah Creshkoff, Author, NYC; Cathy Drew, The River Project, NY; Mitschka Hartley, PhD, Forest Ecologist, Cornell Laboratory of Ornithology, NY; Tedor Whitman, The Wetlands Institute, NJ; Peter Murphy, Author, NJ; Ulla Dalum Berg, PhD Candidate, NYU Anthropology, NY; Jack Connor, Professor of Writing, Richard Stockton College of New Jersey, NJ; Scott Weidensaul, Author, PA; Wendy Hill, PhD, Professor and Chair of Neuroscience, Department of Psychology, Lafayette College, PA; Wendy Stanton, Wildlife Biologist, Pocosin Lakes NWR, NC; Feather Phillips, Director, Pocosin Arts, NC; William R. Stott III,

Research Professor; Director, Albemarle Ecological Field Site, The Carolina Environmental Program, University of N.C., NC; Jan DeBlieu, Author, NC; Ernie Marshall, Bird Watcher, NC; Marimar McNaughton, Marketing Director, Pocosin Arts, NC; Whit McMillan, South Carolina Aquarium, SC; Ann Shahid, Education Director, Francis Beidler Forest Audubon Center and Sanctuary, SC; Brooke Vallaster, Sapelo Island NERRS, GA; Brian Mealey, Director of the Department of Environmental Science, Miami Museum of Science, FL; Frankie Aranzamendi, Bilingual Interpretive Park Ranger, Everglades National Park, FL; Alan Farago, Chairman of the Board, Everglades Defense Council, FL; Brenda Marshall, Director, Trust for Public Land, FL; Jane Gilbert, Executive Director, Arts for Learning/Miami, FL; Janet McAliley, Miami River Commission, FL; Captain Beau Payne, Miami River Marine Group, FL; Mario Gonzalez, Director, Programa Sibarimar, Cuba; Alina Gonzalez, Education Director, Programa Sibarimar, Cuba; Rogelio Diaz-Fernandez, Investigator/Researcher. Population Genetics, Universidad de la Habana, Centro de Investigaciones Marinas, Cuba; Jordana Ayala, Coordinadora de Educacion Ambiental, Fundacion Tierra Viva, Venezuela; Xiomara Bastardo, Coordinadora de Educacion Ambiental, Fundacion Tierra Viva, Venezuela; Ernesto Fernandez Badillo, President, Henri Pittier National Park, Venezuela (Monsoon 2011).

5. All Journal entries available from Monson 2011 at http://www.birdbraindance.org/projects.cfm?id=3&sel=4

10

Belly Dancing in Israel

Body, Embodiment, Religion, and Nationality

Tovi Fenster

In the past ten years there has been a growing interest among Israeli-Jewish women in practicing belly dancing. In Jerusalem I have identified fifteen schools of belly dancing, which have opened in the last five to ten years. All the schools are located in the Western Jewish side of the city. This practice is not unique to Israel. Keft-Kennedy (2005) notes that women have taken up belly dancing in the West as a popular feminist activity. Similarly, Downey, Reel, SooHoo and Zerbib (2010) indicate the wide popularity of belly dancing in the United States. Within this framework, this chapter wishes to explore not only the reasons for the popularity of this trend in Israel and the choice of belly dancing out of a large variety of dance styles available to women, but mainly to investigate how the subjectivities of bodily performance and performativity in the studio change women's social identities. In particular, this chapter explores the implications of practicing belly dancing on women's ethnic, religious, and national identities. This last point is connected to the fact that many belly dancing students are *Jewish* observant women for whom there is a dramatic contrast between the bodily movements, clothing, eye contact, expressions of femininity and sexuality that they perform in belly dancing classes in the studio and in their daily life. Indeed, these differences are more significant for religious women but they are dramatic for secular women too.

My interest in this topic derives from my own personal experience of practicing belly dancing for the last four years and studying for one year in a belly dancing teacher's training course. Throughout these years I have become an insider-outsider experiencing belly dancing as a student in the studio from an intimate perspective as well as exploring the issue from an academic perspective. I then noticed how identity politics became an important element for the women practicing belly dancing, and began investigating how representations of religion, age, and ethnicity (especially Askenazi or Mizrachi) are present and presented in this form of dance. Ashkenazi and Mizrachi Jews are two (general) groups coming from different geographies as well as political, social, and cultural backgrounds. The former are from central and Eastern Europe, the latter from Arab and Middle Eastern countries. These ethnic divisions have evoked a significant amount of research regarding differences in housing, education, identity issue, and gender. In this paper, I focus on religion and age as two major identity components.

I base my analysis on three scales: Firstly, I look at the *body* as the basic unit of analysis in the practice and performance of belly dancing. This scale points not only to the unique performances of the dancing body as opposed to everyday activity, but also to the clothing, eye contact, makeup, use of the mirror, and intimacy developed between the women in belly dancing classes. These contrasting performances of the body in and outside the studio may lead to the assumption that the choice to practice belly dancing results from a repressed sense of the female body and femininity on the base of religious or cultural gendered norms and thus the body and embodied performances practiced in belly dancing classes can be interpreted as a form of resistance and of expressions of forbidden emotions and feelings. The second scale of analysis is the *studio space*. From women's experiences it seems that the studio becomes an heterotopic space (Foucault 2003) that is a space of liberation which is free of cultural and religious dictations; and this is precisely what enables women to dress up and perform their bodies in totally different and perhaps even in ways directly opposite to how they use their bodies on their daily life. On a third scale, the *ethnic and national*, the perceptional distinction between the practice of belly dancing and its cultural, ethnic, and political meanings as part of the Arab culture is investigated. It is assumed that the practice of belly dancing has no effect on women's perceptions of the Israeli-Arab/Palestinian conflict. What I present here is based on my own insider-outsider perspective and in-depth interviews I carried out with three students of belly dancing; all Ashkenazi from middle- to upper-class background who live in West Jerusalem.

THE ORIGINS AND HISTORY OF BELLY DANCING

Belly dancing is a term coined in the West for traditional Middle Eastern dance. The term 'belly dance' is a misnomer as every part of the body is involved in the dance: the most featured body part being the hips. Belly dance takes many different forms depending on country and region, costume and dance styles differ, and new styles have been invented in the west as its popularity has spread globally. As with any dance of folkloric origin, the roots of belly dance are uncertain. The authenticity of even 'traditional' or 'classical' forms of belly dance is open to question and often hotly disputed. The reasons for this uncertainty about the roots of belly dancing are, first, that belly dance was originally danced by women for women in the Levant and North Africa. This explanation is very popular in Western dance schools because it helps to counteract negative sexual stereotyping, but there is no written evidence to support it. Another explanation is that belly dance may have roots in the ancient Arab tribal religions as a dance to the goddess of fertility. A third explanation is that belly dance was always danced as entertainment. Some belly dance historians believe that the movements of dancing girls depicted in carvings during the time of the Pharaohs in ancient Egypt are typical of belly dancing. While these explanations may have some foundation, none of them can be proved to be the origin of belly dance. It is more likely that *all* these factors contributed to the development of belly dance as we know it today. In Middle Eastern society two specific belly dance movements have been used in childbirth for generations, but this is not sufficient evidence to prove that belly dancing arose from birthing rituals—the birthing rituals could equally have arisen from belly dancing.

The first recorded Western encounter with belly dance is during Napoleon's invasion of Egypt in 1798, when his troops encountered the gypsy dancers of the Ghazawee and the more refined dancing of the Almeh, special belly dancers of that period. Belly dance was later popularized during the Romantic movement of the 18th and 19th centuries, when Oriental artists and colonial travelers depicted romanticized images of harem life in the Ottoman Empire (Keft-Kennedy 2005). Around this time, dancers from Middle Eastern countries began to perform at various World Fairs, often drawing crowds in numbers that rivaled those for the science and technology exhibits. The 1893 World's Columbian Exposition in Chicago was famous for its belly dance performances, which raised public outrage over the dancers' movements of their bodies (Keft-Kennedy 2005). From the 1920s onward and with the beginning of the film industry in Egypt, belly dancing has changed dramatically. The rather spontaneous manner of the dance was replaced with choreography and soon a Casino Opera opened in Cairo mostly for westerners where belly dancing became to be perceived by westerners as a sensual, seductive, erotic dance with specific costumes. In 1952 with the revolution of the young officers in Egypt belly dancing was banned. This ban was abolished in 1954 but the prestige of belly dancing has been declined in Egypt since then but at the same time is flourished in Europe and the United States.

WHAT IS BELLY DANCE IN ISRAEL?

First of all, let's define what belly dancing is for those practicing it in Israel, and then what it means for the women practicing it. From conversations with my teacher I understand that there is not just one strict belly dancing style in general. She says she was very influenced by her first teacher in the United States—Serina Wilson. She went there to practice and learn the dance. She then started teaching and along the years studied with other teachers such as Ibrahim Facha, Yusef Sharif, and Lila Hadad. She can't really identify the style of belly dancing that she teaches in the studio as one single style. She obviously was very influenced by the U.S. style of dancing but as she says,

"Belly dancing is like modern dance—each dancer put her personal interpretation in the dance. There are basic movements to which every dancer adds her own style. To my dance I've put all I've learnt along the years including classic ballet, Israeli folk dances, etc. But Serina Wilson was the one who influenced mostly my dancing style." (Interview, June 22, 2011)

Nevertheless, she points to some uniqueness of Israeli belly dancing as compared to the American variation. First, she says that Israelis dance with bare feet, compared to Americans and Turkish women who dance wearing high heels. She also says that "we are part of the Middle East so the weather affects us and the body structure is different than the one of the American women" (ibid). Her style, she says, is minimalistic and simple. It's not seductive and sensual but is based on technique. She put a lot of emphasis on technique in her dancing and teaching. Her belly dancing is definitely different than the traditional Egyptian one and is a mixture of her personal imagination based on some bodily gestures significant to belly dancing.

I now move to discuss how the students in her classes experience belly dancing. In one of the lectures in class we associated the word *belly dance* for each of us. The words mentioned were "femininity; beauty; Jerusalem; to connect to body and soul; soul; freedom; arabesque; happiness; growing; eternity; body control; sensuality; knowledge of oneself; holiday; investment; love; women; Yael and Dorit" (the teachers) (Interview, June 22, 2011). These widespread positive connotations of the word belly dancing tell us about the personal meanings of belly dancing which go beyond the technicality and the physicality of the dance to emotions of growth, happiness, body contact, and so on.

PERFORMATIVITY, DANCING, BODY, AND EMBODIMENT

The literature on performativity, dancing and representation is not new. Dance theorists have already raised a series of issues that may temper as well as inspire the growing interest in the geography of embodiment, performativity, and play. Kemp for example argues that all dance is made up of complex "intersections of speech writing text and body" (quoted in Wolff 1995, 80; and Nash 2000, 656). In her review article in *Progress in Human Geography*, Cathrine Nash (2000) mentions the rich literature on this subject stating that "along with the new language of performativity, the vocabulary of dance is being enlisted in order to rethink ideas of subjectivity, embodiment and social identities" (Nash 2000, 653). By developing a new theoretical vocabulary of performance, the language of performance and dance has been taken up beyond dance and theatre studies. As Nash states, "the meaning of the moving body in dance and the migration of dance forms, traditions and styles as cultural practices are shaped by specific located and interconnected histories" (Nash 2000, 654).

The appearance of dance in geography is also inspired by feminist work on the body and especially Judith Butler's theories of performance of gender and sexuality together with other works of dance studies. According to Butler, gender doesn't exist outside its *doing*, but its performance is also a reiteration of previous *doings* that become naturalized as gender norms. The performativity rather than fixity of identity at least allows the possibility of challenging and parodying these naturalized codes. Butler focuses on gender and sexual identities but this sense of performativity of sex and gender has recently influenced the thinking about the performance of nationhood and ethnic identities. In my chapter, I'd like to re-define the studio as a heterotopic space liberated of these naturalized codes and therefore a space where there is the potential to affect social identities through performance and embodiment.

Thrift links performativity and bodily practices in what he terms *nonrepresentational theory* or the *theory of practice* (Thrift 1996, 1997). Nonrepresentational theory focuses on "practices, mundane everyday practices, that shape the conduct of human beings toward others and themselves in particular sites." This theory, he argues, is concerned with "presentations, showings and manifestations of everyday life" (Thrift 1997, 126–127). He maintains that it is through practices that people become *subjects*—decentered, affective, but embodied, relational, expressive, and involved with others and objects in a world continually in process. Thrift's ideas center around *body-subject* relations and the emphasis is on practices that cannot adequately be spoken of, that words cannot capture, that texts cannot convey but on forms of experience and movement that are not only or never cognitive. This theory moves away from a concern with representation and especially text since, it is argued, text only inadequately commemorates ordinary lives since it values what is written or spoken over multi-sensual practices and experiences. In line with this, Blumen (2011) further distinguishes between performance and performativity as two concepts that help explore how the human body functions from a non-representational perspective. Performance is a concept that analyzes activities as actions that combine materiality, body, and movement. Performativity emphasizes daily practices and the repetitive nature of bodily performances that actually transform identities because we come to perceive them as natural or 'normal.' Examples of performative body-practices are horse riding, swimming, running, or pet owning. Thrift chooses dancing as a "concentrated example of the expressive nature of embodiment" (Thrift 1997, 125). Dance, Thrift argues, connects to other social actions such as rituals, rhythmic work, and play. It is the playfulness of dance that is characterized as gratuitous, free, noncumulative, rule-bound, yet difficult to control, that explains its neglect in the social sciences and humanities. But at the same time these qualities are the source of its capacity to elude power. He argues that playful dance eludes rather than confronts or subverts power through its capacity to hint at different experiential frames, different ways of being that cannot be written or spoken, a point that I will elaborate on later in the paper. By this he suggests a new and demanding direction for cultural geography away from the analysis of texts, images, and discourses and toward understanding the *micro-geographies* of habitual practices, departing from deconstructing representations to explore the non-representational. Nash takes this line of thinking and argues that "the value of ideas of performance and practice is their challenge to forms of interpretation which focus on the representation of meaning in visual or literary texts or use textual analysis to understand the world" (Nash 2000, 657). Nash also sees in dancing the rejection of the modern in favor of the primitive. She identifies two directions of research on the body and embodiment that exist in the literature (Nash 2000). The first focuses on the understanding and denaturalizing of the social differentiation of bodies through practices, and the second focuses on a more generic and celebratory notion of the embodied nature of human existence. Out of these two directions, this paper takes the first one and perceives actual dancing, body gestures and clothing as associated with embodied discourses of resistance to patriarchal social control (Metha and Bondi 1999). By embodied discourses I follow Metha and Bondi's definition (1999) that these are both nonlinguistic and linguistic forms of knowledge and practice that reflect the ways we use our living bodies to give substance to the social distinctions and differences that underpin social relations. After all, as Metha and Bondi suggest following Csordas (1990, 5), arguing that "the body is not an object to be studied in relation to culture but . . . is to be considered as the subject of culture." As Davidson and Milligan (2004) note, our first and foremost, and most immediate and experienced felt geography is the body, the site of emotional experience and expression *par excellence*. Emotions to be sure take place within and around this closest of spatial scales. So, the body and emotions are closely related because the articulation of emotions is spatially related (Davidson and Milligan 2004). As elaborated later, this e/motion perspective is expressed in the studio activities as well.

DANCING

The gendered, cultural, national, and ethnic meanings of dancing have attracted the attention of many researchers. For example, the research of Savigliano (1995) on tango claims that it was never simply about the straight eroticism of the dance but rather about the cultural history and geography of who could tango, where, with whom, for what audience and how. The story of tango tells about concepts of culture, masculinity, class, and nationhood in Argentina, Paris, and Japan. With body gestures and costumes, tango is a performance of the play of power between men and women and between the colonizer and colonized. Likewise, Sanchez Gonzales (1999) discusses the specificity of the salsa's origins in the working class Puerto Rican diaspora in New York and challenges its exoticization and commodification in white salsa venues in North America. In a similar manner, Nash mentions the popularity of Salsa and Tango in Japan as a reminder of the travels of cultural forms that are linked but also bypass circuits of culture centered on Anglo-America. She gives an example of a Japanese company dancing salsa as an expression of hybridity when the Japanese salsa expresses a version of Japanese identity by incorporating and also maintaining the difference of the imported cultures. Other papers explore the dilemmas projected on dancers in specific cultural and political contexts such as the Indian female dancers whose dancing arise critique from contemporary Indian audiences because of the perceptions of the female body as sexual, articulate, and independent (Mitra 2006). Another paper (Wulff 2005) explores the Irish dancing body literally and metaphorically by combining the growing social science interest in mobility with the research on the body as a site of culture. Recently, there are a number of researchers that focus on belly dancing such as Keft-Kennedy's paper (2005), which investigates the process of bodily transformation through the practice of belly dance and explores the mechanisms by which women attain empowerment through the moving body. Downey, Reel, SooHoo and Zerbib's paper (2010) present survey data from a sample of 103 belly dancers in Salt Lake City, Utah, that addresses issues of body image and gender identity and emphasizes how belly dance offers a counter-example to unhealthy body image influences of other dances such as modern dancing where conditions of anorexia are more common because thin bodies are a pre-requisite for successful dancers.

WOMEN'S EXPERIENCES OF BELLY DANCING: SOME METHODOLOGICAL NOTES

This research is based on an insider-outsider perspective, with the author as an academic practicing belly dancing in the studio for the last four years and thus being an observer from within, but also interviewing my other belly dance students. The method I used both in my own observations and in the interviews is based on the distinction made in the literature on non-representation theory between performance and performativity—where the former helps me to connect between the body specific belly dancing movements and women's changing identities while the latter helps me to distinguish between the daily 'automatic' and perhaps banal use of the body and its use in the studio. That is, I want to draw a line between the different body performances in and out the studio and how these differences affect women's identities. By that, I want to find out what it is in the performance of the body in belly dancing classes in the studio that is so different from the banal and daily performativity of these women and to what extent these performances become significant in women's changing identities.

My own experience practicing belly dancing helps me to pinpoint these differences. They are expressed in the following: the *verbal discussions in classes on the e/motional effects of dancing; in the different clothing, makeup, eye contact, and body movements that dance creates; in working in front of the mirror; and in the bodily contacts and gestures between the women themselves.* These interpretations move beyond Thrift's point of the dance as an example of an expressive nature of embodiment as they illustrate that it's not just the *dance* itself that is an expressive nature of embodiment but the *belly dance* that becomes an identity change. Let me elaborate on these points.

In some of the classes there are *verbal discussions on the emotional and even the psychological effects of belly dancing* and of how to perform the body differently after learning it. In one of the classes the teacher said that the body is our musical instrument through which we play the music we hear. In response, one of the students who is a dance movement therapist said that dancing in general expresses "emotions through motions"—she said it in English to emphasize the strong linguistic connection of e/motion in the English language (this is not the case in Hebrew). Quick discussions like this with the emphasis on how different body motions express emotions emphasizes a process of change in multiple expressions of emotions. It is also interesting to notice how the teacher translates the body gestures inside the studio to those outside of it. She emphasizes how women should adopt a straight position—that is the starting point in the studio—in daily life. She uses an example of what one's body looks like in the different positions when it's loose and flabby and when it's straight and upright. She says, "[T]his is how we wait for the bus (loose) and this is what we look like when we dance (upright)" (Interview, June 22, 2011). This use of a scene in womens' daily lives and its accompanying body gesture (as oppose to the body gesture in class) expresses a message of encouragement and of adaptation of the studio body gestures to daily life, that is, a change in the body's configuration in daily life which expresses a change in women's self-image. Not all gestures of course are used outside of the studio, but those that help change women's self-esteem and self-perception certainly are.

The different *clothing* in belly dancing classes, which expose more than cover, are also a part of expressing women's sensuality and female intimacy in the studio. Clothing usually serves as a social definer. It is a choice of how to look like within clear and known social boundaries (Blumen 2011). All women dressed differently outside the studio within what they perceive as their own social boundaries: especially religious women who are dressed outside the studio in a very modest way (including long sleeves and tight collar shirts, long skirts, no trousers, and head cover). The belly dancing clothing on the contrary lacks normative social boundaries or in fact presents space without boundaries for those women. It is meant to expose and emphasize women's sexuality and her body figure. The clothing is usually very bright with lots of shiny colors and items such as rings bracelets, hair items, necklets, and earrings, which are all very big and meant to attract men's attention. Heavy makeup on the eyes, red lipstick on the lips, and a red nail color are part of the bodily costume.

Direct *eye contact* with the audience is very important in belly dancing and the teacher illustrates the seductive look even though the classes are in a studio and not in front of a public audience. This is in contrast to daily performance of eye contact, which is forbidden for religious women, and even secular women make sure they don't look too seductively at other men in order not to attract unwanted attention.

Of course, not all women dress in traditional belly dancing costumes or put on makeup or adopt a seductive look, but even those who don't wear traditional belly dance dress, dress differently and make sure they are dressed with tight pants and ropes or colorful scarfs on their hips to emphasize their dancing movements. Most of them also put some unusual decorations in their hair to emphasize that they dress differently in class. The same relates to the *body movements*. Social boundaries dictate how we move our bodies. Some movements are normative while others are extreme, unacceptable, or mediocre. The body movements in belly dancing are meant to break social boundaries in that they express what are considered to be sensual body movements especially with the hips and the pelvis—gestures that are considered to be seductive and tempting and therefore are forbidden in women's daily lives. In our studio we practice in front of a big mirror so that it becomes a kind of a theatre where we watch ourselves perform unusual performances. And lastly, women hug and kiss before, after, and also in the middle of the class as gestures of support to each other more than in their daily lives. These signs of affection are no dance movements, of course, but are created by the emotional intensity and intimacy created between the women in the studio. These specific performances transform the classes into a *third space* (Bhahba 1994), which crosses the binary division of forbidden and permitted and enables women to perform out of their everyday performativity.

My own insider's experiences were the basis for asking whether these observations in the studio space which act as an heterotopia or as a third space are relevant to other women dancers and to what extent it affected their self-perception. I therefore carried out in-depth interviews with other students of belly dancing classes. In this paper I include three interviews with Ashkenazi Jewish women: Diane, seventy, secular; Leah, thirty-eight, secular; and Esther, fifty-two, religious.

PRACTICES OF BELLY DANCE IN ISRAEL: BODY, EMBODIMENT, AND EMPOWERMENT

The interviews began with discussing how and why the women chose belly dancing. Diane, who is a mother of two, says that she has always liked dancing but felt very clumsy. She is a musician and very connected to music. She looked for ways to maintain her health in old age and looked for fitness activities. She saw belly dancing on TV and after a year her friend invited her to go to the belly dancing festival in Eilat so she thought it would be fun to do that. Leah, is a psychologist and a mother of two children, came to know belly dancing at a conference for psychologists when she went to a belly dancing workshop. She also likes dancing and she thinks it is fun to practice belly dancing. Esther, who is a mother of six and a grandmother to one grandchild, danced folk dances for many years and also was introduced to belly dancing in a workshop. She says she had the impression of it being vulgar because of watching Egyptian movies. When she saw it, she thought it was a piece of art and she decided to start studying it. For Diane and Leah belly dancing is associated with fun more than other types of dancing. For Esther belly dancing is associated with art more than other types of dancing.

I then discussed with them the extent to which belly dancing performances and body performances affect their self-esteem and how they connect to their perceptions of their bodies. Diane says that she dances for fitness. She feels that the dancing does something good to her body. She feels very feminine and sexy when she dances. She

herself is dressed very modestly. She is dressed with tights and a loose t-shirt and usually uses a scarf on her hips. She doesn't use makeup, lipstick or nail color. Moreover,
she doesn't like the way some women dress. She thinks this way of dressing vulgar and
distasteful. She herself feels good with how she dresses. She even grew out her hair
because of the belly dancing. She likes the body gestures she uses while dancing. She
feels free, feminine and elegant (Interview, January 22, 2010). For her, the mere fact
that she, at her age, does belly dancing is a challenge to age stereotypes, to notions of
femininity, sexuality, and old age. The actual fact that she can dance and perform in
class challenges existing assumptions about what seventy-year old women should do
and feel. In her case, it is not so much the clothing that makes the difference but the
body movements, the music, and the growing of her hair that increased her self-esteem.

Leah feels divine (Interview, June, 13, 2010). She really likes belly dancing. She
feels light and feels like a dancer, which she doesn't feel in her daily life. She loves the
music. She doesn't criticize her body anymore; she is not frustrated if her body movements are not correct. She likes to look at herself in the studio mirror. She loves to see
the progress of the other women. She emphasizes that the mirror in the studio is not
depressing as the ones in the shopping malls are where she says to herself that she is
very fat. In the studio she is friendly with the mirror and with her body. Before she
danced she was very critical about herself and her body. She still wants to lose weight
but she doesn't think about it during her dancing classes. This acceptance of her body
in belly dancing classes reminds her of the period she was pregnant. Back then, she
also liked her body because in was "legitimate to be fat" (Interview, June 13, 2010).
Leah's feelings coincide with the findings of a survey carried out in the United States
which revealed that weight pressures among belly dancers is lower than in other
forms of dance and their body satisfaction is higher (Downey et al. 2010). Leah
continues to say that she is sure that the body movements in belly dancing and the
clothing are a form of resistance: resistance against the masculine clothing that suit
only very thin women. Instead, the colorful clothing and the scarfs represent softness
and femininity. She feels that it emphasizes her femininity, but this feminine power is
not meant to tempt men. She says that empowerment is from inside and argues, "In
classes I feel it's great to be a woman while in real life it's difficult to be a woman. It's
the same in pregnancy. I am so happy that I as a woman can be pregnant and men
can't. They are the inferiors" (Interview, June 13, 2010). She associates specific body
gestures with resistance. For her it's the movement of her shoulders and breasts. At
the beginning she was embarrassed to move her breasts as if she is proud of them.
She thought it is very blunt and immodest but now she loves this movement, and she
even dances like this in parties. It is done to express her femininity in a provocative
way without feeling cheap or indecent. This is the opposite of the feminine type of a
woman who is restrained and who is afraid of social criticism. This is the way women
are educated from childhood and in this respect belly dance is a kind of a challenge
and resistance to dominant perceptions of femininity. Leah illustrates the various
connections between the changes in her self-esteem while dancing.

Esther's views highlight another perspective on experiencing belly dancing, that of feeling separated and disconnected from outside world when she dances. "I am in the dance," she says, "for one and a half hour it is only me and the dance" (Interview, June 21, 2010). She feels very much connected to her body. She feels the control of her body and the ability to separate between its parts, which are two of the principles of belly dancing. For her, the discussion of the body is actually a discussion of body parts. She feels a lot of power and freedom. She studies coaching and belly dancing at the same time and like Davidson and Milligan (2004) experiences how the body and mind are the same: "The ability to reach separation and connection between body parts (as we do in belly dancing) and between body and mind, to accept yourself as you are, to be happy about every small movement, to disconnect. I began to dance belly dancing only because I accepted my body. Physically it did well to me. I sit straight now" (Interview, June 21, 2010). She is dressed modestly according to the codes of clothing of her religion and this doesn't diminishes her deep connection with belly dancing because she thinks it's the dancing of the body and not the showing off of the body that matters. "It's something internal," she says and thinks she actually doesn't like the typical belly dancing clothing and perceives it as vulgar. She goes to the belly dancing studio with her hair covered although it's a women-only place because she is used to keeping her hair covered. She doesn't feel the dance is a form of protest or resistance but she can see how for some women the dance is a kind of resistance or protest.

For Diane, Leah, and Esther belly dancing expresses different connection with their bodies. Their attitude to clothing and movements are different but for all three, but for all belly-dancing performances is a matter of boundary changes and of a personal change. For Leah it takes the form of a protest. She says that there is a protest which is directed to emphasize femininities—tits, sparkling dress, and "a kind of a costume that I as mature women don't have the freedom to wear." Indeed, she dresses with special clothing when she dances. Sometimes she says she debates with herself whether to change her clothing to regular ones, perhaps as a challenge. The protest for her is perhaps against the binary values—kitch versus modesty, beautiful versus ugly, modesty versus immodesty, decent versus indecent; and so on. Although binaries are significant in modernist thinking, the practice of belly dancing allows for the mix up of these binaries, and the creation of heterotopia or a third space. "It's temporary—only when I dance—but it's part of everyday life" and by that it becomes repetitive—once or twice a week and thus a performativity. She continues: "I send women with clinical depression to practice belly dancing. For us it is a target to project these good feelings not only in belly dancing classes but also in our lives. So far I didn't succeed" (Interview, June 21, 2010).

It is clear from the narratives of the three women that the practice of belly dancing even without the clothing or with only modest gestures is liberating and changes their self-perceptions and esteem and by that they practice perceptional border crossing about their age, their performances and the weight and form of their bodies.

THE STUDIO IN BELLY DANCING

My second assumption refers to the studio as a liberating, heterotopic, third space or safe space, free of cultural and religious norms, which enables women to dress up and perform bodily gestures that are perceived as immodest and forbidden in their daily lives. In particular, this is relevant to religious Jewish women and perhaps old women but I claim that this is true to secular women as well. The notion of 'safe spaces' has been coined elsewhere by Jewish students regarding their women studies classrooms because they felt relatively secured and more comfortable than in other mixed classes courses because women were the majority in such classes and thus more powerful (Halevi and Blumen 2005). Here too, the studio is a safe female space. Men are not allowed to enter the studio space. Even male maintenance workers do not enter the studio area during classes. This is why religious and even ultra-religious women can wander around the studio area dressed freely in traditional belly dancing clothes. By being mainly non-verbal (differently from university classes) belly dancing classes create a different atmosphere of less competition and more support. Of course there are still power relations especially between the students and the teacher and also among the students themselves who look at who is dancing better but there is also a lot of support and affection between the students. This description is also reflected in the three women's perceptions of the studio.

Diane for example says that the studio is the only place where she dares to dance. She also dances at home but there she has furniture and a dog and she needs to move it all to make a space for dance. It is more comfortable in the studio she says, because it's all very spacious and the mirror is helpful. It makes her feel comfortable and liberated. Leah says that the studio is a *protected space*. It's also located in a basement with very small windows so it feels protected, safe, and pleasant. She says that part of it is not only the physicality of the space but the fact that there is no criticism from other women and that the groups are age mixed: "there is diversity . . . when all are young and friends I feel outsider but in our group it feels very comfortable . . . At the beginning it is important to have a protected space that nobody sees you and its not exposed" says Esther, the religious woman. She continues: "This is the *natural space to dance*. I feel most liberated there although at home I feel the same but in the studio I feel that it is more interesting because somebody (the teacher) leads it. It's one and a half hour of only dancing with no interruption" (Interview, June, 21, 2010). It is quite obvious that the studio is a *unique space* for the women dancers. It is a liberating space not only in the sense that they can dance freely but it is liberating from their own self-criticism. The mirror is a crucial element in this. As Leah said, she can look at the mirror without criticizing herself, while usually it is more difficult for her not to be critical of herself.

The freedom and happiness that the women expressed about belly dancing reminds us of the original role and practice of belly dancing among rural Arab women where it served as a mechanism of entertainment and mutual support. It seems that this purpose is dominant in belly dancing classes in the female-only studio and in this respect there is not much change between traditional belly dancing and modern belly dancing. Here this insight that belly dance is *emotions through motions* becomes clearer. It is expressed in the physical body contact between the women. Women hug and kiss before, after, and even during classes. There is a lot of loud laughing and a feeling of free spirits in class, which makes it a safe space. The classes are a powerful moment in daily life that for most women are not easy to find. This atmosphere in the studio is the modernized version of the traditional function of belly dance.

ETHNICITIES AND NATIONALITIES IN BELLY DANCING

In contrast to the significant effect of belly dancing on women's identities, the connection between belly dancing and Arab culture—and the change in the perceptions toward the Arabs—is not as evident as I had assumed. *Nationally* speaking, belly dancing has not influenced women's perceptions of the Israeli-Arab/Palestinian conflict.

Diane for example, says she that is aware of the fact that belly dancing is part of the Arab culture but doesn't think about this connection when she dances. It seems that for her there is a total separation between politics and dance. Leah too says that her passion for belly dancing doesn't make her feel closer to the Arab culture but it does make her ask questions about Arab and Egyptian culture, especially when the teacher explains the meanings of the songs. It doesn't make her feel closer to Arab culture perhaps because there are no Arab women in class and also because the songs are not sung by Arabs but Algerians or Tunisians. "It's a pity," she says, "I would be happy to be invited to a wedding in East Jerusalem and to take part in it." She says, "I dance in a clean and beautified studio in west Jerusalem with Ashkenazi Jewish women. It's all very organized and intellectualized (so it is hard to talk about a political change). If the studio was in East Jerusalem and Arab women would have danced with us it would have been different" and she summarizes, "I live in lots of separations" (Interview, June 21, 2010).

Esther, who is a headmaster in a girl's school, said that she studied the history of belly dancing in a special course she took and from what she learned that religious Arab women also practice belly dancing. She can associate belly dancing with biblical stories of Miriam the Prophet, for example, who danced when the people of Israel crossed the Red Sea on their way from Egypt to Israel. For her, belly dancing is beyond specific nationality or ethnicity or any other specific context. She says she is not interested in its origins except for its biblical origins. She says that she grew up in a home that was open to other cultures. Her father was involved with the peace treaty with Egypt so other cultures are not strange to her. Belly dancing did made her feel closer to Arab culture but she stressed that she doesn't mix religion, culture, and politics and she separates the Arab nationalism, oriental music, and belly dancing. I find it very interesting that this principle of separation goes all the way from the bodily separated movements—which is the highlight of belly dancing—to the mental separation of body movements inside and outside the studio, to the awareness of separation between belly dancing and their representations of Arab cultures.

CONCLUSION

In this paper I have looked at the performative practices of belly dancing as a *concentrated example of the expressive nature of embodiment* (Thrift 1996). I have also viewed this practice as a way to understand women's perceptions of their bodies and embodiment and the extent to which their experiences of liberation and happiness reflect identity changes in their everyday life. In addition, I wanted to understand whether belly dancing effects political or nationalized perspectives.

I have based my analysis on some major ideas that came up in women's narratives, and I connected them to some of the arguments made by researchers in this field. The first is Thrift's argument that dance is connected to other social actions—to rituals, to rhythmic work, to play. Thrift posits that the playfulness of dance is characterized as gratuitous, free, noncumulative, rule-bound yet difficult to control, and that this explains its neglect in the social sciences and humanities. Women's experiences of practicing belly dancing reaffirms this direction of analysis especially in that these qualities are sources of eluding power rather than confronting or subverting power. The three women, each in her own way, elude power, especially gendered patriarchal power through belly dance. This capacity of belly dance is expressed in different experiential frames, different ways of being that cannot be written or spoken.

The second point is Butler's focus on gender and sexual identities, especially with regards to the performance of nationhood and ethnic identities. In my paper, I redefined the belly dance studio as a heterotopic space liberated of these naturalized codes and therefore a space with the potential to effect social identities through performance and embodiment. From the narratives of the three women it did impact social identities but not their ethnic or national ones—these remained unchanged. However, the gendered identities and women's self-esteem indeed have changed and in this respect the studio became a heterotopic space liberated of patriarchal and masculine perceptions.

Another point I emphasized in the paper is the connection made by the women between motion and e/motion, a perspective that is expressed in the activities of the women at the belly dance studio as well. The last point highlighted in the literature is Blumen's (2011) distinction between performance and performativity as two concepts that help explain how the human body functions as part of the non-representational perspective. As I illustrated at the beginning of the paper, performance is a concept that analyzes activities that combine material, body and movement. Performativity emphasizes daily practices and the repetitive nature of bodily performances that actually transform identities and perceive them as natural or normal. The women's experiences as presented in the paper provide deeper insights to such transformations.

For each of the three women belly dancing performances empower them in different ways and they all expressed better relationships with the body and better self-perception of their bodies. These positive feelings are associated with a challenge to common perceptions of the female body, weight, and figure. This means that the belly dancing performances actually changed women's performativity in their daily life.

The studio turned out to be a *safe space, protected space, unique space*, a space with different codes of behavior, conduct, or dressing. The studio enabled the women to practice different attitudes of their bodies and their existence. It acted as a liberating space, where they can get away from their everyday duties and be themselves and not wives, mothers, or grandmothers. But the studio hadn't turned into a heterotopic space yet, that is, the connection between belly dancing and national perceptions and identities regarding Arab culture and the Israeli/Palestinian conflict did not emerge in the interviews.

In summary, my research exposed the bodily and embodied reflections of belly dancing as a new language of performativity that investigates social and power relations with other means then words and texts. By looking at how bodily experiences of belly dancing affect and are absorbed in women's everyday life I have presented another layer of women's everyday life in the city that hasn't been thoroughly researched yet. As I showed, belly dancing has significant effects that cut across age, class, level of education, and ethnicity.

Conclusion

Embodied Movement, Agency, and the Negotiation of Space

When a body is at dance it sometimes feels invincible and free from the strictures of everyday life: people in mosh pits ricochet off one another with reckless abandon, swing dancers fly through the air like syncopated acrobats, and people go to dance clubs to lose themselves in the trance of rhythm and movement. It is this feeling of invincibility that makes dance such a compelling object of analysis; while the movements feel as though they are fresh and new, in reality they are often choreographed, mimetic, or actions that are imbued with site-specific meanings from which they have long been unmoored. But dancing bodies do not so much *conquer space* as they *engage in space*: they contort to the specific sites where they are dancing, the cultural codes that constrict what movements are acceptable, the particularities of what they can and cannot do, and negotiate with an unseen choreographer over what is proper and expected. This engagement in space places dance as just one part of the complex social system of the dance site. As Lefebvre (1991) argues, dance is

> a gestural system whose organization combines two codes, that of the dancer and that of the spectator (who keeps time by clapping or with other body movements): thus, as evocative (paradigmatic) gestures recur they are integrated into a ritually linked gestural chain.

In this conclusion we briefly review the main conceptual and methodological themes of the volume and look forward to the themes and tensions of the next volume. Throughout we underscore the primacy of the relationship between space and dance. By recognizing the movement arts as engaging in a spatial project, we recognize the special relationship between the body and movement: Tim Cresswell, for example, in his analysis of efforts by the Imperial Society of Teachers of Dancing in the United Kingdom to codify correct and incorrect dance steps argues that incorrect dance steps were raced as belonging to the ethnic "other" outside and distanced from the United Kingdom (2006a). Hence incorrect movements of the body were observed and policed by the dance authorities, who in so doing were not only controlling movements, but also continuing the process of marginalization of the specific places which those movements evoked. In understanding how dance engages with space, our authors have questioned the sites of dance, the corporeality of dance, and how to understand what the dancing body signifies—or if it can actually be understood.

The spatial context of dance changes how audiences perceive dances and how dancers understand their movements. The site of dance is therefore critical to its meaning, and both audiences and dancers take great pains to manipulate sites in order to change how their dance is perceived. Moriah McSherry McGrath in this volume, for example, explored how moving exotic dance out from the traditional LULU ghettos where it is relegated by most cities out into the neighborhoods of Portland changed both the performance of the dance, and how non-dancers viewed these movements. Exotic dance in Portland involved non-traditional body types and unusual music choices, highlighting how lenient planning laws helped to create a unique local dance culture. Similarly, McGrath notes that exotic dance establishments are often "seedy bars" as opposed to "grand theaters or concert halls" where more respected forms of dance occur. Likewise, Matthew Kurtz examined how changing the context of Iñupiaq dance completely transforms its message and intent: the quality of play and mimicry present in Inuit dance was lost on tourists who understood dance to be an authentic representation of culture. To this end, Kurtz views dance as an artifact of the political and colonial history of Alaska that demands that dance scholars better understand the cultural specific roles of dance.

Space always has a specific *cultural* history that is imbued with the national and social history of its inhabitants, and it also has a specific history of *construction* that tells the story of how individual architects and engineers have created and altered spaces to fit their own needs. Frances Bronet, drawing on the work of Bruno Latour, analyzes how converting a performance hall from static container of dance to a fluid and pliable one transforms how the audience experiences dance. She chronicles how in *Beating a Path* and *SpillOut* how the space of the dance is designed concurrently with the dance itself. These changes pulled audience members into the performers and illustrated the ways in which landscapes are designed. Katrinka Somdahl-Sands, in perhaps the most jarring illustration of the agency that we have to influence the spatial context of dance, followed the relationships between migration, dance, dancers, and audience as the Bird Brain Dance troupe mimics the seasonal movement of birds. This motion highlighted the relationship between landscape and motion and how specific places evoke certain emotions. Jennifer Monson, the choreographer of Bird Brain Dance talks about how bodies soften as they interact with nature and become more open to the feelings of the place in which they are located.

A central tenet of how bodies engage in space is the fact that bodies are living and unique entities that cannot perform the same gesture exactly the same every time. Instead, bodies are intrinsically fragile and perform differently based on conditions such as mood, location, and climate. To this end dancing bodies differ from machines in that they not only affect space, but also carry with them memory, emotion, and affect. Tamara Johnson, for example, explored how Cape Town's history of racial oppression and marginalization was embodied in the movements on the dance floors of jazz clubs. To Johnson, the "emotional politics" of dance helps dancers find a way to locate themselves in the world where concepts of global and local and viscous and difficult to navigate. Most importantly, the body is not a spectator to memory, instead it is the vehicle through which experiences happen. In the same way that scholars must often dance in order to understand stand, we must interrogate bodies in order to explore memory. To Paromitra Kar, the body becomes a site where questions of identify are negotiated and the body serves as a liminal spaces where divergent ideas about the self converge. For dancers who are involved in transnational movement, their bodies are truly the only thing that does not change as they move from one continent to another. Our analysis of the bodies of dancers therefore has to take note of how racialized structures of power and land use change the atmosphere and character of movement and suggest that the facial expressions of dancers and the pace at which they move illustrate as much as the steps they take. Likewise, as Teresa Heiland analyzed, *HyperDance* may present bodies as indestructible, but this presentation is only made possible through the various media that edit and transform how distant spectators view dancing bodies. These images are broadcast out from Los Angeles—the entertainment capital of the United States—and media consumer's understanding of dance becomes dislodged from what is physically possible for human bodies to perform. Similarly, Georgia Connover explored how American Tribal Style (ATS) dancers attempt to create new identities in tandem with creating an entirely new dance style. In this instance dance is *conceived* as a space of liberation, as though movement can erase the colonial, gender, and power markers that exist in all systems of movement. To this end, Connover concludes that despite the deliberate reworking of movements styles ATS engages in its own process of otherness, for example, by crediting choreographers with the creation of new dances, not the specific cultures from their movements are derived.

The corporeality of bodies thus demands that we approach the process of understanding the meanings of movement through an embrace of the fragmentary and illusory nature of the body. This contentious relationship between body in movement and meaning is further problematized in this volume by a variety of scholars that employ non-representational theory to their reading of dance. In contrast to the representational work on dance in this volume that engages with the multitude of ways in which the body at dance is either representing or contesting a fixed or temporary identity, non-representational approaches highlight that the relationship between dance, identity, and place is much more about the energy felt, and the lived experience of movement. As we stated earlier, when we dance, we are not only concerned about the representational meaning of our movement, but what equally matters is the sense of *community* we create. Through movement in a certain place, the feeling, the energy of that material or place is absorbed by us, and absorbs us in it. Rather than being controlled by discourse, power, and ideology, the body at dance is a body at play, meaning that the power of movement lies in showing feelings and identity that words cannot and should not name, yet simultaneously making these visible. In this volume, it is particularly the work of Kurtz, Bronet, Somdahl-Sands, and Fenster that illustrates how bodies come together in dance and form a collective, meaningful, and expressive conglomerate without explicitly wanting to be tied to one kind of particular identity and corporeality. The most poignant example in our collection is Tovi Fenster's analysis of belly dancing in Israel. In a society dominated by real, imaged, enforced, and perceived boundaries, the belly dancing studio is often the sole escape from a world where fixed identities are inscribed on women's bodies—it offers a playground for expression beyond the societal discourse outside, and creates a community beyond representation.

In the final analysis, and regardless of a representational or non-representational approach to this phenomenon, dance remains a ubiquitous signifier of place: Maypole dances, salsa, square dancing, and Bharatanatyam each tell the reader a story about how class, culture, and identity have been structured in their local milieu. While these dance forms corporealize local structures and relationships, they are also sites of contestations: people dance as a way of escaping the ordinary and see dance as a space of play where new identities can be tried on and proposed. To this end, Kar explored how South Indian choreographers negotiate their cosmopolitan identities through movement and engagement with different dance styles. She employed the metaphor of the term *pas de deux* from ballet to symbolize how the 'self' and 'other' move in tandem with each other. Similarly, to Jonathan Skinner salsa became a way to understand how individuals situate themselves within the struggles of Northern Ireland. The dancing body migrates elsewhere for the length of time of only one dance, even though at the beginning of the dance partners can talk to another and 'sort-out' where they fit within the local tensions. Dance space here is activated by our actions, and in contemporary Belfast—emerging as it is from its violent history of colonialism and violence—the transnational site of the dance floor is a place for many different types of migrants to come together. And Tovi Fenster found that for Israeli Jewish belly dancers, their identity was not altered through their engagement with belly dance, even though the dance's Middle Eastern roots seem to situate it directly at the tensions of the Arab/Israeli conflict. Therefore our analysis of dance has to be attuned to the constant back and forth between representation and creation, and our theoretical lens needs to be as diverse as the movements of dancing bodies.

Methodologically, our contributors chose research techniques that highlighted the need for a direct understanding of how and why bodies move: mixed methods and participant observations were dominant research tactics. Many, such as Fenster, Johnson, Skinner, Somdahl-Sands, and Heiland are dancers themselves and conducted first-person ethnographies that approach their material from their unique perspective as participants. Combined with interviews with dancers and historical/archival research this research methodology views dance as an embodied representation of both the past and present. The prevalence of ethnographies within this volume suggests that there is a brief and fleeting quality of dance and that the body must be engaged in the research through direct participant in order to represent to the reader what it means to move.

The difficulty documenting dances through dance notation highlights this tension between dance and representation. Choreographed performances are not the same every night because movements change and the entire mood and affect of the performance hall is not static. Derek McCormack (2008) perhaps most famously has looked for ways to structure academic articles in ways that mimic the fluidity and spontaneity of dance. However, the medium of academic scholarship is so different from both social and formal dance that these attempts at decentering the traditional paragraphs and pages of academic writing have not yet established a language of their own. This remains a future project for scholars of dance.

McGrath stands out as a researcher who mapped the location of dance establishments and used this as part of her mixed-methods approach. This embrace of GIS opens up the door to other applications of spatio-temporal datasets to dance (for example, Ahlqvist et al. 2010). Perhaps this technology can add to ethnographic accounts and help scholars of dance understand the micro-geography of the social dance floor is organized, how individuals move around the dance floor, and how dancers in choreographed dance performances change from performance to performance. Adding this type of technology to dance research could strengthen the qualitative research by adding visualizations of often-brief encounters on the dance floor as well bringing into dance scholarship the literature on visualization, representation, and time-space geographies.

In the next volume of our *Geographies of Dance*, we shift our theoretical gaze from bodies that are manipulated and altered through dance, and focus on identity, nationhood, globalization, and the situation of the dancing body as a force that moves to global rhythms. In changing the scale of our analysis we are in no way setting up a hierarchy between the body and the global: as bodies engage in space they are constantly influenced by movements from all over the world. Sallie Marston, John Paul Jones, and Keith Woodward approach this tension by attempting to move away from both hierarchical *and* network-based understandings of scale in favor of what they term a "flat ontology" of interlinked sites. Based on the work of Theordore Schatzki (2002), Marston et al. "propose a spatial ontology that recognizes a virtually infinite population of mobile and mutable sites and that is *ontologically flat* by virtue of its affirmation of immanence—or self organization—as the fundamental process of material actualization" (2005, 51). Hence dance emerges as an act of creative place-making through which dancers engender their connections with other spaces.

Our second edited collection explores such tensions through a diverse range of case studies and theoretical perspectives. In brief, we examine how dance serves as a unifying force that helps to forge new identities, novel forms of hybridization of identity, and helps to gel the corporeal negotiations of groups of people to bind them together. For example, Olaf Kuhlke explores how the Love Parade in post-unification Berlin, Germany, emerged as a material and sexualized signifier of a newly confident and merged nation of Germany. Similarly, Jade Gibson analyzes salsa dancing in post-apartheid South Africa serves as a culturally unifying force. In this instance the diverse communities of Cape Town came together to involve themselves in a dance that was becoming part of the new post-apartheid South Africa.

We also explore the ways in which dance helps to keep people attached to local traditions and serves as a bulwark against the forces of commodification and globalization. For example, Katherine Cornell explores how Francophone dance in Quebec emerged as a signifier of Quebec identity and difference within a larger Anglo-oriented Canada. Similary, Ayoko Aoyama's work on flamenco explores the ways in which the global flamenco industry helped to support this local tradition, but also worked to reform just what the term flamenco meant in a transnational context as a dance whose origins come from the diverse populations of Andalusia but that now connects global communities.

Similar to this volume, neat dichotomies highlight the tensions inherent in dance, but don't do justice to the complex ways that dance brings people together and separates them, fosters community, and corporealizes differences between people in ways that are perhaps more lasting than other ways of signifying difference. Adam Pine, for example, explores how salsa in the United States serves, to borrow Jean Leca's term, as a "reservoir of citizenship" where people of different backgrounds can come together and level out the inequalities existent in society. Instead, dance style, space on the dance floor, and manner of dress all serve to make this space just as marginalizing as various other areas of society, *even as non-Latinos diligently work to corporealize the supposed body motions of Latinos.* In the end, what our second volume will accomplish is to provide a comprehensive understanding of multiple scales of identity, place and dance, to show both the attempts to fix identities to a space though dance and the purposeful disruption of such intended mappings through movement.

Bibliography

Adams, Paul C. 2001. "Peripatetic Imagery and Peripatetic Sense of Place." In *Textures of Place Exploring Humanist Geographies*, edited by Paul C. Adams, Steven Hoelscher, and Karen Till, 186–206. Minneapolis: University of Minnesota Press.

Adey, Peter, Lucy Budd and Phil Hubbard. 2007. "Flying Lessons: Exploring the Social and Cultural Geographies of Global Air Travel." *Progress in Human Geography.* 31:773–791. Accessed September 13, 2011. DOI: 10.1177/0309132507083508.

Adhikari, Mohamed. 2009. *Burdened by Race: Coloured Identities in Southern Africa.* Cape Town: University of Cape Town Press.

Ahlqvist, O., H. Ban, N. Cressie and N. Z. Shaw. 2010. "Statistical Counterpoint: Knowledge Discovery of Choreographic Information Using Spatio-Temporal Analysis and Visualization." *Applied Geography* 30 (4), 548.

Ahluwalia, P. and A. Zegeye. 2003. "Between Black and White: Rethinking Coloured Identity." *African Identities* 1(2): 253–280.

Albright, Ann Cooper. 1997. *Choreographing Difference: The Body and Identity in Contemporary Dance.* Middletown: Wesleyan University Press.

Alderman, D. 2003. "Street Names and the Scaling of Memory: The Politics of Commemorating Martin Luther King Jr. Within the African American Community." *Area* 35: 163–73.

Allen, M. and S. Brown. 2011. "Embodiment and Living Memorials: The Affective Labour of Remembering the 2005 London Bombings." *Memory Studies* 4(3): 312–327.

Amin, Ash and Nigel Thrift. 2002. *Cities: Reimagining the Urban.* Cambridge, UK: Polity.

Anawalt, Sasha. 2008. "Endangered Dance Species...Another Critic Bites the Dust." *Articles: The Blog of the National Arts Journalism Program.* Accessed November 18, 2013. http://www.najp.org/articles/2008/03/lewis–segal–chief–dance–critic.html.

Anchorage Daily Times. 1946. "Group Plans Gambell Trip." May 3.

Anderson, Ben. 2009. "Non-Representational Theory." in *The Dictionary of Human Geography,* edited by Derek Gregory, Ron Johnston, Geraldine Pratt, Michael J. Watts, and Sarah Whatmore, 503–505. West Sussex UK: John Wiley and Sons.

Anderson, Carol. "Choreographic Dialogue with Lata Pada: Questions and Answers." accessed 9/01, 2011, http://www.dcd.ca/latapadaqanda.html.

Aoyama, Y. 2007. "The Role of Consumption and Globalization in a Cultural Industry: The Case of Flamenco." *Geoforum* 38 (1): 103–113.

Aparicio, F. 1998. *Listening to Salsa: Gender, Latin Popular Music, and Puerto Rican Cultures*. Hanover and London: Wesleyan University Press/University Press of New England.

Argyle, Michael. 1981. "The Experimental Study of the Basic Features of the Situation." In *Toward a Psychology of Situations: An Interactive Perspective*, edited by David Magnusson. Hillsdale, NJ: Lawrence Erlbaum Associates.

Arnakak, Jaypetee. 2000. "What is Inuit Qaujimajatuqangit?" *Nunatsiaq News*, August 25.

Arnold, Robert. 1978. *Alaska Native Land Claims*. Anchorage: Alaska Native Foundation.

Arrighi, Giovanni. 1994. *The Long Twentieth Century*. New York: Verso.

Arshi, Sunpreet, Carmen Kirstein, Riaz Naqvi, and Falk Pankow. 1994. "Why Travel? Tropics, En-tropics and Apo-tropics." In *Travellers' Tales: Narratives of Home in Displacement*, edited by George Robertson, Melinda Mash, Lisa Tickner, Jon Bird, Barry Curtis, and Tim Putnam, 225–244. London: Routledge.

Atkin, N. 2006. "Carolena Nericcio and Her American Tribal Style." *Tribal*: 24–25.

Attali, Jacques. 2000. "How Hollywood Rules." *Civilization* 7, 1 (February–March): 644–665.

Auge, Marc. 1995. *Non-Places: Introduction to an Anthropology of Supermodernity*. London and New York City: Verso.

Austin, Tom. 2007. American Eden. *Travel + Leisure* 37 (8): 204, http://www.travelandleisure.com/articles/american-eden.

Bachelard, Gaston. 1994. *The Poetics of Space*. Translated by M. Jolas. Originally published 1969. Boston: Beacon Press.

Bairner, Alan. 2006. "'The Flâneur and the City': Reading the 'New' Belfast's Leisure Spaces." *Space and Polity* 10(2): 121–134.

Bakht, Natasha. "Natasha Bakht Bio." Canada Council for the Arts. Accessed September 2001, 2011, http://www.canadacouncil.ca/equity/nk129096798609196686.htm.

Banham, Reyner. 1971. *Los Angeles: The Architecture of Four Ecologies*. Harmondsworth, England: Penguin.

Barber, Mary. 1954. "Visiting the Top of the World." *Travel*. July 1.

Barker, Roger G. 1968. *Ecological Psychology*. Palo Alto: Stanford University Press.

Barthes, Roland. 1977. *Image, Music, Text*. Translated by Stephen Heath. New York, NY: Noonday.

Barton, Bernadette. 2006. *Stripped: Inside the Lives of Exotic Dancers*. New York: New York University Press.

———. 2007. "Managing the Toll of Stripping: Boundary Setting among Exotic Dancers." *Journal of Contemporary Ethnography* 36 (5): 571–596.

Barton, Bernadette and Constance L. Hardesty. 2010. "Spirituality and Stripping: Exotic Dancers Narrate the Body Ekstasis." *Symbolic Interaction* no. 33 (2):280–296. doi: 10.1525/si.2010.33.2.280.

Bauman, Zygmunt. 2000. *Liquid Modernity*. Cambridge: Polity Press.

Beck, Ulrich and Natan Sznaider. 2006. "Unpacking Cosmopolitanism for the Social Sciences: A Research Agenda." *The British Journal of Sociology* 57:1–23.

Beechey, Frederick. 1831. *Narrative of a Voyage to the Pacific and Beering Strait, Volume I*. London: Colburn and Bentley.

Bell, David and Gill Valentine. 1995. "The Sexed Self." In *Mapping the Subject: Geographies of Cultural Transformation*, edited by Steve Pile and Nigel Thrift, 143–157. London and New York: Routledge.

Benjamin, Walter. 1969. *Illuminations*, edited by Hannah Arendt. New York: Schocken Books.

———. 1978. "On the Mimetic Faculty." in *Reflections,* edited by Peter Demetz. New York: Schocken Books.

Bergson, Henri. 1988. *Matter and Memory*. New York: Zone Books.

Berleant, Arnold. 1970. *The Aesthetic Field: a Phenomenology of Aesthetic Experience*. Springfield, IL: Charles C Thomas, Publisher.

Berry, Chris, Soyoung Kim, and Lynn Spigel. 2010. "Here, There, and Elsewhere." In *Electronic Elsewheres*, edited by Chris Berry, Soyoung Kim, and Lynn Spigel, vii–xxvii. Minneapolis, MN: University of Minnesota Press.

Berthoz, Alain. 2000. *The Brain's Sense of Movement*. Cambridge, MA: Harvard University Press.

Besteman, C. 2008. *Transforming Cape Town*. Berkeley: University of California Press.

Beyers, C. 2009. "Identity and Forced Displacement: Community and Colouredness in District Six." In *Burdened by Race: Coloured Identities in Southern Africa*, Adhikari, M. (Ed.) 79–103. Cape Town: University of Cape Town Press.

Bhabha, Homi K. *The Location of Culture*. 1994. London, New York: Routledge.

Bhattacharya, Nova. "Nova Bhattacharya Bio." Accessed September 2001. http://www.ipsita novadance.com/bio.html

Bickford-Smith, V. 1995. "South African Urban History, Racial Segregation and the Unique Case of Cape Town?" *Journal of Southern African Studies* 21(1): 63–78.

Bissell, David. 2009. "Travelling Vulnerabilities: Mobile Timespaces of Quiescence." *Cultural Geographies* 16 (4), 427–445.

Blumen, O. 2011. "(Non)Representation of the Human in the Landscape." In *Cultural Landscape Patterns*, edited by A. Soffer, J. Maos, and R. Cohen-Seffer, 31–46. Haifa: University of Haifa.

Blunt, Alison and Robyn Dowling. 2006. *Home*. New York: Routledge.

Bockstoce, John. 2009. *Furs and Frontiers in the Far North: The Contest among Native and Foreign Nations for the Bering Strait Fur Trade*. New Haven, CT: Yale University Press.

Boddy, Trevor. 1992. "Underground and Overhead: Building the Analogous City." In *Variations of a Theme Park*, edited by Michael Sorkin, 123–153. New York: Hill and Wang.

Bodenhorn, Barbara. 1997. "'People Who Are Like Our Books': Reading and Teaching on the North Slope of Alaska." *Arctic Anthropology* 34 (1): 117–134.

Bourdieu, Pierre. 1980. *The Logic of Practice*. Translated by Blackwell. Stanford, CA: Stanford University Press.

———. 1977. *Outline of a Theory of Practice*. Cambridge: Cambridge University Press.

Bradley, Mindy S. 2008. "Stripping in the New Millennium: Thinking about Trends in Exotic Dance and Dancers' Lives." *Sociology Compass* no. 2 (2):503–518. doi: 10.1111/j.1751-9020.2007.00083.x.

Bradley-Engen, Mindy S. 2009. *Naked Lives: Inside the Worlds of Erotic Dance*. Albany: State University of New York Press.

Bradley-Engen, Mindy S., and Jeffery T. Ulmer. 2009. "Social Worlds of Stripping: The Processual Orders of Exotic Dance." *Sociological Quarterly* 50 (1): 29–60.

Braun, Bruce. 2002. "Colonialism's Afterlife: Vision and Visuality on the Northwest Coast." *Cultural Geographies* 9: 202–247.

———. 2004. "Nature and Culture: On the Career of a False Problem." In *A Companion to Cultural Geography*, edited by James Duncan, Nuala Johnson, and Richard H. Schein. 151–179. Malden, Oxford, Victoria: Blackwell.

Brennan, Denise. 2004. *What's Love Got to Do with It? Transnational Desires and Sex Tourism in the Dominican Republic*. Durham: Duke University Press.

Brenner, N. 2001. "The Limits to Scale? Methodological Reflections of Scalar Structuration." *Progress in Human Geography* 25 (4): 591–614.

Brents, Barbara G. and Kathryn Hausbeck. 2010. "Sex Work Now: What the Blurring of Boundaries around the Sex Industry Means for Sex Work, Research, and Activism." In *Sex Work Matters: Exploring Money, Power, and Intimacy in the Sex Industry*, edited by Melissa Hope Ditmore, Antonia Levy and Alys Willman, 9–22. New York: Zed Books.

Brents, Barbara G. and Teela Sanders. 2010. "Mainstreaming the Sex Industry: Economic Inclusion and Social Ambivalence." *Journal of Law and Society* no. 37 (1):40–60.

Briggs, Jean. 1991. "Expecting the Unexpected: Canadian Inuit Training for an Experimental Lifestyle." *Ethos* 19/3: 259–287.

———. 1997. "From Trait to Emblem and Back: Living and Representing Culture in Everyday Inuit Life." *Arctic Anthropology* 34/1: 227–235.

———. 1998. *Inuit Morality Play: The Emotional Education of a Three Year Old*. New Haven CT: Yale University Press.

Bronet, F. and Schumacher, J. 1999 "Design in Movement: The Prospects of Interdisciplinary Design," *Journal for Architectural Education* 53, no. 2: 97–109.

Brooks, Peter. 1993. *Body Work: Objects of Desire in Modern Narrative*. Cambridge, London: Harvard University Press.

Brooks, Siobhan. 2001. "Exotic Dancing and Unionizing: The Challenges of Feminist and Antiracist Organizing at the Lusty Lady Theater." In *Feminism and Antiracism: International Struggles for Justice*, edited by France Winddance Twine and Kathleen M. Blee, 59–70. New York: New York University Press.

———. 2010a. "Hypersexualization and the Dark Body: Race and Inequality among Black and Latina Women in the Exotic Dance Industry." *Sexuality Research and Social Policy* no. 7 (2):70–80. doi: 10.1007/s13178-010-0010-5.

———. 2010b. *Unequal Desires: Race and Erotic Capital in the Stripping Industry*. Albany: State University of New York Press.

Brown, Steven, Michael J. Martinez, and Lawrence M. Parsons. 2005. "The Neural Basis of Human Dance." *Cerebral Cortex* 16: 1157–1167.

Bruckert, Chris. 2002. *Taking It Off, Putting It On: Women in the Strip Trade*. Toronto: Women's Press.

Bruckert, Chris, Colette Parent, and Pascale Robitaille. 2003. Erotic Service/Erotic Dance Establishments: Two Types of Marginalized Labour. Ottawa: Law Commission of Canada.

Brunner, Jim. 2006. "When It Comes to Strip Clubs, Portland Has Nothing to Hide." *Seattle Times*, November 20.

Brush, Stephen B. and Doreen Stanbinsky. 1996. *Valuing Local Knowledge: Indigenous People and Intellectual Property Rights*. Washington DC and Covelo, California: Island Press.

Bull, Cynthia Jean Cohen. 1997. "Sense, Meaning, and Perception in Three Dance Cultures." In *Meaning in Motion: New Cultural Studies of Dance*, edited by Jane. C. Desmond, 269–288. Durham and London: Duke University Press.

Buonaventura, Wendy. 1989. *Serpent of the Nile: Women and Dance in the Arab World.* London: Saqi.

Burch, Ernest Jr. 1975. *Eskimo Kinsmen: Changing Family Relationships in Northwest Alaska.* St. Paul MN: West Publishing.

———. 1977. *Draft—The Cultural and Natural Heritage of Northwest Alaska: Volume VII, International Affairs.* Anchorage AK: National Park Service.

———. 1994. "The Iñupiat and the Christianization of Arctic Alaska." *Etudes / Inuit / Studies* 18/1–2: 81–108.

———. 1998. *The Iñupiaq Eskimo Nations of Northwest Alaska.* Fairbanks: University of Alaska Press.

Bureau of Labor Statistics. *Occupational Outlook Handbook, 2008–09 Edition: Dancers and Choreographers.* Department of Labor 2009 [cited September 12, 2009. Available from http://www.bls.gov/oco/ocos094.htm.

Butler, Judith. 1997. *Excitable Speech: A Politics of the Performative.* New York, NY: Routledge.

———. 2006. *Gender Trouble: Feminism and the Subversion of Identity.* New York: Routledge.

Buttimer, Anne. 1976. "Grasping the Dynamism of the Lifeworld." *Annals of the Association of American Geographers* 66, no. (2): 277–292.

Calvo-Merino, Beatriz, Julie Grèzes, Daniel E. Glaser, Richard E. Passingham, and Patrick Haggard. 2006. "Seeing or Doing? Influence of Visual and Motor Familiarity in Action Observation." *Current Biology* 16, 19: 1905–1910.

Calvo-Merino, Beatriz, Corinne Jola, and Patrick Haggard. 2008. "Towards a Sensorimotor Aesthetics of Performing Art." *Consciousness and Cognition* 17, 3: 911–922.

Cameron, Samuel. 2004. "Space, Risk and Opportunity: The Evolution of Paid Sex Markets." *Urban Studies* no. 41 (9):1643–1657. doi: 10.1080/0042098042000243084.

Card, David, Kevin F. Hallock, and Enrico Moretti. 2010. "The Geography of Giving: The Effect of Corporate Headquarters on Local Charities." *Journal of Public Economics* 94: 222–234.

Carlton, Donna. 1995. *Looking for Little Egypt.* Bloomington: IDD Books.

Casey, Edward S. 2001. "Body, Self, and Landscape: A Geophilosophical Inquiry into the Place-World." In *Textures of Place Exploring Humanist Geographies*, edited by Paul C. Adams, Steven Hoelscher, and Karen Till, 403–425. Minneapolis: University of Minnesota Press.

Chapkis, Wendy. 2000. "Power and Control in the Commercial Sex Trade." In *Sex for Sale: Prostitution, Pornography, and the Sex Industry*, edited by Ronald Weitzer, 181–201. New York: Routledge.

Charmaz, Kathy. 2005. "Grounded Theory in the 21st Century: Applications for Advancing Social Justice Studies." In *Handbook of Qualitative Research*, edited by Norman K. Denzin and Yvonna S. Lincoln, 507–37. Thousand Oaks, CA: Sage Publications.

Chatfeild, Michael. 1974. *A History of Accounting Thought.* Hinsdale, IL: Dryden Press.

Chatterjea, Ananya. 2004. *Butting Out: Reading Resistive Choreographies through Works by Jawole Willa Jo Zollar and Chandralekha.* Middletown: Wesleyan University Press.

Chatterjee, Sandra and Shyamala Moorty. "BiDentities, not Binaries: Using Choreography and Writing to Investigate Bicultural Experiences." *Mots Pluriel* online archive accessed September 2011. http://motspluriels.arts.uwa.edu.au/MP2303scsm.html.

Clark, VeVe. 1994. "Performing the Memory of Difference in Afro-Caribbean Dance: Katherine Dunham's Choreography, 1938–87." In *History and Memory in African-American Culture*, edited by Genevieve Fabre and Robert O'Meally, 188–204. Oxford: Oxford University Press.

Clarke, Adele E. 2003. "Situational Analyses: Grounded Theory Mapping after the Postmodern Turn." *Symbolic Interaction* no. 26 (4):553–576.

———. 2005. *Situational Analysis: Grounded Theory after the Postmodern Turn*. Thousand Oaks, CA: Sage Publications.

———. 2007. "Grounded Theory: Critiques, Debates, and Situational Analysis." In *The Sage Handbook of Social Science Methodology*, edited by William Outhwaite and Stephen P. Turner, 423–442. Los Angeles: Sage Publications.

Cohen, Jason. 2007. "There's Something about Mary's." *Portland Monthly*: 94.

Colls, Rachel. 2012. "Feminism, Bodily Difference and Non-Representational Geographies." *Transactions of the Institute of British Geographers* (forthcoming).

Committee for the Community Relations of the President's Council on Principles in Respect of the Provision of Amenities for All Races in Towns, Cities, and Along the Open Road 1984. South African Institute of Race Relations.

Coorlawala, Uttara Asha. 1994. "Classical and Contemporary Indian Dance: Overview, Criteria and a Choreographic Analysis." PhD Diss., New York University.

Copeland, Roger. 1990. "Founding Mothers: Duncan, Graham, Rainer, and Sexual Politics." *Dance Theatre Journal* 8, 3(Fall): 27–29.

Coplan, D. 2008. *In Township Night: South Africa's Black City Music and Theatre*. Chicago: University of Chicago Press.

Corbett, John. 2000. "Experimental Oriental: New Music and Other Others." In *Western Music and Its Others: Difference, Representation, and Appropriation in Music*, edited by David Hesmondhalgh and Georgina Born, xi, 360 p. Berkeley, CA, London: University of California Press.

Corsín Jiménez, Alberto. 2003. "On Space as a Capacity." *Journal of the Royal Anthropological Institute*, 9: 137–153.

Coulmont, Baptiste J. and Philip J. Hubbard. 2010. "Consuming Sex: Socio-legal Shifts in the Space and Place of Sex Shops." *Journal of Law and Society* no. 37 (1):189–209. doi: 10.1111/j.1467-6478.2010.00501.x.

Crampton, Jeremy and John Krygier. 2006. "An Introduction to Critical Cartography." *ACME: An International E-Journal for Critical Geographies* 4, no. (1): 11–33.

Cressey, G. 2006. *Diaspora Youth and Ancestral Homeland British Pakistani/Kashmiri Youth Visiting Kin in Pakistan and Kashmir*. Brill: Leiden.

Cresswell, Tim. 1996. *In Place/Out of Place Geography, Ideology, and Transgression*. Minneapolis, MN: University of Minnesota Press.

———. 2001. "Making Up the Tramp: Toward a Critical Geosophy." In *Textures of Place Exploring Humanist Geographies*, edited by Paul C. Adams, Steven Hoelscher, and Karen Till, 167–185. Minneapolis: University of Minnesota Press.

———. 2006a "'You Cannot Shake That Shimmie Here': Producing Mobility on the Dance Floor." *Cultural Geographies* 13 (1): 55–77.

———. 2006b. *On the Move: Mobility in the Modern Western World*. New York: Routledge.

———. 2010. "Toward a Politics of Mobility." *Environment and Planning D: Society and Space*, 28: 17–31. Accessed August 9, 2011. doi: 101068/d11407.

Creswell, John W. 2003. *Research Design: Qualitative, Quantitative, and Mixed Methods Approaches*. 2nd ed. Thousand Oaks, CA: Sage.

Cross, Emily S., Antonia F. de C. Hamilton, and Scott T. Grafton. 2006. "Building a Motor Simulation de Novo: Observation of Dance by Dancers." *NeuroImage* 31: 1257–1267.

Csordas, Thomas. 1990. "Embodiment as a Paradigm for Anthropology". *Ethos* 18/1: 5–47.

Culcasi, Karen. 2006. "Cartographically Constructing Kurdistan within Geopolitical and Orientalist Discourses." *Political Geography* 25: 680–706.

Curti, G. H. 2008. "From a Wall of Bodies to a Body of Walls: Politics of Affect | Politics of Memory | Politics of War. *Emotion, Space and Society* 1(2): 106–118.

Daly, Ann. 1992. "Dance History and Feminist Theory: Reconsidering Isadora Duncan and the Male Gaze. In *Gender in Performance: The Presentation of Difference in the Performing Arts*, edited by Laurence Senelick, 239–259. Medford, MA: Tufts University Press.

Dance Resource Center of Greater Los Angeles: Southern California's Source for Everything Dance. "Southern California Dance Map." Accessed October 11, 2011. http://www.drc-la .org/pages/other_organizations.

———. "Mission & History." http://www.drc-la.org/pages/mission_history. Accessed October 11, 2011.

Dando, Christina E. 2009. "'Whore-Friendly People': Heritage Tourism, the Media and the Place of Sex Work in Butte, Montana." *Gender, Place & Culture* no. 16 (5):587–607. doi: 10.1080/09663690903148440.

Davidson, J. and C. Milligan. 2004. "Embodying Emotion Sensing Space: Introducing emotional Geographies." *Social & Cultural Geography* 5(4): 523–532.

Davis, Mike. 1999. *Ecology of Fear: Los Angeles and the Imagination of Disaster*. New York: Vintage Books.

Dawe, Gerald. 2006. "The Revenges of the Heart: Belfast and the Poetics of Space." In *The Cities of Belfast*, edited by Nicholas Allen and Aaron Kelly, 199–210. Dublin: Four Courts Press.

Dear, Michael J. 2003. "The Los Angeles School of Urbanism: An Intellectual History." *Urban Geography* 24, 6: 493–509.

Dear, Michael J. and Steven Flusty. 2000. "Postmodern Urbanism." *Annals of the Association of American Geographers* 90, 1: 50–72.

De Certeau, Michel. 1984. *The Practice of Everyday Life*. Berkeley, CA: University of California Press.

Defrantz, Thomas F. 2004. "The Black Beat Made Visible: Hip Hop Dance and Body Power." In *Of the Presence of the Body: Essays on Dance and Performance Theory*, edited by Andre Lepecki, 64–81. Middletown, CT: Wesleyan University Press.

Delaney, D. and H. Leitner. 1997. "The Political Construction of Scale." *Political Geography* 16 (2): 93–97.

Delgado, Celeste and José Muñoz. 1997. "About the Series." In *Everynight Life: Culture and Dance in Latin/o America*, edited by Celeste Delgado and José Muñoz, ix–x. London: Duke University Press.

Dempster, Elizabeth. 1995. "Women Writing the Body: Let's Watch a Little How She Dances." In *Bodies of the Text: Dance as Theory, Literature as Dance,* edited by Ellen W. Goellner and Jacqueline Shea Murphy, 21–38. New Brunswick, NJ: Rutgers University Press.

Derrida, Jaques. 1974. *Of Grammatology*. Baltimore: John Hopkins University Press.

Desmond, Jane C. 1997. "Embodying Difference: Issues in Dance and Cultural Studies." In *Meaning in Motion: New Cultural Studies of Dance*, edited by Jane. C. Desmond, 29–54. Durham and London: Duke University Press.

———. "Introduction." 1997. In *Meaning in Motion: New Cultural Studies of Dance*, edited by Jane. C. Desmond, 1–29. Durham and London: Duke University Press.

Dewsbury J-D. 2003. "Witnessing Space: 'Knowledge With-Out Contemplation.'" *Environment and Planning A* 35, 1907–1932.

Diprose, Rosalyn. 2002. *Corporeal Generosity: On Giving with Nietzche, Merleau–Ponty, and Levinas.* Albany, NY: State University of New York Press.

Dittmer, Jason. 2010. *Popular Culture, Geopolitics, and Identity.* Lanham, Boulder, New York, Toronto, and Plymouth, UK: Rowman & Littlefield Publishers, Inc.

Dixon Gottschild, Brenda. 2000. *Waltzing in the Dark.* New York, NY: Palgrave.

Djoumahna, Kajira. 2003. *The Tribal Bible: Exploring the Phenomenon That Is American Tribal Bellydance.* Santa Rosa: Kajira Djoumahna/BlackSheep BellyDance.

Dolfman, Michael L., Richard J. Hodlen, and Solidelle Fortier Wasser. 2007. "The Economic Impact of the Creative Arts Industries: New York and Los Angeles." *Monthly Labor Review* (October): 21–34.

Domosh, Mona. 1999. "Sexing Feminist Geography." *Progress in Human Geography* no. 23 (3):429–436. doi: 10.1177/030913259902300306.

Downey, D. J, J. J. Reel, S. Soohoo and Zerbib, S. 2010. "Body Image in Belly Dance: Integrating Alternative Norms into Collective Identity." *Journal of Gender Studies* 19, no. 4: 377–393.

Dumbrell, K. 1998. Athlone in the Early 20th Century—a Precursor to Working Class Housing in the Cape Flats: 1900–1930. BA Honors, University of Cape Town.

Dunbar–Hall, P. 2003. "Tradisi and Turisme: Music, Dance, and Cultural Transformation at the Ubud Palace, Bali, Indonesia." *Australian Geographical Studies*, 41(1): 3–16.

Duncan, James and David Lambert. 2004. "Landscapes of Home." In *A Companion to Cultural Geography*, edited by James Duncan, Nuala Johnson, and Richard H. Schein. 382–403. Maldon, Oxford, Victoria: Blackwell.

Edensor, Tim. 2000. "Moving through the City." In *City Visions,* edited by David Bell and Azzedine Haddour, 121–140. Harlow: Prentice Hall.

Edley, Paige P., and Ginger Bihn. 2005. "Corporeality and Discipline of the Performing Body: Representations of International Ballet Companies." In *Intercultural Communication and Creative Practice: Dance, Music and Women's Cultural Identity*, edited by Laura Lengel, 213–228. Westport, CT: Praeger.

Edwards, Michelle L. 2010. "Gender, Social Disorganization Theory, and the Locations of Sexually Oriented Businesses." *Deviant Behavior* no. 31 (2):135–158. doi: 10.1080/01639620902854852.

Egan, R. Danielle. 2004. "Eyeing the Scene: The Uses and (RE)uses of Surveillance Cameras in an Exotic Dance Club." *Critical Sociology* no. 30 (2):299–319. doi: 10.1163/156916304323072125.

———. 2006. "Resistance under the Black Light: Exploring the Use of Music in Two Exotic Dance Clubs." *Journal of Contemporary Ethnography* no. 35 (2):201–219.

Eichenbaum, Rose. 2000. "Stubborn Dance in L.A." *Dance Magazine,* (April): 68–72.

Elocution Solution. "Elocution Solution: A Professional Speech Makeover." 2011. Accessed October 9, 2011. http://www.elocutionsolution.com/blog/what-is-an-accent/.

Erasmus, Z. 2001. "Introduction: Re-imagining Coloured Identities in Post-Apartheid South Africa." In *Coloured by History, Shaped by Place: New Perspectives on Coloured Identities in Cape Town,* Erasmus, Z. (ed.) 1–20. Cape Town: Kwela Books.

Erasmus, Z. and Pieterse, E. 1997. "Conceptualising Coloured Identities in the Western Cape Province of South Africa." Bellville: Maribuye Centre, University of the Western Cape. Paper presented at the conference "National Identity and Democracy." Cape Town, South Africa, 14–18 March, 1997.

Escobar, A. 2001. "Culture Sits in Places. Reflections on Globalism and Subaltern Strategies of Globalization." *Political Geography* 20: 139–174.

———. 2009. "Other Worlds Are (Already) Possible: Self-organization, Complexity, and Post-capitalist Cultures." In *World Social Forum: Challenging Empires*, edited by Jai Sen and Peter Waterman, 393–404. Montreal: Black Rose Books.

———. 2006 "Post Development." In *The Elgar Companion to Development Studies*, edited by David Alexander Clark, 448–451. Northampton, MA: Edward Elgar Publishing Ltd.

Fairbanks Daily News-Miner. 1946. "Wien Opens Sight Seeing Flight Trips." May 16.

Farrer, Gracia. 2004. "The Chinese Social Dance Party in Tokyo: Identity and Status in an Immigrant Leisure Subculture," *Journal of Contemporary Ethnography* 33(6): 651–674.

Farrer, James. 2002. *Opening Up: Youth Sex Culture and Market Reform in Shanghai*. Chicago: University of Chicago Press.

Featherstone, M. 2010. Body, Image and Affect in Consumer Culture. *Body & Society* 16(1): 193–221.

Febres, Mayra. 1997. "Salsa as Translocation." In *Everynight Life: Culture and Dance in Latin/o America*, edited by Celeste Delgado and José Muñoz, 175–188. London: Duke University Press.

Fenster, T. 2004. *The Global City and the Holy City: Narratives of Knowledge, Planning and Diversity*. Pearson: London.

Ferreday, Debra. 2008. "'Showing the Girl': The New Burlesque." *Feminist Theory* no. 9 (1):47–65. doi: 10.1177/1464700108086363.

Fienup-Riordan, Ann. 1994. *Boundaries and Passages: Rule and Ritual in Yupik Eskimo Oral Tradition*. Norman: University of Oklahoma Press.

Fleischman, Richard and Thomas Tyson. 1999. "Opportunity Lost? Chances for Cost Accountants' Professionalization under the National Industrial Recovery Act of 1933." *Accounting, Business and Financial History*, 9/1: 51–75.

Florida, Richard L. 2002. *The Rise of the Creative Class: And How It's Transforming Work, Leisure, Community and Everyday Life*. New York: Basic Books.

Ford, N. and Brown, D. 2006. *Surfing and Social Theory: Experience, Embodiment and Narrative of the Dream Glide*. New York: Routledge.

Forsyth, Craig J. and Tina H. Deshotels. 1997. "The Occupational Milieu of the Nude Dancer." *Deviant Behavior* no. 18 (2):125–142. doi: 10.1080/01639625.1997.9968049.

Foster, Susan Leigh. 1996. "Introduction." In *Corporealities: Dancing Knowledge, Culture and Power*, edited by Susan Leigh Foster. New York: Routledge.

———. 1996. "The Ballerina's Phallic Pointe." In *Corporealities: Dancing Knowledge, Culture and Power*, edited by Susan Leigh Foster. New York: Routledge.

———. 1998. "Choreographies of Gender." *Signs, Journal of Women in Culture and Society* 24: 1–33.

———. 2011. *Choreographing Empathy*. New York, NY: Routledge.

Foucault, Michel. 1978. *The Care of the Self*. New York: Pantheon Books.

———. 2003. *Heterotopia*. Resling Publishers, Tel Aviv (Hebrew Edition).

———. 1991 "Governmentality." In *The Foucault Effect: Studies in Governmentality* edited by Graham Burchell, Colin Gordon, and Peter Miller, 87–104. Chicago, IL: University of Chicago Press.

Franck, Harry. 1939. *The Lure of Alaska*. New York: Frederick Stokes.

Frascella, F. 2003. "The Beginning of ATS: A Series of Women Artists." *Bennu*. 5: 9–11.

Fraser, A. and N. Ettlinger. 2008. "Fragile Empowerment: The Dynamic Cultural Economy of British Drum and Bass Music." *Geoforum* 39 (5): 1647–1656.

Frenken, Geerte M. N. and Stephen J. Sifaneck. 1998. "Sexworkers and Dope: An Ethnography of Heroin Using Lap Dancers in New York City." *Addiction Research* no. 6 (4):341–370. doi: 10.3109/16066359808993311.

Fulkerson, Mary O'Donnell. (n.d.). "A Time Seeking Its Name." Accessed June 25, 2012. http://streamxs.nl/releasedance/ReleaseDance/pdf/A%20TIME%20SEEKING%20ITS%20NAM1.pdf.

Gaffney, Michael. 1982. "The Human Resources Approach to Native Rural Development: A Special Case." in *Alaska's Rural Development*, edited by Peter Cornwall and Gerald McBeath. Boulder CO: Westview.

Gagen, Elizabeth. 2004. "Making America Flesh: Physicality and Nationhood in Early Twentieth-Century Physical Education Reform." *Cultural Geographies*, 11: 417–442.

Gallup. 2012. *Mississippi Is Most Religious U.S. State*. Gallup 2012 [cited July 8 2012]. Available from http://www.gallup.com/poll/153479/mississippi-religious-state.aspx.

Gazzola, Valeria, Lisa Aziz-Zadeh, and Christian Keysers. 2006. "Empathy and the Somatotopic Auditory Mirror System in Humans." *Current Biology* 16, (September 19): 1824–1829.

George, Nelson. 2005. *Hip Hop America*, 2nd ed. New York, NY: Penguin.

George, Rosemary Marangoly. 1996. *The Politics of Home: Postcolonial Relocations and Twentieth-Century Fiction*. Cambridge: Cambridge University Press.

Gibson-Graham, J.K. 2006. *A Postcapitalist Politics*. Minneapolis: University of Minnesota Press.

Giddens, Anthony. 1992. *The Transformation of Intimacy: Sexuality, Love and Eroticism in Modern Societies*. London: Polity Press.

Glasscock, Jessica. 2003. *Striptease: From Gaslight to Spotlight*. New York: H.N. Abrams.

Goldberg, Marianne. 1997. "Homogenized Ballerinas." In *Meaning in Motion: New Cultural Studies of Dance*, edited by Jane C. Desmond, 304–319. Durham and London: Duke University Press.

Goodman, Karen. "Talkin' 'bout My Generation: Dancing in L.A. 1970–2000." *The Dance History Project of Southern California*. May 5, 2012. Accessed July 14, 2012. http://www.dancehistoryproject.org/spotlight/dance-in-la-60s-80s/#comment-30.

Goffman, Erving. 1974. *Frame Analysis*. Cambridge, MA: Harvard University Press.

Gotfrit, Leslie. 1988. "Women Dancing Back: Disruption and the Politics of Pleasure." *Journal of Education* 170(3): 122–141.

Gould, Joe. 2005. The Best Strip Clubs in America: With a Client, a Friend, or Alone. *Men's Fitness* 21 (7): 62, http://www.mensfitness.com/lifestyle/entertainment/10-best-strip-clubs-america.

Green, Ashbel S. 2002. "Ruling Challenges Oregon's Unique Speech Protections." *Oregonian*, May 6.

Green, Paul. 1959. *I Am Eskimo, Aknik My Name*. Juneau: Alaska Northwest Publishers.

Green-Rennis, Lesley L., Lourdes J. Hernandez-Cordero, Kjersti Schmitz, and Mindy Thompson Fullilove. In press. "'We Have a Situation Here!': Using Situation Analysis for Health and Social Research." In *Qualitative Research Methods for Social Work Research*, edited by Robert A. Miller. New York: Columbia University Press.

Greenberg, Michael R., Dona A. Schneider, Karen Lowrie, and Ann Dey. 2008. "The Theory of Neighbourhood Decline Due to Pariah Land Uses: Regaining Control of the Downward Cycle." *Local Environment* no. 13 (1):15–26.

Gregory, Derek. 1995. "Between the Book and the Lamp: Imaginative Geographies of Egypt, 1849–1850." *Transactions of the Institute of British Geographers*, 20/1: 29–57.

Gregory, D., R. Johnston, G. Pratt, M. G. Watts and S. Whatmore (Eds.). 1995. *The Diction-ary of Human Geography*. West Sussex UK: John Wiley and Sons.

Grosvenor, Elsie. 1956. "Alaska's Warmer Side." *National Geographic*, 59/6 (June): 737–775.

Grosz, E. 1994. *Volatile Bodies: Toward a Corporeal Feminism*. Bloomington, IN: Indiana University Press.

———. 1995. *Space, Time, and Perversion: Essays on the Politics of Bodies*. New York & London: Routledge.

Gross, Matt. 2009. "Frugal Portland." *New York Times*, May 10.

Halbwachs, M. 1992. *On Collective Memory*. L. A. Coser. (Trans. and ed.) Chicago: University of Chicago Press.

Hagendoorn, Ivar. 2004. "Some Speculative Hypotheses about the Nature and Perception of Dance and Choreography." *Journal of Consciousness Studies* 11, 3–4: 79–110.

Hagerman, Chris. 2007. "Shaping Neighborhoods and Nature: Urban Political Ecologies of Urban Waterfront Transformations in Portland, Oregon." *Cities* no. 24 (4):285–297.

Halberstam, Judith. 2005. *In a Queer Time and Place: Transgender Bodies, Subcultural Lives*. New York: New York University Press.

Halevi, S. and Blumen, O. 2005. "Obviously They Were There But . . .: Men's Presence in Women's Studies—An Israeli Perspective." *Feminist Teacher* 15, no. 3: 203–212.

Hall, Stuart. 1990. "Cultural identity and diaspora." In *Identity, community, culture, difference*, edited by Jonathan Rutherford. London: Lawrence & Wishart.

———. 1993. "What is this 'Black' in Black Popular Culture?" *Social Justice* 20, 1–2 (Spring): 104–115.

———. 1997. *Representation: Cultural Representations and Signifying Practices*. London: Sage Publications.

Hanna, Judith Lynne. 1998. "Undressing the First Amendment and Corsetting the Striptease Dancer." *TDR: Drama Review* no. 42 (2):38–69. doi: 10.1162/dram.1998.42.2.38.

———. 2010. "Dance and Sexuality: Many Moves." *Journal of Sex Research* no. 47 (2–3):212–241. doi: 10.1080/00224491003599744.

Hannerz, Ulf. 1990. "Cosmopolitans and Locals in World Culture." *Theory Culture & Society* 7: 237–251.

———. 1996. *Transnational Connections: Culture, People, Places*. London: Routledge.

Haraway, Donna. J. 1991. "A Cyborg Manifesto: Science, Technology, and Socialist-Feminism in the Late Twentieth Century." In *Simians, Cyborgs and Women: The Reinvention of Nature*, 149–181. London: Free Association Books.

Harkness, J. L. 2003. "In the Choreography Biz: Los Angeles Choreographer Kitty McNamee Tells It Like It Is." *Dance Spirit*, March: 53–55.

Harley, John Brian. 1988. "Maps, Knowledge, and Power." In *The Iconography of Landscape: Essays on the Symbolic Representation, Design and Use of Past Environments*, edited by C. U. Press.

———. 1989 "Deconstructing the Map." *Cartographica* 26, no.(2): 1.

Harris, Cole. 1997. *The Resettlement of British Columbia*. Vancouver BC: UBC Press.

Harrison, Paul. 2010. "Testimony and the Truth of the Other." In *Taking-Place: Non-Repre-sentational Theories and Geography*, edited by Ben Anderson and Paul Harrison. Burlington VT: Ashgate.

Hart, G. 2006. "Denaturalising Dispossession: Critical Ethnography in the Age of Resurgent Imperialism." *Antipode* 38 (5): 977–1004.

Harvey, David. 1990. *The Condition of Postmodernity: An Enquiry into the Origins of Cultural Change*. Oxford: Blackwell.

Hayden, Dolores. 1995. *The Power of Place: Urban Landscapes as Public History*. Boston: MIT Press.

Hayden, Dolores. 2002. *Redesigning the American Dream: The Future of Housing, Work, and Family Life*. New York: W.W. Norton.

Hazzard-Gordon, Katrina. 1990. *JOOKIN': The Rise of Social Dance Formations in African-American Culture*. Philadelphia: Temple University Press.

Healy, Michael. 1889. *Report of the Cruise of the Revenue Marine Steamer Corwin in the Arctic Ocean in the Year 1884*. Washington DC: Government Printing Office.

Heidegger, Martin. 1962. *Being and Time*. Translated by John Macquarrie. London: SCM Press.

———. 1971. "Building Dwelling Thinking." In *Poetry, Language, Thought*. Translated by Albert Hofstadter, Harper Colophon Books, New York.

Heiland, Teresa, Paige Edley, and Darrin Murray. 2008. "Body Image of Dance in Los Angeles: The Cult of Slenderness and Media Influence among Dance Students." *Research in Dance Education* 9, 3 (November): 257–75.

Higgins, Dalton. 2009. *Hip Hop World*. Berkeley, CA: Groundwood Books.

Hoelscher, S. and D. H. Alderman, 2004. "Memory and Place: Geographies of a Critical Relationship." *Social & Cultural Geography* 5(3): 347–355.

Holtzman, G. 2006. *A Treatsie on Langarm in Cape Town*. Undergraduate Honors Thesis, University of Cape Town.

Hopwood, Anthony. 1987. "The Archaeology of Accounting Systems." *Accounting, Organizations and Society*, 12/3: 207–234.

Housee, Shirin. 1999. "Journey through Life: *The Self in Travel*." In *Travel Worlds: Journeys in Contemporary Cultural Politics*, edited by Raminder Kaur and John Hutnyk, 137–154. London: Zed Books.

Howard, Rachel. "Hagen and Simone and TONGUE." *Voice of Dance*, August 30, 2004. Accessed October 2, 2011. http://www.voiceofdance.com/v1/features.cfm/1075/Dance -Review-Hagen-Simone-and-Tongue075.html.

Hubbard, Philip J. 1998a. "Community Action and the Displacement of Street Prostitution: Evidence from British Cities." *Geoforum* no. 29 (3):269–286. doi: 10.1016/S0016 -7185(98)00014-1.

———. 1998b. "Sexuality, Immorality and the City: Red-light Districts and the Marginalisation of Female Street Prostitutes." *Gender, Place & Culture* no. 5 (1):55–76. doi: 10.1080/ 09663699825322.

———. 2008. "Encouraging Sexual Exploitation? Regulating Striptease and 'Adult Entertainment' in the UK." In *Globalization, Media and Adult/Sexual Content: Challenges to Regulation and Research*. Athens.

———. 2009. "Opposing Striptopia: The Embattled Spaces of Adult Entertainment." *Sexualities* no. 12 (6):721–745. doi: 10.1177/1363460709346111.

———. 2012. *Cities and Sexualities*. New York, NY: Routledge.

Hubbard, Philip J., Roger Matthews, and Jane Scoular. 2009. "Legal Geographies—Controlling Sexually Oriented Businesses: Law, Licensing, and the Geographies of a Controversial Land Use." *Urban Geography* 30 (2): 185–205.

Hubbard, Philip J., Roger Matthews, Jane Scoular, and Laura Agustín. 2008. "Away from Prying Eyes? The Urban Geographies of 'Adult Entertainment.'" *Progress in Human Geography* 32 (3): 363–381.

Hubbard, Philip J. and Teela Sanders. 2003. "Making Space for Sex work: Female Street Prostitution and the Production of Urban Space." *International Journal of Urban and Regional Research* no. 27 (1):75–89. doi: 10.1111/1468-2427.00432.

Huggan, Graham. 2009. *Extreme Pursuits: Travel/Writing in an Age of Globalization.* Ann Arbor: The University of Michigan Press.

Huq, Rupa. 2006. *Beyond Subculture: Pop, Youth and Identity in a Postcolonial World.* London; New York: Routledge.

Ikuta, Hiroko. 2004. *"We Dance because We Are Iñupiaq"—Iñupiaq Dance in Barrow: Performance and Identity.* MA thesis: University of Alaska Fairbanks.

Jacobs, Jane. 2002/1961. *The Death and Life of Great American Cities.* 2002 ed. New York: Random House.

Jacobs, Jane and Catherine Nash. 2003. "Too Little, Too Much: Cultural Feminist Geographies." *Gender, Place and Culture* 10/3: 263–279.

Jameson, Fredric. 1991. *Postmodernism, or the Cultural Logic of Late Capitalism.* London: Verso.

Jazeel, T. 2005. "The World is Sound? Geography, Musicology and British–Asian Soundscapes." *Area* 37(3): 233–241.

Jazeel, Tariq and Colin McFarlane. 2007. "Responsible Learning: Cultures of Knowledge Production and the North-South Divide." *Antipode,* 39/5: 781–789.

———. 2010. "The Limits of Responsibility: A Postcolonial Politics of Academic Knowledge Production." *Transactions of the Institute of British Geographers,* 35: 109–124.

Jeffreys, Sheila. 2008. "Keeping Women Down and Out: The Strip Club Boom and the Reinforcement of Male Dominance." *Signs* no. 34 (1):151–73. doi: 10.1086/588501.

Jencks, Charles. *Heteropolis: Los Angeles, the Riots and the Strange Beauty of Hetero-architecture.* New York, NY: St. Martin's Press, 1993.

Joiner, Gene. 1950. "News about Town." *Mukluk Telegraph,* June 15.

———. 1951. "Arctic Expeditions for All." *Mukluk Telegraph,* July 28.

Joint Town Planning Committee of the Cape and Stellenbosch. Joint town Planning Scheme, Section 3. Preliminary Statement as adopted by the technical sub–committee on February 6, 1969. Outline Development Plan for the Cape Flats.

Johnson, H. Thomas and Robert Kaplan. 1987. *Relevance Lost: The Rise and Fall of Management Accounting.* Boston, MA: Harvard Business School Press.

Johnson, Merri Lisa. 2006. "Stripper Bashing: An Autovideography of Violence Against Strippers." In *Flesh for Fantasy: Producing and Consuming Exotic Dance,* edited by R. Danielle Egan, Katherine Frank and Merri Lisa Johnson, 159–188. New York: Thunder's Mouth Press.

Johnson, N. and G. Pratt. 2009. Memory. In *Dictionary of Human Geography,* D.

Johnson, T. 2011. "Salsa Politics: Desirability, Marginality, and Mobility in North Carolina's Salsa Nightclubs." Aether, *The Journal of Media Geography* 7(20): 10–31.

Johnston, Holly. Interview by Teresa Heiland January 15, 2009.

Johnston, Lynda and Robyn Longhurst. 2010. *Space, Place, and Sex: Geographies of Sexualities.* Lanham: Rowman & Littlefield.

Johnston, Thomas. 1975. "Alaskan Eskimo Dance in Cultural Context." *Dance Research Journal* 7/2: 1–11.

———. 1978. "Humor, Drama, and Play in Alaskan Eskimo Mimetic Dance." *Western Canadian Journal of Anthropology* 8/1: 47–64.

———. 1990. "Context, Meaning, and Function in Inupiaq Dance." in *Dance: Current Selected Research, Volume 2*, edited by Lynnette Overby and James Humphrey. New York: AMS.

Joly, Rebecca. 2007. "Beautiful, Striking: Modern Los Angeles Dances Presented by Grand Performances September 8." *LA Yoga Ayurveda and Health Magazine* 6, 8 (October 12): 12.

Jonas, Andrew E. G. 2006. "Pro Scale: Further Reflections on the 'Scale Debate' in Human Geography." *Transactions of the Institute of British Geographers* no. 31 (3):399–406. doi: 10.1111/j.1475-5661.2006.00210.x.

Jones, John, I. Paul and Wolfgang Natter. 1999. "Space 'and' Representation." In *Text and Image: Constructing Regional Knowledges*, edited by Anne Buttimer, Stanley Brunn, and Ute Wardega, 239–247. Leipzig, Germany: Institut fur Laenderkunde, Universitaet Leipzig.

Jones, O. 2005. "An Emotional Ecology of Memory, Self and Landscape." In *Emotional Geographies*. J. Davidson, L. Bondi and M. Smith (Eds). Oxford: Ashgate, 205–218.

Kabachnik, Peter. 2010. "The Myth of the Placeless Gypsy." *Area* 42(20), 198–207.

Kaiser, R. and Nikiforova, E. 2008, "The Performativity of Scale: The Social Construction of Scale Effects in Narva, Estonia." *Environment and Planning D: Society and Space* 26 (3): 537–562

Kassabova, Kapka. 2011. *Twelve Minutes of Love: A Tango Story*. London: Portobello Books.

Katrak, Ketu. 2008. "The Gestures of Bharata Natyam: Migrating into Diasporic Contemporary Indian Dance." In *Migrations of Gesture*, edited by Cary Noland and Sally Ann Ness. Minneapolis: University of Minnesota Press.

Katz, Cindi. 2004. *Growing Up Global: Economic Restructuring and Children's Everyday Lives*. Minneapolis: University of Minnesota Press.

Kay, Kerwin. 2000. "Naked but Unseen: Sex and Labor Conflict in San Francisco's Adult Entertainment Theaters." *Sexuality and Culture* no. 3 (3):39–67.

Kaye, Nick. 2000. *Site-specific Art: Performance, Place and Documentation*. New York: Routledge.

Kealiinohomoku, Joann. 1969. "An Anthropologist Looks at Ballet as a Form of Ethnic Dance." In *Moving History/Dancing Cultures: A Dance History Reader*, edited by Ann Dils and Ann C. Albright, 33–43. Middletown, CT: Wesleyan University Press.

Keft-Kennedy, V. 2005. "How Does She Do That? Belly Dancing and the Horror of a Flexible Woman." *Women's Studies* 34: 279–300.

Kendall, Gavin, Ian Woodward, and Zlatko Skrbis. 2009. *The Sociology of Cosmopolitanism: Globalization, Identity, Culture and Government*. Basingstoke: Pallgrave Macmillan.

Kershaw, Baz. 1992. *The Politics of Performance: Radical Theater as Cultural Intervention*. London and New York: Routledge.

Keysers, Christian and Valeria Gazzola. 2009. "Expanding the Mirror: Vicarious Activity for Actions, Emotions, and Sensations." *Current Opinion in Neurobiology* 19: 666–671.

Killen, Patricia O'Connell and Mark Silk. 2004. *Religion and Public Life in the Pacific Northwest: The None Zone*. Walnut Creek, CA: AltaMira Press.

Kirchberg, Volker. 1995. "Arts Sponsorship and the State of the City." *Journal of Cultural Economics* 19: 305–20.

Kloetzel, Melanie and Carolyn Pavlik, editors. 2010. *Site Dance: Choreographers and the Lure of Alternative Spaces*. Gainesville: University Press of Florida.

Knopp, Lawrence M., Jr. 1995. "Sexuality and Urban Space: A Framework for Analysis." In *Mapping Desire: Geographies of Sexualities*, edited by David Bell and Gill Valentine, 149–161. New York: Routledge.

Kuokkanen, Rauna. 2008. "What is Hospitality in the Academy? Epistemic Ignorance and the (Im)Possible Gift." *Review of Education, Pedagogy, and Cultural Studies* 30: 60–82.

Kurtz, Matthew. 2006. "Ruptures and Recuperations of a Language of Racism in Alaska's Rural / Urban Divide." *Annals of the Association of American Geographers*, 96/3: 601–621.

———. 2010. "Heritage and Tourism." in *Understanding Heritage in Practice*, edited by Susie West. Manchester UK: University of Manchester Press.

Laffey, Susan. 1995. *Representing Paradise: Euro-American Desires and Cultural Understandings in Touristic Images of Montserrat, West Indies*. MA Anthropology Thesis, Texas University, Austin.

Lamothe, Daphne. 2008. *Inventing the New Negro: Narrative, Culture, and Ethnography*. Philadelphia: University of Pennsylvania Press.

Landzelius, Michael. 2004. "The Body." In *A Companion to Cultural Geography*, edited by James Duncan, Nuala Johnson, and Richard H. Schein. 279–297. Maldon, Oxford, Victoria: Blackwell.

Langer, Suzanne. 1953. *Feeling and Form*. London: Routledge and Kegan Paul.

Larner, Wendy and Richard Le Heron. 2002. "The Spaces and Subjects of a Globalizing Economy: A Situated Exploration of Method." *Environment and Planning D: Society and Space*, 20: 753–774.

Las Vegas, Viva. 2009. *Magic Gardens (or, the Starry–Eyed Saviors of the Western Night)*. Portland, OR: Dame Rocket Press.

Latham, Alan and Derek McCormack. 2004. "Moving Cities: Rethinking the Materialities of Urban Geographies." *Progress in Human Geography* 28, 701–24.

Latour, B. 1987. *Science in Action*. Cambridge: Harvard University Press.

Layne, V. 1995. *A History of Dance and Jazz Band Performance in the Western Cape in the Post-1945 Era*. MA Thesis, University of Cape Town.

Leitner, Helga, Eric Sheppard, and Kristin M. Sziarto. 2008. "The Spatialities of Contentious Politics." *Transactions of the Institute of British Geographers* no. 33 (2):157–172. doi: 10.1111/j.1475-5661.2008.00293.x.

Lefebvre, Henri. 1991. *The Production of Space*. Translated by Donald Nicholson–Smith. Malden, MA: Blackwell Publishing .

Levy, Ariel. 2005. *Female Chauvinist Pigs: Women and the Rise of Raunch Culture*. New York: Free Press.

Leyshon, A., D. Matless and G. Revill (Eds.) 1998. *The Place of Music*. New York City: The Guilford Press

Liepe-Levinson, Katherine. 2002. *Strip show: Performances of Gender and Desire*. Edited by Susan Bassnet and Tracy C. Davis, *Gender in Performance*. New York: Routledge.

Lippard, Lucy. 1997. *Lure of the Local: Sense of Place in a Multicentered Society*. New York City: The New Press.

Loft, Anne. "Towards a Critical Understanding of Accounting: The Case of Cost Accounting in the UK, 1914–1925." *Accounting, Organizations and Society*, 11/2 (1986): 137–169.

———. 1994. "Accountancy and the First World War." Pp. 116–137 in *Accounting as Social and Institutional Practice*, edited by Anthony Hopwood and Peter Miller. Cambridge, UK: Cambridge University Press.

Lorimer, Hayden. 2005. "Cultural Geography: The Busyness of Being 'More-Than-Representational.'" *Progress in Human Geography*, 29/1: 83–94.

Lukinbeal, Chris and Jim Craine. 2009. "Geographic Media Literacy: An Introduction." *GeoJournal* 74: 175–182.

Lyons, Jacob. Interview by Teresa Heiland October 10, 2008.

Lysaght, Karen. 2005. "'Catholics, Protestants and Office Workers from the Town': The Experience and Negotiation of Fear in Northern Ireland." In *Mixed Emotions: Anthropological Studies of Feeling*, edited by Maruska Svašek and Kay Milton, 127–143. Oxford: Berg Publishers.

Macpherson, Hannah. 2010. "Non-Representational Approaches to Body–Landscape Relations." *Geography Compass* 4(1), 1–13. Accessed April 7, 2012. doi: 10.1111/j.1749-8198.2009.00276.x

Madison, Soyini and Judith Hamera. 2000. *Sage Handbook of Performance Studies*. London: Sage Publications.

Maginn, Paul and Christine Steinmetz. 2011. Sex in the City: The Changing Face of Adult Retailing. *The Conversation* (September 5), http://theconversation.edu.au/sex-in-the-city -the-changing-face-of-adult-retailing-3083.

Mandy. 2006. "Reader's Letters." *Tribal*: 3.

Maniilaq Association. 1985. *NANA Regional Strategy: 1979–1982*. Kotzebue: Maniilaq.

Marston, S. A. 2000. "The Social Construction of Scale." *Progress in Human Geography* 24 (2): 219–242.

———. 2003. "Mobilizing Geography: Locating Space in Social Movement Theory." *Mobilization: An International Quarterly* no. 8 (2): 227–233.

Marston, Sallie A., John Paul Jones, and Keith Woodward. 2005. "Human Geography without Scale." *Transactions of the Institute of British Geographers* no. 30 (4):416–432. doi: 10.1111/j.1475-5661.2005.00180.x.

Martin, Deborah G. and Byron Miller. 2003. "Space and Contentious Politics." *Mobilization: An International Quarterly* no. 8 (2):143–156.

Martin, D-C. 2000a. "The Burden of the Name: Classifications and Constructions of Identity: The Case of the 'Coloureds' in Cape Town." (South Africa). *African Philosophy* 13(2): 99–124.

Martin, D-C. 2000b. "Cape Town's Coon Carnival: A Site for the Confrontation of Competing Coloured Identities." In *Senses of Culture: South African Cultural Studies*, S. Nuttall and C-A Michael, 363–379. Oxford: Oxford University Press.

Martin, John. 1939. *Introduction to the Dance*. New York, NY: Dance Horizons.

Martin, Randy. 1998. *Critical Moves: Dance Studies in Theory and Politics*. Durham & London: Duke University Press.

Massey, Doreen. 1994. *Space, Place and Gender*. Cambridge, MA: Polity.

———. 2005. *For space*. London; Thousand Oaks, Calif.: Sage.

Massumi, B. 2002. *Parables for the Virtual: Movement, Affect, Sensation*. Durham: Duke University Press.

Maticka-Tyndale, Eleanor, Jacqueline Lewis, Jocalyn P. Clark, Jennifer Zubick, and Shelley Young. 2000. "Exotic Dancing and Health." *Women & Health* no. 31 (1):87–108. doi: 10.1300/J013v31n01_06.

Maticka-Tyndale, Eleanor, Jacqueline Lewis, and Megan Street. 2005. "Making a Place for Escort Work: A Case Study." *Journal of Sex Research* 42 (1): 46–53.

McCann, Eugene. 2010. "Urban Policy Mobilities and Global Circuits of Knowledge: Toward a Research Agenda." *Annals of the Association of American Geographers*, 101/1: 107–130.

McCormack, Derek. 2003. "An Event of Geographical Ethics in Spaces of Affect." *Transactions of the Institute of British Geographers*. 28, 488–507. Accessed April 12, 2012. http://www.jstor.org/stable/3804394

——. 2008. "Geographies for Moving Bodies: Thinking, Dancing, Spaces." *Geography Compass,* 2/6: 1822–1836.

McDowell, Linda. 1999. *Gender, Identity and Place Understanding Feminist Geographies.* Minneapolis: University of Minnesota Press.

McFarlane, Colin. 2006. "Crossing Borders: Development, Learning and the North-South Divide." *Third World Quarterly,* 27/8: 1413–1437.

——. 2010. "The Comparative City: Knowledge, Learning, Urbanism." *International Journal of Urban and Regional Research,* 34/4: 725–742.

McMains, Juliet. 2006. *Glamour Addiction inside the American Ballroom Dance Industry.* Middletown, CT: Wesleyan University Press.

McNabb, Steven. 1985. *Interaction Conventions and the Creation of Stereotypes in Northwest Alaska: An Ethnography of Communication.* PhD dissertation: Brown University.

McNair, Brian. 2002. *Striptease Culture: Sex, Media and the Democratization of Desire.* London; New York: Routledge.

McRobbie, Angela. 1997. "Dance Narratives and Fantasies of Achievement." In *Meaning in Motion: New Cultural Studies of Dance,* edited by Jane. C. Desmond, 207–231. Durham and London: Duke University Press.

Media, Wesleyan University Press and the Academic. "Appendix B: Elizabeth Streb Biography." Accessed September 20, 2011. http://acceleratedmotion.wesleyan.edu/primary_sources/ texts/bodiesandmachines/elizabeth_streb_bio.pdf.

Mercer, Kobena. 2007. "Diaspora Culture and the Dialogic Imagination: The Aesthetics of Black Independent Film in Britain." In *Theorizing Diaspora,* edited by Jana Evans Braziel and Anita Mannur. Malden: Blackwell Publishing.

Merrill, H. and D. Carter. 2002. "Inside and Outside Italian Political Culture: Immigrants and diasporic politics in Turin." *Geojournal* 58: 167–175.

Merrill, H. 2004. "Space Agent: Anti-racist Feminism and the Politics of Scale in Turin, Italy." *Gender, Place and Culture* 11 (2): 189–204.

Merriman, Peter, George Revill, Tim Cresswell, Hayden Lorimer, David Matless, Gillian Rose, and John Wylie. 2008. "Landscape, Mobility, Practice." *Social & Cultural Geography,* 9:2, 191–212. Accessed September 6, 2011. doi: 10.1080/14649360701856136

Metha, A. and Bondi, L. 1999. "Embodied Discourses: On Gender and Fear of Violence." *Gender, Place and Culture* 6: 67–84.

Michaud, Bradley. Interview by Teresa Heiland October 15, 2008.

Miles, Matthew B. and A. Michael Huberman. 1994. *Qualitative Data Analysis: An Expanded Sourcebook.* 2nd ed. Thousand Oaks, CA: Sage Publications.

Miller, C. 2007. "An Oral History of Jazz in Cape Town from the Mid-1950s to the Mid-1970s." In *Imagining the City: Memories and Cultures in Cape Town Field,* eds., Meyer, and Swanson (eds.), 133–150. Cape Town: Human Science Research Council Press.

Miller, C. 2007b. What is Cape Jazz? http://www.jazzrendezvous.co.za/readarticle.php?artcl=00000029, accessed June 28, 2010

Miller, Peter. 1992. "Accounting and Objectivity: The Invention of Calculating Selves and Calculable Spaces." *Annals of Scholarship* 9/1–2: 61–86.

Miller, Peter and Ted O'Leary. 1989. "Hierarchies and American Ideals, 1900–1945." *Academy of Management Review,* 14/2: 250–265.

Mitchell, J. Clyde. 1983. "Case and Situation Analysis." *Sociological Review* no. 31 (2):187–211.

Mills, Amy. 2010. *Streets of Memory: Landscape, Tolerance, and National Identity in Istanbul.* Athens: University of Georgia Press.

Mitchell, Timothy. 1992. "Orientalism and the Exhibitionary Order." in *Culture and Colonialism,* edited by Nicholas Dirks. Ann Arbor MI: University of Michigan Press.

Mitra, R. 2006. "Living a Body Myth, Performing a Body Reality: Reclaiming the Corporality and Sexuality of the Indian Female Dancer." *Feminist Review* 84: 67–83.

Monmonier, Mark. 1996. *How to Lie with Maps.* Chicago: University of Chicago Press.

Monson, Jennifer. 2011. "Bird Brain Dance." Accessed September 15, 2011. http://www.birdbraindance.org/

Moore, Adam S. 2005. "Bump and Grind." *Portland Mercury*, March 9. ATLAS.ti 5.2. ATLAS.ti GmbH, Berlin.

Morocco. 1985. "Dance Directions: Old Forms and New Influences." *Backstage.*

Morrison, Toni. 1992. *Playing in the Dark: Whiteness and the Literary Imagination.* New York: Random House.

Morrow, Phyllis. 1990. "Symbolic Actions, Indirect Expressions: Limits to Interpretation of Yupik Society." *Etudes / Inuit / Studies* 14/1–2: 141–158.

Muhr, Thomas. Atlas. Ti Version 5.2. ATLAS. ti GmbH, Berlin.

Muller, C. 2004. South African Music: A Century of Traditions in Transformation. Santa Barbara: ABC-CLIO.

Nagle, John. 2012. "Between Trauma and Healing: Tourism and Neoliberal Peacebuilding in Divided Societies." In *Writing the Dark Side of Travel*, edited by Jonathan Skinner, 29–46. Oxford: Berghahn Books.

Nally, Claire. 2009. Grrrly Hurly Burly: Neo-burlesque and the Performance of Gender. *Textual Practice* 23 (4):621–643.

NANA. *Annual Report.* 2003. http://www.nana.com (accessed March 6, 2005).

———. 2008. *Red Dog Mine.* http://www.nana.com (accessed September 3, 2011).

Nash, Catherine. 2000. "Performativity in Practice: Some Recent Work in Cultural Geography." *Progress in Human Geography,* 24/4: 653–664.

Naske, Claus-M. 1973. *An Interpretive History of Alaskan Statehood.* Anchorage: Alaska Northwest Publishers.

Naske, Claus-M. and Merman Slotnick. 1989. *Alaska: A History of the 49th State*, 2nd Edition. Norman: University of Oklahoma Press.

Nast, H. and Pile, S. (Eds.) 1998. *Places through the body.* London, UK: Sage

Nericcio, C. 2004 "The Art of Bellydance: A Fun and Fabulous Way to Get Fit." New York, Barnes & Noble Books.

———. 2007. "FatChanceBellyDance." Retrieved September, 1, 2007, from http://www.fcbd.com/about/.

Nixon, Rob. 1994. *Homelands, Harlem, and Hollywood: South African Culture and the World Beyond.*

Nome Nugget. 1946. "Alaska Airlines Brings Tourist Group." May 6.

Nora, P. 1989. Between Memory and History: Les Lieux de Mémoire. *Representations* 26 (Spring): 7–25.

Noxolo, Pat, Parvati Raghuram and Clare Madge. (2012). "Unsettling Responsibility: Postcolonial Interventions." *Transactions of the Institute of British Geographers.*

O'Neill, Maggie, Rosie Campbell, Philip J. Hubbard, Jane Pitcher, and Jane Scoular. 2008. "Living with the Other: Street Sex Work, Contingent Communities and Degrees of Tolerance." *Crime, Media, Culture* no. 4 (1):73–93. doi: 10.1177/1741659007087274.

O'Shea, Janet. 2007. *At Home in the World: Bharata Natyam on the Global Stage*. Middletown: Wesleyan University Press.

Osumare, Halifu. 2002. "Global Break Dancing and the Intercultural Body." *Dance Research Journal* 34, 2 (Winter): 30–45.

Pada, Lata. *Shunya* Programme Notes. 2009. *Contemporary Choreography in Indian Dance, Conference Brochure*.

Papastergiadis, Nikos. 2012. *Cosmopolitanism and Culture*. Cambridge: Polity.

Papayanis, Marilyn Adler. 2000. "Sex and the Revanchist City: Zoning Out Pornography in New York." *Environment and Planning D-Society & Space* no. 18 (3):341–353. doi: 10.1068/d10s.

Parr, Adrian. 2008. *Deleuze and Memorial Culture: Desire, Singular Memory and the Politics of Trauma*. Edinburgh: Edinburgh University Press.

Pasko, Lisa. 2002. "Naked Power: The Practice of Stripping as a Confidence Game." *Sexualities* no. 5 (1):49–66.

Perkins, Chris. 2008. "Cultures of Map Use." *The Cartographic Journal* 45, no.(2): 150–158.

Perlmutter, Donna. 1995. "Mehmet Sander Dance Company: Lace, Los Angeles, California—Dance Reviews." *Dance Magazine*, (December):108–10.

Peterson, Marina. 2010. *Sound, Space, and the City*. Philadephia, PA: Univeristy of Pennsylvania Press.

Pichon, Swann, Beatrice de Gelder, and Julie Grezes. 2008. "Emotional Modulation of Visual and Motor Areas by Dynamic Body Expressions of Anger." *Social Neurosciences* 3, 3–4: 199–212.

Pietrobruno, Sheenagh. 2006. *Salsa and Its Transnational Moves*. Lanham, MD: Lexington Books.

Pile, S. 2009. Emotions and Affect in Recent Human Geography. *Transactions* 35: 5–20.

Popke, Jeff. 2009. "Geography and Ethics: Non–Representational Encounters, Collective Responsibility and Economic Difference." *Progress in Human Geography* 33(1): 81–90.

Potluri, K. 2004. "The Return to District Six: 'Looking Down the Line with Rose-Tinted Glasses'?" MA Thesis, University of Cape Town.

Pitts-Taylor, Victoria. 2003. *In the Flesh: The Cultural Politics of Body Modification*. New York; Houndmills, England: Palgrave Macmillan.

Popke, Jeff. 2009. "Geography and Ethics: Non-Representational Encounters, Collective Responsibility and Economic Difference." *Progress in Human Geography*, 33/1: 81–90.

Popper, Frank J. 1981. "Siting LULU's." *Planning* no. 47 (4):12–15.

Radley, A. 1995. "The Illusory Body and Social Constructionist Theory." *Body and Society* 1: 3–24.

Raghuram, Parvati. 2011. "The Spaces of Development and Migration—A Journey." Paper presented at University of Utrecth, October 25.

Rajan, Geeta and Shailja Sharma. 2006. *New Cosmopolitanisms: South Asians in the US*. Stanford: Stanford University Press.

Rapport, Nigel and Andrew Dawson. 1998. "The Topic of the Book." In *Migrants of Identity* edited by Nigel Rapport and Andrew Dawson, 3–18. London: Berg.

Rapport, Nigel and Andrew Dawson. 1998. "Home and Movement: A Polemic." In *Migrants of Identity* edited by Nigel Rapport and Andrew Dawson, 19–38. London: Berg.

Rasmussen, L. 2001. *Cape Town Jazz 1959–1963: The Photographs of Hardy Stockmann*. Copenhagen: The Booktrader.

Regehr, Kaitlyn. 2012. The Rise of Recreational Burlesque: Bumping and Grinding towards Empowerment. *Sexuality & Culture* 16 (2):134–157.

Relph, Edward. 1976. *Place and Placelessness*. London: Pion, Ltd.

Revill, George. 2004. "Performing French Folk Music: Dance, Authenticity, and Nonrepresentational Theory." *Cultural Geographies,* 11: 199–209.

Reynolds, Nancy and Malcom McCormick. 2003. *No Fixed Points: Dance in the Twentieth Century.* New Haven, CT: Yale University Press.

Robinson, Jennifer. 2006. *Ordinary Cities: Between Modernity and Development*. London: Routledge.

———. 2011. "Comparisons: Colonial or Cosmopolitan?" *Singapore Journal of Tropical Geography,* 32: 125–140.

Ronai, Carol Rambo. 1989. "Turn-ons for Money: Interactional Strategies of the Table Dancer." *Journal of Contemporary Ethnography* no. 18 (3):271–198.

Rose, Gillian. 2000. "Practicing Photography: An Archive, a Study, Some Photographs and a Researcher." *Journal of Historical Geography,* 26/4: 555–571.

Rose, N. 1996. *Inventing Our Selves*. Cambridge, UK: Cambridge University Press.

———. 1999. *Powers of Freedom: Reframing Political Thought*. Cambridge: Cambridge University Press.

Ross, Becki L. 2009. *Burlesque West: Showgirls, Sex and Sin in Postwar Vancouver*. Toronto: University of Toronto Press.

Ross, Becki L. and Kim Greenwell. 2005. "Spectacular Striptease: Performing the Sexual and Racial Other in Vancouver, B.C., 1945–1975." *Journal of Women's History* no. 17 (1):137–164. doi: 10.1353/jowh.2005.0012.

Ruiters, M.R. 2006. "Elite (Re)Constructions of Coloured Identities in a Post-Apartheid South Africa: Assimilations and Bounded Transgressions." Ph.D. Diss., Rutgers University.

Safran, William. 1991. "Diasporas in Modern Societies: Myths of Homeland and Return." *Diaspora: A Journal of Transnational Studies* 1:83–99.

Said, Edward. 1978. *Orientalism*. New York: Vintage Books.

———. 2006a. "Vision and Viscosity in Goa's Psychedelic Trance Scene." *ACME: An International E-Journal for Critical Geographies,* 4(2): 172–193.

———. 2006b. "Reontologising Race: The Machinic Geography of Phenotype." *Environment and planning D: Society and Space,* 24: 9–24.

Saldanha, Arun. 2005. "Trance and Visibility at Dawn: Racial Dynamics in Goa's Rave Scene." *Social and Cultural Geography* 6 (5): 707–721.

Saldanha, Arun. 2007. *Psychedelic White: Goa Trance and the Viscosity of Race*. Minneapolis: University of Minnesota Press.

Salem, L. A. 1995. "The Most Indecent Thing Imaginable: Sexuality, Race and the Image of Arabs in American Entertainment, 1850–1990." *Education,* Temple University: 286.

Sanchez, Lisa E. 1997. "Boundaries of Legitimacy: Sex, Violence, Citizenship, and Community in a Local Sexual Economy." *Law and Social Inquiry-Journal of the American Bar Foundation* no. 22 (3):543–580. doi: 10.1111/j.1747-4469.1997.tb01081.x.

Sanchez Gonzales, L. 1999. "Reclaiming Salsa." *Cultural Studies* 13: 326–350.

Sanders, Teela. 2004. "Controllable Laughter: Managing Sex Work through Humour." *Sociology: The Journal of the British Sociological Association* no. 38 (2):273–291.

———. 2005. "It's Just Acting: Sex Workers' Strategies for Capitalising on Sexuality." *Gender, Work, and Organization* no. 14 (4):319–342.

Sasha Anawalt Blog/The Blog of the National Arts Journalism Program. http://www.najp.org/articles/2008/03/lewis-segal-chief-dance-critic.html.

Savigliano, M. 1995. *Tango and the Political Economy of Passion.* Boulder, CO: Westview.

Schatzki, Theodore R. 2002. *The Site of the Social. A Philosophical Account of Social Life and Change.* University Park PA: Penn State University Press.

Schively, Carissa. 2007. "Understanding the NIMBY and LULU Phenomena: Reassessing Our Knowledge Based and Informing Future Research." *Journal of Planning Literature* no. 21 (3):257–266. doi: 10.1177/0885412206295845.

Schlosser, Eric. 1997. "The Business of Pornography." *U.S. News and World Report,* February 10, 42–50.

Schneider, Jane and Ida Susser. 2003. *Wounded Cities: Destruction and Reconstruction in a Globalized World.* Oxford: Berg Publishers.

Schneider, R. 1997. *The Explicit Body in Performance.* New York City: Routledge.

Scott, David. 1995. "Colonial Governmentality." *Social Text* 13/2: 191–220.

Scoular, Jane, Jane Pitcher, Rosie Campbell, Philip J. Hubbard, and M. O'Brien. 2007. "What's Anti-social about Sex Work? The Changing Representation of Prostitution's Incivility." *Community Safety Journal* no. 6 (1):11–17.

Seattle Times. 1946. "First Tourists Welcomed by Nome Eskimos." May 7.

Segal, Lewis. 1994. "Cover Story: Dance to the Edge: A Controversial L.A. Modern Dance Trend That Some Are Calling Hyperdance Emphasizes Athleticism, Endurance and Risk, Serving as a Timely Metaphor for Survival in an Age of Disaster." *Los Angeles Times,* (March 6): 8.

———. 2007 "'Foreign Bodies': Life on the Edge; Music, Sculpture and Dance Meld in the Stunning Diavolo piece." *Los Angeles Times,* September 6,: E–5.

———. 2006 "Five Things I Hate about Ballet." *Los Angeles Times,* August 6,: E–31.

———. 2007 "The Body-Bruising Career of a Performer." *Los Angeles Times,* April 21: E–8.

Seveck, Chester. 1973. *Longest Reindeer Herder.* Fairbanks AK: Arctic Circle Enterprises.

Shanks, Alyssa. 2009. "Northwest Arctic Borough." *Alaska Economic Trends* 29/8: 12–16.

Sharif, Keti. 2004. *Bellydance: A Guide to Middle Eastern Dance, Its Music, Culture and Costume.* Crows Nest: Allen and Unwin.

Sharp, Elaine B. 2004. "Metropolitan Structure and the Sex Business." In *Metropolitan Governance: Conflict, Competition, and Cooperation,* edited by Richard C. Feiock. Washington, DC: Georgetown University Press.

Shteir, Rachel. 2004. *Striptease: The Untold History of the Girlie Show.* New York: Oxford University Press.

Shuttleton, David, Diane Watt, and Richard Phillips. 2000. *De-centring Sexualities: Politics and Representations beyond the Metropolis.* London; New York: Routledge.

Sides, Josh. 2006. "Excavating the Postwar Sex District in San Francisco." *Journal of Urban History* no. 32 (3):355–379. doi: 10.1177/0096144205282713.

Siegel, Marcia B. 1988. "The Truth about Apples and Oranges." *TDR* 32(4): 24–31.

Silvey, R. 2006. Geographies of Gender and Migration: Spatializing Social Difference. *International Migration Review* 40 (1): 64–81.

Skelton, T. and Valentine, G. (Eds.) 1998. *Cool Places: Geographies of Youth Cultures.* New York: Routledge.

Skinner, Jonathan. 2012. "Globalization and the Dance Import/Export Business: The Jive Story." In *Dancin' Culture: Knowledge, Transformation and Identity in the Anthropology of Dance*, edited by Helene Neveu-Kringelbach and Jonathan Skinner, 29–45. Oxford: Berghahn Books.

Skinner, Jonathan. 2010. "Work/Leisure Balances and the Creation of a Carnival Cosmopolitanism amongst Salsa Dancers." *Intergraph: Journal for Dialogic Anthropology* 2(2). Accessed February 28, 2012. http://intergraph-journal.com/enhanced/vol2issue2/12.html.

———. 2009. "'Live in Fragments No Longer': Imagination and the Connection in Human Nature." In *Human Nature as Capacity: An Ethnographic Approach*, edited by Nigel Rapport, 207–230. Oxford: Berghahn Publications.

———. 2008. "Women Dancing Back—and Forth: Resistance and Self-Regulation in Belfast Salsa." *Dance Research Journal* 40(1): 65–77.

———. 2007. "The Salsa Class: A Complexity of Globalization, Cosmopolitans and Emotions." *Identities* 14(4): 485–506.

Sloan, Lacey and Stéphanie Wahab. 2000. "Feminist Voices on Sex Work: Implications for Social Work." *Affilia-Journal of Women and Social Work* no. 15 (4):457–479.

Sloterdijk, Peter. 2011. *Bubbles: Spheres 1*. Cambridge: MIT Press.

Smart Travel Info. "Los Angeles: Where Dreams Are Made." July 6, 2011. Accessed October 9, 2011. http://www.smarttravelinfo.com/los-angeles-where-dreams-are-made/.

Smith, Valene. 1966. *Kotzebue: A Modern Eskimo Community*. PhD dissertation: University of Utah.

———. 1989. "Eskimo Tourism: Micro-Models and Marginal Men." in *Hosts and Guests: The Anthropology of Tourism*, edited by Valene Smith. Philadelphia: University of Pennsylvania Press.

Snyder, G. 1990 *The Practice of the Wild*. San Francisco: North Point Press.

Soja, Edward W. 1986. *Postmodern Geographies: The Reassertion of Space in Critical Social Theory*. New York, NY: Verso.

———. 1996. *Thirdspace*. Cambridge, Oxford: Blackwell Publishers, Inc.

Somdahl-Sands, K. 2006. "Triptych: Dancing in Thirdspace." *Cultural Geographies* 13 (4): 610–616.

———. 2007. *Dancing in Place: The Radical Production of Civic Spaces*. PhD Dissertation. University of Texas, Austin.

Spencer, Paul. 1985. "Introduction: Interpretations of the Dance in Anthropology," in P. Spencer (ed.), *Society and the Dance*. Cambridge: Cambridge University Press, pp. 1–46.

Spice, William. 2007. "Management of Sex Workers and Other High-Risk Groups." *Occupational Medicine* no. 57:322–8. doi: 10.1093/occmed/kqm045.

Spivak, Gayatri Chakravorty. 2003. *Death of a Discipline*. New York: Columbia University Press.

———. 2008. *Other Asias*. Malden MA: Blackwell Publishing.

Spring, Bob and Ira Spring. 1953. "Air Trip to Eskimo Villages." *Sunset* 110/4 (April): 29–32.

Spring, Norma. 1953. "The Kids of Kotzebue." *Seattle Times* pictorial section, November 23.

Stants, H. 2006. "About 'Tribal-Fusion.'" Evolution DVD, Hollywood Music Center.

Sternberg, Donna. 1994. "The Edge of Dance." *The Los Angeles Times*, March 20,: 91. Accessed July 14, 2012. http://articles.latimes.com/1994-03-20/entertainment/ca-36196_1_rudy-perez-performance-ensemble-modern-dance-dance-artists.

Strickler, Fred. "Working with Bella Lewitzy, 1967–75." *The Dance History Project of Southern California*. May 10, 2012. http://www.dancehistoryproject.org/genre/modern/working-with-bella-lewitzky-1967-1975/. Accessed July 14, 2012.

Strom, Elizabeth. 2003. "Cultural Policy as Development Policy: Evidence from the United States." *International Journal of Cultural Policy* no. 9 (3):247–263. doi: 10.1080/1028663032000161687.

Sussman, Leila. 1998. "Dance Audiences: Answered and Unanswered Questions." *Dance Research Journal* 30, 1 (Spring): 54–63.

Swyngedouw, E. 2004. *Glocalisations*. Philadelphia: Temple University Press.

Tani, Sirpa. 2002. "Whose Place Is This Space? Life in the Street Prostitution Area of Helsinki." *International Journal of Urban and Regional Research* 26 (2): 343–359.

Taussig, Michael. 1993. *Mimesis and Alterity: A Particular History of the Senses*. New York: Routledge.

Taylor, Diana. 2003. *The Archive and the Repertoire: Performing Cultural Memory in the Americas*. Durham: Duke University Press.

Thapar, Romila. 1996. "The Tyranny of Labels." *Social Scientist* 24: 3–23.

Thomas, Helen. 2003. *The Body, Dance and Cultural Theory*. New York: Palgrave Macmillan.

Thomas, William I. and Dorothy S. Thomas. 1928. *The Child in America*. New York: Alfred A. Knopf.

Thrift, Nigel. 1983. "On the Determination of Social Action in Space and Time." *Environment and Planning D: Society and Space,* 1: 23–57.

———. 1996. *Spatial Formations*. Thousand Oaks CA: Sage.

———. 1997. "The Still Point: Resistance, Expressive Embodiment and Dance." in *Geographies of Resistance,* edited by Steve Pile and Michael Keith, . London: Routledge.

———. 2000. "Afterwords." *Environment and Planning D: Society and Space,* 18: 213–255.

———. 2004. "Summoning Life." in *Envisioning Human Geographies*, edited by Paul Cloke, Philip Crang, and Mark Goodwin. London: Arnold.

———. 2004. "Driving in the City." *Theory Culture Society* 21, 41–59. Accessed September 13, 2011. doi: 10.1177/0263276404046060

———. 2005. *Knowing Capitalism*. Thousand Oaks CA: Sage.

———. 2007. *Non-Representational Theory: Space / Politics / Affect*. London: Routledge.

———. 2008. "Pass It On: Towards a Political Economy of Propensity." *Emotion, Space and Society,* 1: 83–96.

———. 2009. "Different Atmospheres: Of Sloterdijk, China, and Site." *Environment and Planning D: Society and Space,* 27: 119–138.

Till, Karen. 1999. "Staging the Past: Landscape Designs, Cultural Identity and Erinnerungspolitik at Berlin's Neue Wache." *Cultural Geographies* 6 (3): 251–283.

Till, Karen. 2005. *The New Berlin: Memory, Politics, Place*. Minneapolis: University of Minnesota Press.

Tolia-Kelly, Divya. 2006. "Affect—An Ethnocentric Encounter? Exploring the 'Universalist' Imperative of Emotional / Affectual Geographies." *Area,* 38/2: 213–217.

Trautner, Mary Nell. 2005. "Doing Gender, Doing Class: The Performance of Sexuality in Exotic Dance Clubs." *Gender & Society* no. 19 (6):771–788.

Trotter, H. 2006. "Trauma and Memory: The Impact of Apartheid-Era Forced Removals on Coloured Identity in Cape Town." In *Burdened by Race: Coloured identities in southern Africa*, Adhikari, M.(ed.) 49–78. Cape Town: University of Cape Town Press.

Urish, Ben. 2004. "Narrative Striptease in the Nightclub Era." *The Journal of American Culture* no. 27 (2):157–165. doi: 10.1111/j.1537-4726.2004.00126.x.

U.S. Census. 1913. *Thirteenth Census of the United States: Volume III, 1910*. Washington DC: Government Printing Office.

———. 1952. *Census of the Population: 1950, Volume I.* Washington DC: Government Printing Office.

———. "Kotzebue city, Alaska, 2010." http://www.factfinder2.census.gov (accessed September 3, 2011).

Van den Berghe, P. L. 1960. "Miscegenation in South Africa." *Cahiers d'Études Africaines* 1(4): 68–84.

VanStone, James. 1955. "Archaeological Excavations at Kotzebue, Alaska." *Anthropological Papers of the University of Alaska* 3/2: 75–155.

Venkat, Lalitha. "Hari Krishnan: Pushing the Parameters of Narrative Expression." Accessed online on September 1, 2011. http://www.narthaki.com/info/intervw /intrvw82.html.

Wachtel, N. 1986. "Memory and History: Introduction." *History and Anthropology* 12: 207–224.

Wahab, Stéphanie, Lynda Baker, Julie Smith, Kristy Cooper, and Kari Lerum. 2011. "Exotic Dance Research: A Review of the Literature from 1970 to 2008." *Sexuality & Culture* 15 (1): 56–79.

Warbelow, Willy Lou. 1990. *Empire on Ice.* Anchorage AK: Great Northwest Publishing.

Warren, Larry. 1977. *Lester Horton: Modern Dance Pioneer.* Princeton, NJ: Princeton Book Company.

Waxer, L. (Ed.) 2002. *Situating Salsa: Global Markets and Local Meanings in Latin Popular Music.* New York: Routledge.

Weedon, Chris. 1998. "Feminism and the Principles of Poststructuralism." In *Cultural Theory and Popular Culture: A Reader.* Second Edition. Ed. John Storey. Athens: University of Georgia Press.

Weisz, Steven. 2008. "Philadelphia Dance Projects Hosts Jennifer Monson: BIRD BRAIN Projects." *The Dance Journal* December 29. Accessed September 15, 2010. http://phila delphiadance.org/blog/2008/12/29/philadelphia-dance-projects-hosts-jennifer-monson -bird-brain-projects/

Weitzer, Ronald. 2000. "Why We Need More Research on Sex Work." In *Sex for Sale: Prostitution, Pornography, and the Sex Industry,* edited by Ronald Weitzer, 1–13. New York: Routledge.

West, Charles. 1985. *Mr. Alaska: Forty Years of Alaska Tourism, 1945–1985.* Seattle: Weslee Publishing.

West, Darrell M. and Marion Orr. 2007. "Morality and Economics: Public Assessments of the Adult Entertainment Industry." *Economic Development Quarterly* no. 21 (4):314–324.

Western Cape Archives, 3/CT 4/1/5/579

Western Cape Archives, CDC 385, 32/1/4400/177

Western Cape Archives, KAB CDC 384 32/1/4400/122

Western Cape Archives, KAB CDC 383 32/1/4400/67

Whitehead, Kally and Tim Kurz. 2009. "'Empowerment' and the Pole: A Discursive Investigation of the Reinvention of Pole Dancing as a Recreational Activity." *Feminism & Psychology* 19 (2):224–244.

Wieschiolek, Heike. 2003. "'Ladies, Just Follow His Lead!': Salsa, Gender and Identity." In *Sport, Dance and Embodied Identities,* edited by Eduardo Archetti and Noel Dyck, 115–138. Oxford: Berg Publications.

Wilkinson, P. 2000. "City Profile: Cape Town." *Cities* 17(3): 195–205.

Wolff, Janet. 1997. "Reinstating Corporeality: Feminism and Body Politics." In *Meaning in Motion: New Cultural Studies of Dance,* edited by Jane C. Desmond, 81–100. Durham and London: Duke University Press.

———. 1995. "Dance Criticism: Feminism, Theory and Choreography." In *Resident Alien: Feminist Cultural Criticism*, edited by J. Wolff, 68–87. Cambridge: Polity Press.

Wood, Denis, John Fels, and John Krygier. 2010. *Rethinking the Power of Maps*. New York London: The Guilford Press.

Woodward, K. 2007. *Affect, Politics, Ontology*. Ph.D. Diss., University of Arizona.

Wulff, H. "Memories in Motion: The Irish Dancing Body." *Body & Society* 11, no. 4 (2005), 45–62.

Wylie, John. 2010. "Non-Representational Subjects?" in *Taking-Place: Non-Representational Theories and Geography*, edited by Ben Anderson and Paul Harrison. Burlington VT: Ashgate.

Y Royo, Alessandria. 2003. "Classicism, Post-classicism and Ranjabati Sircar's Work: Redefining the Terms of Indian Contemporary Dance Discourses." *South Asia Research* 23:153–169.

———. 2004. "Dance in the British South Asian Diaspora: Redefining Classicism." *Postcolonial Text* 1, no. 1. September 28, 2009. www.postcolonial.org/index.php/pct/article/viewArticle/367/809.

Yin, Robert K. 2003. *Case Study Research: Design and Methods*. Edited by Leonard Bickman and Debra J. Rog. 3rd ed, *Applied Social Research Methods*. Thousand Oaks, Calif.: Sage.

Zatz, Noah D. 1997. "Sex Work/Sex Act: Law, Labor, and Desire in Constructions of Prostitution." *Signs* no. 22 (2):277–308.

Index

About the Contributors

Frances Bronet is Dean of the School of Architecture and Allied Arts at the University of Oregon. She has been developing work in multidisciplinary design curricula between architecture; engineering; science, technology, and society; dance; and electronic arts for the past twenty years. She has been published in *Feminist Technologies*; *Performing Nature: Explorations in Ecology and the Arts*; the *International Journal for Engineering Education*; and the *Journal for Architectural Education*, among others. Bronet is currently working with nationally acclaimed choreographer Alito Alessi and his award-winning mixed-abilities company DanceAbility on a set of choreographed action installations. She recently completed a series of funded interactive full-scale architecture, construction, and dance installations with the Ellen Sinopoli Dance Company which received national and regional acclaim. She has worked with Terry Creach, Doug Verone, and Elizabeth Streb. Bronet has been named an Association of Collegiate Schools of Architecture Distinguished Professor, a DesignIntelligence Educator of the Year and the Carnegie Foundation for the Advancement of Teaching New York Professor of the Year.

Georgia Conover is both a critical dance scholar and a health geographer pursing a Ph.D. in human geography from the University of Arizona. She also owns and teaches in a small dance studio in Tucson. Before moving to Arizona, she spent twelve years as a political journalist, documentary producer, and news director in Tallahassee, Florida, where she earned an Emmy nomination for television documentary and a national Edward R. Murrow award for radio documentary.

Professor Tovi Fenster is the head of the Planning for the Environment with Communities (PEC) Lab at the Department of Geography and Human Environment, Tel Aviv University. She is the former head of the Institute of Diplomacy and Regional

Cooperation (2011–2012), former NCJW Women and Gender Studies Program head (2007–2009), and former chair of IGU Gender and Geography Commission (2004–2008). She has published articles and book chapters on ethnicity, citizenship, and gender in planning and development. She is the editor of *Gender, Planning and Human Rights* (1999) and the author of *The Global City and the Holy City: Narratives on Knowledge, Planning and Diversity* (2004) and *Planning, Knowledge and Everyday Life* (2012). She is co-editor (with Haim Yacobi) of *Remembering, Forgetting and City Builders* (2011). In 1999, she initiated the establishment and has been the first chair (2000–2003) of *Bimkom-Planners for Planning Rights* in Israel (an NGO).

Teresa Heiland, PhD, is assistant professor of dance at Loyola Marymount University, a Certified Laban Movement Analyst, Language of Dance Specialist, and Franklin Method and Pilates practitioner, works at the intersection of dance education, dance science and wellness, body image, and multi-literacies. She seeks to produce teaching and research activities that inform disciplinary practices, provoke personal development, and deepen dancers' understanding of their potential as artists, educators, and writers. In her scholarly work, she investigates learning through dancing and writing, examining the nature of literacy through dance notation, teaching and learning, investigating body image, and assessing imagery's affects on dance technique. She has authored articles and chapters about motif notation and literacy in college choreography courses, effects of Hollywood media pressures on college dance majors, and how dance training is affected by imagery interventions during training.

Tamara M. Johnson received her doctorate in geography from the University of North Carolina at Chapel Hill in 2011. She was funded through a Fulbright grant to conduct field work in South Africa from 2009 to 2011. Her selection of Cape Town as a research site for a project on dance and urban change was driven by her broader research interest in urban contexts marked by rapid and significant change. Her previous studies in North Carolina examined Latino migration and the changing contexts and demography of social interaction in leisure spaces. She is interested in the ways in which continued conflicts over changes in the material and symbolic infrastructure of the city play out in urban social spaces. Tamara has been dancing salsa socially and semi-professionally since 2000, and has performed salsa, samba, mambo, tango, and Afro-Cuban in the United States, Canada, and South Africa. While conducting research in Cape Town, Tamara participated in dance classes (either as an instructor or a participant) with eight salsa and jazz dance companies, and performed or taught with four salsa schools and three other loosely organized companies. Tamara is currently at the Office of International Programs at the University of North Carolina at Charlotte.

Paromita Kar is a PhD candidate in dance studies at the Department of Dance, York University, Toronto, and also an independent dance artist and choreographer.

She holds a master's degree in dance from York University, and a bachelor's degree in history, with a minor in drama from Queen's University. She is a practitioner of the classical Indian dance style of Odissi, and her research interests lie in traditional lineage styles of the Indian classical dance forms, twentieth century Odissi revival history, and German Expressionist dance.

Matthew Kurtz is a socio-economic research consultant in Ottawa and an adjunct research professor at Carleton University, where he teaches courses in research methodology and economic geography. His research explores the ways that "economic knowledge" has been produced in multi-cultural North America. He was a member of the Open University course teams that authored the textbooks *Arctic Approach* and *Understanding Heritage in Practice*.

Moriah McSharry McGrath is a researcher and educator whose interests center on place, marginalization, and health. She holds master's degrees in urban planning and public health from Columbia University and a bachelor's degree in feminist and gender studies from Haverford College. She conducted the research presented in this book at the Portland State University School of Urban Studies and Planning.

Dr. Jonathan Skinner is senior lecturer in social anthropology at the Queen's University Belfast. His interests are in tourism and dance–modern social dancing communities especially. He is the author of *Before the Volcano* (2004), editor of *Writing Dark Travel* (2012), and co-editor of *Great Expectations* (2012) and *Dancing Cultures* (2012).

Dr. Katrinka Somdahl-Sands has held a tenure-rack assistant professor position at Rowan University in Glassboro, New Jersey since 2009. After finishing her dissertation "Dancing in Place: The Radical Production of Civic Spaces" at the University of Texas at Austin (2007), she spent a year teaching at the National University of Ireland at Galway. She is a political/cultural geographer with interests in performance, cultural politics, and the spaces of political citizenship. Her most recent challenge is becoming the interim coordinator for the New Jersey Geographic Alliance.